7

D1187724

THE GROWTH OF ROYAL GOVERNMENT
UNDER HENRY III

THE GROWTH OF ROYAL
GOVERNMENT UNDER HENRY III

Edited by
David Crook and Louise J. Wilkinson

THE BOYDELL PRESS

First published 2015
The Boydell Press, Woodbridge

ISBN 978 1 78327 067 5

The Boydell Press is an imprint of Boydell & Brewer Ltd
PO Box 9, Woodbridge, Suffolk IP12 3DF, UK
and of Boydell & Brewer Inc.
668 Mount Hope Ave, Rochester, NY 14620–2731, USA
website: www.boydellandbrewer.com

A catalogue record for this book is available
from the British Library

The publisher has no responsibility for the continued existence or accuracy of
URLs for external or third-party internet websites referred to in this book, and
does not guarantee that any content on such websites is, or will remain, accurate
or appropriate.

This publication is printed on acid-free paper

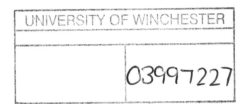

Contents

II. Government in Action

Illustrations

Tables

Figures

Contributors

Nick Barratt obtained his PhD from King's College London in state finance and fiscal history, and has researched and written on royal revenue and the development of the medieval Exchequer. He is currently Head of Medieval, Early Modern, Legal, Maps and Photographs at The National Archives.

Paul Brand is an emeritus fellow of All Souls College, Oxford. He works and writes on English medieval legal history, mainly of the long thirteenth century.

David Carpenter is Professor of Medieval History at King's College London. He was principal investigator of the AHRC-funded Henry III Fine Rolls project (2005–11) and has recently published a book on Magna Carta for Penguin.

David Crook is a former Assistant Keeper of Public Records. He has continued to be involved in the Henry III Fine Rolls project, and in a number of other research and publication projects, especially ones relating to the East Midlands. He has a particular interest in forest law and the legend of Robin Hood.

Paul Dryburgh is a medieval records specialist at The National Archives. He works principally on the records of royal government in the thirteenth and early fourteenth centuries, particularly the reign of Edward II. He is also Honorary Secretary of the Lincoln Record Society and Joint General Editor of the Pipe Roll Society.

Beth Hartland has held postdoctoral research positions at the universities of Durham and Glasgow, and King's College London. She is currently an independent historian, working on the medieval histories of Cheltenham and Cirencester for *Victoria County History Gloucestershire*. Her publications include the Fine Roll volumes, contributions to the website People of Northern England, 1216–1286 (www.pone.ac.uk), and numerous articles on medieval Ireland.

Philippa Hoskin is Reader in Medieval History at the University of Lincoln. She is general editor of the British Academy's English Episcopal Acta series, and also honorary general editor of the Canterbury and York Society's publications and of the Lincoln Record Society Kathleen Major Series. She publishes on thirteenth-century ecclesiastical, social and cultural history.

Charles Insley is a senior lecturer in medieval history at the University of Manchester. His recent publications include *Cathedrals, Communities and Conflict in the Anglo-Norman World*, ed. P. Dalton, C. Insley and L. Wilkinson (2011). He is currently writing a book on Athelstan.

Adrian Jobson is a former senior medieval records specialist at The National Archives. His most recent publication is *The First English Revolution: Simon de Montfort, Henry III and the Barons' War* (2012).

Tony Moore is a research associate at the ICMA Centre, Henley Business School, University of Reading. His research interests focus on the relationship between centre and locality in medieval England, and the history of finance. He is currently working on a Leverhulme Trust-funded project on medieval foreign exchange; he has previously participated in projects investigating medieval English sovereign debt and the aftermath of the loss of Normandy in 1204.

Alice Taylor is Lecturer in Medieval History at King's College London. She is the author of the forthcoming book *The Shape of the State in Medieval Scotland* and is preparing an edition of the early legal compilations of Scotland entitled *The Auld Lawes of Scotland*. She has published on Scottish history of the central Middle Ages, including its chronicle tradition, the experience of unfreedom, and crime and its punishment. She is Co-Investigator on the AHRC-funded project 'Models of Authority: Scottish Charters and the Emergence of Government' from 2014 to 2017, run jointly at the University of Glasgow, Cambridge University and King's College London.

Nicholas Vincent is Professor of Medieval History at the University of East Anglia and a Fellow of the British Academy.

Scott Waugh is the executive vice chancellor and provost of the University of California, Los Angeles (UCLA). His publications include *The Lordship of England* (1988), and *England in the Reign of Edward III* (1991). He has a long-standing interest in the office of escheator and its records.

Louise Wilkinson is Professor of Medieval History at Canterbury Christ Church University. She was a co-investigator of the AHRC-funded Henry III Fine Rolls project. Her most recent book is *Eleanor de Montfort: A Rebel Countess in Medieval England* (2012). She is Joint General Editor of the Pipe Roll Society.

The publication of this book has been made possible by a grant from
The Scouloudi Foundation
in association with the Institute of Historical Research

Acknowledgments

Many of the papers in this volume were first presented at the Henry III Fine Rolls Project conference held at King's College London in June 2012. The editors are grateful to Charles Insley and Nicholas Vincent for also agreeing to contribute chapters to our collection. We would also like to extend our thanks to Caroline Palmer, Robert Kinsey and the rest of the staff at Boydell & Brewer for their patience and support in seeing this volume through to publication. Although 2015 is the 800th anniversary of the 1215 Magna Carta, it was, of course, during the reign of King Henry III (1216–72) that Magna Carta became fully embedded within English political life. It is therefore hoped that the essays within this volume will make another timely contribution to the national and international celebrations focused on Magna Carta in 2015.

David Crook, Grantham
Louise J. Wilkinson, Canterbury

Abbreviations

AALT, IMG_0001	Anglo-American Legal Tradition Website, R. C. Palmer, E. K. Palmer and S. Jenks, available at aalt.law.uh.edu/aalt. html, image number(s) under the appropriate document
Annales Monastici	*Annales Monastici*, ed. H. R. Luard, Rolls Series, 5 vols (London, 1864–9)
APS	*Acts of the Parliaments of Scotland*, ed. T. Thomson and C. Innes, 11 vols (Edinburgh, 1814–24)
AWR	*The Acts of Welsh Rulers, 1120–1283*, ed. A. H. Pryce with C. L. G. Insley (Cardiff, 2005)
BF	*Liber Feodorum, or Book of Fees, commonly called Testa de Nevill*, ed. H. C. Maxwell Lyte, 3 vols (London, 1920–31)
BIHR	*Bulletin of the Institute of Historical Research*
BL	British Library, London
Bracton	*Bracton: On the Laws and Customs of England*, ed. G. E. Woodbine, trans. S. E. Thorne, 4 vols (Cambridge, MA, 1968–77)
C&S	*Councils and Synods with other Documents relating to the English Church*, part 2: *1205–1313*, ed. F. M. Powicke and C. R. Cheney, 2 vols (Oxford, 1964)
CChR	*Calendar of Charter Rolls*, 6 vols (London, 1903–27)
CDI	*Calendar of Documents Relating to Ireland, 1171–1307*, ed. H. S. Sweetman, 5 vols (London, 1875–86)
CFR	*Calendar of Fine Rolls of the Reign of Henry III*, at http://www.finerollshenry3.org.uk/content/calendar/calendar. html
Chronica Majora	*Matthaei Parisiensis Chronica Majora*, ed. H. R. Luard, Rolls Series, 7 vols (London, 1872–83)
CIM	*Calendar of Inquisitions Miscellaneous (Chancery)*, vol. 1 (London, 1916)
CIPM	*Calendar of Inquisitions Post Mortem*, vol. 1 (London, 1904)
CIRCLE	*A Calendar of Irish Chancery Letters, c. 1244–1509*, ed. P. Crooks (Dublin, 2012), at https://chancery.tcd.ie/
CLR	*Calendar of Liberate Rolls Henry III*, 6 vols (London, 1916–64)
CPR	*Calendar of Patent Rolls Henry III*, 4 vols (London, 1906–13)

CR	*Close Rolls of the Reign of Henry III*, 14 vols (London, 1902–38)
CRR	*Curia Regis Rolls*, 20 vols (London and Woodbridge, 1922–2006)
Dialogus	*Dialogus de scaccario and constitutio domus regis*, ed. and trans. E. Amt and S. D. Church (Oxford, 2007)
Documents	*Documents of the Baronial Movement of Reform and Rebellion, 1258–1267*, ed. R. F. Treharne and I. J. Sanders (Oxford, 1973)
EHR	*English Historical Review*
ER	*The Exchequer Rolls of Scotland*, ed. J. Stuart, G. Burnett *et al.*, 23 vols (Edinburgh, 1878–1908)
HMC	Historical Manuscripts Commission
HR	*Historical Research*
JMH	*Journal of Medieval History*
NRS	National Records of Scotland
ODNB	*Oxford Dictionary of National Biography* (Oxford, 2004), available to subscribers online at www.oxforddnb.com
PR	*Patent Rolls of Henry III*, 2 vols (London, 1901–3)
PRS	Pipe Roll Society
PRS n.s.	Pipe Roll Society new series
RGE	D. Crook, *Records of the General Eyre*, Public Record Office Handbooks 20 (London, 1982)
RLC	*Rotuli Litterarum Clausarum in Turri Londinensi Asservati*, ed. T. D. Hardy, 2 vols (London, 1833–4)
RLP	*Rotuli Litterarum Patentium in Turri Londinensi Asservati*, ed. T. D. Hardy (London, 1835)
Rot. Chart.	*Rotuli Chartarum in Turri Londinensi Asservati, Vol. I, Pars 1, 1199–1216*, ed. T. D. Hardy (London, 1837)
Rot. de Lib.	*Rotuli de Liberate ac de Misis et Praestitis Regnante Iohanne*, ed. T. D. Hardy (London, 1844)
Rot. de Ob. et Fin.	*Rotuli de Oblatis et Finibus in Turri Londinensi Asservati Tempore Regis Johannis*, ed. T. D. Hardy (London, 1835)
RRS, i	*Regesta Regum Scottorum*, vol. 1: *The Acts of Malcolm IV, King of Scots, 1153–65*, ed. G. W. S. Barrow (Edinburgh, 1960)
RRS, ii	*Regesta Regum Scottorum*, vol. 2: *The Acts of William I, King of Scots, 1165–1214*, ed. G. W. S. Barrow (Edinburgh, 1971)
RRS, iii	*Regesta Regum Scottorum*, vol. 3: *The Acts of Alexander II, King of Scots, 1214–49*, ed. K. J. Stringer (Edinburgh, forthcoming)
Select Charters	W. Stubbs, *Select Charters*, 9th edn, revised by H. W. C. Davis (Oxford, 1913)

Select Pleas	*Select Pleas of the Forest*, ed. J. G. Turner, Selden Society 13 (1901)
TCE I	*Thirteenth Century England I: Proceedings of the Newcastle Upon Tyne Conference 1985*, ed. P. R. Coss and S. D. Lloyd (Woodbridge, 1986)
TCE II	*Thirteenth Century England II: Proceedings of the Newcastle Upon Tyne Conference 1987*, ed. P. R. Coss and S. D. Lloyd (Woodbridge, 1988)
TCE III	*Thirteenth Century England III: Proceedings of the Newcastle Upon Tyne Conference 1989*, ed. P. R. Coss and S. D. Lloyd (Woodbridge, 1991)
TCE IV	*Thirteenth Century England IV: Proceedings of the Newcastle Upon Tyne Conference 1991*, ed. P. R. Coss and S. D. Lloyd (Woodbridge, 1992)
TCE V	*Thirteenth Century England V: Proceedings of the Newcastle Upon Tyne Conference 1993*, ed. P. R. Coss and S. D. Lloyd (Woodbridge, 1995)
TCE VII	*Thirteenth Century England VII: Proceedings of the Durham Conference 1997*, ed. M. Prestwich, R. Britnell and R. Frame (Woodbridge, 1999)
TCE VIII	*Thirteenth Century England VIII: Proceedings of the Durham Conference 1999*, ed. M. Prestwich, R. Britnell and R. Frame (Woodbridge, 2001)
TCE X	*Thirteenth Century England X: Proceedings of the Durham Conference 2003*, ed. M. Prestwich, R. Britnell and R. Frame (Woodbridge, 2005)
TCE XI	*Thirteenth Century England XI: Proceedings of the Gregynog Conference 2005*, ed. B. K. Weiler, J. E. Burton, P. Schofield and K. Stöber (Woodbridge, 2007)
TCE XII	*Thirteenth Century England XII: Proceedings of the Gregynog Conference 2007*, ed. J. E. Burton, P. Schofield and B. K. Weiler (Woodbridge, 2009)
TCE XIII	*Thirteenth Century England XIII: Proceedings of the Paris Conference 2009*, ed. J. Burton, F. Lachaud and P. Schofield (Woodbridge, 2011)
TNA	The National Archives, Kew
TRHS	*Transactions of the Royal Historical Society*
Wendover	*Rogeri de Wendover Flores Historiarum*, ed. H. G. Hewlett, Rolls Series, 3 vols (London, 1886–9)

Introduction

David Carpenter, David Crook and Louise J. Wilkinson

King Henry III succeeded his father, King John, at the age of nine in 1216 and reigned for fifty-six years until his death in 1272. His reign was a period of momentous change. The spiritual life of the country was transformed by the arrival of the friars and the work of pastorally minded bishops. The population increased rapidly so that, according to some calculations, it neared six million by the end of the century, roughly three times its size at the time of Domesday Book. Meanwhile the money supply greatly increased and an extended network of chartered markets and fairs came into place. However, the rise in the population was outrunning the ability of the land to sustain it, creating growing numbers of peasant smallholders living on the edge of subsistence and quite literally starving to death in years of bad harvest. There were other sufferers, too. The king broke the financial capacity of the Jews through heavy taxation, and also sanctioned the belief that they crucified Christian boys in macabre parody of the crucifixion of Christ. The way was being prepared for the eventual expulsion of the Jews from England in 1290.[1]

In the first phase of his reign, even when the minority was formally ended in 1227, Henry ruled with great ministers inherited from his father by his side. What historians sometimes call his 'personal rule' began in 1234. During that period an increasingly important part was played by Henry's queen, Eleanor of Provence, whom he married in 1236. The patronage which Henry gave both to Eleanor's Savoyard relations and also to his own Poitevin half-brothers was widely criticised, and growing hostility to foreigners served to sharpen a sense of English national identity. Henry's personal rule ended in the great revolution of 1258. A magnate council seized power and carried through wide-ranging reforms of law and local government. After his victory at the battle of Lewes in May 1264, Simon de Montfort, earl of Leicester, became the virtual ruler of England until his defeat and death at the battle of Evesham in August 1265. It was another two years before peace and order returned to England.[2]

---

[1] An illuminating new account of this period may be found in John Gillingham, *Conquests, Catastrophe and Recovery: Britain and Ireland 1066–1485* (London, 2014). See also D. Carpenter, *The Struggle for Mastery: Britain 1066–1284* (London, 2004), chapters 1, 9–13.

[2] Works on this period include H. Ridgeway, 'Foreign Favourites and Henry III's Problems of Patronage, 1247–58', *EHR* 104 (1989), 590–610; J. R. Maddicott, *Simon de Montfort* (Cambridge, 1994); D. A. Carpenter, *The Reign of Henry III* (London, 1996); M. Howell, *Eleanor of Provence: Queenship in Thirteenth-Century England* (Oxford, 1998); L. J. Wilkinson, *Eleanor de Montfort: A Rebel Countess in Medieval England* (London, 2012); A. Jobson,

Politically and constitutionally the most important developments of the reign were the establishment of Magna Carta and the emergence of parliament. It was Henry III's Magna Carta, issued in 1225, which became the final and definitive version, not King John's Charter of 1215 or the revised versions of the early minority in 1216 and 1217. It is chapters from Henry's Charter of 1225 that are still on the statute book of the United Kingdom today. Alongside Magna Carta, Henry III also issued both in 1217 and 1225 a quite separate Charter dealing with the law and administration of the royal forest, and thereafter the two Charters were always linked together. The first assembly to be called 'parliament' in an official document met in 1237. The first parliament to which were summoned knights representing the counties and burgesses representing the towns, the 'House of Commons' in embryo, was that convoked in January 1265 when Simon de Montfort was in control of government. The pattern of Montfort's parliament was repeated with increasing frequency under Henry III's son, Edward I (1272–1307). By the end of his reign the presence of knights and burgesses in parliament was more or less fixed. The political community had thus become much wider. The national assembly envisaged in King John's 1215 Magna Carta was one composed of earls, barons, bishops, abbots and other tenants-in-chief. They alone were thought sufficient to represent the realm. In the second half of the century the growing power and independence of knights at the head of county society, and the increasing wealth of towns, meant that they too had to be represented.[3]

The workings of royal government were inseparable from these developments in politics, government and society. The vast corpus of records they produced reveals an increasingly sophisticated governmental machine around which turned much of the kingdom's life. The great bulk of these records were produced by the Chancery, the Exchequer and the law courts. In the reign of Henry III, the Chancery for the most part followed the king, which was not difficult given Henry's relatively sedentary lifestyle, so different from that of his father.[4] The Chancery issued the charters, letters patent, letters close and writs through which England was governed. Through them, Henry dispensed patronage, spent money, gave a myriad of orders, and enabled his subjects to initiate litigation according to the forms of the common law. Much of this output was recorded on the great series of Chancery rolls: charters on charter rolls, letters patent on patent rolls, and letters close both on the close rolls and (for letters dealing with the expenditure of money) the *liberate* rolls.[5] In addition, the fine rolls recorded

The First English Revolution: Simon de Montfort, Henry III and the Barons' War (London, 2012). There are many pertinent individual studies in the fourteen volumes of *Thirteenth Century England* (*TCE*) published between 1985 and 2013.

[3]   The definitive work on Parliament is now J. R. Maddicott, *The Origins of the English Parliament, 924–1327* (Oxford, 2010).

[4]   See J. E. Kanter, 'Peripatetic and Sedentary Kingship: The Itineraries of John and Henry III', in *TCE XIII*, pp. 11–26.

[5]   See D. A. Carpenter, 'The English Royal Chancery in the Thirteenth Century', in *English Government in the Thirteenth Century*, ed. A. Jobson (Woodbridge, 2004), pp. 49–70.

the offers of money to the king for concessions and favours. A new set of rolls was begun at the start of each regnal year, so the sets ran from 28 October (the day of Henry III's first coronation in 1216) to 27 October. Thanks to labours of nineteenth- and twentieth-century editors, working under the auspices of the old Public Record Office, nearly all these rolls are in print, in the form of either full Latin text or English calendar. The omission of the fine rolls was remedied by the Henry III Fine Rolls project, funded by the Arts and Humanities Research Council. Between 2007 and 2012 the project made freely available online electronically searchable translations of the roughly two million words found in the Henrician rolls (www.finerollshenry3.org.uk). It also published three hardback volumes covering the period from 1216 down to 1242.[6]

The Chancery was not the only office travelling with the king and producing records. The Wardrobe, which stored the king's treasure, did so too, and also had its accounts audited by the Exchequer.[7] The departments responsible for the court's daily food, drink and alms-giving likewise recorded their expenditures. When these wardrobe and household records survive, as they do all too rarely, they can be very illuminating.[8]

The function of the Exchequer was to collect and audit the Crown's annual revenue.[9] The results of the annual audit were recorded on documents later called 'pipe rolls', because each roll looked like a pipe when rolled up. The sequence of surviving pipe rolls begins in 1155 and they are now in print down to 1224, thanks to the work of the Pipe Roll Society (http://www.piperollsociety.co.uk).[10] Two later pipe rolls have been printed, those for 1230 and 1242, while that of 1259, edited by Richard Cassidy, is forthcoming. Images of the pipe rolls after 1224 can be found on the Anglo-American Legal Tradition website (http://aalt. law.uh.edu). The Exchequer also produced memoranda rolls, receipt and issue rolls, and plea rolls, and some of this material has been published both by the Pipe Roll Society and Selden Society (http://www.selden-society.qmw.ac.uk).[11]

[6]   *Calendar of the Fine Rolls of the Reign of Henry III preserved in The National Archives*, ed. P. Dryburgh and B. Hartland; technical eds A. Ciula, J. M. Vieira and T. Lopez, 3 vols (Woodbridge, 2007–9).

[7]   See *The Wardrobe Accounts of Henry III*, ed. B. L. Wild, PRS n.s. 58 (London, 2012).

[8]   See D. A. Carpenter, 'The Household Rolls of King Henry III of England (1216–1272)', *HR* 80 (2007), 22–46.

[9]   For the Exchequer in this period, see N. Barratt, 'Finance on a Shoestring: The Exchequer in the Thirteenth Century', in *English Government in the Thirteenth Century*, ed. A. Jobson (Woodbridge, 2004), pp. 71–86.

[10]   For the one earlier pipe roll to survive, see *The Great Roll of the Pipe for the Thirty-First Year of the Reign of King Henry I, Michaelmas 1130*, ed. J. A. Green, PRS n.s. 57 (London, 2012). See also M. Hagger, 'A Pipe Roll for 25 Henry I', *EHR* 122 (2007), 133–40.

[11]   *Receipt Rolls for the Fourth, Fifth and Sixth Years of the Reign of King Henry III: Easter 1220, 1221, 1222*, ed. N. Barratt, indexes by L. Napran and D. Crook, PRS n.s. 52 (London, 2003); *Receipt Rolls for the Seventh and Eighth Years of the Reign of King Henry III: Easter 1223, Michaelmas 1224*, ed. N. Barratt, indexes by L. Napran and D. Crook, PRS n.s. 55 (London, 2007); *Receipt and Issue Rolls for the Twenty-Sixth Year of the Reign of King Henry III, 1241–42*, ed. R. C. Stacey, PRS n.s. 49 (London, 1987–8); *The Memoranda Roll of the King's Remembrancer for Michaelmas 1230-Trinity 1231*, ed. C. Robinson, PRS n.s. 11 (London,

A branch of the Exchequer dealt with Jewish affairs, and its plea rolls, where they survive, have been published by the Jewish Historical Society (http://www.jhse. org).[12]

The king held a variety of courts for which records survive. The court *coram rege*, later called the court of King's Bench, followed his person. The 'Bench', later called the court of Common Pleas, sat at Westminster. The king's judges in the localities held a series of courts, with different jurisdictions. There were also courts held by the justices appointed to try breaches of the forest law, and a good number of their plea rolls, too, are extant from the 1250s onwards. A high proportion of this judicial material has been published both by The Public Record Office / The National Archives and, in the case of the plea rolls of judges in the counties, by the Selden Society and local record societies.[13] Images of the original rolls can again be found on the Anglo-American Legal Tradition website (http://aalt.law.uh.edu).

During the course of Henry's reign, there was a great increase in the scale of this record-keeping. The first volume of patent rolls to be calendared in England, covering the fifteen years between 1232 and 1247, ran to 660 printed pages. The volume covering just the six years between 1266 and 1272 contains 930 pages.[14] It took 89 membranes to record the business of the Bench in 1220 (itself an unusually high figure for that period), and 352 in 1275.[15] Some of pipe rolls from late in Henry's reign are nearly double the size of those from the start. It is from the study of these records that the chapters in this book flow.

The first section of this book, 'Records and their Uses', explores the practice and purpose of record-keeping in Henry III's England. David Carpenter's chapter discusses the importance of the fine rolls for charting the growth of government records during the reigns of King John and King Henry III, the transformation in the wealth and breadth of business dealt with in the rolls under the latter, and the new light that their contents shed on the motivating

---

1933); *Select Cases in the Exchequer of Pleas*, ed. H. Jenkinson and B. E. R. Fermoy, Selden Society 48 (London, 1931).

[12] *Calendar of the Plea Rolls of the Exchequer of the Jews Henry III and Edward I*, ed. J. M. Rigg, H. Jenkinson and H. G. Richardson, Jewish Historical Society, 4 vols (London, 1905–72); *Plea Rolls of the Exchequer of the Jews*, vol. 5: *Edward I, 1275–77*, ed. S. Cohen, Jewish Historical Society (London, 1992); *Plea Rolls of the Exchequer of the Jews*, vol. 6: *Edward I, 1279–81*, ed. P. Brand, Jewish Historical Society (London, 2005).

[13] *CRR*. The publication of eyre rolls is noted in D. Crook, *Records of the General Eyre* (London, 1982). Rolls from the reign of Henry III published since 1982 include *Crown Pleas of the Devon Eyre of 1238*, ed. H. Summerson, Devon and Cornwall Record Society new series 28 (Torquay, 1985); *The Civil Pleas of the Suffolk Eyre of 1240*, ed. E. J. Gallagher, Suffolk Records Society 52 (Woodbridge, 2009); *The 1258–59 Special Eyre of Surrey and Kent*, ed. A. H. Hershey, Surrey Record Society 38 (Woking, 2004); *The 1263 Surrey Eyre*, ed. S. Stewart, Surrey Record Society 40 (Woking, 2006); *Crown Pleas of the Wiltshire Eyre 1268*, ed. B. Farr, C. Elrington and H. Summerson, Wiltshire Record Society 65 (Chippenham, 2012).

[14] *CPR 1232–47*; *CPR 1266–72*.

[15] P. Brand, *The Origins of the English Legal Profession* (Oxford, 1992), p. 24.

forces behind the revolution of 1258. Paul Dryburgh considers the relationship between the fine rolls and the originalia rolls, a hitherto neglected series of government records, and the range of bureaucratic functions that those rolls served at the royal Exchequer. Paul Brand examines the value of the fine rolls for legal historians, principally through the information they reveal about foreign pleas, the operation of the 'four knights' system and criminal justice, the treatment of aliens (men or women born outside England), the alienation of lands by tenants-in-chief, the drafting of special writs, and the punishment of persons convicted of redisseisin. The expansion of English royal justice under Henry III is the focus of Tony Moore's chapter. In it, he surveys evidence drawn from the extant plea rolls and fine rolls to trace the increased workload of the royal courts, identifying the period in or around 1250 as a key turning point, when the range of business dealt with by the county courts was eroded, and the scope of that dealt with by the royal courts increased dramatically.

Beth Hartland's chapter is the first of three that focus on record-keeping practices in other parts of the British Isles during the thirteenth century. One of the chief ways in which English lordship over Ireland was enforced under Henry III was through the work of the Irish Chancery. Hartland investigates why the Irish Chancery did not follow or imitate English bureaucratic practice by compiling fine rolls of its own, and how Irish fines were administered by the English Crown and its agents. The processes of financial auditing and record-keeping adopted by Scottish kings in the thirteenth century are then explored by Alice Taylor, who offers a firm rebuttal to the idea that administrative developments in Scotland were modelled, albeit on a more modest scale, on those of England. Charles Insley's chapter, meanwhile, addresses the question of the relationship between English administrative practices and those of the rulers of twelfth- and thirteenth-century Gwynedd. Drawing on the *acta* of the Welsh rulers, Insley argues that it is time to adopt a more nuanced approach to understanding diplomatic practice in Wales, an approach that acknowledges more fully native, as well as English, influences, the complex political context in which they operated, and the identities and conflicting claims to authority that they articulated. Through its focus on a little-studied inventory of gifts made to Henry III in 1234–5, now preserved in The National Archives, Nicholas Vincent draws the first section of the book to a close by reminding us of the diplomatic, political, financial and personal importance of the precious objects presented to King Henry III as gifts by foreign potentates and rulers and the king's English subjects.

The chapters in the second section, 'Government in Action', explore the operation of English royal government at the centre and in the localities during the reign of Henry III. Nicholas Barratt brings into focus the restoration of the machinery of government during the minority of Henry III, tracing the recovery of Exchequer authority, namely the process of reconstruction and the re-establishment of procedures to facilitate the collection of royal revenues in the aftermath of the civil war over Magna Carta. The administration of the royal forest was another controversial aspect of royal government under Henry III, as it had been under his predecessors. David Crook's chapter examines the significance of Roger of Wendover's account of the boundary clauses of the implementation of the Charter of the Forest in 1225–7. Relating to the time when Wendover was prior of Belvoir, Crook argues that his description of these events was informed by his own experiences, as the manager of a small monastic estate in Leicestershire and Nottinghamshire, of the operation of forest eyres and the local grievances to which they gave rise. Adrian Jobson traces the restoration of royal administration in England after the Barons' War, exploring the speed, level of efficiency and processes whereby the Exchequer, the law courts and the Chancery, the three chief organs of government, resumed their operations.

Not only was Henry III's reign a pivotal period in the history of English royal government, it was also an important time for ecclesiastical legislation within the English Church. Philippa Hoskin analyses the occasionally fraught relationship between the Church and the Crown under Henry III, and the emergence of epis-copal opposition to the king in the late 1250s and early 1260s. These tensions came to a head in 1261, when a set of statutes for the English Church were pre-sented to, and rejected by, the pope, paving the way for the bishops to ally with the Montfortian barons at Lewes in 1264. The final two chapters of the volume focus on different groups of personnel of English royal government under Henry III. Louise Wilkinson explores the contribution made by aristocratic women to English political life, and the roles that some of them assumed in local govern-ment as sheriffs, castellans and foresters. Scott Waugh charts in detail the long line of administrative experiments that culminated in the final emergence of the office of escheator just before 1250. He explicitly links the development of the office to broader efforts to stabilise and reform royal finances, and therefore authority, during the king's minority. The office's subsequent development was characterised by the government's growing reliance on local men to manage its feudal resources. Waugh's research was greatly facilitated by the calendaring of the previously unpublished fine rolls, which made readily accessible a great many of the detailed pieces of information needed to reconstruct the later stages of this complex administrative process.

The chapters in this volume promise to enhance significantly our understand-ing of the processes, machinery, mechanisms and personnel of Henrician royal government and its record-keeping practices; it is also hoped that they will pave the way for future research into this pivotal era in English administrative, consti-tutional, legal and political history that lay between Magna Carta and the birth of the parliamentary state.

I

Records and their Uses

1

Between Magna Carta and the Parliamentary State: The Fine Rolls of King Henry III, 1216–72

David Carpenter

If a fire in The National Archives at Kew was spreading towards the Chancery rolls, and there was time to save only one portion of them from the thirteenth century, without question I would save the fine rolls of the reign of Henry III. Far more than any other rolls from the period, they reflect fundamental changes in the nature of kingship, government and society, changes in that hinge period between the implantation of Magna Carta into English life and the development of the parliamentary state. The other Chancery rolls of this time – those recording charters, letters patent and letters close – remain much the same across the reigns of John and Henry III, apart that is from the hiving off of the financial business of the close rolls into a separate *liberate* roll.[1] The fine rolls, by contrast, change absolutely. More than the other series, they illustrate the growth in record-keeping, that movement 'from Memory to Written Record', which is the subject of Michael Clanchy's classic book.[2] The fine rolls also illustrate two of the central developments of Henry's reign: on the one hand, the increase in the benefits of monarchy with the huge expansion of the common law; on the other, the decline in the burdens of monarchy because Magna Carta made it so much more difficult to extract money from the king's subjects in an arbitrary fashion. Indeed, the fine rolls, more than any other source, demonstrate the triumph of Magna Carta and thus show the need for a new monarchy in the thirteenth century. The king had now to find alternative sources of revenue, the most obvious and lucrative being general taxation. Since such taxation, as the 1215 Magna Carta made clear, needed the general consent of the kingdom, here were the origins of the tax-based parliamentary state. Given the burgeoning benefits of the common law, one might think that Henry III was well placed to conciliate local society and secure the consent of parliament to taxation. In fact, of course, such was the unpopularity of his rule that after 1237 he never succeeded in doing so. In 1258 a great revolution stripped him of power and carried through wide-ranging reforms of local government. In seeking to explain the revolution, historians like myself have had a tendency to treat as separate strands the unpopularity of the king's government in the shires, the factional struggles at a court dominated (or so it might seem) by

---

[1] *CLR 1226–40*, pp. v–xiii.
[2] M. T. Clanchy, *From Memory to Written Record*, 3rd edn (Oxford, 2012).

Henry's foreign relatives, and the collapse of Henry's scheme to place his second son on the throne of Sicily. Another value of the fine rolls is to show how far these strands were in fact connected. The rolls provide the main evidence for the extraordinary effects of a policy that Henry developed in the 1250s, that of distraint of knighthood. This alienated county society and gave it an insight into the nature both of Henry's court and foreign policy. The fine rolls therefore shed new light on the revolution of 1258.

Although they had a long earlier history, the fine rolls survive only from the start of John's reign, in 1199.[3] When they first appear their contents are very different from those of the other rolls kept by the Chancery, which also survive from around the same time. Whereas the latter record Chancery output, in the form of copies of charters, letters patent and letters close, the fine rolls are simply lists of the fines made with the king. A fine essentially was an offer of money accepted by the king for a concession or favour. It could be virtually compulsory, as when made by a tenant-in-chief to enter his inheritance, or by an individual to recover the king's favour. It could also be entirely voluntary, as when purchasing a charter to establish a new market, or a writ to prosecute a law case. In the first half of John's reign the records of individual fines on the rolls only rarely mention the accompanying royal letters to the sheriffs ordering them to take security for payment. Where a letter is noted it rarely includes the clause with the date of issue. This format is explained by the function of these rolls, which was simply to keep a record of the money offered to the king. Such a record was absolutely necessary because, although those making offers were often, in the rolls, said to 'give' the money, the money was very rarely given immediately in coin. Rather payment was to be in the future, so schedules of payment were often included when the fine was noted in the rolls. Moreover, although all fines were made at the itinerant court, and were sometimes called 'offers of the court' (*oblata curie*), it was nearly always the Exchequer at Westminster which had the job of actually collecting the money and auditing the payments. So that it knew what money to collect, copies of the fine rolls, known as 'originalia rolls', were sent to it in

---

[3] For what follows, see P. R. Dryburgh and B. Hartland, 'The Development of the Fine Rolls', in *TCE XII*, pp. 193–205; D. Carpenter, 'Historical Introduction', in *Calendar of the Fine Rolls of the Reign of Henry III preserved in The National Archives*, vol. 1: *1216–1224*, ed. P. Dryburgh and B. Hartland, technical eds A. Ciula and J. M. Vieira (Woodbridge, 2007), pp. vii–xxiii; P. R. Dryburgh, 'The Language of Making Fine', Fine of the Month June 2007, available at http://www.finerollshenry3.org.uk/content/month/fm-06-2007.html (accessed 2 April 2015); and Dryburgh, 'Originalia Rolls 11 and 17 Henry III', in *Calendar of the Fine Rolls of the Reign of Henry III preserved in The National Archives*, vol. 2: *1224–1234*, ed. P. Dryburgh and B. Hartland, technical eds A. Ciula and J. M. Vieira (Woodbridge, 2008), pp. x–xxiv. For debate about the origins of the Chancery rolls, see N. Vincent, 'Why 1199? Bureaucracy and Enrolment under John and his Contemporaries', in *English Government in the Thirteenth Century*, ed. A. Jobson (Woodbridge, 2004), pp. 17–48; D. Carpenter, '"In testimonium factorum brevium": The Origins of the English Chancery Rolls', in *Records, Administration and Aristocratic Society in the Anglo-Norman Realm*, ed. N. Vincent (Woodbridge, 2009), pp. 1–28, together with Vincent's reply at pp. xvi–xix. It might be added that Carpenter saw no need to change what he had written in the light of Vincent's amusing remarks.

stages through the year. When the Exchequer got the rolls, it included the new debts in the lists of debts, called 'the summonses', which the sheriffs were ordered to collect and pay into the Exchequer. The resulting payments (or lack of them) were recorded on the pipe roll for the year under the heading of 'new offerings' (*nova oblata*), the pipe rolls, one for each financial year, being the Exchequer's record of its annual audit of the money owed to the Crown.

The early fine rolls, therefore, are merely lists of money owed to the king for specified concessions, together on occasion with schedules of payment and lists of sureties.[4] Very soon, however, the desire to record more information brings about a change. All the surviving rolls down to that for 1207–8 have the form described above. The rolls for the next five years are lost. When the series resumes with the roll for 1213–14, the pattern is different. Much more regularly than before, a record is made of the letters issued to the sheriffs in relation to the fines. Now, moreover, the letters are always given their concluding clause stating the place and date of their attestation. So the first four letters on the roll are those witnessed by the king at Wingham (Kent) on 31 May, at Aldingbourn (Sussex) on 14 June, and at Corfe on 22 and 23 June.[5] For the first time, therefore, it is possible to put a date to the fines.

There was another development which transformed the nature of the fine rolls. This was the inclusion of more and more letters unrelated to fines.[6] The reason for putting such letters on the fine rolls, letters usually addressed to local officials or the Exchequer, was that they were often related, as were fines, to the financial administration of the country. We can see a start of this in John's reign when the roll for 1207–8 records the terms on which local officials – sheriffs and keepers of manors – are to hold office. John fitz Hugh, for example, is to answer for a 100-mark increment as sheriff of Surrey.[7] Gradually, it became the practice to record all such appointments on the fine rolls. The fine roll of 1256–7 has twenty-seven of them. The rolls also came to include letters dealing with such matters as money demanded from the Jews, tallages levied on towns and royal manors, and concessions over the rates of debt repayment.

In the 1220s the increase in non-fine business prompted a change to the marginal annotations made to each entry.[8] In the early fine rolls these had been limited to the name of the county to which the entry belonged. When the great majority of entries related to fines that made perfect sense. The county annotations were carried over into the originalia rolls and thus helped the Exchequer assign each fine to its correct county, both in the list of debts that the sheriffs were to collect and in the pipe rolls, themselves organised county by county. However, once a significant proportion of the entries was no longer about fines and did not need sorting in this way, it made more sense to label these entries

---

4   John's fine rolls are printed in *Rot. de Ob. et Fin.*
5   *Rot. de Ob. et Fin.*, pp. 464–5.
6   Dryburgh and Hartland, 'Development of the Fine Rolls', pp. 199–205.
7   *Rot. de Ob. et Fin.*, pp. 379, 400, 411, 427.
8   Carpenter, 'Historical Introduction', pp. xix–xxi.

not relating to fines according to their subject matter and/or the people to whom they related. A reform of the marginalia in the 1220s precisely brought that about.

During the course of Henry's reign the fine rolls hugely increased in size. The roll for 1220–1 has 352 entries; fifty years later the roll for 1270–1 has 1,581. The increase in non-fine business is one reason for that. Another, more important, was the expansion in the number of writs purchased to initiate or facilitate common law litigation.[9] Here, to be sure, the fine rolls only reveal one strand of the writ business, for they have nothing about the standard form writs 'of course' (*de cursu*), which initiated a large proportion of the common law litigation. This is because, costing only 6*d.*, the money for such writs went straight into the Chancery. Thus of the approximately 130 writs surviving from the writ file of the 1248 Berkshire eyre, writs that is which initiated litigation at the eyre, not one has an entry on the fine rolls.[10] In the 1320s, when we have the first evidence from the financial records of the Chancery, it looks as though over 20,000 writs *de cursu* were being issued every year. The problem with such writs in the thirteenth century was that they only initiated litigation before the justices in eyre, which could mean waiting for years until they came to hear pleas. If litigants wished to speed matters up, then they had to secure different types of writ. Since such writs cost more than 6*d.* they *do* feature on the fine rolls.[11] Their increasing number is another telling witness to the popularity of the common law.

The scale of this increase can be illustrated by a direct comparison between two sets of fine rolls fifty years apart, namely those for 1207–8 and 1256–7.[12] These are the rolls which cover John's ninth regnal year, from 31 May 1207 to 30 May 1208, and Henry's forty-first, from 28 October 1256 to 27 October 1257. When it comes to the ease with which writs could be obtained from the Chancery, these years are comparable, for both kings were entirely in England, apart from three weeks in August and September 1257 when Henry was engaged on an ineffective campaign in north Wales. One thinks, of course, of John as itinerating much more quickly and widely than his sedentary son, yet in 1207–8 the furthest north he reached was Nottingham, in August 1207.[13] Both kings spent time at Winchester, Clarendon, Woodstock and London, though John's visits were much briefer than Henry's.[14]

---

[9]   For an analysis of this down to 1233–4, see Dryburgh and Hartland, 'Development of the Fine Rolls', pp. 197–9.

[10]   *The Roll and Writ File of the Berkshire Eyre of 1248*, ed. M. T. Clanchy, Selden Society 90 (London, 1972–3), pp. lxvi, cxii–cxiii, and nos a1–a231.

[11]   D. Carpenter, 'The English Royal Chancery in the Thirteenth Century', in *English Government in the Thirteenth Century*, ed. A. Jobson (Woodbridge, 2004), pp. 49–70, at pp. 55–6.

[12]   *Rot. de Ob. et Fin.*, pp. 371–464; *CFR 1256–57*, nos 1–1037.

[13]   John was in the Welsh marches both in November 1207 and April 1208. His itinerary, worked out by T. Duffus Hardy, is in the introduction to *RLP*. See J. Kanter, 'Peripatetic and Sedentary Kingship: The Itineraries of John and Henry III', in *TCE XIII*, pp. 11–26.

[14]   For Henry's itinerary, see T. Craib, 'The Itinerary of Henry III, 1216–1272' (Public Record Office, 1923), edited and annotated by S. Brindle and S. Priestley (English Heritage,

In the fine roll of 1207–8 there are around seventy fines purchasing writs connected in some way with common law legal actions. Thirty-three of these are for writs of *pone*, which transferred cases either into the court held by the king's judges at Westminster, the Common Bench, or into the court of King's Bench, which followed the king himself. Fifty years later, in the roll of 1256–7, the equivalent number of fines is 462, a six-fold increase. Sixty are for writs of *pone*, 130 for writs *ad terminum* (writs which gave a date or 'term' for the hearing of a case), and 270 were for having a case heard by specific judges, so as not to have to wait for the eyre. Most of the leading judges of the period were active in this work: Bath, Bracton, Briewes, Erdington, Preston, Turri, Thirkleby, Whitchester and Walton all feature in the fines. Since the roll includes 1,037 items of business, the 462 purchases of writs take up 44% of the whole. The percentage rises to over 55% if we exclude the many fines in the roll from a one-off sale of privileges, as discussed later. In the last phase of the reign the percentage is even higher. In the rolls between 1265–6 and 1271–2, purchases of writs never take up less than 90% of the whole. In 1220–1 the equivalent percentage had been around 25%.

The demand for litigation by common law had been there in John's reign, but he had failed to exploit it. The fine roll of 1207–8 has not a single example of a commission for the hearing of individual assizes which became so common under Henry III. What was worse, between 1209 and 1214 John shut down the Bench at Westminster and the routine eyres in the counties. Instead he made all common law litigation follow the King's Bench, which was impossibly inconvenient for litigants, given his frenetic itinerary. The condemnation in Magna Carta was emphatic. Under chapter 17 common pleas were not to follow the king's court but be heard in a fixed place. That meant either before the Bench at Westminster or before the king's judges in the counties.[15] When it came to the visitations of the counties, the Charter went on to stipulate that the king's judges were to visit the counties four times a year and hear the most popular of the assizes in the county courts, with four knights elected in the county court. In the Charter of 1217 this was moderated, perhaps by the intervention of the king's judges, aware of the burdens four visitations a year would impose. Instead, they were only to come once a year, and hear the assizes simply with the knights of the county, rather than having to work with four elected knights. Even the once-yearly visitations do not seem to have been implemented in practice. But in spirit the demand was fulfilled, as the fine rolls show, by the commissions to judges to hear individual assizes. At first, between 1218 and 1240, these commissions were very often to four county knights, which harked back to the four knights of the 1215 Charter. Thereafter, as we see in the roll of 1256–7, they were to individual judges.[16] The latter, however, probably co-opted county knights to sit with them,

no date), forthcoming in the List and Index Society series.

[15] M. T. Clanchy, 'Magna Carta and the Common Pleas', *Studies in Medieval History Presented to R. H. C. Davis*, ed. H. Mayr-Harting and R. I. Moore (London, 1985), pp. 219–32.

[16] For discussion, see A. Musson, 'The Local Administration of Justice: A Reappraisal of

as probably envisaged in the 1217 Magna Carta. The cost of writs for such commissions was significant, but not impossibly high. In the fine roll for 1256–7, 246 of the writs cost half a mark, 197 one mark, and forty-three 20 shillings.

The fine rolls of Henry III come, therefore, to look very different from those of John in the area of judicial administration. They also look very different when it comes to the financial burdens the king was placing on his subjects, as the pioneering work of Paul Dryburgh and Beth Hartland has shown.[17] According to their calculations, the amount offered to John in the fine rolls of 1199–1200, in the heavy business at the start of the reign, was an astonishing £40,704. In 1204–5, a more normal year, it was £17,971. In 1213–14 the total was £25,379, although it was only £12,036 if we exclude the £13,333 fine of Geoffrey de Mandeville to marry Isabella of Gloucester. But by this time John was losing his grip and making concessions in the aftermath of the plot of 1212. By contrast, the most offered in any Henrician fine roll down to 1242 was £11,294 in the roll for 1241–2, and this sum falls to £4,628 if one fine of £6,666 from Joan, widow of Hugh Wake, for the custody of his lands during the minority of the heir, is excluded. The average offered in the eight rolls between 1226–7 and 1233–4 was £6,941. In the eight rolls between 1234–5 and 1241–2 it drops to £3,980.

In order to extend the range of these comparisons, I have added up the amounts offered to the king in the fine rolls for 1207–8 and 1256–7. These years are very comparable, since during both the kings needed enormous sums to fund their ambitions overseas. John was building up a treasure to support the campaign which, he hoped, would recover his Continental empire. Henry was doing the same for the campaign intended to place his second son on the throne of Sicily. Simply in terms of ready cash from fines, John's needs were actually less pressing in 1207–8 than Henry's fifty years later. John remained comfortably funded by the proceeds of the great tax on rents and movable property agreed at the Oxford council in February 1207. The fine rolls of 1207–8 themselves include six fines relating to the collection of the tax.[18] On the dorse of the roll the total receipts are noted as being £57,421, with the auditors noting that they would give more information to the king 'when we come to you'.[19] Henry, by contrast, was desperately in need of ready cash. His income had been reduced by the appanage created for his son, the Lord Edward, and by the assigning of Jewish revenue, in

---

the "Four Knights" System', in *English Government in the Thirteenth Century*, ed. A. Jobson (Woodbridge, 2004), pp. 97–110; and J. Kanter, 'The Four Knights' System and the Evidence for it in the Fine Rolls', Fine of the Month March 2007, available at http://www.fine-rollshenry3.org.uk/content/month/fm-03-2007.html (accessed 2 April 2015).

[17] For Dryburgh and Hartland's figures, see *Fine Rolls of the Reign of Henry III*, vol. 2: *1224–1234*, pp. vi–ix; *Calendar of the Fine Rolls of the Reign of Henry III preserved in The National Archives*, vol. 3: *1234–1242*, ed. P. Dryburgh and B. Hartland, technical eds A. Ciula and J. M. Vieira (Woodbridge, 2009), pp. xii–xiii; and Hartland and Dryburgh, 'Development of the Fine Rolls', pp. 194–5.

[18] *Rot. de Ob. et Fin.*, pp. 372, 393, 395, 401, 413, 430.

[19] *Rot. de Ob. et Fin.*, p. 459.

return for a loan, to his brother Richard of Cornwall. Meanwhile he continued to shower patronage on his foreign relations. 1,000 marks of the income from fines in the roll of 1256–7 were assigned to Edward, and another 1,000 marks to the queen's uncle Thomas of Savoy. Something of Henry's immediate need is shown in the orders, enrolled on the fine rolls, for the selling off of woods in the royal forest in order to raise 4,000 marks.[20]

In 1257–8, therefore, one might expect Henry's need for fine income to be actually greater than John's in 1207–8. The comparison is in Henry's favour. Yet the victory is John's, crushingly so. The total amount offered to King John in the roll of 1207–8 is some £22,000. The total offered to Henry III in the roll of 1256–7 is some £4,000. Of course, in giving figures of this kind it is necessary to be aware of possible distortions arising from one exceptional fine, like those of Geoffrey de Mandeville or of Joan Wake. There are, however, no comparable distortions in the rolls of 1207–8 and 1256–7. In the former roll the two largest fines are both of 3,000 marks, while another eight are for 1,000 marks or more. In 1256–7 the largest fine is one of 2,000 marks offered by the executors of the bishop of Ely. Then there is one fine of £500 and four of over 100 marks. Underlying the very different amounts promised, there is another contrast. There were far more fines under Henry but they were of smaller amounts. John's £22,000 came from 260 fines with an average value of £84. Henry's £4,000 came from around 900 fines with an average value of £4 4s. 6d. Indeed, 500 of Henry's fines were for amounts of between half a mark and 20s., many of them for the judicial writs already analysed.

There are several factors behind the sharp decline in the number of high-value individual fines. While Henry wanted money just as much as his father, he had none of John's energy and acuity in obtaining it. There was also the fact that John had more to give, especially from the English lands seized from those Normans who had taken the French allegiance in 1204. Thus Roger de Mortimer and his wife, Isabella, gave 700 marks for the manor of Oakham in Rutland, while William, earl of Warenne, gave 3,000 marks for the lands of Gilbert de Laigle.[21] Above all, however, the change was due to the fact that Henry was restricted by the provisions and spirit of Magna Carta in a way that John was not.

The Charter had laid down that the relief to be paid by earls and barons on entering their inheritances was to be £100. The relief for a whole knight's fee was to be £5, with less if less was held. In the fine roll of 1256–7 there are references to fifteen reliefs. All came within the terms of Magna Carta. That paid by the baron Philip de Columbars, for example, was precisely £100.[22] That of Henry of Lexington, bishop of Lincoln, for the one fee held in chief by his brother John, was £5, although he had lands in seven counties, as well as property in London.[23] Smaller reliefs were paid by those inheriting less than a fee. Alan de Chekehull

---

20 *CLR 1256–57*, nos 454, 565.
21 *Rot. de Ob. et Fin.*, pp. 398–9, 401–2.
22 *CFR 1256–57*, no. 710.
23 *CFR 1256–57*, no. 434. For the one fee, see *CIM*, no. 378.

was charged only 2 marks. A note on the roll explained that the relief was so modest because a survey of his lands (which survives) showed them to be worth only 24*s*. 6*d*. a year.[24]

The pattern in the roll of 1207–8 is quite different. There are five clear examples of reliefs exceeding the limits which would soon be laid down in Magna Carta, and several others which probably come into that category. The relief of Henry de Pomeroy to inherit his barony of Berry Pomeroy in Devon was £400.[25] That of William of Well for one knight's fee was 50 marks, or £33 6*s*. 8*d*. In this case, in striking contrast to what happened to Alan de Chekehull, an inquiry into the value of the property had done him little good. It showed that his fee was worth only £7 10*s*. a year.[26] Since this was half the income which later obliged people to take up knighthood, William might have hoped for relief at the very least in accord with Magna Carta's £5 for a knight's fee; in fact, he was required to pay more than six times as much.

The rolls also reveal a striking contrast in the treatment of widows.[27] Magna Carta laid down that widows should not pay for entry into their dowers, marriage portions and inheritances. The rolls for 1207–8 have three cases where they precisely have to do so.[28] The Charter also stipulated that widows should not be compelled to remarry. John occasionally paid lip service to this principle. In four instances on the 1207–8 roll the marriage is made in some way conditional on the widow's consent.[29] In the case of Alice, widow of John Belet, her marriage to Thomas de Burgh required the consent both of her father, Fulk d'Oyry, and herself.[30] On the other hand, John in the same roll gave away the marriages of four widows without any reference to consent at all.[31] The pressure which could be brought to bear on widows is very clear. Sometimes it was no more than letters being sent by the king begging the widow to accept her new husband 'without

[24] *CFR 1256–57*, no. 431; *CIM*, no. 388. For the other reliefs, see *CFR 1256–57*, nos 212, 216, 354, 458, 460, 469, 568, 721, 745, 735.

[25] *Rot. de Ob. et Fin.*, p. 407; I. J. Sanders, *English Baronies: A Study of their Origin and Descent* (Oxford, 1960), p. 106.

[26] *Rot. de Ob. et Fin.*, p. 372. For other reliefs, see pp. 403, 406, 414, 419, 523, 528.

[27] For a detailed discussion of the contrast between John and Henry III in their treatment of widows, and the effect of Magna Carta, which bears out the contrast made here, see S. L. Waugh, *The Lordship of England: Royal Wardships and Marriages in English Society and Politics, 1217–1327* (Princeton, 1988), pp. 85–7, 158–61. See also S. Annesley, 'The Impact of Magna Carta on Widows: Evidence from the Fine Rolls, 1216–1225', Fine of the Month November 2007, available at http://www.finerollshenry3.org.uk/content/month/fm-11-2007.html (accessed 2 April 2015); M. Ray, 'The Lady is Not for Turning: Margaret de Redvers' Fine not to be Compelled to Marry', Fine of the Month December 2006, available at http://www.fin-erollshenry3.org.uk/content/month/fm-12-2006.html (accessed 2 April 2015); D. Carpenter, 'Hubert de Burgh, Matilda de Mowbray and Magna Carta's Protection of Widows', Fine of the Month March 2008, available at http://www.finerollshenry3.org.uk/content/month/fm-03-2008.html (2 April 2015).

[28] *Rot. de Ob. et Fin.*, pp. 420, 430, 438.

[29] *Rot. de Ob. et Fin.*, pp. 371, 375, 440, 441.

[30] *Rot. de Ob et Fin.*, p. 440.

[31] *Rot. de Ob. et Fin.*, pp. 378, 383, 402, 429.

delay and objection'.[32] On other occasions John went beyond polite persuasion. In the roll we find Thomas of Galloway offering 1,000 marks for the land of Hugh de Say. He was to pay this off at 60 marks a year until he had married Margaret, Hugh's daughter and heir, when he was to pay a larger sum to be determined. Clearly, until the recently widowed Margaret (she had been the wife of Hugh de Ferrers) agreed to marry Thomas, she was going to be deprived of her inheritance. Acting completely contrary to the terms of Magna Carta, John had simply given it to Thomas of Galloway. In the event, before he had managed to marry Margaret, Thomas fell from favour and lost the Say lands. This time John was having no nonsense. Without making any reference to consent, he sold Margaret's marriage and all her inheritance to Robert de Mortimer for 1,000 marks.[33] John was also ready to accept money offered by widows to escape forced remarriage. In the 1207–8 roll Avelina, widow of Osbert de Longchamp, gave 200 marks and two palfreys both for that privilege and for recovering the inheritance of which she had been disseised by the king's order, the very reverse of receiving it without charge. However, 200 marks was not enough for John's household knight, Walter of Tew, who intervened and offered 400 marks to have Avelina as his wife, with John stipulating that if she did not agree he was in any case to have her lands. In the end Avelina had to offer 500 marks in order to escape.[34]

When we look at the roll of 1256–7, the contrast is great. There are no examples of widows offering money to escape forced remarriage. There are no examples of them having to offer money to gain possession of their dowers, marriage portions and inheritances. When Joan, widow of Roger of Huntingfield, gave 100 marks for the wardship of her son together with his lands, that was all the fine was for.[35] There was no clause, routine under John, which protected her from forced remarriage, or allowed her to marry whom she wished. The roll for 1256–7 is not untypical here. During the ten calendar years between 1248 and 1257, ten widows fined for the wardship of their children and their lands, without any provision about remarriage, save that Amice, countess of the Isle of Wight, agreed that she would not marry while she was still paying her fine.[36] There are nine orders assigning widows dower without any mention of payment.[37] There

---

[32] *Rot. de Ob. et Fin.*, pp. 371, 375.

[33] *Rot. de Ob. et Fin.*, pp. 407–8; *The Great Roll of the Pipe for the Twelfth Year of the Reign of King John*, ed. C. F. Slade, PRS n.s. 26 (London, 1951), pp. 170, 172, 173.

[34] *Rot. de Ob. et Fin.*, pp. 430, 432–3, 463–4; *The Great Roll of the Pipe for the Ninth Year of the Reign of King John*, ed. A. M. Kirkus, PRS n.s. 22 (London, 1946), p. 49; *The Great Roll of the Pipe for the Tenth Year of the Reign of King John*, ed. D. M. Stenton, PRS n.s. 23 (London, 1945), pp. 100–1. For an earlier example of competitive bidding, see the case of the widow of Stephen de Faucumberg: *Rot. de Ob. et Fin.*, pp. 51, 56.

[35] *CFR 1256–57*, no. 1018.

[36] *CFR 1248–49*, nos 23, 142, 176 (Amice's fine); *CFR 1249–50*, no. 377; *CFR 1250–51*, nos 709, 781, 935, 995; *CFR 1251–52*, no. 1231; *CFR 1255–56*, no. 1024; *CFR 1256–57*, no. 1018.

[37] *CFR 1249–50*, no. 824; *CFR 1250–51*, nos 153, 931; *CFR 1252–53*, no. 363; *CFR 1253–54*, nos 263, 509; *CFR 1255–56*, nos 518, 737; *CFR 1256–57*, no. 434; *CFR 1257–58*, no. 55.

are also no examples of widows fining to avoid compulsory remarriage, and only three for permission to marry whomever the widow wished.[38] These three fines, moreover, were arguably compatible with Magna Carta, since it allowed the king to take security that a widow would not marry without his consent. It was thus not unreasonable to charge for waiving the consent.[39] It is true that the fine rolls, like other government records, still state that the marriages of widows of tenants-in-chief are in the king's gift,[40] but in these ten years only four fines were accepted from men purchasing such marriages. One of them, moreover, says that what is being sold is the marriage 'as much as pertains to the king'.[41] Under the terms of Magna Carta, that would simply mean the king's right to assent to the marriage and to take security that the widow would not remarry without that assent; this left open, as we have said, the possibility of charging for waiving the right. That this was how the king himself understood such grants is clear from a fine in 1244. Here Henry gave Bartholomew Pecche

> that which would have pertained to the king of the marriage of Philippa, who was the wife of William Sifrewast, if the custody had remained in his hands, namely that the same Philippa might not marry herself without licence of the same Bartholomew, just as she would not be able to do without the king's licence if he had retained that custody in his hand.[42]

In another concession in 1253, what is sold is the widow's marriage 'if she shall wish to marry herself', which would seem to mean any fine that she might make to marry as she wishes.[43]

The most famous chapter in Magna Carta was designed to put a stop to John's arbitrary treatment of individuals, to end the 'vis et voluntas' and the 'ira et malevolentia' of which J. E. A. Jolliffe wrote.[44] Chapter 39 reads:

> No free man is to be arrested, or imprisoned, or disseised, or outlawed, or exiled or in any way destroyed, nor will we go against him, nor will we send against him, save by the lawful judgment of his peers or the law of the land.

The fine roll of 1207–8 bears striking testimony to the need for this chapter. It contains twelve fines made to escape the king's rancour and recover his favour, fines coming from a cross-section of society.[45] The burgesses of Beverley, for example, gave 50 marks; the men of Cornwall 200 marks; the knight Hugh of Chacombe, former sheriff of Warwickshire and Leicestershire, 800 marks; the knight Roger fitz Adam, former sheriff of Hampshire, 1,000 marks; the baron

---

[38]   *CFR 1247–48*, no. 388; *CFR 1250–51*, no. 573; *CFR 1253–54*, no. 509.
[39]   There is very little evidence in the fine rolls that Henry routinely took such security, other than sometimes demanding an oath from the widow that she would not marry without the king's license. See *CFR 1255–56*, no. 627; Waugh, *Lordship of England*, pp. 116–17.
[40]   For example, *CFR 1251–52*, no. 405.
[41]   *CFR 1255–56*, no. 1230.
[42]   *CFR 1244–45*, no. 55.
[43]   *CFR 1252–43*, no. 431.
[44]   J. E. A. Jolliffe, *Angevin Kingship*, 2nd edn (Oxford, 1963), chs 3 and 4.
[45]   *Rot. de Ob. et Fin.*, pp. 372, 375, 382, 384, 386–7, 389, 392, 396, 398, 412–14.

Roger de Cressy 1,200 marks; and William, archdeacon of Taunton, 2,000 marks. The total offered was some £5,500. According to Nicholas Barratt, between 1207 and 1211 there was a dramatic rise in the actual revenue paid into the Exchequer from such fines. They produced £2,252 in 1209, £3,414 in 1210 and £2,731 in 1211.[46] These fines were closely linked to others, ten in all, from those who had evidently already suffered from the results of the king's displeasure, and now had to offer money for the recovery of land seized into his hands.[47] Of course, those making fines of these kinds had all transgressed in some way. The offence was often unspecified, but Hugh of Chacombe had probably failed to appear in court when summoned.[48] Roger de Cressy had certainly married an heiress without permission. Roald fitz Alan, the constable of Richmond, had resisted the tax of 1207, and had to give 200 marks and four palfreys to recover Richmond Castle, of which he had consequently been disseised.[49] Yet the disseisins from which the offenders suffered were highly unlikely to have been the result of any kind of legal process. Indeed, that was sometimes admitted. Although the knight William fitz Roscelin maintained he had nothing to do with Roger de Cressy's offence, he still had to offer 60 marks and a good hawk to recover his lands seized 'by order of the king'.[50] The sheer number of these fines shows that angry threats and extra-legal disseisin were part of John's normal pattern of rule.

If we turn to the fine roll of 1257–8, we are in a different world. There are no fines to recover land seized into the king's hands. In total contrast to 1215, lawless disseisin 'by will of the king' was simply not an issue in 1258. Under chapter 52 of the 1215 Magna Carta, anyone unlawfully disseised by John was to be immediately restored. If there was any dispute, the issue was to be adjudged by the twenty-five barons named in the security clause of the Charter. In the event, in the days after Magna Carta a series of restorations were made. Nothing like that happened in 1258. The office of chief justiciar was resurrected, and was filled by Hugh Bigod. Hugh's brief was certainly to hear complaints and redress grievances, but he only dealt with one case of alleged disseisin by the king. This was brought by Roger de Mortimer over the manor of Lechlade. His claim was hardly clear-cut, and no judgment was ever pronounced in his favour.[51]

There was an equally great contrast when it came to fines to secure the king's grace and benevolence. In the fine roll of 1257–8 there is only one of these, a

---

[46] N. Barratt, 'The Revenue of King John', *EHR* 111 (1996), 835–55, at p. 849. Barratt's figures come from the pipe rolls. He does not give figures for the years before 1209.
[47] *Rot. de Ob. et Fin.,* pp. 372, 373, 376, 377, 379, 381, 395, 402, 409, 430.
[48] *The Memoranda Roll for the Tenth Year of the Reign of King John*, ed. R. A. Brown, PRS n.s. 31 (London, 1955), p. 28; *CRR*, v, p. 18.
[49] *Rot. de Ob. et Fin.*, pp. 398, 372.
[50] *Rot. de Ob. et Fin.*, p. 373.
[51] See D. Carpenter, 'A Noble in Politics: Roger Mortimer in the Period of Baronial Reform and Rebellion, 1258–1267', in *Nobles and Nobility in Medieval Europe: Concepts, Origins, Transformations*, ed. A. J. Duggan (Woodbridge, 2000), pp. 186–200. For Bigod's eyres, see *The 1258–59 Special Eyre of Surrey and Kent*, ed. A. H. Hershey, Surrey Record Society 38 (Woking, 2004); and A. H. Hershey, 'Success or Failure? Hugh Bigod and Judicial Reform during the Baronial Movement, June 1258–February 1259', in *TCE V*, pp. 65–88.

fine of £500 made by John de Balliol.[52] Admittedly at around the same time an amercement was imposed on another northern magnate, Robert de Ros, probably of 1,000 marks (although Henry, in a fit of passion, may have wanted one of 100,000 marks!). The treatment of Balliol and Ros was, however, quite exceptional. It was the only time that Henry, during his personal rule, disciplined great men in his father's fashion.[53] His reasons were equally exceptional. Both Balliol and Ros had been accused of mistreating Henry's young daughter, Margaret, wife of King Alexander III of Scotland. They were keeping her in the gloomy castle of Edinburgh, and preventing her from sleeping in the same bed as her husband. Henry and his wife, Queen Eleanor, were doting parents and nothing was more calculated to raise their anxieties and incite their anger. The punishment of Balliol and Ros was the result. In the fine rolls from 1236 to 1257 there are only three comparable fines: the clerk Walter de Burgh's of 400 marks for various transgressions as keeper of the king's demesne manors; Henry of Bath's of 2,000 marks for malpractices as a judge; and Peter de Maulay's of 60 marks for failing to send knights to the 1257 campaign in Wales.[54]

Henry, therefore, opened up the common law to his subjects in a way that John completely failed to do. Unlike John, he did not in general disseise people of property 'by will' or demand fines to recover his grace. Why then was there so much opposition to his rule in parliament, and a revolution in 1258? There are of course several answers to that question. The revolution of 1258 was very much a revolution within the court of Henry III, the result of factional struggles aggravated by the level of patronage Henry had given to his foreign relatives.[55] One can see a trace of that in the fine rolls, where half the greatest fine in 1256–7, that of 2,000 marks owed by the executors of the bishop of Ely, was given to the queen's uncle Thomas of Savoy. It was given, moreover, as a note on the fine roll shows, on 9 April 1258, at the very start of the Westminster parliament that sparked the revolution. There was nothing hidden about the gift, either, for it was recorded by an indignant Matthew Paris.[56]

Factional struggles at court, however, spread out into much wider discontent. There was a widespread belief that Henry placed those he favoured, notably his foreign relatives, above the law, making it impossible to bring legal actions against them. He thus broke Magna Carta chapter 40 and failed in one of the most basic tasks of kingship, that of being an impartial judge. Some of the victims were rival magnates, others were also knights, free-tenants and peasants in the shires who suffered from the local officials of those protected.[57] There were

[52] CFR 1256–57, no. 894.
[53] For a full discussion, see D. Carpenter, 'The *vis et voluntas* of Henry III: The Downfall and Punishment of Robert de Ros', Fine of the Month November 2012, available at http://www.finerollshenry3.org.uk/redist/pdf/fm-08-2012.pdf (accessed 2 April 2015).
[54] CFR 1250–51, nos 359, 822; CFR 1257–58, no. 37.
[55] See above all H. Ridgeway, 'The Lord Edward and the Provisions of Oxford (1258): A Study in Faction', in TCE I, pp. 89–99.
[56] CFR 1256–57, no. 916; Chronica Majora, v, pp. 677–8.
[57] See D. Carpenter, The Reign of Henry III (London, 1996), pp. 80–5, 30–6.

other ways in which Henry's rule bore down on local society. Denied general taxation, he had no alternative but to raise more money from his sheriffs and justices in eyre.[58] This created a vicious circle, for it made it all the more likely that no taxes would be granted. In 1254 the regents told Henry (who was then overseas in Gascony) that he could not expect a tax unless he ordered the sheriffs to obey Magna Carta, for many complained that they were not doing so.[59] When four knights representing each county were summoned to parliament to say what tax they would give, their answer was that there would be no tax at all.[60] It is true that this is the only example of knightly representation in parliament before the 1260s, but the summoning of minor tenants-in-chief meant that knights had always had a voice there.[61]

The fine rolls are a key source for the pressure Henry was bringing to bear on local society. It is here that we find the harsh financial terms, with their ever increasing increments, that he was imposing on the sheriffs. It is here also that we find the evidence for the extraordinary policy Henry developed in the 1250s, one which attacked the very people on whom local government depended. This was Henry's great campaign to distrain men to become knights.[62] The policy had begun as a genuine attempt to strengthen the military forces of the kingdom. It ended as little more than an attempt to make money, since Henry was only too ready to sell exemptions from the honour. Here Henry was developing a source of revenue untapped by his father. John never made a concerted attempt to force men to take up knighthood or make money from fines for respite. In the fine roll of 1213–14, when William Hervei offered 80 marks and one palfrey to have the land of his father while at the same time enjoying exemption from knighthood during the two years he had to pay the debt.[63] This, however, is an isolated example.

Under Henry III, all this changed. In November 1224 came the first general attempt to force men to take up knighthood.[64] Those deemed to be qualified

---

[58]   See J. R. Maddicott, 'Magna Carta and the Local Community, 1215–1259', *Past & Present* 102 (1984), 25–65, at pp. 44–8.

[59]   *Royal and Other Historical Letters Illustrative of the Reign of Henry III*, ed. W. W. Shirley, Rolls Series, 2 vols (1862, 1866), ii, pp. 101–2.

[60]   For this parliament, see J. R. Maddicott, *The Origins of the English Parliament, 924–1327* (Oxford, 2010), pp. 210–18.

[61]   Maddicott, *Origins of the English Parliament*, pp. 198–204; J. R. Maddicott, '"An infinite multitude of nobles": Quality, Quantity and Politics in the Pre-Reform Parliaments of Henry III', in *TCE VII*, pp. 17–46.

[62]   For what follows, see M. Powicke, *Military Obligation in Medieval England: A Study in Liberty and Duty* (Oxford, 1962), ch. 4; and S. L. Waugh, 'Reluctant Knights and Jurors: Respites, Exemptions, and Public Obligations in the Reign of Henry III', *Speculum* 58 (1983), 937–86.

[63]   *Rot. de Ob. et Fin.*, p. 497.

[64]   For the costs of knighthood and the decline in the number of knights, which forms the background to Henrician policies, see K. Faulkner, 'The Transformation of Knighthood in Early Thirteenth-Century England', *EHR* 111 (1996), 1–23; and P. Coss, *The Knight in Medieval England, 1100–1400* (Stroud, 1993), ch. 3.

were not simply the king's tenants-in-chief. Rather, the sheriffs were to proclaim that 'each single layman of full age' having at least one knight's fee was to be knighted by the following Easter 'as he loves his fee or fees'.[65] The aim here was to increase the pool of knights for a possible campaign in France, following the death of Philip Augustus. The aim was much the same in the next set of measures, those introduced between 1240 and 1242 with first a campaign in Wales looming and then one in Poitou. Here again the scope was general, but two new elements were introduced. The first was to extend the obligation to assume knighthood beyond those who held a knight's fee. Thus in July 1240 the sheriffs were to proclaim that all those who held a whole knight's fee, and also those who had less than a fee but could still sustain knighthood, were to assume the honour.[66] The names of those who did not take up knighthood were to be sent to the king, together with the value of their lands. Perhaps these valuations led to the decision, taken sometime before December 1241, to remove the question of who could sustain knighthood from the discretion of the sheriffs. Instead, the alternative to a whole fee as a qualification was defined as land worth £20.[67] The second innovation was to enforce the taking up of knighthood. In 1240 the sheriffs, much as in 1224, had merely been to proclaim that those qualified must take up knighthood 'as they love their tenements'. At some point before December 1241, the decision was taken to go further. Now the sheriffs were to enforce the taking up of knighthood by distraint. Indeed, under a writ of March 1242, those distrained 'by their lands and their chattels' were to have no 'administration' of their properties until they gave security for taking up the honour.[68]

In November 1252 the policy of compulsory knighthood took a new and pecuniary turn. As before, the sheriffs were to distrain all those who had a whole knight's fee or £20 worth of land to assume the honour. As before the order was related to Henry's military necessities, this time his forthcoming campaign in Gascony. Now, however, the order mentioned that those who did not want to take up knighthood might fine with the king to have respite.[69] That potential knights might have royal letters giving them respite had been mentioned in the order of March 1242,[70] but this was the first time that fining with the king to obtain such letters had been openly advertised as a possibility. For the first time the aim of the measure was as much to make money from selling respites as it was to increase the pool of knights.

All these previous measures concerning knighthood paled before that introduced in April 1256.[71] This was far more exacting in a number of ways. First, it set

---

[65] *RLC*, ii, p. 69b.

[66] *CR 1237–42*, p. 239.

[67] *CR 1237–42*, p. 428. This order (to the sheriff of Bedfordshire–Buckinghamshire, but probably sent more widely) refers to earlier orders which do not survive since they were not enrolled.

[68] *CR 1237–42*, pp. 428, 430, 434–5.

[69] *CR 1251–53*, pp. 430–1.

[70] *CR 1237–42*, p. 434.

[71] *CR 1254–56*, pp. 293, 418.

a lower bar for qualification and thus put pressure on a wider range of people. The criterion of a knight's fee was dropped altogether and the value of the land held by military service was made the sole qualification. But instead of the level being set at land worth £20, as before, it was now brought down to land worth £15. The aim of the measure, far more than before, was also simply to make money. True, Matthew Paris says that the hope was that knighthood of England would be made strong like that in Italy.[72] Henry may indeed have been thinking of the army he had to raise for the campaign in Sicily. It is also true that the first writ about the measure, in April 1256, says nothing about the alternative of fines.[73] But there must have been other un-enrolled writs sent to the sheriffs which made the alternative of fining abundantly clear. Paris himself wrote of a 'royal edict' being 'proclaimed through the whole kingdom of England' to the effect that those with £15 worth of land should take up knighthood, while 'those not wishing to do so, or not able to sustain the honour of knighthood, should redeem themselves through money'.[74] A letter of July 1256 to the sheriff of Buckinghamshire and Bedfordshire referred to earlier orders to that effect. Indeed, the July letter made very plain the real purpose of the initiative. Henry expressed his anger and aston-ishment at the sheriff's failure to carry out the order as 'we can see quite clearly from the few men who have come to us from your bailiwick in order to obtain respite'.[75] The £15 level of qualification was, of course, directly related to making money since it was bound to increase the numbers of those who felt they could not afford the honour and were prepared to pay to avoid it.[76]

The measure of April 1256 was also pushed forward with a new ruthlessness through pressure on the sheriffs. The fine roll for 1255–6 has a special schedule recording the amercements imposed at the Michaelmas Exchequer of 1256 on all the sheriffs for failing to carry out the distraint effectively.[77] News of their punishment reached Matthew Paris, who recorded it in his *Chronica Majora*.[78] This certainly roused the sheriffs into action. As commanded, they sent in long lists of those in their counties who were eligible for knighthood, together with a valuation of their lands.[79] There were eighteen victims each in Oxfordshire and Wiltshire, nineteen in Kent and fifty-one in Lincolnshire. In all, the surviving returns from over twenty counties reveal that there were well over 550 victims of the policy.[80] The true number must have been much larger, given that the

---

[72]   *Chronica Majora*, v, p. 560.
[73]   *CR 1254–56*, p. 293.
[74]   *Chronica Majora*, v, p. 560.
[75]   TNA, C 47/1/1, no. 17. This appears to be the original of a letter which was not enrolled.
[76]   For the financial motives, see Waugh, 'Reluctant Knights', p. 961.
[77]   *CFR 1255–56*, nos 1196–1220; *CFR 1256–57*, nos 593, 599; and *CR (Supplementary) 1244–66*.
[78]   *Chronica Majora*, v, pp. 588–9.
[79]   The surviving returns are brought together now as TNA, C 47/1/1, nos 1–31. For the order for returns to be sent in, see *CR 1254–56*, p. 418.
[80]   My figure includes those whose names are lost through damage. This may be why it is larger than the 'more than 400' given in Waugh, 'Reluctant Knights', p. 951. On the other hand, Waugh may just have counted more accurately.

returns for some of the most populous counties (Yorkshire, Norfolk, Suffolk and Essex) are lost, while many of those which do survive are damaged. Scott Waugh, indeed, found some 200 men who do not appear on the lists of those purchasing respites.[81] It would not be surprising if the number of potential knights affected by the policy was around a thousand.

The hand of the policy thus fell heavily on the knightly class. Just how many actually assumed knighthood we do not know, but if those on the lists who did not obtain respites assumed the honour, then it was a good number. Scott Waugh found that of the fifty-seven men in the returns for Shropshire, only twenty-one, 30%, received respites. The figures in Bedfordshire and Buckinghamshire were 27% and Northamptonshire 48%.[82] The thoroughness with which the sheriffs eventually did their work is also shown in the numerous complaints from those who felt they had been unfairly assessed. No fewer than fifty potential knights made a fine with the king for an inquiry into the value of their lands, alleging that it was less than £15. Twenty-five were proved correct and secured exemptions.[83] The sheriffs were thus damned if they did and damned if they didn't. They were amerced for a lack of zeal in carrying out the distraint, and an excess of zeal in assessing the incomes.

We know far more, thanks to the fine rolls, about those who purchased respites, and here the results were spectacular and quite different from earlier years. The orders for distraint between 1240 and 1242 produced only a dozen fines for respite. In 1252–3, there were thirty-six. There then followed a lull with only four fines in the rolls for 1253–4 and 1254–5. The fine rolls for 1255–6 and 1256–7 are quite different, and betray the result of the measure of April 1256. In that for 1255–6 there are 202 fines for respite, and in the roll for 1256–7, 163, a total of 365. In addition there are, as we have seen, some fifty fines for a valuation of land. Altogether then some 415 individuals were forced to make fines as a result of the policy.[84]

The fines secured a respite from knighthood, not, it should be stressed, a total exemption. In most cases the respite was for three years, running from Michaelmas 1256, Christmas 1256, or Michaelmas 1257, depending on when the fine was made. The usual cost for a respite or an inquiry was 5 marks, that is £3 6s. 8d., which approached a quarter of the annual income of a £15-a-year knight. Many of those caught by the policy had incomes greater than that, but many did not. In Oxfordshire six of the eighteen men on the list were put down as having lands worth £15 a year; in Worcestershire it was ten of the twenty-one.[85] Although the fines did not have to be paid cash down (the two feasts of the Confessor on 13 October and 15 January were common terms), relatively few

[81] Waugh, 'Reluctant Knights', p. 951.
[82] Waugh, 'Reluctant Knights', p. 952.
[83] *CR (Supplementary) 1244–66*, nos 124–48.
[84] A copy of some, but far from all, of the fines was made, for which see *CR (Supplementary) 1244–66*, nos 8–207. Virtually all of the fines here are enrolled on the fine rolls.
[85] TNA, C 47/1/1, nos 28, 25. The Lincolnshire return (no. 15) unhelpfully gives everyone an income of £15.

seem to have been left unpaid by July 1258.[86] The policy brought the potential knights into direct and evidently acrimonious contact with the sheriffs. It was the sheriff who had to convoke the juries to value the lands, and return the lists of those eligible.[87] It was equally the sheriff who had then to distrain those who did have £15 worth of land either to take up knighthood or make a fine to avoid it. In some of the returns the sheriff noted that he had indeed distrained everyone on the lists.[88] Once a fine was made, the sheriff had then to take security for its payment. This clearly gave wide scope for shrieval abuse, and one of the articles of inquiry in 1258 concerned sheriffs who had taken bribes not to distrain those who ought to have been knights.[89]

The policy also had wider ramifications, for it gave the potential knights an insight into the nature of Henry's court, and the extent to which it was dominated by foreign ministers and favourites. All the fines were made at court, and all the money was paid into the Wardrobe. Once payments were made, a note to that effect was made on the fine rolls against the original entry. This seems to have been the chief record of the payment, with the absence of such notes being the chief record of an outstanding debt.[90] So little was the Exchequer involved in either the collection or audit of the fines that it was not even told about them, and they were omitted entirely from the originalia rolls. Since, as we have said, few of the fines were paid cash down, the potential knights, in person or by proxy, had to make two visits to court: once when they made the fine and once when they paid it. This involved contact with the Chancery, which issued the letters to the sheriffs about the respites or the inquiries, and with the Wardrobe, which received the money. The potential knights must have been very aware of 'the wardrobe [being] in foreign hands', to quote a section heading in Tout's classic book.[91] Many of the entries have a note stating that payment has been made either to Artald de Saint Romain or Peter des Rivallis. Indeed, over eighty fines were stated as paid to Peter. Fewer than forty lack notes recording their payment. Both Artald and Peter, of course, were foreigners. Artald, keeper of

---

[86] See below, n. 90.

[87] The names of the jurors are given in two of the returns: TNA, C 47/1/1, nos 18, 19.

[88] TNA, C 47/1/1, nos 7, 11, 20, 21.

[89] E. F. Jacob, *Studies in the Period of Baronial Reform and Rebellion, 1258–1267* (Oxford, 1925), p. 30, cap. xi.

[90] The payments to Peter had been made by July 1258, when he was dismissed. Many notes just record payment into the Wardrobe, so with these there is no *terminus ad quem*. However, when the reform government in the second half of 1258 placed the fines for knighthood, along with other related fines, under the control of the Exchequer (see R. Cassidy, 'The Reforming Council Takes Control of Fines of Gold, 1258–1259', Fine of the Month October 2011, available at http://www.finerollshenry3.org.uk/content/month/fm-10-2011.html (accessed 2 April 2015)), it found only twenty-nine fines connected with knighthood unpaid: *CFR 1257–58*, nos 1186, 1189–92, 1195, 1197, 1200–1, 1215–20, 1223–6, 1231, 1235, 1237, 1242, 1262–3, 1266, 1272, 1286. These fines correspond with those in the fine rolls lacking notes of payment.

[91] T. F. Tout, *Chapters in Mediaeval Administrative History: The Wardrobe, the Chamber and the Small Seals*, 6 vols (Manchester, 1920–33), i, p. 260.

the Wardrobe from January 1255 until his death around Michaelmas 1257, was from Burgundy or Provence. Peter des Rivallis, his successor, 'an alien after an alien' as Matthew Paris put it, remained in post until 8 July 1258, when he was dismissed by the reforming barons.[92] He was, of course, the nephew or son of Peter des Roches, the notorious Tourangeau bishop of Winchester.[93] Although it is doubtful whether the potential knights necessarily saw the king or his favourites in person, they must surely have soaked up the atmosphere of the court. The fourteen potential knights fining for respite in the first half of December 1256, for example, would have found there (for they all witness royal charters in the period) the king's half-brothers William de Valence and Guy and Geoffrey de Lusignan, as well as the queen's uncle Peter of Savoy, the Savoyard steward of the royal household Imbert Pugeys, and the king's Italian jester, Fortunatus de Luka, whom Henry had ordered to be thrown into the bath at Bath.[94] Hostility to the king's half-brothers was a major feature of the crisis of 1258 when, of course, the Lusignans were expelled from England. If resentment of foreigners was widespread in England, it was partly due to the stories about the brutality of their local agents. It was also due to the impression of Henry's very foreign court gained by many hundreds of men from the shires when they came to make fines for respite of knighthood.

The fines also meant that the potential knights felt the impact of Henry's disastrous foreign policy, with its attempt to place his second son on the throne of Sicily. They thus came to understand very well the lack of judgment Henry had shown in undertaking the enterprise. Awareness of the king's 'simplicity', as contemporaries put it, thus spread to the shires alongside knowledge of his foreign court. We have said that the great majority of the fines were worth £3 6s. 8d., but there was something else about them, too: the very great majority were paid not in silver but in gold. In the fine rolls they are stated as being worth half a mark of gold. Since the ratio between gold and silver at this time was ten to one, half a mark of gold was worth ten half-marks of silver, or five whole marks, and so £3 6s. 8d. That the fines were really paid in gold is clear from the Wardrobe accounts, which reveal that Henry was indeed building up a treasure in gold in part from fines made in the metal.[95] The fine rolls do not reveal the form in which the gold came to the king, but the Wardrobe accounts show

[92] *Chronica Majora*, v, pp. 298, 655; *Annales Monastici*, iii, p. 194; Tout, *Chapters*, i, p. 278, and p. 282 note 7.

[93] For both Peters, see Nicholas Vincent's magisterial *Peter des Roches: An Alien in English Politics, 1205–1238* (Cambridge, 1996).

[94] *The Royal Charter Witness Lists of Henry III*, ed. M. Morris, List and Index Society 291–2, 2 vols (Kew, 2001), ii, p. 102; *CFR 1256–57*, nos 171, 177, 179, 187–91, 196, 197, 201, 208, 209, 211. For Fortunatus, who was probably from Lucca, see D. Carpenter, 'Henry III's Sense of Humour', Fine of the Month November 2011, available at http://www.finerollshenry3.org.uk/content/month/fm-11-2011.html (accessed 2 April 2015).

[95] There are no accounts for Peter de Rivallis. Artaud's accounts only run from January 1255 to April 1256 (not 1257 as Tout says), so they do not cover the fines for distraint of knighthood. However, they show that gold was indeed being received into the Wardrobe from fines: *The Wardrobe Accounts of Henry III, 1224–72*, ed. B. L. Wild, PRS n.s. 58 (London, 2012),

that the great bulk of it was 'in folio', that is, in leaf.[96] Presumably those fining bought the leaf from goldsmiths, thus incurring additional expense. The victims of the policy must all have asked why the king was demanding money in gold. The answer was to fund the army Henry was pledged to send to Sicily to wrest the kingdom from its Hohenstaufen rulers, the Sicilian currency being in gold. It was not, therefore, merely the Church which was being called upon to fund this mad scheme. English local county society was also doing its bit. It too came to see that England was being governed by a very foolish king.[97]

Quite apart from these wider consequences, the policy of distraint of knighthood had long been unpopular. It was probably protests from the shires which led to Henry, in March 1242, making clear that the knight's fee which was the qualification for knighthood had to be 'in demesne'. This was to retreat from his earlier position that it merely needed to be 'whole' (*integrum*).[98] Three years later, in 1245, it was probably protests in parliament which led to another retreat by Henry III on the issue. He had initially ordered the sheriffs to distrain all who had £20-worth of land or 'the fee of a knight by which they ought to be knights'. But on 8 June, shortly after the meeting of a parliament, he told the sheriffs of eight counties that, because of 'the complaints of many people', they were now to distrain only those with £20-worth of land or a 'whole knight's fee in demesne' worth as much. In other words, that the knight's fee, too, had to be worth £20 was now specified, whereas before it had merely to be 'the fee of a knight by which they ought to be knights'.[99] Opposition may also be the reason why very little seems to have come from Henry's order in November 1252 that those with land worth £20 a year or a whole knight's fee worth as much should come before him the following Easter to receive knighthood or make a fine for exemption.[100]

Despite this background, the only reference to distraint of knighthood in 1258–9 comes in the articles of inquiry sent to the four knights in each county where, as we have seen, there was a clause about sheriffs taking bribes to let people avoid the distraint.[101] One reason for the absence of visible protest may be that the king's right to force those qualified to take up knighthood was unquestioned. It was related to the king's wider right to enforce on everyone in the

---

p. 84. The fines in gold for distraint of knighthood were part of a much broader effort to have fines made in gold, for which see Carpenter, *Reign of Henry III*, pp. 120–2.

[96] *Wardrobe Accounts*, p. 84; Carpenter, *Reign of Henry III*, pp. 120–1.

[97] For the foolishness of the Sicilian enterprise, see D. Carpenter, 'Henry III and the Sicilian Affair', Fine of the Month February 2012, available at http://www.finerollshenry3.org.uk/redist/pdf/fm-02-2012.pdf (accessed 01 October 2014). For a different view, see B. Weiler, 'Henry III and the Sicilian Business: A Reinterpretation', *HR* 184 (2001), 127–50.

[98] *CR 1242–47*, pp. 434–5, 428.

[99] *CR 1242–47*, pp. 350, 354, 356–7; Maddicott, *Origins of the English Parliament*, p. 222.

[100] *CR 1251–53*, pp. 430–1; Powicke, *Military Obligation*, pp. 75–6. It may also be that the home government refused to implement an order of Henry's from Gascony in the following year to distrain all ten-pound landholders to be knights: *Annales Monastici*, i, p. 154; Powicke, *Military Obligation*, p. 76.

[101] Jacob, *Studies in the Period of Baronial Reform and Rebellion*, p. 30 cap. xi.

country the obligation to bear arms. That obligation was itself graded according to the income of the king's subjects. Thus, under the 1181 Assize of Arms, those with a knight's fee were to have a lorica, helmet, shield and lance; freemen with rents or chattels worth 16 marks were to have the same equipment; freemen who had chattels or rents worth 10 marks were to have a hauberk, a cap of iron and a lance. All this was to be rigorously enforced, with those who failed to have the appropriate arms being arrested.[102] The obligation here was to have the appropriate equipment rather than to take up knighthood itself, but the two were very closely linked. Indeed, the orders to the sheriffs to distrain men to be knights spoke of them 'taking knightly arms' ('ad arma militaria capienda').[103]

The king's right to enforce knighthood had thus deep roots, but it would be very surprising if the distraint of 1256, with its low threshold of £15, did not contribute to the unpopularity of royal government in the shires and thus to the revolution of 1258. The king was alienating the very people on whom local government depended. Indeed, he was giving them a particular reason for wanting a change of regime. Without that, there was a danger they would be distrained all over again once their three years' exemption expired in 1259 or 1260. As it was, the revolution of 1258 ended the policy of making money from distraint of knighthood. The fine rolls of the rest of the reign have virtually no offers for respites.[104] Henry attempted only one more general distraint. That was in June 1260, when he was trying to reassert his authority and break through the restrictions imposed on him in 1258. To qualify, however, it was now necessary to have lands worth £30 a year, double the level of 1256. Nothing was said about buying respites, and none seem to have been bought. When the ruling council reasserted its authority in October 1260, it brought the distraint to an end.[105]

For all its unpopularity, Henry's distraint of knighthood policy had made no decisive difference to his financial position. The total paid into the Wardrobe from the fines made in 1256 and 1257 was some £1,640. By the end of 1257, no more was coming in. In the roll of 1257–8 the fines for respite were worth a paltry £26.[106] Henry's fine income remained pathetically small compared to that of his father. Of course, this owed something to Henry's personality, but even the hard-driving Edward I was unable to revive the income from fines. In the roll for 1304–5 the total amount offered to Edward was £1,120, of which

---

[102]   *The Chronicle of the Reigns of Henry II and Richard I commonly known as Benedict of Peterborough*, ed. W. Stubbs, Rolls Series, 2 vols (London, 1867), i, pp. 278–80.

[103]   For example, *CR 1251–53*, pp. 430–1; *CR 1254–56*, pp. 294, 295.

[104]   For a rare later fine, see *CFR 1266–67*, no. 443. The fine of Godfrey le Fauconer mentioned in *CR 1264–68*, p. 423, had been made in 1256: *CFR 1255–56*, no. 687.

[105]   *CR 1259–61*, pp. 171, 220. One reason for the distraint was to have a good showing of tenants-in-chief at the feast of the Confessor on 13 October 1260, where they could be knighted with John of Brittany. For later distraints apparently in individual counties: *CR 1261–64*, p. 125; *CR 1264–68*, p. 110 (during Montfort's regime); *CFR 1266–67*, no. 284; *CPR 1266–72*, p. 260. For distraint of knighthood and compulsory military service under Edward I (where the level varies between £20 and £100), see Powicke, *Military Obligation*, pp. 105–9.

[106]   Carpenter, *Reign of Henry III*, p. 124.

£500 effectively was pardoned, and thirty-eight 'reasonable reliefs', which were presumably levied in accordance with Magna Carta. That £1,120 provides some contrast to John's £22,000 of a hundred years before.[107]

There had to be a different way forward for royal finance and, of course, there was. The way was general taxation. Here the fine rolls of 1207–8 were prophetic. Alongside £22,000 promised in fines, they also record the £57,000 actually produced by John's great tax of 1207. The problem with such taxation was that it needed the general consent of the kingdom. That had been laid down in the 1215 Magna Carta, and though the chapter was omitted from the subsequent versions of the Charter, the principle remained.[108] The fine rolls reveal as much in a remarkable alteration to an entry in 1245. In this, a Chancery clerk indicated that general taxation paid by everyone, as opposed to taxation simply paid by the king's tenants-in-chief, needed to be 'conceded by all the community of the realm', in other words it needed the consent of parliament.[109] The way was being pointed towards the tax-based parliamentary state. No government record shows the need for that state better than the fine rolls.

[107] Carpenter, 'The English Royal Chancery', pp. 54–5.
[108] Maddicott, *Origins of the English Parliament*, p. 133.
[109] D. Carpenter, 'Consent to Taxation, the Community of the Realm, and the Development of Parliament: The Aid of 1245', Fine of the Month May 2010, available at http://www.fine rollshenry3.org.uk/content/month/fm-05-2010.html (accessed 2 April 2015).

2

The Form and Function of the Originalia Rolls

Paul Dryburgh

Ever since its inception in 2005, the Henry III Fine Rolls project has been bringing to greater public attention the rolls upon which are recorded the offers made from all sections of society for the favour of medieval England's longest-reigning monarch. The fine rolls, as is splendidly demonstrated throughout this volume, reveal much regarding the nature of kingship and royal patronage, politics and government, and of changes to law, society and the environment in the thirteenth century. They also provide important clues to the workings of the royal administration during key phases in the development of the written record.[1] The project has also explored a supplementary series of rolls that occasionally sheds light on the Crown's financial management practices in thirteenth-century England and enhances our understanding of the bureaucratic processes behind securing the king's goodwill.

The originalia rolls (TNA series E 371) consist essentially of heavily abridged extracts of entries from the fine rolls. Drawn up by Chancery clerks, these extracts were periodically sent membrane by membrane to the Exchequer to provide it with the financial information it needed to pursue debtors, process accounts and oversee the management of the Crown's estates. However, since they ostensibly repeat the information found on the fine rolls they have been largely ignored by historians, particularly since the publication by Charles Roberts in 1835–6 of his two volumes of excerpts from the Henrician fine rolls.[2] Today, indeed, the originalia rolls are no longer stored at The National Archives but in deep storage at a former Cheshire salt mine, a mark of their apparent lack of utility.[3]

---

[1] For which, see, particularly, M. T. Clanchy, *From Memory to Written Record: England 1066–1307*, 3rd edn (London, 2012); R. C. Stacey, *Politics, Policy, and Finance under Henry III* (Oxford, 1987). For the fine rolls context, see D. A. Carpenter, 'Historical Introduction', in *Calendar of the Fine Rolls of the Reign of Henry III preserved in The National Archives*, vol. 1: *1216–1224*, ed. P. Dryburgh and B. Hartland, technical eds A. Ciula and J. M. Vieira (Woodbridge, 2007), pp. vii–xxix.

[2] *Excerpta e Rotulis Finium in Turri Londinensi asservatis, Henrico tertio Rege*, ed. C. Roberts, 2 vols (London, 1835–6). These volumes themselves, of course, provide a limited guide to the content of the fine rolls, including only about 10–15% of total entries. Extracts from the originalia rolls were published in the nineteenth century in H. Playford, *Rotulorum Originalium in Curia Scaccarii Abbreviatio* (London, 1805).

[3] For more on these deep storage facilities, see Anna E. Bülow and Tom Gregan, 'An Alternative for the Long-Term Storage of Archival Records: A Salt Mine in Cheshire', in *Where Shall We Put It? Spotlight on Collection Storage Issues: Papers given at the National Preservation Office Annual Conference Held 4 October 2004 at the British Library*, available through http://www.bl.uk/blpac/pdf/conf2004.pdf (accessed 7 April 2015).

By contrast, I want to suggest that their relationship with the fine rolls was more nuanced; their position in the bureaucratic chain acted as a check on the enrolment of fines, while at the Exchequer they became an alternative source for various key legal and administrative matters, for which they may have retained some currency over time and may still have valuable things to tell modern scholars.

The Originalia Rolls

For the reign of Henry III only two originalia rolls survive before 1235: those for 1226–7 and 1232–3.[4] Thereafter, they survive in an almost unbroken sequence.[5] In three years – 1236–7, 1237–8 and 1239–40 – they provide the main evidence of fines, as the corresponding fine rolls do not survive. The originalia rolls' main role was fiscal. As H. G. Richardson noted, the Angevin kings' method of governing necessitated constant communication between an itinerant court and Chancery and a sedentary Exchequer.[6] In order for promises entered into with the king, wherever he might have been, to be recovered, it was 'plainly necessary that a notification of all sums due to be collected should be sent to the Exchequer'. This was achieved by Chancery clerks copying entries from the fine rolls that specified from whom debts should be collected or, as the nature of the fine rolls themselves changed, to whom custodies, for example of a royal demesne manor, were being committed and from whom an account should therefore be expected.[7] Once copied, each membrane of extracts would be sent to the Exchequer. This is entered on the fine roll usually by the note 'Hinc mittendum est ad scaccarium' (From here it is to be sent to the Exchequer), which signified that all entries up to that point had been extracted, copied and dispatched. Once at the Exchequer most entries on each membrane of extracts would be annotated, in two or more stages, with, firstly, '*s*', showing that a summons was to be drawn up for the sheriff of the county in which the debtor resided to collect the debt, and/or 'in Rotulo' (in the Roll), showing that the entry had been transferred to the pipe roll, the Exchequer's central roll of audit. I have discussed some aspects of the form and content of the rolls, and these marginal annotations, in

---

4   TNA, E 371/1B, 2. Evidence from the memoranda rolls for 1219–20, 1221–2 and 1222–3 points to originalia rolls being compiled during Henry's first six regnal years: E 159/3, rot. 4d. (1216–17); E 368/4, rots 9 (1219–20), 9d (1220–1); E 368/5, rot. 8 (1221–2). I intend to edit and publish these early memoranda rolls for the Pipe Roll Society.
5   Rolls do not survive for Henry's 27th (1242–3), 30th (1245–6), 31st (1246–7) and 37th (1252–3) regnal years.
6   *The Memoranda Roll for the Michaelmas Term of the First Year of the Reign of King John (1199–1200)*, ed. N. Blakiston with an introduction by H. G. Richardson, PRS n.s. 21 (London, 1943), p. xvii.
7   For the development of material on the fine rolls, see P. R. Dryburgh and B. Hartland, 'The Development of the Fine Rolls', in *TCE XII*, pp. 193–205.

my introduction to volume II of the fine roll calendars.[8] Instead of retracing my steps, I now want to look at the part the originalia rolls played in record-making and record-keeping.

Making and Keeping Records: The Evidence from the Originalia Rolls

Despite their fiscal role, the originalia rolls are Chancery rather than Exchequer documents. Looking at their compilation and transmission reveals something of general Chancery practice. While the task of copying the extracts from the fine rolls no doubt fell to some of the most junior clerks, due to the relatively simple nature of abstracting and transcribing entries to remove formulae and leave in the key details, extraction should nonetheless be seen as a key task in executing the Chancery's aim of passing on full and accurate financial and administrative information to the Exchequer.[9] It is noteworthy that membranes of extracts were, according to notes on the dorse of the originalia rolls, submitted to the treasurer by the hand of either the chancellor himself or senior officials. Ralph de Neville, keeper of the seal from 1213 and then chancellor from 1226 until his death in 1244, frequently delivered extracts.[10] Later in the reign prominent Chancery clerks like John le Francis and Adam of Chesterton were given the task of transmission.[11] Neville was a chancellor whose influence was keenly felt in changes to Chancery procedure and who exerted a firm control over his office, while Chesterton apparently had special responsibility for dealing with moneys emanating from Chancery grants.[12] It is clear that the Chancery perceived the transmission of financial information to the Exchequer as integral to its role, and kept it under close, top-level supervision until the moment of deposit. In order to exercise this function proficiently, however, the Chancery had to ensure that what it sent enabled the Exchequer to exercise *its* functions equally effectively.

[8]   'Originalia Rolls', in *Calendar of the Fine Rolls of the Reign of Henry III preserved in The National Archives*, vol. 2: *1224–1234*, ed. P. Dryburgh and B. Hartland, technical eds A. Ciula and J. M. Vieira (Woodbridge, 2008), pp. x–xxv.

[9]   Richardson argued that from 1200 it was only through the originalia rolls that the Exchequer could draw up the pipe rolls: *Memoranda Roll 1 John*, p. xvii.

[10]   See, for example, *CFR 1218–19*, no. 435 (c. 25 October 1219) where a note concerning the extracts reads: 'From here it is to be sent to the Exchequer and what is above has been delivered to the Treasurer by the hand of R. de Neville'; and *CFR 1232–33*, nos 90 (c. 22 January 1233), 169 (c. 12 April 1233), and 270 (29 July 1233). For biographical information on Ralph de Neville, see F. A. Cazel, Jr, 'Neville, Ralph de (*d.* 1244)', *ODNB*, available through http://www.oxforddnb.com (accessed 7 April 2015).

[11]   Le Francis: *CFR 1238–39*, no. 397 (c. 1239); *CFR 1247–48*, no. 243 (1248). Chesterton: *CFR 1247–48*, no. 625 (c. 15 June 1248); *CFR 1258–59*, no. 909 (c. 25 November 1259); *CFR 1259–60*, no. 485 (30 October 1260). The first of these entries for Chesterton confirms Paul Brand's suggestion in his recent biography that he had begun his career as a Chancery clerk several years earlier than 1252: P. A. Brand, 'Adam of Chesterton (*d.* 1268/9)', *ODNB*, available through http://www.oxforddnb.com (accessed 7 April 2015).

[12]   Carpenter, 'Historical Introduction', pp. xvii–xxiii.

The creation of extracts basically involved ruthless editing, rewriting or consolidating of fine roll entries to remove unnecessary verbiage and to bring out the facts most relevant to the Exchequer: the name of the debtor(s) or official(s); the amount of fine(s) or farm(s); the terms of repayment; the place(s) and/or county or counties concerned. An entry in the 1249/50 fine roll dated 16 December 1249, for instance, reads:

> Because H. of Wingham is gravely ill, the king asks R. Passelewe, archdeacon of Lewes, to take up the custody of the abbey of Peterborough and to substitute in his place such a person who shall be sufficient to answer for the issues of the same abbey to the king at the Exchequer.

This is rewritten in the originalia roll to read:

> The king has committed to Robert Passelewe, archdeacon of Lewes, the abbey of Peterborough, vacant by the cession of William de Hotot, [formerly abbot] of the same place.[13]

This gave the Exchequer all it required to summon Passelewe to account for the issues of the vacant abbey through his deputy, and removed extraneous information. In the originalia roll for the year 1264–5, during the Montfortian ascendancy, three fines made by the prior of Tutbury were reordered to ensure that the two of them which summoned the prior in Derbyshire were isolated from the other fine, which was to be summoned by the sheriff of Staffordshire, and that a fine by Robert fitz Payn, entered in their midst on the fine roll, was more easily picked out by Exchequer clerks when writing the summons.[14]

There was, however, room for interpretation. Even those originalia roll entries that transfer the barest of details can be at variance with the fine roll entries from which they are copied, especially in terms of the spelling of personal and place names – the bane of every editor's life. On occasion, one might argue that certain names had been misread and miscopied, as was probably the case in the originalia roll for 1269–70 where 'Robert de Holm' looks suspiciously like 'Robert de Hibn'.[15] In other instances the spellings are too different. Take the justice and royal official William of Axmouth. Whereas the fine roll gives 'Essemuthe', the corresponding originalia roll entry gives 'Axemue'.[16] We must assume that the copying clerk glanced at the fine roll, absorbed the name and gave his own version, presumably as he knew who the person was and expected his colleagues to know, and both versions clearly referred to the same man.[17] Whether this version

---

[13] *CFR 1249–50*, no. 79; TNA, E 371/15, m. 1.

[14] *CFR 1264–65*, nos 227–30; TNA, E 371/29, m. 3 (16 March 1265).

[15] *CFR 1269–70*, no. 219; TNA, E 371/34, m. 3. For a similar copying mistake in Chancery, this time in the duplicate fine rolls, see *CFR 1220–21*, no. 5 (2 November 1220), where the abbot of Kirkestall (Kirkstall, Yorkshire WR) is transcribed as 'Brickestall'.

[16] See the online indexes to the first four volumes of fine rolls for all variant spellings: http://www.frh3.org.uk/content/indexes/place/ao-az.html (accessed 7 April 2015).

[17] I am grateful to David Carpenter for his advice here. We should not, however, completely close our minds to the possibility that these variants are the result of entries being dictated by the more senior clerk to the junior and of mishearing or problems with accent or pronunciation.

would be a more standard form better known to the Exchequer cannot really be ascertained, but it might be argued that it was. Overall, though, this process of extracting entries both smoothed the flow of information between the Chancery and the Exchequer and saved parchment.

Moreover, the process of copying and abstracting would, by its very nature, give the clerks compiling the originalia rolls the perfect opportunity to immerse themselves in what had been enrolled on the fine rolls, to query anything odd and to spot mistakes. The process of extraction, then, served an important secondary function of reviewing and correcting the fine rolls, perhaps being part of a general process of review in Chancery. If we compare the text of the fine and originalia rolls, as can now be done on the website (although images of the originalia rolls are not available apart from those highlighted above), we find that many corrections made to the text of the fine rolls have been silently amended in the originalia rolls, such as familial relationships or Christian names.[18] Additions are also made in the text of the originalia rolls – to indicate status, for instance, or to associate places to differentiate individuals for the summons.[19] The originalia roll clerks were, in short, creating clean copy for the Exchequer.

How would this review have worked? How would a clerk know what he needed to correct? We should, I think, imagine the clerk compiling the current membrane of extracts sitting with both rolls laid out before him and a pile of parchment scraps on which drafts for fine roll entries had been made, perhaps even with a more senior clerk standing over him giving him access to other documents and decisions. It would be natural when attempting to create a full and accurate record to refer to more than one source, documentary and human. What follows are some examples to demonstrate the products of this process.

On occasion, the originalia rolls give different dates of witness for entries from those in the fine rolls; there are twenty-one such discrepancies in the first thirty-two regnal years, and many more thereafter.[20] Information about different dates must come from a source other than the fine rolls. One suspects that the clerk was referring to a draft or some kind of list and added his new date on comparing these with the fine rolls. Most often these only change the dating by a day or so, but it still suggests that dating undated entries on the fine roll by the previous dated entry, as scholars have done, is not always safe. It also suggests that there may have been more than one version of the documents from which fines were enrolled circulating in Chancery. One such possible document is a schedule carrying a fine of the burgesses of Derby for having a charter that no Jew should henceforth reside in their town, which is sewn onto the membrane of the fine roll for 1260–1 rather than simply enrolled in its chronological position,

[18] See, for example, *CFR 1244–45*, no. 183, where Peter son of Matthew is given as the 'son' rather than the 'brother' of Herbert son of Matthew.

[19] *CFR 1250–51*, no. 661; TNA, E 371/16, m. 7 (c. 21 May 1251), where Hugh de Botiun is described as 'the king's valet'.

[20] *CFR 1235–36*, nos 41, 153, 187, 199, 230, 233, 306, 404, 410; *CFR 1238–39*, no. 251; *CFR 1240–41*, nos 506, 509; *CFR 1241–42*, no. 211; *CFR 1242*, no. 411; *CFR 1243–44*, nos 114, 120, 420; *CFR 1244–45*, nos 147, 189; *CFR 1247–48*, nos 112, 431.

as would generally have been the case.[21] A similar case involves an entry from 1227 in which Hugh of Wells, bishop of Lincoln, offered 20 marks to have a charter that the market of Chipping Warden (Northamptonshire), established by Henry of Braybrooke, might not be permitted to stand, as in the bishop's charter, for sole market rights in Northamptonshire. This is modified in the originalia roll, where we are told that the bishop's charter was issued after the king's first coronation, and that he should similarly be permitted to hold his markets in Thorney (Cambridgeshire) and Biggleswade (Bedfordshire) as he had held them by a grant of King John.[22] Here we have a conundrum. Entries on the charter roll reveal a general charter for the bishop's markets witnessed on 5 February, and the more specific one on 30 April.[23] The undated fine roll entry comes at 27 May in the sequence of enrolment. Could it be that the fine roll clerk had access to a draft of the former only, from which he made his enrolment, and that the originalia clerk had managed to get hold of, or had been supplied with, the fuller version? Of course, he may have had access to the charter roll, given the similarity of the two texts. The discrepancy in enrolment is puzzling: the bishop was presumably in prolonged negotiation with the minority government over his privileges, and it is doubtful that two charters would have been enrolled without a fine having been made; maybe the later enrolment in the fine rolls connects the formal acceptance of the fine with the collection by the supplicant of the engrossed charter, at which point a draft would have been filed for enrolment.[24] In any case, it was deemed necessary for the Exchequer to know that the fine covered these markets beyond Northamptonshire. The extra details were presumably added in a review by the originalia roll clerk in the days leading up to 15 June, when that set of extracts went to the Exchequer.[25]

Medieval Chancery practice is not something of which we have more than an impressionistic view;[26] there is no equivalent for the Chancery of the *Dialogue of the Exchequer*, Richard fitz Nigel's didactic account of how the financial arm of government functioned in the late twelfth century.[27] Clearly, the Chancery was full of parchment for documents in various stages of preparation by teams

---

[21]   TNA, C 60/58, m. 9 (*CFR 1260–61*, no. 630).

[22]   *CFR 1226–27*, no. 241; TNA, E 371/1B, m. 5.

[23]   *CChR*, i, pp. 2, 33.

[24]   This issue is the subject of a fascinating Fine of the Month by Adam Chambers, a PhD student at King's College London: 'The Bordesley Charter: A Window on Chancery Procedure?', Fine of the Month September 2011, available at http://www.frh3.org.uk/content/month/fm-09-2011.html (accessed 7 April 2015).

[25]   *CFR 1226–27*, no. 266.

[26]   The most useful studies of enrolment in Chancery are: T. F. Tout, *Chapters in the Administrative History of Mediaeval England: The Wardrobe, the Chamber and the Small Seals*, 6 vols (Manchester, 1920), i, pp. 10–17, 121–50, 177–87, 284–94; Clanchy, *From Memory to Written Record, passim*; N. C. Vincent, 'Why 1199? Bureaucracy and Enrolment under John and his Contemporaries', in *English Government in the Thirteenth Century*, ed. A. L. Jobson (Woodbridge, 2004), pp. 17–49.

[27]   *Dialogus de Scaccario (The Dialogue of the Exchequer) and Constitutio Domus Regis (The Disposition of the King's Household)*, ed. and trans. E. Amt and S. D. Church (Oxford, 2008).

of clerks working on drafting, engrossing and enrolling, and there were routines and procedures to be followed. Entries such as these seem to indicate that the fine rolls themselves were similarly compiled from drafts, which clerks might also check and correct before enrolment. It is possible that clerks accumulated piles of drafts and enrolled them at intervals sometimes distant from a grant or order. Pressure of events and the peripatetic nature of the court could certainly make things difficult. In the most extreme case, in the years of Lewes and Evesham, large gaps are left on the fine roll as if in the expectation that more entries would follow but, as Sophie Ambler has demonstrated, an ancillary roll of fines was taken up by Henry in the campaign that ultimately led to his defeat at Lewes, and fines on that roll were not entered onto the main fine roll at any time thereafter.[28] The corresponding originalia roll for 1263–4, however, bears scarcely a trace of the turmoil beyond a simple but triumphant 'Lewes' mid-membrane to demarcate the two administrations of Henry III and Simon de Montfort.[29]

Conversely, alongside possible periodic reviews, there is evidence that Chancery clerks on occasion enrolled at the behest of senior royal officials. Take the fine by which the sons of Master Mosse, Jew of London, offered 300 marks for custody of the lands, rents and houses formerly of another prominent Jew, Salomon le Eveske. This is dated by its position on the roll to 10 August 1260. However, an addition, possibly by the same hand, after the terms of payment are laid out notes that 'It is to be known that the enrolment of this fine was made by the testimony of Simon Passelewe at Windsor on Thursday next before the Assumption of the Blessed Mary', in that year 12 August.[30] The testimony of Passelewe, a justice of the Jews, perhaps indicates the urgency in providing a proper record of this agreement, which had probably been made before him and his associates, and the immediacy with which the fine roll was compiled.

More research among Chancery records is needed before firmer and rounded conclusions can be formed. Having said that, it might be fruitful to speculate that the compilation of the originalia rolls sometimes ran parallel with the correction of the fine rolls to ensure the Chancery's enrolment was an accurate and up-to-date record for both the king and the recipients of his favour. A note on the fine roll for 1219–20 which reads 'Amended up to here' is a pointer to this.[31] Two entries dated in sequence to 23 March 1258 record that Geoffrey de

---

[28] Sophie Ambler, 'The Loans and Fines of Montfortian Bishops and the Missing Fine Roll in *expedicione* of 1264', Fine of the Month November 2008, available at http://www.frh3.org.uk/content/month/fm-11-2008.html (accessed 7 April 2015). For the gaps, see *CFR 1263–64*, nos 108–15 (TNA, C 60/61, m. 4). For the best modern narrative of the Lewes campaign, see J. R. Maddicott, *Simon de Montfort* (Cambridge, 1994), pp. 256–78.

[29] TNA, E 371/28, m. 4. Clearly this was entered some time after the battle. Only about six lines are left blank either side of this word.

[30] *CFR 1259–60*, no. 588 (TNA, C 60/57, m. 4).

[31] 'Emendatum est usque huc': *CFR 1219–20*, no. 94. This may at that time be a result of the compilation of the duplicate series of fine rolls, for which, see Carpenter, 'Historical Introduction', pp. xvii–xxiii.

Gotheleston gave half a mark for a writ *ad terminum*.[32] The second of these is can-celled 'because it is the same writ'. Perhaps the clerk who had originally enrolled these entries on the fine roll had two drafts and assumed they were different writs. During his review the clerk enrolling the originalia thought something about this looked amiss and was able to check a draft or take advice and ensure the cancellation of the second entry without enrolling it on his own membrane. Other entries point in the same direction: a note beside a fine of £500 for the confirmation of his liberties granted by King John to Peter des Roches, bishop of Winchester, in March 1227 reads 'It has not yet been sent', in other words to the Exchequer via the originalia roll;[33] just a few lines below is a note that the extracts up to that point had been sent. There is no record of this fine in the originalia roll at that point, and we can perhaps see the originalia roll clerk being told not to copy the fine for whatever reason and making a note to that effect for reference.[34] It was only when the next extraction took place that a second version of this fine, enrolled eleven entries on in sequence, reached the originalia roll and thus the Exchequer for action to be taken.[35]

It is also possible to suggest that the compilation of the originalia roll mem-branes may have sometimes gone hand in hand with the addition of marginal headings to the fine roll. We might therefore see a small team of clerks reviewing, refining and correcting the fine rolls as they scrolled down preparing the mar-ginal headings or checking the entries ready for copying, or vice versa. Practice probably varied. It is clear that marginal headings were added after the drafting of the main body of the entries in the fine rolls. In the fine roll for 1264–5 there are no headings after 10 January; the disturbed state of the kingdom prevented clerks from returning to insert them.[36] The clerk compiling the originalia roll, though, does add them; it apparently made greater sense that the Exchequer should have an indication of the county whose sheriff would receive summons to raise the debt than it did the Chancery.[37]

Of course, much of this is inference. The suggestion here is not that a mass of corrections in the fine roll were made during this review process; more detailed palaeographical analysis is required, and this is something the interactive nature of the fine rolls website permits. An indeterminate but large number of scribal corrections in the fine rolls was no doubt instantaneous in any case, to correct minor slips in spelling or words omitted in enrolling. Nevertheless, it would make sense for a periodic review to take place, particularly at moments as oppor-tune as supplying marginalia or copying entries onto the originalia roll, when substantial quantities of entries could be handled.

---

[32]   *CFR 1257–58*, nos 384–5.
[33]   *CFR 1226–27*, no. 161.
[34]   N. C. Vincent, *Peter des Roches: An Alien in English Politics, 1205–1238* (Cambridge, 1996), pp. 227–8.
[35]   *CFR 1226–27*, no. 172.
[36]   *CFR 1264–65*, no. 62.
[37]   TNA, E 371/29, mm. 2–3.

The Originalia Rolls as Working Documents

This is not to say that the relationship between the fine and originalia rolls is straightforward; on the contrary, it is actually rather complex. For though the two rolls are intimately linked in the bureaucratic chain, their paths as working documents have usually been seen to have diverged to some degree. While the fine rolls retained some currency for reference, it has always been supposed that the originalia rolls were merely ephemeral, their purpose being to transfer debts to the Exchequer for summons and enrolment, and nothing more. This only tells part of the story, for there is a sizeable amount of material of genuine significance in the originalia rolls that is not found in the fine rolls, most of which came through other Chancery channels. This statement, in turn, suggests that the bureaucratic chain had its kinks and that for the Exchequer itself the originalia rolls did not simply outlive their purpose once summons had been issued and debts transferred to the pipe roll.

Table 1 Entries in the originalia rolls (1256–66) not recorded in the fine rolls

Regnal Year	Number of Entries	Nature of Entries
1255–6	53	Farming out of royal demesne
		Commissions of castles
1256–7	2	Fines
		Pledges
1257–8	120	Fines of gold and silver
1258–9	8	Miscellaneous grants, fines, homages
1259–60	23	Commissions of counties/castles
1260–1	29	Commissions of castles
		Memoranda concerning stock
1261–2	10	Commissions of offices/royal demesne
1262–3	28	Fines
		Commissions
1263–4	68	Fines
		Commissions
		Royal demesne
1264–5	76	Commissions (mostly in lead up to and aftermath of the battle of Evesham)
1265–6	114	Letters patent of commission

Table 1 outlines precisely how many of these new entries there are in the originalia rolls during the years 1255–66, a period which witnessed the breakdown and reassertion of Henry's royal authority and the struggle for mastery at the heart of politics. There are 531 entries enrolled only in the originalia rolls, which add just over 5% to the total number of fine roll entries for that period. These entries consist of a variety of material but are weighted heavily towards commissions to hold office. Most noteworthy among them are the frequent changes of castle custodians and farmers of manors throughout these years of protest and upheaval, especially the 182 in 1264–5 and 1265–6, which chart the rapidly changing fortunes of men in whom the king and his Montfortian rivals placed their trust.[38] These entries also include the commitment of the Leicestershire manors of Great Bowden and Market Harborough, whose story David Carpenter has brought to life so vividly in some of his more important Fines of the Month articles on the fine rolls website.[39]

These commissions are, of course, also enrolled on the patent rolls.[40] However, the late-Victorian calenderers of those rolls do not include in their edition details of the fees, profits and increments payable, which was what the Exchequer really needed to know. This flags up a gradual change in the content of the originalia rolls. By the time Edward II ascended the throne in 1307 these documents included extracts from the three major series of Chancery rolls – patent, close and fine – from entries of importance to the Exchequer's accounting and financial management functions, of which fines played a very small and insignificant part.[41] It may be that this practice developed out of the tensions of the 1250s and 1260s. As counties, castles, demesne lands and other royal offices changed hands so frequently, and sometimes in large numbers, and as the Montfortians attempted to bring greater rigour to government, it was perhaps deemed expedient in order for the Chancery to keep control of the number and variety of membranes of extracts sent to the Exchequer, where, given their nature and provenance, they would be tacked onto the record of fines in the originalia roll. The Exchequer would then have the information it needed to draw up the pipe roll, and for future reference, in one place. The suspicion is that this type of material would be compiled to order in Chancery, at least initially, and not as part of the process of extracting fine roll entries. Yet, as the weight of material deemed worthy of transmission increased, so this process became routine.

The originalia rolls had long acted as a conduit of information on royal demesne lands and other rights not found in the fine rolls, but which had come into the Exchequer through the Chancery. The roll for 1240–1, for example, has three scrappy membranes sewn into it.[42] These detail those demesne manors leased to tenants, the annual farms, the extents, and in some cases provide unique snapshots of livestock and farm equipment on those manors. The king's stock committed to the Worcestershire manor of Feckenham, for example, consisted

---

[38]   *CFR 1264–65*, nos 620–95; *CFR 1265–66*, nos 740–852.
[39]   *CFR 1264–65*, no. 641. For more details about peasant protest in this period, see D. A. Carpenter, 'The Peasants of Rothley in Leicestershire, the Templars and King Henry III', Fine of the Month April 2009, available at http://www.frh3.org.uk/content/month/fm-04-2009.html), and both parts of D. A. Carpenter, '"The greater part of the vill was there": The Struggle of the Men of Brampton against their Lord', Fine of the Month December 2008, available at http://www.frh3.org.uk/content/month/fm-12-2008.html, and March 2009, available at http://www.frh3.org.uk/content/month/fm-03-2009.html (all accessed 7 April 2015).
[40]   Most of those for 1260–1 are to be found at *CPR 1258–66*, pp. 163–4.
[41]   See TNA, E 371/68, the first originalia roll of Edward II's reign.
[42]   *CFR 1240–41*, nos 756–828; TNA, E 371/8A, m. 4 (and schedules 1 & 2).

of thirty-five oxen, ten cows, a bull, ten bullocks, fifty pigs, four piglets, four plough-horses, two ploughs without any iron, two carts with iron harness, and another four ploughs.[43] Such detailed information may well have emanated from inquisitions returned into Chancery in response to the king's desire to lease his demesne to raise income, whereupon the letters of commission would be composed. A delivery note on the dorse of the third membrane of the originalia roll for that year reveals that it arrived in the Exchequer by the hand of a Chancery clerk, William of St Albans, on 8 October, close therefore to the end of Henry's twenty-fifth regnal year and as the Michaelmas Exchequer opened.[44] The next set of extracts from the fine rolls was dispatched in the following January, so we can assume that the Chancery considered the information it had gathered had to be sent in time for the account.[45]

Perhaps a majority of these extra membranes and schedules of material that are sewn into the originalia rolls was also transmitted to the Exchequer aside from the extraction process to meet a perceived pressing need for the information conveyed. Unusually, this body of material also includes amercements from judicial eyres. In the rolls for 1232–3, for instance, is a short membrane of amercements from an assize session at King's Lynn in Norfolk held shortly after Easter 1233.[46] Eyre or assize estreats usually reached the Exchequer directly without being enrolled among the originalia: on 25 September 1231 the fine rolls record an order to the sheriff of Yorkshire to deliver a roll of amercements taken before Stephen of Seagrave in his county into the Exchequer on the morrow of All Souls, perhaps with his account.[47] But, in cases such as these justices were maybe playing it safe: their commission came from the Chancery and they considered it politic to return their estreats there first, from whence they could be transmitted to the Exchequer. The speed with which the membrane arrived at the Exchequer is also striking. The King's Lynn assizes took place on 11 April and the treasurer received the record by the hand of the chancellor only sixteen days later. A batch of extracts was delivered into the Exchequer on 16 April,[48] and perhaps this membrane was transmitted by the chancellor along with it, as if it were a membrane of the originalia roll.

There was, then, some information deemed worthy of dispatch outside the routine flow. It is, though, much more problematic to account for the few dozen fines that find their way onto the originalia roll only, usually in chronological sequence in the main text of the extracts; these include six fines on the roll for 1262–3 which consist of offers for respite of knighthood, to take custody of lands and heirs, and the restoration of lands and revenues of religious houses, all

---

[43] *CFR 1240–41*, no. 775.
[44] *CFR 1240–41*, no. 828.
[45] For another schedule of stock, this time from Windsor Castle, see *CFR 1260–1*, nos 1091–3; TNA, E 371/25, m. 9 (schedule 3).
[46] *CFR 1232–33*, no. 333, n. 1. See also *CFR 1241–42*, nos 369–74.
[47] *CFR 1230–31*, no. 306.
[48] *CFR 1232–33*, no. 169.

of which would normally be enrolled among the fines.[49] Why are they omitted from the fine roll? We know that clerks compiling the originalia rolls worked in Chancery, so these extra entries would have been added there. Is it conceivable that the drafts from which fines were enrolled strayed, so that when the originalia roll clerk sat down with the two rolls and his pile of drafts, such strays had been gathered up without first being enrolled among the fines?

The Afterlife of the Originalia Rolls

From all these possibilities, it would appear that the lines of communication between Chancery and Exchequer were not always clear. Another key question is to ask what happened after the originalia rolls had served their purpose of transmitting financial and administrative information from Chancery to the Exchequer, in what we might call the 'afterlife' of the originalia rolls? On one level the answer is disappointingly little; there appears only sporadic evidence of later additions being made on the rolls. Nevertheless, the fact that additions were made at all, and their very nature, suggests the originalia rolls did retain some measure of currency over a number of years. Obviously, one of their most important functions was to give the Exchequer a record of the pledges taken for fines, and since the time between initial offer and actual payment might be many months, and might ultimately involve default, this record would be an important medium-term information source for the Exchequer. Throughout the corpus of originalia rolls, moreover, are scattered a variety of marginal remarks relating to administrative business that appear to have been added by Exchequer clerks. The first of these is 'Finitum' (Finished), which makes a brief appearance in the mid-1230s.[50] It is generally associated with orders to cause individuals to have seisin of inheritances, dower or escheated estates, or the arrest or release of chattels, and is probably associated with the supplementary conditions given in grants. In 1237, Payn de Chaworth, for instance, was granted full seisin of the lands of his late mother, Margaret de la Ferté, in Hampshire and Wiltshire, on condition that he answered for the issues of the lands at the Exchequer until he made fine with the king for the grant.[51] The order to the sheriff is annotated 'Finitum', suggesting that in this case Payn did make fine and that no more action needed to be taken. Similarly, the annotation 'Finitum' by an order to the escheator Roger of Essex to cause Alice, widow of Ralph Paynel, to have her dower and to permit Hugh of Pattishall to cause Ralph's lands in Lincolnshire to be cultivated, suggests that one of these transactions, perhaps the latter, had been completed.[52] Slightly more sporadically distributed throughout the rolls are similar marginal

---

49 *CFR 1262–63*, nos 815, 817, 818, 820, 821, 838.
50 The twentieth regnal year has eleven of these entries: *CFR 1236–37*, nos 26, 44, 68, 104, 109, 141, 156, 164, 207, 251, 258.
51 *CFR 1236–37*, no. 44 (4 February 1237).
52 *CFR 1236–37*, no. 68 (c. 3 March 1237).

annotations to the effect that 'The sheriff received nothing', as in an order from the roll for 1243–4 to the sheriff of Northumberland to take into the king's hand the lands of John Vicecomes for outstanding debts to a Jew.[53] It is tempting to see this annotation being added by Exchequer clerks as a result of the accounting and audit process. In this particular case the evidence does not survive. In two other examples on the same roll, it seems this possible inference might be misleading. Orders for the escheat of the lands of William Pippard in Devon and of the manors of Swindon in Wiltshire, Hintlesham in Suffolk and Wingrave in Buckinghamshire are supplemented in the fine roll by notes that the sheriffs concerned were amerced for failing to take these lands into the king's hand.[54] Notification of the amercement does not figure in the originalia rolls. In the case of the sheriff of Devon the amercement is pardoned him by the king, and the assumption is that this pardon must have taken place before the clerk compiled the originalia roll, or that clerk himself knew of the pardon and made a note to inform the Exchequer that they need not summon the sheriff for the debt.

By contrast, however, it is relatively common in the originalia rolls to find a marginal annotation that proves certain fines were never paid. This is 'in Rotulo compendii' (in the compendium Roll) and the annotation was definitely made by Exchequer clerks but at a distant remove from the original offer to the king. As part of a programme of Exchequer reform in 1323–4 led by Walter de Stapelton, bishop of Exeter and treasurer of Edward II, Exchequer records were scrutinised, and outstanding, ancient debts brought together in the so-called 'compendium rolls'. Clerks annotated the relevant debts on the originalia rolls before extracting them. A note was then made on the dorse of the originalia roll to the effect that all such fines had been extracted.[55] This, of course, means that we can trace the failure of individuals to make good on their promises to the king, and we must assume without other evidence that the favour they had requested was not granted.

Finally, there is tantalising evidence of a revival of interest in the information supplied by the originalia rolls almost three centuries after their compilation. There is a marginal annotation in the originalia roll for 1269–70 which appears to read 'in the Roll of the tenth year of [King] H. the seventh'.[56] There are entries throughout Henry III's originalia rolls that refer to future rolls for further processing of debts, but with the development of the compendium rolls it might have been safely assumed that debts enrolled in the originalia rolls would be ignored and left to die. The entries to which this annotation is attached concern annual rents of 12d. owed by the abbots of Flaxley in Gloucestershire and Pershore in Worcestershire, which were perhaps neither summoned nor

53   *CFR 1243–44*, no. 61 (1 January 1244); TNA, E 371/11, m. 1.
54   *CFR 1243–44*, nos 189 (25 April 1244), 207 (c. 3 May 1244).
55   See, for example, TNA, E 371/1B, m. 9d. – 'Fines et alia debita que debebantur per hunc rotulum anno regni Regis E. filii E. xvij extrahebantur mense Septembris eodem anno xvijº'.
56   TNA, E 371/34, m. 1: 'in Rotulo anno xº H. septimi'. I am very grateful to Dr Beth Hartland for locating this entry while editing that originalia roll, and to Dr Sean Cunningham of The National Archives for discussing Henry VII's interest in reviving old debts with me.

contemporaneously annotated to show that they reached that year's pipe roll.[57] However, in the Gloucestershire account on the pipe roll for 10 Henry VII (1494–5) we do indeed find two entries recording outstanding debts of £11 5s. from each abbot as 'in the originalia of the fifty-fourth year of King Henry III in the first membrane …'.[58] Henry VII, it seems, or some of his more determined Exchequer officials, initiated a drive to recover ancient debts, scouring earlier versions of the rolls in their care, and we can imagine Henry rubbing his hands in anticipation of clawing back ancient prerogatives that had been allowed to lapse, even though this could well have provoked accusations of outrageous enforcement of that royal prerogative.[59]

Conclusion

The medieval English Chancery is an institution that does not give up its secrets very easily. If an individual wanted the king's favour in the thirteenth century, he or she almost invariably had to pay for it. It was in the interests of both parties, king and supplicant, that this agreement was recorded – enrolled – centrally. By these means rights could be pursued and defended in equal measure. For the entirety of the reign of Henry III it was on the fine rolls that these agreements were recorded; but, there remained one main channel by which this information could be transmitted to the Exchequer for collection, and this was by the copying out of salient details onto the originalia rolls. These were simple in form and simple in purpose, and it seems highly likely that such simplicity allowed them to meet their purpose. However, it also produced secondary benefits. A detailed comparison between the fine and originalia rolls, now made possible by the project website, has highlighted a more delicate balance and nuanced relationship between these two cognate sets of rolls than has been previously imagined. The processes that have been outlined here may only be inferred, but the comparison between the two sets of rolls is strongly suggestive that the Chancery was able to employ the originalia rolls to monitor some of its administrative procedures and better marshal what were often disparate scraps of parchment, a mass of working documents, in the service of the Crown.

---

[57] *CFR 1269–70*, nos 1588, 1589. The annotations regarding summons are illegible in the originalia roll.

[58] TNA, E 372/340, rot. 7, m. 2. Marginal annotations record that these are extracted debts.

[59] Recently, the medieval and early modern team at The National Archives have discovered a roll of James I's reign, recording Crown debts and recognisances dating back to the 1450s, indicating the early modern Exchequer appears to have appreciated the uses to which its treasure trove of ancient records could be put.

3

The Fine Rolls of Henry III as a Source for the Legal Historian

Paul Brand

Legal historians are omnivorous animals. Almost every kind of official governmental record from thirteenth-century England is something which the legal historian can draw on. The fine rolls of Henry III's reign are no exception to this general rule. For most purposes, their evidence is only part of a wider palette of material on which the legal historian must draw in constructing his or her picture, and not something that can be used by itself. But the rolls do often provide important evidence which we would otherwise lack, and the legal historian can certainly not afford to neglect them.

One of the most important types of evidence that the Henry III fine rolls provide for the legal historian is that which Tony Moore discusses in this volume: for the payment of fines by individual litigants to ensure that cases which might otherwise have gone to county courts or other local courts went instead to the Common Bench or to King's Bench; and for the removal of cases out of the county court into the central courts, or rather primarily into the Common Bench, by writs of *pone* and also, probably, *recordari*. The phenomenon is an important one and shows how much the drawing of litigation into the central courts was litigant-driven. Another related, but lesser, phenomenon that the fine rolls illustrate well is of payments to ensure that cases from counties other than the county where an eyre was being held were heard at sessions of the general eyre (and always on particular return days). This was not something of which I had been aware till I looked at the fine rolls. In general, 'foreign' (out of county) pleas on the eyre plea rolls seem to be cases from a county where an eyre had just been held and which had not been determined before the justices left that county. Payments recorded on the fine rolls indicate that it was also possible for a relatively small sum of money (generally half a mark or 1 mark, and rarely as much as 20 shillings or 2 marks) to bring cases from counties other than that in which the eyre was sitting to be heard in a 'foreign' county. These seem generally to be brought by original writ rather than by a writ transferring litigation already begun in the county court, and appear never to be transfers of cases out of the Common Bench to an eyre session. The earliest seems to be in early December 1226 when Felice the widow of William Clerk of Warwick gave half a mark for a writ of dower claiming land in several Warwickshire villages to be heard before the justices at Gloucester at the octaves of Hilary 1227 (described somewhat awkwardly as 'in uno comitatu in alium').[1] Normally the number of such pleas initiated in eyres in 'foreign' counties seems to have been relatively small. The largest number of such cases identified comes from 1263, when payments were made (in March and April) for eleven such pleas (from the counties of Nottinghamshire, Northamptonshire, Yorkshire and Leicestershire) to be heard in the Lincolnshire eyre of April to June 1263.[2] The clerks of Chancery seem to have had instructions as to which counties pleas could be drawn from. In late June 1269 a single litigant had an offer of half a mark accepted to bring a Yorkshire plea before the justices itinerant then in session at Newcastle, and another half mark to bring a Lincolnshire plea before the justices itinerant at Leicester, though this did not open till late September.[3] The litigant's own convenience would surely have suggested bringing both pleas at the same time in the same county, and it was the same team of justices who held both eyres.

The fine rolls are also part of the evidence for another type of litigation that should, in theory, have come to the Common Bench being heard by other justices locally instead. Magna Carta as enacted in 1215 (in chapter 18), and as re-enacted in a revised version in 1216 (in chapter 13), required that assizes of *darrein presentment* (determining who was entitled to present to a vacant ecclesiastical living on the basis of a jury finding as to who had presented the last rector, who had recently died) should in future be heard locally in the county concerned, together with assizes of *novel disseisin* and *mort d'ancestor*, by two royal justices holding four sessions in the county each year with four local knights as associates.[4] In the 1217 reissue this chapter was significantly amended. Although assizes of *novel disseisin* and *mort d'ancestor* were to continue being heard locally in this way, assizes of *darrein presentment* (chapter 15 said) were always to be taken and determined before the justices of the (Common) Bench, and it was in this amended form that the chapter was further reissued in 1225.[5] However, as Julie Kanter noted in 2007, when the 'four knights' system for hearing assizes of *novel disseisin* and *mort d'ancestor* outside (but in addition to) the general eyre was created in 1218 we also find the same arrangement being used for the hearing of some assizes of *darrein presentment* as well, notwithstanding the provisions of the 1217 reissue of Magna Carta.[6]

Kanter gives the impression that the four knights system only existed down to 1232, but this is mistaken. The only significance of 1232 is that it is the date at which the Public Record Office stopped publishing a full transcript of the patent rolls and went over to publishing a calendar – one that omitted what were considered to be routine judicial commissions. Exactly when the 'four knights'

---

[1]   *CFR 1226–27*, no. 37.
[2]   *CFR 1262–63*, nos 305, 310, 312, 356, 361, 363, 364, 366, 395, 452, 455.
[3]   *CFR 1268–69*, nos 435, 436.
[4]   *Select Charters*, pp. 295, 337.
[5]   *Select Charters*, pp. 342, 350.
[6]   For the 'Fine of the Month' in which she dealt with this, see J. Kanter, 'The Four Knights' System and the Evidence for it in the Fine Rolls', available at http://www.finerollshenry3.org.uk/content/month/fm-03-2007.html (accessed 7 April 2015).

system came to an end is more difficult to say because of the loss of two relevant patent rolls for 23 and 24 Henry III. The system was still apparently in operation in 22 Henry III (1237–8) but it had apparently disappeared by 25 Henry III (1240–1). It was replaced, however, not by total compliance with the provisions of Magna Carta but by a continuation of the system of commissioning at least some local hearings, but before royal justices and others rather than before four local knights. A register of writs which seems in the main to belong to the later years of the reign of Henry III tells us that assizes of *darrein presentment* were *de cursu* at the Common Bench and also in the eyre in the county where the church was located, and *de levi gracia* before justices in eyre in other counties, but *de magna gracia* before other specially commissioned justices.[7] The fine rolls suggest that even this last rule may be misleading, for in three entries in 1265–6 we find plaintiffs making fines to obtain assizes of *darrein presentment* before Richard of Middleton (in late October 1265), before Richard of Middleton and Peter de Percy (in early January 1266) and before Martin of Littlebury (in late March or early April 1266), but we also see that it was offerings of no more than 1 mark or (in the latter two cases) half a mark which secured these commissions.[8] The fine rolls also provide confirmation that assizes of *darrein presentment* were (despite the provisions of Magna Carta) from early on also being summoned before the justices in eyre. Early in March 1220 we find a plaintiff paying 1 mark to have an assize of *darrein presentment* which had been summoned before the next eyre in Warwickshire heard instead before the justices at Westminster one month after Easter.[9]

The fine rolls are rather less useful in helping to track and understand other institutional changes connected with the longer intervals between sessions of the general eyre in individual counties, in particular the beginnings of regular gaol deliveries conducted by four knights from the counties whose gaols were being delivered, or by other smaller groups of royal justices. There seems to be no trace of payments being made for these sessions, whether by the prisoners who were being tried at these gaol deliveries or by the communities of those counties whose gaols were being delivered. Nor does there seem to be any trace of payments being made for writs *de bono et malo* specially authorising the justices of gaol delivery to try prisoners accused of homicide.[10] This significant development in the legal system is only mentioned in passing in, for example, the order sent in 1230 to Walter de 'Envermeu' and Simon of Hales to send to the Exchequer the estreats of fines, perquisites and amercements made before them at Lincoln when they last delivered the gaol there before the king's crossing.[11] The fine roll

---

[7]   *Early Registers of Writs*, ed. E. de Haas and G. D. G. Hall, Selden Society 87 (1970), CC 49 (p. 49).

[8]   *CFR 1264–65*, no. 11; *CFR 1265–66*, nos 112 and 256.

[9]   *CFR 1219–20*, no. 106.

[10]   R. B. Pugh, 'The writ *de bono et malo*', *Law Quarterly Review* 92 (1976), 258–67; J. M. Kaye, 'Gaol Delivery Jurisdiction and the Writ *de bono et malo*', *Law Quarterly Review* 93 (1977), 259–72.

[11]   *CFR 1229–30*, no. 388.

for 17 Henry III likewise contains a copy of the estreats from a gaol delivery held at Lincoln before Simon of Ropsley and his colleagues recording the valuations of the chattels of three men hanged by the justices, one payment for the king's year-and-a-day of the land of one of the three hanged men, and the amercement of one surety when the man he had pledged did not appear.[12]

There is also other revealing and interesting material on the working of the criminal justice system. In 1250 a payment of 20 shillings was proffered by the prior of St Neots for an order to the sheriff of Cambridgeshire to receive into the king's prison at Cambridge a prisoner (Roger Cusin) who had been detained for larceny in the prior's prison.[13] Here we see some evidence as to why one of the clauses of the Petition of the Barons in 1258 (clause 20) complained that when an earl, baron, bailiff or other who had a liberty, whether in a city or in a village, took a malefactor and offered him to the sheriff or his bailiff to imprison him till judgment was made, the sheriff refused unless he made a fine for receiving him.[14] Evidently one way of getting round this, even though it also presumably required payment, was to get the king to order a prisoner's acceptance into the sheriff's or king's prison.

There is also the long and complicated story of the death of Thomas of Charlecote. The fine rolls are an essential part of this story, but other sources are also essential to rounding it out. The first entry on a fine roll is a simple one, belonging to a date sometime in late August or early September 1249. It orders the sheriff of Warwickshire to make an enquiry as to the chattels of Thomas of Charlecote, who was believed to have drowned himself; the sheriff was to establish into whose hands Thomas's chattels had fallen, and to take them into safe custody so that he could answer for them at the king's Exchequer.[15] So far so simple. Seizure into the king's hands of the movable goods of a man who had committed suicide was in line with the normal practice for those who had committed *felonia de se* by the mid-thirteenth century.[16] The story gets a little more complicated when we look at an entry in the fine roll for 14 February 1263. The sheriff of Warwickshire was now told that the king had discovered, by inspecting the eyre rolls of Roger of Thirkleby and his colleagues (the justices of the 1247 Warwickshire eyre), that there had been two presentments relating to the death of Thomas in that eyre. One had been by the hundred of Kineton. The jurors of this hundred had presented his death as a suicide by drowning in the pond of Haseley, but had done so 'ignorantly' (*ignoranter*) because that village was not even in the hundred. This had led to a judgment adjudging Thomas's chattels (to the value of £71 5s. 4d.) to the king. But there had subsequently been a second presentment, by the hundred of Barlichway (which did include Haseley, where

12   *CFR 1232–33*, no. 99.
13   *CFR 1249–50*, no. 166.
14   *Documents*, p. 84.
15   *CFR 1248–49*, no. 423.
16   R. D. Groot, 'When Suicide became Felony', *Journal of Legal History* 21 no. 1 (2000), 1–20.

the death had occurred). This had found that Thomas had in fact been strangled and thrown into the fish-pond of Haseley by three of his servants, Hugh the cook, Richard le Westreys and Christine the dairywoman, who had been executed for the killing before the same justices. Thus the chattels should not have been forfeited. The sheriff was therefore ordered to restore the chattels to the heirs and the kin of Thomas to distribute for the benefit of his soul.[17] The 1247 Warwickshire eyre roll survives only in a damaged condition, and only the first of these two presentments can now be read on it.[18]

To round out the story, however, we need also to look at the records of the Exchequer of the Jews. From these we learn that Thomas of Charlecote had been seriously indebted to at least one Jewish creditor. In 1244 the king had granted Thomas a respite of a debt allegedly owed to David of Oxford when he produced a starr of acquittance and also a chirograph recording jewels he had delivered to David on account of this debt.[19] David had died in 1244 and some of his debts had passed to his widow, Licorice of Winchester. In 31 Henry III (1246–7) Thomas had apparently made a fresh acknowledgement to Licorice (by chirograph), acknowledging a debt of £180 secured on all his lands.[20] The record of an action of account brought by Thomas's son Thomas against Licorice in the Exchequer of the Jews in Easter term 1253 shows that Licorice claimed that Thomas (senior) had subsequently, at the Exaltation of the Cross 32 Henry III (14 September 1248), acknowledged (by chirograph) a debt of £400 repayable at Michaelmas 38 Henry III (1254), for which Thomas was also to pay 20 marks a year during the six years prior to the repayment date, and another debt of £60 also allegedly made on the same day.[21] Thomas's initial objection to the first of these acknowledgments was that its terms were contrary to the *statuta judaismi* (the rules governing the Jewish community), since it was, in effect, compounding the interest on a loan. He did not make the (to us) obvious objection that the chirographs had been made after his father's death. But later in the record this did emerge, even though the record of the case rather obscures it. It records his argument that soon after 'dictum chirographum' was made (and this must be a reference to the chirograph recording the initial loan of £180 made in 1246–7) Thomas had been killed and Licorice had accused Thomas's steward (whom the record identifies, perhaps wrongly and certainly confusingly, as another Thomas of Charlecote) of that killing. The steward had retained his late master's seal in his custody until sued for it in the king's court, and had surrendered it a little before Christmas 1252. The steward had had the chirograph (this seems to be a reference to the bond for £400) made in order to secure peace from Licorice and

---

[17] *CFR 1262–63*, no. 254; the writ is also summarised (but with errors) in TNA, E 159/37, m. 16d.

[18] TNA, JUST 1/952, rot. 38d.

[19] *Calendar of Plea Rolls of the Exchequer of the Jews*, vol. 1: *1218–1272*, ed. J. M. Rigg (London, 1905), p. 78.

[20] *Select Pleas, Starrs etc., of the Jewish Exchequer, 1220–1284*, ed. J. M. Rigg, Selden Society 15 (1901), p. 19.

[21] *Select Pleas, Starrs etc.*, pp. 19–27.

to disinherit the heirs of Thomas. This Thomas (meaning the steward) had also been in seisin of the lands as the serjeant of Licorice once she took seisin in late September 1249. A subsequent jury verdict, however, found that she had only taken seisin a little later, at the feast of St Andrew the Apostle 34 Henry III (30 November 1249), and that she had then taken goods and chattels belonging to Thomas worth £100 6s. 7d. This suggests that the judgment in the 1247 eyre adjudging the chattels as forfeit to the king may not in fact have been executed. A second jury verdict indicates that Thomas had possessed land in Haseley worth £15 3s. 10d. a year, and land in Whitnash worth £10 2d. a year. Although the king had intervened on Licorice's behalf, eventually an afforced court consisting of Philip Lovel (the treasurer), Roger of Thirkleby, Henry of Bath, John of Wyville and Simon Passelewe decided that Thomas only owed the original £180 plus interest up to the time of his father's death and less anything received by Licorice. So the whole story is rather more complicated than the fine rolls alone seem to suggest.

There are also entries on the fine rolls which help to shed light on the development of other areas of English law in the reign of Henry III. One related set of entries provides an interesting side-light on the law relating to alien status and allegiance in the middle of the thirteenth century. Most of the cases about alien status and allegiance from this period relate to claims for land in England made by those born elsewhere but claiming to be the heirs of those who had once held the land, while their opponents said that birth outside the king's allegiance should disqualify them from making such claims. An entry on the fine roll of 27 Henry III, dated 15 March 1243, provides a stern reminder that birth within England might not, in itself, be enough to secure the right to inherit. It orders the sheriff of Essex to take into the king's hands all the land which falls hereditarily to Roger Bataille, even though he was born in England ('licet idem Rogerus oriundus fuerit in Anglia'), as he was living ('manens') in Calais and in the allegiance of the king of France, and also to arrest Roger if he should find him either at Barstable in Essex, where he had been recently ('ubi nuper fuit'), or anywhere else in his bailiwick, and to detain him in prison till further order.[22] There was what looks like a follow-up order in August of the same year addressed to the same sheriff and ordering the seizure of all the lands formerly belonging to Geoffrey Bataille, and their transfer to the custody of the bailiff of the hundred of Barstable to hold on the king's behalf.[23] A further follow-up in January 1249 (also recorded on the fine roll) records a grant of 60 acres with appurtenances in Barstable, formerly belonging to Roger Bataille and purportedly part of 'the lands of the Normans' ('et sunt de terris Normannorum'), though Roger Bataille was not a 'Norman' but an Englishman, to William Gifford for an annual rent of 20 shillings, to hold until the king returned the land to the right heirs by peace or his own wishes.[24]

[22] *CFR 1242–43*, no. 203.
[23] *CFR 1242–43*, no. 347.
[24] *CFR 1248–49*, no. 80.

A royal ordinance of 1256 affirmed what the king had perhaps begun asserting before that: that tenants-in-chief could not alienate the lands they held in chief without the king's permission. The great historian of the control of alienation, Malcolm Bean, while admitting that it was difficult to track the king's control of such alienations before the reign of Edward I, nonetheless thought the measure effective.[25] The evidence of the fine rolls makes this a little less sure. Take the mandate to the escheator north of the Trent issued on 6 May 1262 on the fine roll for 46 Henry III.[26] This ordered him to seize the manor of Manchester into the king's hands because its recently deceased tenant-in-chief, Thomas Gresle, had enfeoffed his son, Peter Gresle, of it, but had not enfeoffed him at such a time ('tali tempore') and 'in such a way' that he could have had free tenement in it ('et eo modo quod inde liberum tenementum habere possit'), and so wardship of the manor belonged to the king by reason of the wardship of the land and heir of Thomas. The grant was invalid because it had not been made long enough before the death of Thomas to be effective, but there seems to be no suggestion that the grant was invalid because it had not received the king's prior approval.[27] Peter was the younger son of Thomas and was perhaps already in 1262 warden of the church of Manchester; the elder son of Thomas, Robert, had died in 1261, leaving an infant son, also Robert, who did not come of age till c. 1275. Another fine roll entry of May 1269, recording another mandate to the escheator north of the Trent, recited the finding of an inquisition made by the same escheator, which had found that Matthew of Sandiacre and his wife Christine had enfeoffed John of Stokes of nine bovates in Sandiacre in Derbyshire and put him in seisin of them, and had then affirmed this grant by a fine made in the Warwickshire eyre (probably that of 1262).[28] John had been in seisin for eight years and more and had then granted the land back to them for the term of their lives for 30 shillings annually. When they had recently died John had re-entered the land and held it till the sub-escheator for Derbyshire had entered it, since it was held of the king for 30 shillings a year. The entry ordered the escheator to let John have the land back once he had found surety for payment of relief. Nowhere is there any suggestion that the original grant had been invalid as having been made without the king's consent, or even that a fine needed to be paid for entering land held in chief without that consent. All that was required was the payment of relief.

The fine rolls also cast some light on the process of drafting and approving special writs of legal significance. An entry on the fine roll for 41 Henry III records an agreement by William de Bonevile in November 1256 to pay half a gold mark in the Wardrobe at Easter 1257 for the removal of a Devonshire assize of *mort d'ancestor* in which the bishop of Bath (who was currently overseas) has been vouched to warranty to the Common Bench.[29] Here the interest lies in

[25] J. M. W. Bean, *The Decline of English Feudalism* (Manchester, 1968), pp. 67–71.
[26] *CFR 1261–62*, no. 414.
[27] The grant itself is enrolled on *CR 1261–64*, p. 124.
[28] *CFR 1268–69*, no. 348.
[29] *CFR 1266–67*, no. 86.

the note at the end of the entry. This carefully notes that this writ 'was issued on the advice of the king's justices' ('istud breve processit de consilio justiciari-orum regis'). The point seems to be that the normal rule (established by chapter 14 of the 1217 reissue of Magna Carta and reaffirmed in the 1225 reissue) was that such assizes could be transferred to the Common Bench only if some spe-cific point of legal difficulty had arisen, and that it might be thought doubtful whether it really had in this instance.[30] Perhaps only the justices of the Common Bench were trusted to deal properly with the difficulty created by the vouchee's absence. But the clerk seems very concerned to note that the writ was only issued after taking expert legal advice.

In a second entry in the same roll, from July 1257, we find a brief note recording that Hawise de Longchamp has given the king half a mark for a writ drafted by Henry of Bratton ('pro uno brevi formato per H. de Bratton') against Reginald de Grey to be heard before the justices of the Common Bench.[31] Although there is no trace of such a writ on the close rolls (where newly drafted writs are sometimes to be found), there is a case enrolled on the Common Bench plea roll for Hilary term 1259 which seems almost certainly to be the case initiated by this writ.[32] From this we can see that Hawise was the widow of Henry de Longchamp and was suing Reginald de Grey and his wife Maud (who was Henry de Longchamp's daughter and heiress) for not allowing her free tenants in the Herefordshire village of Wilton (whose services had been assigned to her as part of her dower) to perform suit to her court in Wilton as they were obliged to do and had customarily done, and for not allowing her to use the franchises which belonged to her dower. She claimed Reginald and Maud were distraining her tenants to prevent them performing suit to her court, and claimed damages. They denied obstructing her right to her tenants' suit and said her free tenants were at liberty to do this suit if they wished. This litigation is also clearly connected with a prior suit heard in the 1256 Herefordshire eyre in which Hawise had sued twenty-one free tenants (many with Welsh names) for the suit they owed and had customarily performed to her court at Wilton every two weeks and of which she had been seised until a year previously.[33] They too, however, acknowledged owing suit to the court as she claimed, and agreed to do it in future, and the sheriff was to distrain them if they failed.

However, the chief interest of the entry is, for the legal historian interested in the reviser of *Bracton*, in adding to the relatively small amount of evidence from the 1250s which shows Henry of Bratton drafting special writs for the use of litigants. The final entry relating to writs is one I wish I had noticed before publishing my

---

[30] *Select Charters*, pp. 342, 350.
[31] *CFR 1256–57*, no. 823.
[32] TNA, KB 26/162, m. 28. *The Complete Peerage*, vol. 6, ed. H. A. Doubleday, D. Warrand and Lord Howard de Walden (London, 1926), p. 171 note 'f' shows Maud was the daughter and heiress of Henry.
[33] TNA, JUST 1/300C, rot. 11d.

book on the legislation of the period of baronial reform.[34] One of the provisions added to the Provisions of Westminster when it was reissued in a revised form in 1263 was a new clause 25 relating to writs of entry, the category of land action which allowed land to be claimed on the basis of a single specific flaw in the chain of title through which the current tenant possessed the land he held. Hitherto there had been a limit (which varied from type to type of writ of entry) on the number of links in the chain of title which linked the initial flawed acquisition and the current possessor. The new clause provided that this limit should no longer apply; instead plaintiffs should be allowed to have a writ which mentioned the initial flaw but did not necessarily specify the links in the chain. The clause also stated that the original writs for this purpose were to be 'provided by the king's council'.[35] Draft writs of entry in the *post* of the kind authorised by the legislation are found on the dorse of the close roll in early March 1263 and an actual writ of entry in the *post* in the Rutland eyre of April 1263, but then no more are to be found until Hilary term 1267 (in the Common Bench), when such a writ was challenged as being 'outside the common form of the writ of entry'.[36] This was all of the story that I knew. But the fine rolls provide at least a footnote to that story. Sometime in early October 1263 Laurence of Amersham offered half a mark specifically for a writ of entry leviable in Buckinghamshire. This is in itself remarkable since writs of entry were normally issued without payment. But even more remarkable is the qualification added to the words 'writ of entry'. The payment is for a writ of entry 'to the fourth degree' ('pro uno brevi de ingressu ad quartum gradum habendo ad bancum'). Though different forms of counting the degrees existed, there was general agreement that a writ of entry 'to the fourth degree' (with four chains of title since the flawed transaction) lay 'outside the degrees'. Such a writ was not authorised by the legislation since that envisaged the omission of the chain of title we find in writs of entry in the *post*. But someone in October 1263 seems to have been willing to authorise the issuing of a writ to cover a chain of title longer than that covered by the pre-1263 degrees but still expressed in terms of those degrees. This has, I think, to be someone who positively disapproved of dropping the chain of title but was willing to see it extended in writs of entry.

Finally, there is evidence in the fine rolls concerning the punishment of those convicted of redisseisin. Chapter 3 of the Provisions of Merton of 1236 had established a new procedure for use when a successful plaintiff in an assize of *novel disseisin*, or any other land action, who had been put in seisin by the judgment of the king's court was disseised by the person against whom the land had been recovered. This was a special new action of redisseisin authorised by royal writ but heard locally by the sheriff in association with the coroners and using a jury partially drawn from the jurors of the previous jury. If the defendant(s) was or were found guilty of redisseisin they were to be arrested and imprisoned until the king

---

[34] P. Brand, *Kings, Barons and Justices: The Making and Enforcement of Legislation in Thirteenth-Century England* (Cambridge, 2003).

[35] Brand, *Kings, Barons and Justices*, p. 449.

[36] Brand, *Kings, Barons and Justices*, pp. 181–2.

gave order for their release (whether in return for ransom or in some other way) and the plaintiff put back into seisin of the land.[37] Writs of redisseisin were not initially enrolled (this only began in 1285) and so we have no means of knowing how common they were. Nor do we know much about the mechanisms used to secure the release of those imprisoned for redisseisin. Because the whole process was so unsupervised there must be a suspicion that sheriffs may sometimes have found ways of diverting the fines or ransoms the king should have received into their own pockets. This certainly seems to be the background to chapter 8 of the Statute of Marlborough of 1267, which rehearses the requirement of the 1236 legislation that those arrested and imprisoned for redisseisin were not to be released except on the special order of the king after making fine for their offence, and that sheriffs who released such offenders without such an order were to be heavily amerced and the offenders still to be held liable for punishment.[38]

There are three entries on the published close rolls about the mechanisms for the release of those imprisoned for redisseisin. One (from 1241) delegated to the justices of the Worcestershire eyre of 1241 the responsibility for setting the fine to be paid by Geoffrey de Cure, who was in prison for the offence and whose release was authorised provided he found suitable sureties for appearing before them.[39] An order of 1251 authorised the sheriff of Hampshire to release the prior of Sandford, who had been imprisoned in Winchester for this offence, and pardoned the prior any 'vindictam et amerciamentum'.[40] A 1253 order issued during the king's absence authorised the release of Hugh of Boothby and three others by the sheriff of Huntingdon in return for sureties for their appearance before the king's council to make fine.[41]

The fine rolls add at least seven further pieces of information about the procedure for the release of those imprisoned for redisseisin for the period before 1272. The earliest of these is from 1243 and the latest is from 1271, but the bulk comes from the 1260s. Almost all those mentioned in these entries were currently in custody, with the apparent exception of the John d'Oyry, who was pardoned imprisonment altogether in an entry of 1264.[42] The later entries (from the second 1260 entry onwards) also generally specify where the offender was being held in prison.[43] The earliest of the entries (of 1243) mentions only the plaintiff who has been redisseised,[44] but subsequent entries also mention the

---

37 *CR 1234–37*, pp. 337–8.
38 Brand, *Kings, Barons and Justices*, pp. 195–6.
39 *CR 1237–42*, pp. 285–6.
40 *CR 1251–53*, p. 4.
41 *CR 1251–53*, p. 416.
42 *CFR 1263–64*, no. 156.
43 All are being held in royal prisons: these are Winchester (*CFR 1259–60*, no. 668), Glastonbury (*CFR 1260–61*, no. 181), Shrewsbury (*CFR 1268–69*, no. 274) and Lincoln (*CFR 1270–71*, no. 1204).
44 *CFR 1242–43*, no. 324. Though note the 1269 entry specifies the form of the 'redisseisin' (the re-erection of a pond unjustly erected to the nuisance of someone else's free tenement) without mentioning whose: *CFR 1268–69*, no. 274.

place where the redisseisin had occurred. Three of the seven references (of 1260, 1261 and 1271) mention that the imprisonment has been 'by the king's order', but this may simply refer to the king's writ of redisseisin which had authorised the hearing of the case.[45] Four of the entries mention a specific amount of money as having been paid for release: no more than 1 mark (paid by two men) for release from prison in 1260;[46] 40 shillings paid in advance by John d'Oyry not to be imprisoned in 1264;[47] 100 shillings in 1243;[48] and eight and a half marks paid by the abbot of Shrewsbury and two other men in 1269, with each being assigned a specific share to pay.[49] In the other three cases (in 1260, 1261 and 1271) the sheriff was instructed to accept a reasonable fine for the king's benefit 'according to the quality of the offence and the quantity of the offender's goods but saving his livelihood'.[50] The first two of these simply talked of the sheriff answering for the fine at the Exchequer; the last spelled out that the sheriff was to be able to account for the fine on his account at the Exchequer and reminded that 'we have burdened you by the rolls of our Chancery to answer at the Exchequer for the fine'. Only the first of the enrolments, however, also made release conditional on the offender satisfying his opponent for the damages he had incurred by the disseisin.[51] Perhaps sheriffs did not need to be reminded of this. When I was working on the action of redisseisin in connection with the writing of my doctoral thesis in the 1960s and 1970s, and much more recently when I was revising that thesis for publication, I did not think of looking at the fine rolls for evidence. I now know that I should have done. Medieval legal historians may in principle be omnivorous, but sometimes they are not quite omnivorous enough in practice. At least our 'food' is now available on our screens at the click of a mouse thanks to the Henry III Fine Rolls project.

---

[45] *CFR 1259–60*, no. 668; *CFR 1260–61*, no. 181; *CFR 1270–71*, no. 1204.
[46] *CFR 1259–60*, no. 132, but this may not have been effective.
[47] *CFR 1263–64*, no. 156.
[48] *CFR 1242–43*, no. 324.
[49] *CFR 1268–69*, no. 274.
[50] *CFR 1259–60*, no. 668; *CFR 1260–61*, no. 181; *CFR 1270–71*, no. 1204.
[51] *CFR 1242–43*, no. 324.

4

The Fine Rolls as Evidence for the Expansion of Royal Justice during the Reign of Henry III

Tony K. Moore

The two towering figures in medieval English legal history are Henry II, the founder of the common law, and Edward I, the 'English Justinian'.[1] Henry III has, perhaps inevitably, been overshadowed. For instance, Robert Palmer's 2003 survey of English legal history jumps straight from *Magna Carta* to Edward I, omitting Henry III entirely.[2] This is not to underestimate the importance of a number of recent studies on particular aspects of the legal system during the reign.[3] Equally valuable are the editions of the *Curia Regis Rolls* down to 1250 and an increasing number of published eyre rolls.[4] There is also a general understanding that important changes took place during Henry's reign. According to F. W. Maitland, Henry's reign was 'an age of rapid, but steady and permanent growth … the subsequent centuries will be able to do little more than to fill in the details of a scheme which is set before them as unalterable.'[5] The following discussion aims to use the evidence of the fine rolls to shed new light on this 'scheme'.

To fully understand the significance of the reign of Henry III for English legal history, it is necessary first to sketch the broad outline of the legal system. Indeed, it could be argued that there was no single 'legal system' in medieval England but rather a multiplicity of different jurisdictions: the royal (or common law) courts of the Bench (and, from 1234, *coram rege*) and the itinerant royal justices, sitting in eyre *ad omnia placita* or commissioned to hear individual assizes; the

[1] M. Hale, *The History of the Common Law of England*, ed. C. M. Gray (London, 1971), pp. 88–106. The reign of Henry III merits just over two pages, where Hale focuses on Magna Carta and Bracton.

[2] R. C. Palmer, 'England: Law, Society and the State', in *A Companion to Britain in the Later Middle Ages*, ed. S. H. Rigby (Oxford, 2003), pp. 242–60, at p. 249.

[3] Perhaps the best exemplar of one strand of research is P. Brand, *Kings, Barons and Justices: The Making and Enforcement of Legislation in Thirteenth-Century England* (Cambridge, 2003). For a more quantitative approach, see D. Klerman, 'Settlement and the Decline of Private Prosecution in Thirteenth-Century England', *Law and History Review* 19 (2001), 1–65.

[4] *CRR*; the most recent eyre roll to be edited is *The Civil Pleas of the Suffolk Eyre of 1240*, ed. E. J. Gallagher, Suffolk Records Society 52 (2009). Research has been greatly facilitated by the posting of images of legal and other documents on the Anglo-American Legal Tradition website.

[5] F. Pollock and F. W. Maitland, *The History of English Law before the Time of Edward I*, 2 vols, 2nd edn (Cambridge, 1923), i, p. 174.

communal courts of the hundred, county and borough; the private courts of the manor and honour; and the church courts.[6] The counter-argument would stress the extent to which these different systems were integrated, particularly under Henry II, so that pleas could be transferred from local courts to central courts.[7] This essay will focus on civil litigation over property as conducted in the central courts. As Donald Sutherland pointed out, 'in the course of the thirteenth century, the business of county and feudal courts in judging claims to freehold declined almost to the vanishing point, and this work passed over to the king's court.'[8] But can we be more precise about this process?

There are numerous evidential problems in such an undertaking, particularly the almost complete absence of any surviving records from the communal courts.[9] The earliest county court plea rolls date from the 1330s, by when they had clearly lost their former jurisdiction over property actions.[10] Instead, we have to rely on indirect evidence. Early legal works such as *Glanvill*, or compilations of writs, suggest that the majority of real property actions were initiated before the county courts.[11] The same conclusion could be inferred from the relative lack of business before the *curia regis* in the twelfth and early thirteenth centuries. In addition, there is a previously unrecognised source for the business of the county courts in the form of appointments of attorneys recorded on the close rolls between 1225 and 1238. The status of the litigants and value of the properties under dispute suggest that the county courts were still an important part of the legal system during the first half of Henry's reign. Moreover, a comparison between these appointments and corresponding plea rolls of the central courts and the eyre show that the county courts were not merely acting as a feeder for the royal courts.[12]

---

[6]   A. Harding, *The Law Courts of Medieval England* (London, 1973), is still a good introduction. Since this chapter concerns the thirteenth century, I shall use the contemporary names of the Bench and court *coram rege* for the later Common Pleas and King's Bench.

[7]   P. Brand, 'Henry II and the Creation of the English Common Law', in *Henry II: New Interpretations*, ed. C. Harper-Bill and N. Vincent (Woodbridge, 2007), pp. 215–41, at pp. 222–3 and 239.

[8]   D. W. Sutherland, *The Assize of Novel Disseisin* (Oxford, 1973), p. 82.

[9]   The best study is R. C. Palmer, *The County Courts of Medieval England, 1150–1350* (Princeton, 1982), although this is most detailed for the reign of Edward I, as pointed out in P. R. Coss, 'Knighthood and the Early Thirteenth-Century County Court', in *TCE II*, pp. 45–57, at p. 45. Useful documents can be found in W. A. Morris, *The Early History of the County Court: An Historical Treatise with Illustrative Documents* (Berkeley, CA, 1926).

[10]   *Rolls from the Office of the Sheriff of Bedfordshire and Buckinghamshire, 1332–1334*, ed. G. H. Fowler, Publications of the Bedfordshire Historical Records Society, Quarto Series 3 (1929); H. Jenkinson, 'Plea Rolls of the Medieval County Courts', *Cambridge Historical Journal* 1 (1923), 103–7; T. F. T. Plucknett, 'New Light on the Old County Court', *Harvard Law Review* 42 (1929), 639–75.

[11]   *Brevia Placitata*, ed. G. J. Turner and T. F. T. Plucknett, Selden Society 66 (1951), pp. lvi–lix.

[12]   This source is discussed in brief in T. K. Moore, 'Government and Locality: Essex in the Reign of Henry III, 1216–72' (unpublished PhD thesis, University of Cambridge, 2006), pp. 102–3. A more detailed study is in preparation.

To a certain extent, therefore, the declining business of the county courts has to be deduced from the increasing business before the royal courts, for which the surviving evidence is much more plentiful. A number of historians have attempted to quantify the long-term growth in the business of the royal courts. Palmer compiled some indicative figures that show the number of pleas before the Bench increasing from 452 cases in Trinity term 1205 to 1,482 cases in Trinity term 1275, and 4,491 cases in Trinity term 1305.[13] This suggests that the work of the Bench tripled during the reign of Henry III and again during that of Edward I. Paul Brand offered a more precise chronology: 'a doubling of the business dealt with by the court between 1200 and 1242–3; another doubling of business between then and 1260, a further doubling between 1260 and 1280; a 78 percent increase between 1280 and 1290; and roughly a further doubling between 1290 and 1306.'[14] Finally, N. Neilson estimated that there were around 6,000 cases before the Bench during Trinity term 1332, suggesting that the expansion of business in the central courts continued after the reign of Edward I, but at a slower rate.[15]

The most rigorous method of tracing the increased workload of the royal courts would be to comb through the plea rolls, identifying and collating the different pleas, but this approach is impractical. There are numerous gaps in the series of surviving plea rolls from Henry III's reign,[16] and even with these losses the sheer volume of surviving evidence presents its own difficulties. While it would theoretically be possible to analyse and index the surviving plea rolls case by case, that would be an enormous undertaking. It is more practical to look beyond the legal records to find proxy sources for the business of the royal courts that are more complete and more tractable. Two such proxies can be used to present a new, quantitative perspective on the English legal system during the thirteenth century. The first, and crudest, is to chart the size of the plea rolls of the central courts, as measured by the number of rotuli they include. The second is to study fines for writs to initiate or transfer pleas before the royal courts as recorded in the fine rolls. As David Carpenter has pointed out, 'the gigantic expansion in payments for writs to initiate and further legal actions is key evidence for the widening scope of the common law.'[17] This approach takes advantage of two important features of the fine rolls: first, unlike the plea rolls, they are almost complete for the whole of Henry III's reign; second, they are

---

[13]   Palmer, 'England: Law, Society and the State', p. 248.

[14]   P. Brand, *Origins of the English Legal Profession* (Oxford, 1992), pp. 23–4.

[15]   N. Neilson, 'The Court of Common Pleas', in *The English Government at Work, 1327–1336*, vol. 3: *Local Administration and Justice*, ed. J. F. Willard, W. A. Morris and W. H. Dunham (Cambridge, MA, 1950), pp. 259–85, at p. 273.

[16]   In 1257 the king ordered an inquiry into the location of all eyre, Bench and *coram rege* plea rolls (*CR 1256–59*, p. 281). For a discussion of the survival of eyre rolls over this period, which mirrors in some ways that of the Bench plea rolls, see *RGE*, pp. 12–24.

[17]   D. A. Carpenter, 'Historical Introduction', in *Calendar of the Fine Rolls of the Reign of Henry III preserved in The National Archives*, vol. 1: *1216–1224*, ed. P. R. Dryburgh and B. Hartland, technical eds A. Ciula and J. M. Vieira (Woodbridge, 2007), p. xxiii.

uniquely accessible thanks to the work of the Henry III Fine Rolls project.[18] We will conclude by assessing the fine rolls' significance for our understanding of the legal changes of Henry III's reign.

Before discussing the volume of business before the royal courts in detail, it is important to define what we mean by business and to make an important distinction between 'stocks' and 'flows'. On the one hand, the 'stock' of business represents all the pleas pending before the court at any one time. It could be argued that this gives a good sense of the 'busyness' of the courts. However, as suits increasingly became mired in procedural stages, the same plea could remain before the court for several terms or years, and would be counted a number of times.[19] On the other hand, we could assess the work of the courts in terms of the 'flow' of new pleas into the court and of existing pleas out of the court, as they were resolved. This could be by formal verdict of the court or, perhaps more frequently, by one party dropping a case, possibly as a result of an out-of-court settlement.[20] In this sense, the flow of suits into and out of a court gives a better picture of the number of different pleas dealt with by it. Clearly these two concepts are linked, the stock being the result of accumulated flows into and out of the court in previous years.

The first proxy – namely, the size of the plea rolls, quantified in terms of the number of rotuli – is, in a very literal sense, the most obvious measure of the number of pleas before the royal courts. A similar approach was adopted by Brand to give a rough measure of the expansion of the business of the Bench, although he looked at all the plea rolls from one year and at approximately decennial intervals.[21] Here we use a slightly different methodology, sampling one term from each calendar year.[22] In addition to long-term trends, this should also illuminate the year to year fluctuations in the business of the courts. The current analysis runs from the earliest surviving plea roll of 1194 to the end of Edward I's reign in 1307. After 1272 the plea rolls survive in almost unbroken series. From this point, the roll for each Easter term was chosen.[23] Rotuli dedicated to non-plea business (rolls of attorneys, adjournments, enrolments of charters and protections) were excluded from the count. The period before 1272 presents more difficulties. Non-fragmentary rolls survive for only seventy-one of the 191 terms during which the Bench was in session,[24] so it was not possible to select the

---

[18] A similar approach was adopted in Moore, 'Government and Locality', using the manuscript rolls but limited to fines from Essex. This national analysis confirms the observations drawn from the county sample.

[19] Palmer, *County Courts*, pp. 220–1.

[20] The classic treatment is E. Powell, 'Settlement of Disputes by Arbitration in Fifteenth-Century England', *Law and History Review* 2 (1984), 21–43.

[21] Brand, *Origins*, pp. 23–4.

[22] For the same method applied to the business of the court *coram rege* during the reign of Edward I, see C. Burt, *Edward I and the Governance of England, 1272–1307* (Cambridge, 2013).

[23] P. Brand, 'Lawyers' Time in England in the Later Middle Ages', *Time in the Medieval World*, ed. C. Humphrey and W. M. Ormrod (York, 2001), pp. 73–104, at p. 74.

[24] The Bench reopened in Michaelmas 1217, and there was a total of 220 further terms during the remaining fifty-five years of Henry's reign. However, before 1250, the Bench ceased to sit during eyre visitations, accounting for twenty-nine terms (calculated from *RGE*).

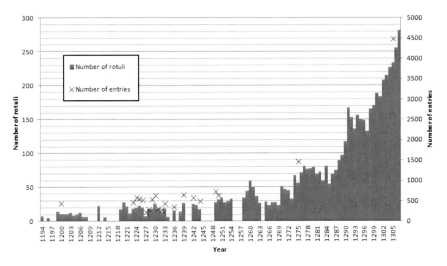

Fig. 1 The size of the plea rolls

same term every year. For each year, the term with the highest (adjusted) number of membranes was selected, again excluding rotuli concerned with non-plea business. Since Michaelmas was longer than the other three terms, comprising eight return days rather than five or fewer, totals for Michaelmas were reduced by three eighths (37.5%). The results are shown in Figure 1.

It is important to highlight some limitations of this evidence. One major weakness is that the number of pleas entered on each rotulus could vary both within a plea roll, depending on the length of the entry recording each case, and over time, reflecting changes in enrolment practice and script. To compensate for this Figure 1 also includes the numbers of entries on selected rolls. This includes the numbers of cases found by Palmer for 1205, 1275 and 1305. In addition, the editions of the *Curia Regis Rolls*, from volume eleven onwards, number each entry, which makes it easy to calculate the number of entries in each roll.[25] This exercise shows that the increase in the number of rotuli correlates with an increase in the number of pleas or entries. Figure 1 shows that there are a number of gaps in the surviving evidence for Henry III's reign, partly from loss of evidence but also reflecting the fact that, before 1250, the Bench did not sit during visitations of the general eyre.[26] Finally, as explained above, the size of plea rolls indicates the 'stock' of new and old business pending before the court. Of course, an increase in the size of the plea rolls could reflect a flow of new business into the court, or that existing suits were pending for longer before being resolved or abandoned. More likely, it results from a mixture of the two.

These caveats notwithstanding, the long-term trend is clear. The plea rolls increased in size from only eight rotuli in 1194 to 282 rotuli in 1307, indicating

---

[25] Note, however, that entries and cases are not necessarily identical.
[26] Brand, *Origins*, p. 22.

the massive rise in the business of the Bench over the course of the long thirteenth century. During Henry III's reign the size of the Bench plea rolls increased from eighteen rotuli in 1219 to forty-six in 1272 (an increase of around 250%) although, as we shall see, the business of the Bench probably peaked in 1260 at sixty rotuli before dropping dramatically during the disturbances of the Barons' Wars. This confirms the general pattern established by Palmer and Brand.[27]

The current analysis facilitates a closer inspection of year-on-year changes in the size of the plea rolls and thus the stock of business before the Bench. There was not a steady increase over the whole period, but rather some spurts of rapid growth between longer periods when the size of the plea rolls remained steady. The scale of the graph makes this quite difficult to see for Henry III's reign. One simple calculation is that the average size of a plea roll from the first half of Henry's reign (to 1244) was nineteen rotuli, compared to thirty-six for the second half of the reign. If the reign is further divided into seven equal periods of eight years, we find a similar story: the first thirty-two years of Henry's reign consistently averaged around twenty membranes (1217–24 = 20, 1225–32 = 18, 1233–40 = 17, 1241–8 = 22), then there is a sharp jump to thirty-one (1249–56) and forty-two (1257–64), before a decline to thirty-five (1265–72). This suggests that there may have been a turning point around 1250, as will be argued below, although its impact may have been masked by a number of particular factors. For instance, even though the Bench remained in session during the eyre visitation of 1252–8, the justices in eyre may well have drawn off business that would otherwise have gone to the Bench. Moreover, the Bench plea rolls between Trinity term 1254 and Michaelmas term 1258 have all been lost. Finally, it is likely that the political unrest of the last years of Henry's reign disrupted the business of the central courts. While the size of the plea rolls peaked during the early years of the reform movement, after reform turned to rebellion in 1263 the rolls halved in size and were still recovering at the end of the reign.[28]

The second proxy source for the expansion of the royal courts during Henry III's reign is to study the numbers of fines for legal writs recorded on the fine rolls. This approach has several advantages. First, the fine rolls survive in almost complete sequence for the whole of Henry's reign.[29] This compensates for the gaps in the plea roll evidence. Moreover, the fine rolls are more readily analysed than the plea rolls, particularly because of the availability of the online translation provided by the Fine Rolls of Henry III project. The fine rolls also provide an alternative perspective on the business of the courts, since they record (part of) the flow of new cases coming before the royal courts rather than the stock

[27] See above, p. 57.
[28] For a general discussion of the legal records for and from the period of reform and rebellion, see E. F. Jacob, *Studies in the Period of Baronial Reform and Rebellion* (Oxford, 1925). For legal discussions and reforms, see Brand, *King, Barons and Justices*. For the disruption to the Bench in 1264, see A. Jobson, *The First English Revolution: Simon de Montfort, Henry III and the Barons' War* (London, 2012), pp. 109, 151.
[29] The fine rolls for the twenty-first, twenty-second and twenty-fourth regnal years are missing. The new edition of the fine rolls fills these gaps using the originalia rolls for those years.

of pending pleas. Finally, simply noting the increasing size of the plea rolls does not help us to understand how and why this increase in the business of the royal courts came about. The fine rolls, on the other hand, reveal one of the important mechanisms whereby the business of the royal courts expanded, in large part at the expense of the local courts.

The common law was structured around the forms of action dictated by the system of original writs that initiated lawsuits.[30] The choice of writ determined the course of pleading, mesne process and nature of proof, as well as in which court the plea would be heard. Until the reforms of the nineteenth century, legal education required the mastery of the forms of action.[31] For the current discussion the key distinction is between those original writs that were granted *de cursu* (as of course) and those granted *de gratia* (of grace).[32] Writs *de cursu* were issued by the Chancery for a set fee of 6*d*. but writs *de gratia* required further authorisation, in least in theory. While writs *de gratia* could always be granted freely of the king's grace, *pro Deo* in the case of poor litigants, or as a sign of royal favour, in practice many recipients had to offer fines, which were recorded in the fine rolls.

At the beginning of Henry's reign it seems that relatively few writs were returnable *de cursu* before the central royal courts of the Bench or *coram rege*. Instead, the majority of writs were returnable *de cursu* before the local courts. For example, the writ of right was presented before the court of the lord of whom the property was held. It could then be transferred to the county court by writ of *tolt*. Many routine actions were initiated by viscontiel writs addressed to the sheriff, and brought litigation before the county court. Subsequently, a writ register from the late thirteenth century lists these formerly viscontiel writs as being returnable to the Bench 'for a price'.[33] Suits could also be brought before the local courts by plaint, and then could be transferred to the royal courts by writ of *pone* or by *recordari* alleging false judgement.[34] It seems as though the rule was that pleas could be transferred to the next visitation of the justices in eyre to that county *de cursu*, but to the Bench or *coram rege* only *de gratia*.[35] The basic argument here is that most of the fines for legal writs after about 1250 were for such writs *de gratia*, and thus represent either the transfer of cases from the local courts to the central courts or the initiation *de novo* before the central courts of pleas that would previously have been heard before the local courts.

---

[30]   For the forms of action, see R. C. van Caenegem, *The Birth of the Common Law*, 2nd edn (Cambridge, 1988), pp. 29–33. Original writs are distinct from judicial writs, which were issued by the courts themselves to enforce process.

[31]   F. W. Maitland, *The Forms of Action at Common Law: A Course of Lectures*, ed. A. H. Chaytor and W. J. Whittaker (Cambridge, 1958), pp. 1–11.

[32]   *Brevia Placitata*, pp. xlviii–lix; *Early Registers of Writs*, ed. E. de Haas and G. D. G. Hall, Selden Society 87 (1970), pp. xix–xx. The earliest detailed discussions date from Edward I's reign, and many of the fines recorded in the fine rolls show that this distinction was evolving over the course of Henry's reign.

[33]   *Early Registers*, p. xxvii.

[34]   Palmer, *County Courts*, pp. 174–219, 229–35.

[35]   *Brevia Placitata*, p. lvi.

The level of detail with which the fine rolls record the purchase of legal writs changes dramatically during Henry's reign. The early fine rolls provide a wealth of detailed information about the writs being issued. See, for example, an entry from the fine roll for the second year:

> 8 *May* [1218]. *Westminster. Suffolk.* William son of Aitrop gives the king one mark for having a *pone*, before the justices at Westminster in the octaves of Trinity, of a plea that is in the county court of Suffolk between William, claimant, and William of Braham, defendant, concerning a carucate of land with appurtenances in Friston, by the king's writ of right. He has the *pone.* Order to the sheriff to take security from William for this mark to the king's use for this writ. Witness the earl [William Marshal, earl of Pembroke].[36]

In addition to the financial details that the Exchequer would need to collect the fine, being the name of the purchaser, the sum involved and the county, the above entry effectively contains a précis of the writ, so providing a great deal of information about the action itself, including the names of both parties (not just the purchaser of the writ), the property at issue, the form of action, the court from which the case is to be removed and that to which it is to be transferred, as well as the return day on which the plea is to be heard. The only information missing is detail about the pleading or arguments advanced by each party. Later entries were briefer. One entry from 1272 reads:

> *Norfolk.* Henry de Bosco gives half a mark for having a *pone.* Order to the sheriff of Norfolk.[37]

This omits nearly all the detailed information contained in the earlier entries. The fine roll entry can be compared with the actual writ of pone, which survives in the writ file for Michaelmas term 1272.

> Henry, by the grace of God, king of England, lord of Ireland and duke of Aquitaine, to the sheriff of Norfolk, greetings. Put, at the petition of the plaintiff, before our justices at Westminster in one month after Michaelmas, the hearing that is in your county court, by our writ, between Henry de Bosco versus Roger Lesseyn and Thomas Lesseyn, whom the same Henry claims to be his serfs. And summon by good summoners the aforesaid Roger and Thomas that they will be there to answer to the aforesaid Henry. And have there the summoners, this writ and the other writ. Witness me myself at Woodstock, the first day of July in the fifty-sixth year of our reign. And take security from the aforesaid Henry for half a mark to our use for this writ.[38]

Many fine roll entries simply refer to the purchase of a writ *ad terminum.* This writ, which should be distinguished from the writ of entry *ad terminum qui*

---

[36]   *CFR 1217–18*, no. 66.
[37]   *CFR 1271–72*, no. 1000.
[38]   TNA, CP 52/1/1A/4, no. 9. The fine roll entry is not dated but is entered between two entries dated 2 July and 3 July respectively. This suggests that the position of an entry in the fine roll roughly reflects when it was issued, if not always exactly.

preteriit,[39] provided for a plea to be heard before a certain court at a certain time. This formulation may conceal valuable information, and an indication of this can be found by comparing the fine roll entries for 1248 with their counterparts on the originalia rolls.[40] In thirty cases the originalia roll entries are abbreviated to a writ *ad terminum*, but the entries on the fine rolls provide more information. One plea was to be returned *coram rege*, and all the others transferred pleas to the justices in eyre, the Bench then being suspended. Ten simply refer to a writ and provide no further details about the plea, but there were three pleas of agreement and of warranty, two of trespass and mesne, and one each of attaint, entry and *pone*.

One way of filling in all the missing details from these abbreviated entries would be to collate all the fines for original writs with the surviving rolls of the Bench, the court *coram rege* and the itinerant justices. A less laborious alternative is to look at the writs themselves, as retained by the courts after their return,[41] but only a handful of early writ files survive.[42] The following discussion focuses on the Bench writ file of Michaelmas term 1272.[43] The majority of the legible writs in this file are judicial writs issued as part of mesne process. Of the original writs, eight were returnable *de cursu* to the Bench and twenty-eight can be classified as *de gratia*.[44] Of the *de gratia* writs, either seven or eight can be matched to a fine roll entry. Most of these writs end with a clause that the sheriff is to take security for payment of the fine, while the others do not include this clause. This means that the majority of the writs *de gratia* did not involve a fine and therefore would not be entered on the fine rolls. This is significant for the value of the fine rolls as a record of the total number of legal writs *de gratia* actually issued.

Whereas a writ *de cursu* only cost 6*d.*, and even this could be waived, a writ *de gratia* was significantly more expensive. By far the most frequently promised fine was half a mark (6*s.* 8*d.*) in 12,590 entries (60.8%). Other common 'price points' were 1 mark (13*s.* 4*d.*) in 4,600 entries (22.2%), or 20*s.* in 1,676 entries (8.1%). Higher sums were unusual but not unknown, particularly earlier in the

---

[39]   *Brevia Placitata*, p. liv.

[40]   *CFR 1247–48, passim.*

[41]   J. Conway Davies, 'Common Law Writs and Returns: Richard I to Richard II', *BIHR* 26 (1954), 125–56.

[42]   For discussion and editions of early writ files, see D. M. Stenton, *Pleas before the King or his Justices, 1198–202*, vol. 1: *Introduction with Appendixes Containing Essoins 1199–1201, a 'King's Roll' of 1200, and Writs of 1190–1200*, Selden Society 57 (1953), pp. 5–33, 350–418; M. T. Clanchy, *The Roll and Writ File of the Berkshire Eyre of 1248*, Selden Society 90 (1973), pp. lx–lxxiv, 401–99.

[43]   TNA, CP 52/1/1A.

[44]   Writs *de cursu*: *precipe in capite* (TNA, CP 52/1/1A/4, no. 14; /6, no. 18); *precipe* of advowson (/4, nos 13, 15); prohibition (/4, no. 1; /8, no. 3); dower *unde nichil habet* (/4, no. 26); *utrum* (/4, no. 2). Writs *de gratia* without fine: TNA, CP 52/1/1A/4, nos 12, 16, 17, 24, 28; /5, nos 10, 11, 19, 23; /6, nos 1, 4, 10, 11, 14, 21; /7, nos 4, 8, 12; /8, nos 8, 14. Writs *de gratia* associated with fines: TNA, CP 52/1/1A/4, nos 9 (*CFR 1271–72*, no. 1000), 27 (1402); /6, no. 26 (1378); /7, nos 6 (1169), 9 (1139); /8, nos 6 (1651), 17 (1229). It is possible that *CFR 1271–72*, no. 492, relates to TNA, CP 52/1/1A/7, no. 7.

reign. Although these fines were much lower than the sums demanded under John, they still involved sizeable amounts of money.[45] However, many writs *de gratia* were issued without charge, which may reflect a genuine concern to ensure that even the poor had access to the courts.[46] Of the twenty writs *de gratia* issued without a fine in the writ file of 1272, for example, three recipients were explicitly described as paupers, while eight of the others were widows and one an unmarried daughter. The fine rolls also contain a small number of entries noting the pardoning of a fine for a writ on account of the poverty of the recipient.[47] However, charity might not be the only reason for a fine not to be levied. There are other examples of fines being pardoned at the instance of influential figures at court, such as the king's daughter Margaret, queen of Scotland, the *curialis* and future earl of Warwick, John de Plescy, and the justice Gilbert of Preston.[48] As ever, the well-connected received preferential treatment.

In summary, the fine rolls measure one part of the flow of new cases into the royal courts, namely those writs that were not returnable *de cursu* into the royal courts. Strictly, they record only part of the total number of such writs, since the Chancery clerks did not always demand a fine for the issue of a writ *de gratia*, so they cannot be taken as a comprehensive source of all new business coming before the royal courts. They do, however, provide an indication of what, judging from the number of fines recorded, must have been a stream of litigation flowing into the royal courts. However, the potential of this source has been rather neglected; Carpenter commented on the 'almost complete absence of work on the legal evidence in the rolls'.[49] This can be partly explained by the omission of fines for writs from previous editions of the fine rolls on the grounds that they contained little matter of interest.[50] It is true that, as we have seen, the very brief entries of fines after about 1250 provide minimal information, but, when aggregated and analysed quantitatively, they can shed light on wider patterns of litigation.

The methodology adopted in the current study is fairly straightforward. In total, there are 39,342 entries in the fine rolls as edited and translated.[51] Again, the ideal approach would have been individually to code each of the fine roll

[45] For John's exactions, see J. C. Holt, *Magna Carta*, 2nd edn (Cambridge, 1992), pp. 123–187.

[46] A. Musson and W. M. Ormrod, *The Evolution of English Justice: Law, Politics and Society in the Fourteenth Century* (Basingstoke, 1999), pp. 127–31.

[47] *CFR 1220–21*, no. 128; *CFR 1241–42*, no. 177; *CFR 1250–51*, no. 451; *CFR 1255–56*, no. 14; *CFR 1270–71*, no. 1047 was 'vacated because the chancellor granted it for God'.

[48] *CFR 1240–41*, no. 416; *CFR 1260–61*, no. 173; *CFR 1271–72*, no. 1118.

[49] *Calendar of Fine Rolls, 1216–72*, p. xxviii. For exceptions, see *Brevia Placitata*; Palmer, *County Courts*; Moore, 'Government and Locality'; B. Hartland and P. Dryburgh, 'The Development of the Fine Rolls', in *TCE XII*, pp. 193–205, at pp. 197–9.

[50] *Excerpta e Rotulis Finium in Turri Londinensi Asservatis*, ed. C. Roberts, 2 vols (London, 1835–6), i, pp. xxiv–xxv, xxx–xxxi; *Calendar of Fine Rolls, 1272–1307* (London, 1911), pp. vii–x.

[51] Entries are not necessarily the same as items, since some entries contain multiple fines or distinct units, while other single items cover more than one entry, for example when an order to deliver seisin to an heir was sent to several sheriffs.

entries as either relating to a writ initiating or transferring a plea to the royal courts or not and, for those identified as relating to such writs, to categorise them by such information as the type of writ, the courts involved, the plea, the identities of the parties to the suit, etc. Such an undertaking is beyond the scope of the current study. Instead, it relies on the relative formalism of the records to automate the process of identifying and analysing fines for original writs. The text of all the fine roll entries was extracted and imported into a database, which was then subjected to a series of logical queries searching for keywords and particular combinations of words characteristic of fines for original writs. This was an iterative process, adjusted by trial and error, involving the application of several stages to filter out 'false positives', such as an entry relating to the pardoning of a fine for a writ, or an amercement made before the royal justices. Ultimately, 20,713 entries (52.6% of the total) were identified as concerning fines for initiating or transferring pleas to the royal courts.

As with the analysis of the size of the plea rolls, a number of qualifications concerning the evidence need to be stressed. For instance, the methodology identifies entries on the fine roll concerning legal writs. A few of these entries record one fine made for multiple legal writs. These have not been differentiated in the following figures, although their impact on the results would be limited. More problematic is the lack of information given in the fines themselves, especially during the second half of the reign, as clearly indicated by the comparison of two fines included above. As a result, the following discussion will only briefly set out a qualitative analysis of these fines and the light they can shed on the English legal system during the reign of Henry III. Rather, the evidence of the fine rolls is more useful when analysed quantitatively, and we will go on to use the fine rolls as a guide to the chronology of the expansion of the business of the royal courts. A final caveat is that it is impossible to be sure to what extent the expansion of the central courts represents the transfer of business from one part of the extended legal system to another (a zero-sum game), or whether it reflects an absolute increase in the amount of litigation across the legal system as a whole. The latter is possible, since the population of England was rising throughout the thirteenth century, leading to greater competition for resources and a consequent increase in disputes and litigation; however, this alone would not account for the dramatic nature of the changes around 1250.[52]

The most frequent information provided in the fines is the type of writ purchased. Nearly half of the fines (9,846) were to have a special assize commission. Of the remaining fines for writs to initiate or transfer pleas to the central courts, the oldest was the *pone* (2,271 instances). This instructed the recipient, usually the sheriff, to put a plea from his court to another court at a specified date. It continued to be used fairly consistently across the reign. Perhaps more important, however, was the writ *ad terminum* (5,215), as discussed above. This first

---

[52]   For the most recent estimates of population growth in the thirteenth century, see S. Broadberry *et al.*, *British Economic Growth, 1270–1870* (Cambridge, 2015), pp. 10–13, 19–27.

appears in significant numbers in 1242 (twenty) and 1243 (seventy), before all but disappearing until 1248. Not coincidentally, writs described as *precipe* (445) increase in frequency between 1244 and 1247, before vanishing entirely after the writ *ad terminum* formula became firmly established. It is therefore likely that the writ *ad terminum* and the *precipe* are largely different ways of describing the same set of writs. Finally, the king had always claimed oversight over the wider legal system, and another large group of fines concerned the attaint of previous verdicts (893), or allegations of false judgement via *recordari* or certification (192).

The fines also provide information about how pleas were transferred between different courts within the wider legal system. Where the original court is specified, it is almost invariably the county court. Moreover, even if some fines – for instance to have a plea that would usually be brought by viscontiel writ instead returned before the Bench – did not technically transfer a plea pending in the county court to the central courts, their ultimate effect would be the same. In addition, there were fines to have decisions made in other courts reviewed (most frequently by attaint, but also by record). These included a number of pleas heard before the itinerant justices as well as the local courts. There is a very small number of other courts mentioned, for example one plea from the manorial court of Writtle, one from the hundred court of Rotherbridge and another from the wapentake of Aswardhurn, as well as one possibly from the borough court of Grimsby.[53]

The fine rolls provide less information about which courts pleas were to be returned to. Where known, the destinations of these pleas is shown in Figure 2. The fine rolls make a clear distinction between fines to have special assize commissions (9,846) and those to have pleas heard before the justices of the Bench, court *coram rege* or in eyre (10,833). Unfortunately, nearly two thirds (6,520) of the latter fines do not specify the court involved and, as noted previously, we should not necessarily assume that all writs *ad terminum* involved writs to the Bench.[54] Of the remaining 4,313 fines, nearly three fifths (58.8%) were to be returned at the Bench, compared to 21.1% before the justices in eyre and 20.1% to the court *coram rege*. In addition, we may note four fines to transfer pleas from one county court to another county court.[55] Two of these date from 1241 and the other two from 1246 and 1247, during a period of judicial experimentation. Unless this was purely a vexatious tactic, it shows that some litigants still preferred to sue in the county court even if, for a similar cost, they could have transferred their pleas to the central courts.

The number of fines to transfer pleas before the itinerant justices is worth exploring further, particularly since most pleas pending could be moved *de cursu* to the next visitation of the justices in eyre to that county. In fact, most of these writs sought to move the plea to an eyre in a different county, presumably for

---

[53] *CFR 1243–44*, no. 276; *CFR 1255–56*, no. 305; *CFR 1235–36*, no. 251; *CFR 1224–25*, no. 280.

[54] This revises Turner's belief that '*ad terminum* for practical purposes meant *ad bancum*' (*Brevia Placitata*, p. lv).

[55] *CFR 1240–41*, nos 305, 315; *CFR 1245–46*, no. 342; *CFR 1246–47*, no. 372.

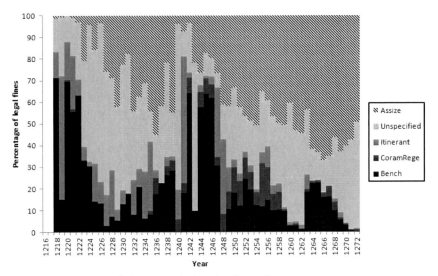

Fig. 2 Destinations of pleas recorded in the fine rolls

timetabling reasons. In addition, litigants who could not wait for the eyre could fine to have justices specially commissioned to hear a possessory assize. Again, it should be noted that, as with writs to initiate or transfer pleas before the central courts, the majority of assize commissions were granted without fines. In the absence of easily accessible information about commissions enrolled on the dorse of the patent rolls, however, the fine rolls provide a convenient indication of trends in the issuing of assize commissions. Figure 2 shows the dramatic increase in the proportion of such fines, especially after 1250. Towards the end of Henry's reign, in fact, fines for assizes overtake those for writs to the Bench or *coram rege*. The fine rolls also highlight another important development, namely from the issuing of such commissions to four local knights to a named royal justice with the power to associate others with him.[56] This change can be dated fairly precisely to 1242; there were 181 fines to have assizes heard by four justices or four knights between 1227 and 1241, compared to four afterwards. As a result, the royal justices may actually have carried out more legal business during the vacations than during the legal terms; Susan Stewart, for instance, has highlighted the busy workload of Gilbert of Preston throughout the year.[57]

It is more difficult to make any valid observations about the pleas involved. The earlier fine roll entries tend to give more details. Early fines for debt had

---

[56] A. Musson, 'Reappraisal of the "Four Knights" System', in *English Government in the Thirteenth Century*, ed. A. Jobson (London, 2004), pp. 97–111; J. Kanter, 'The Four Knights System and the Evidence for it in the Fine Rolls', Fine of the Month March 2007, available at http://www.finerollshenry3.org.uk/content/month/fm-03-2007.html (accessed 9 April 2015).

[57] S. Stewart, 'A Year in the Life of a Royal Justice: Gilbert de Preston's Itinerary, July 1264–June 1265', in *TCE XII*, pp. 155–65.

to promise the king a portion of any sums recovered, with the king's share to be taken from the first monies collected.[58] These were later replaced by writs of debt (presumably the viscontiel writ redirected to the royal courts) at the standard fixed rates. This may seem a better deal for the creditor, although one may wonder if court process proved less expeditious when the king had no stake in the outcome. Another important growth area was trespass.[59] Pleas of trespass first appear in significant numbers in the plea rolls from 1242, but fines for writs of trespass only from 1248, peaking in 1255 and 1256.[60] It should also be noted that fines for trespass were not always directed to the court *coram rege*; of the 493 fines that specify the court in which the plea was to be heard, 280 (56.8%) went *coram rege* but 147 (29.8%) to the Bench and 65 (13.2%) to the justices in eyre.[61] Regarding the later fines, the best evidence can be found in the writ file of Michaelmas 1272.[62] Of the twenty-eight writs *de gratia*, the most common were writs of entry (eleven), followed closely by reasonable dower (eight), then replevin (three), naifty and trespass (both two), with one plea of debt and one assize of *mort d'ancestor*. The great majority of these were viscontiel writs, further strengthening the argument that the expansion of the royal courts was, directly or indirectly, at the expense of the local.

The fine rolls may therefore provide more information when used quantitatively than when used qualitatively. In total, fines for legal writs comprised more than half of all fine roll entries during the reign, but this is greatly skewed towards the later years of the reign, as shown in Figure 3. There was an average of sixty-two fines for legal writs per year up to 1240, followed by an increase to 174 per annum between 1241 and 1249, before a huge rise to 790 per annum after 1250. In fact, by the end of Henry's reign the fine rolls had been almost entirely taken over by judicial business. The rate of increase in the number of fines is massively greater than the overall increase in the size of the plea rolls. This is to be expected, given that the fines were rising from a smaller base, but it also suggests that the increase in fines for writs *de gratia*, particularly considering that many such writs were granted freely and so do not appear in the fine rolls, was one of the main drivers of the general expansion of the business before the Bench. We can also use the fine rolls help to fill in some of the gaps in the sequence of plea rolls and to be more precise about the chronology of the expansion of the royal courts during the reign of Henry III.

---

[58] For example, William de Saint-Michael promised the king a third of 130 marks owed by Thomas Crook, and of £300 owed by Ernald de Mandeville (*CFR 1219–20*, nos 197, 289). See also *CFR 1217–18*, no. 33, and *CFR 1218–19*, no. 61, for disputes about herrings (although the king was to be paid in cash rather than in kind).

[59] S. F. C. Milsom, 'Trespass from Henry III to Edward III', *Law Quarterly Review* 74 (1958), 195–224, 407–36, 561–90.

[60] For the incidence of early pleas of trespass in Essex, see Moore, 'Government and Locality', pp. 160–1, 166–7.

[61] One plea of trespass was specially commissioned to be heard by the royal justice William of Wilton (*CFR 1260–61*, no. 516).

[62] TNA, CP 52/1/1A/4.

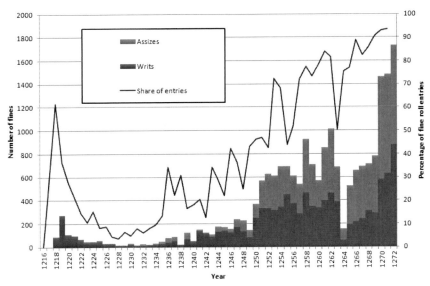

Fig. 3 Judicial business on the fine rolls

The legal fines recorded during the first third of Henry's reign, to 1242, have been analysed by Paul Dryburgh and Beth Hartland.[63] They stress the link between the fines and the visitations of the eyre, a connection further validated by this analysis, as can be seen in Figure 2. In general, the relative lack of fines for writs *de gratia* during this period implies that most of the pleas appearing before the Bench were brought by writs *de cursu*. Although it is possible that more writs *de gratia* were being issued at this time but that the recipients were not being charged with a fine, this can probably be rejected, given the continuing stagnation in size of plea rolls before 1250. This can be taken as negative evidence for the continuing importance of the county courts as judicial venues – an idea confirmed by more positive evidence in the form of appointments of attorneys in the close rolls. One significant innovation in the 1220s was the issuing of special commissions to four local knights to hear specific assizes, although these were only issued in large numbers from the second half of Henry's reign.

There are early indications of change during 1242 and 1243, which may be seen as part of a series of measures taken by the regent, Walter de Gray, archbishop of York, to centralise judicial supervision during the king's expedition to Gascony.[64] Gray used the court *coram consilio* as a form of 'superior eyre', visiting East Anglia to counter disorder. In particular, he heard an increasing number of pleas of trespass.[65] Other developments at this time, as discussed above, include the first consistent use of the writ *ad terminum* and the issuing

---

63 Hartland and Dryburgh, 'Development of the Fine Rolls', pp. 198–9.
64 For the judicial work of the council during the regency, see *CRR*, xvii, pp. xii–xviii.
65 Moore, 'Government and Locality', pp. 165–7.

of assize commissions to named justices of the central courts rather than to local knights. However, these changes may have triggered some opposition, evidence of the English political community's ambivalence towards royal justice, on the one hand desiring greater access to the royal courts but on the other distrusting legal innovation. The parliament of 1244 complained that 'for the lack of a chancellor, many writs against justice were granted'.[66] Further, one of the demands of the 'Paper Constitution' of 1244 was that 'writs obtained against the king and the custom of the realm should be completely revoked'.[67] Robert Stacey has suggested that this complaint refers to writs ordering distraints to collect on Jewish debts, but a more likely explanation is that it concerns the judicial experimentation during the king's absence.[68] If so, it only delayed the inevitable.

A more decisive turning point came in about 1250.[69] We have seen that the size of plea rolls increased by over 50% between that year and the end of the reign. There is also a rise in numbers of fines, from 166 in 1248–9, to 399 in 1249–50, and 580 in 1250–1. This sudden and sustained increase probably reflects a change in royal policy. It may have been associated with a contemporary initiative for the sale of charters granting markets and fairs or free warren, respites from knighthood, and exemptions from service on juries, assizes and recognisances.[70] There may even have been a connection between the rise in fines for writs and the demand for exemptions: as the royal courts expanded, and especially as the numbers of assize commissions increased, the obligation to serve on juries, assizes and recognitions became more onerous. This might be dismissed as another of Henry's fundraising schemes, but there were a number of other legal reforms at that time that seem to suggest a more comprehensive strategy. For the first time, the Bench continued to sit during a nationwide eyre visitation; the sessions of the eyre had to be squeezed into the vacations between legal terms, contributing to the increasing length of visitations.[71] Furthermore, the king began to pay regular salaries to the royal justices.[72] This launched the royal courts into a period of expansion, which was interrupted

---

[66] '… per defectum cancellarii brevia contra justitiam pluries fuerant concessa': *Chronica Majora*, iv, p. 363.

[67] '… brevia contra regem et regni consuetudinem regni impetrata penitus revocentur': *Chronica Majora*, iv, p. 367.

[68] R. C. Stacey, *Politics, Policy and Finance under Henry III, 1216–1245* (Oxford, 1987), p. 217 n. 37.

[69] Turner identified the third decade of Henry's reign, and the ascendancy of William de Raleigh as the king's senior advisor, as a period of reforming zeal (*Brevia Placitata*, p. lix), but the evidence of the fine rolls suggests a somewhat later date.

[70] D. A. Carpenter, 'The Gold Treasure of King Henry III', in *TCE I*, pp. 61–88, at pp. 66–9; S. L. Waugh, 'Reluctant Knights and Jurors: Respites, Exemptions, and Public Obligations in the Reign of Henry III', *Speculum* 58 (1983), 937–86, at pp. 949, 962–71; D. Crook, 'Charters of Free Warren and the Petition of the Barons, 1227–1258', in *TCE VIII*, pp. 33–48, at pp. 37–8.

[71] The increasing length of eyre visitations is clear from *RGE*.

[72] P. Brand, 'Edward I and the Transformation of the English Judiciary', *The Making of the Common Law* (London, 1992), pp. 139–68, at pp. 144–8.

temporarily during the disturbances of the 1260s, but recovered after 1267 and only accelerated under Edward I.

In spite of the lack of information included within the individual entries themselves, the fine rolls are a valuable source for the mechanics of the English legal system, especially when analysed quantitatively. More precisely, the joint evidence of the plea and the fine rolls suggests that there was a qualitative and quantitative shift about 1250 in the business of the royal courts, especially the Bench and court *coram rege*. This had implications for the balance of the legal system. The most immediate impact was on the county courts, which lost, probably relatively quickly, much of their previous jurisdiction.[73] Furthermore, individual assize commissions may have been as significant as pleas before the Bench or court *coram rege* in expanding the scope of royal justice. In turn, the combination of permanent central courts and easy access to individual assize commissions may have helped to make the general eyre redundant.[74] The evidence of the fine rolls thus supports G. J. Turner's opinion that 'the legal reforms of the reign of Henry III, effected in silence behind the lattice of the Chancery, will compare not unfavourably with those embodied in the bulky statutes of Edward I.'[75] The very fact that this expansion in the royal courts was best documented in the fine rolls shows that it was driven by demand from below, not imposed from above. At various points Henry III and his advisors may have made it easier to acquire writs *de gratia*, but the resultant expansion resulted from the actions of thousands of litigants who were willing to pay to have their pleas heard before the royal courts.[76]

---

[73] This had certainly occurred by the time of the earliest surviving plea rolls from the county courts, see above, p. 56.
[74] For the end of the eyre, see D. Crook, 'The Later Eyres', *EHR* 97 (1982), 241–68, at pp. 244–6. See also C. Burt, 'The Demise of the General Eyre in the Reign of Edward I', *EHR* 120 (2007), 1–14, esp. pp. 10–13.
[75] *Brevia Placitata*, p. lix.
[76] Musson and Ormrod, *Evolution of English Justice*, pp. 115–27.

5

Administering the Irish Fines, 1199–1254:
The English Chancery, the Dublin Exchequer and the
Seeking of Favours

Beth Hartland

The events of the political coup in which Hubert de Burgh, justiciar of England and Ireland, was removed from power in 1232 and replaced with Peter des Roches and his nephew, Peter de Rivallis, are well known.[1] One of the results of this coup over control of the mechanisms of power in England was, whether intended or not, to plant the seeds of a new administrative powerhouse in Ireland.[2] This was the Irish Chancery, granted to the English chancellor, Ralph de Neville, the rolls of which have now been brilliantly reconstructed online by the Irish Chancery project. The resulting online edition (*CIRCLE: A Calendar of Irish Chancery Letters, c. 1244–1509*) is the place to find out about, and use, the Irish close and patent rolls.[3] What we cannot find here are the Irish fine rolls (or Irish charter rolls), as the Irish Chancery never produced such series. It is the purpose of this discussion to investigate why the Irish Chancery did not produce fine rolls, and to examine how fines concerning Ireland were dealt with instead.

Attention is often drawn in the historiography of medieval Ireland to the removal of its treasure to England under Henry III and Edward I.[4] Given this, and the primary function of the fine rolls in facilitating the collection of debts

---

[1] See N. Vincent, *Peter des Roches: An Alien in English Politics, 1205–1238* (Cambridge, 1996), ch. 8.

[2] This is discussed in *The Administration of Ireland, 1172–1377*, ed. H. G. Richardson and G. O. Sayles (Dublin, 1963), pp. 22–4. The suggestion there is that the grant of the chancellorship to Ralph de Neville (28 September 1232: *CR 1231–34*, pp. 112–13) was intended to wrest some control back from Peter de Rivallis.

[3] *CIRCLE: A Calendar of Irish Chancery Letters, c. 1244–1509*, ed. P. Crooks (Dublin, 2012), online at http://chancery.tcd.ie/. This work was initiated by Jocelyn Otway-Ruthven: see http://chancery.tcd.ie/content/reconstructing-rolls-medieval-irish-chancery#the-irish-chancery-project (accessed 9 April 2015). Otway-Ruthven's book *A History of Medieval Ireland* (London, 1968) is still an indispensable guide to the history of the medieval lordship.

[4] See, for example, S. Duffy, *Ireland in the Middle Ages* (London, 1997), pp. 125–33, on the period from 1254 to 1307. For primary source examples from an earlier period, see *CR 1227–31*, pp. 302, 303, 342, 434.

by the Exchequer,[5] musings over whether the Dublin administration could have produced its own fine rolls do not seem outrageous. Indeed, given their important place within the workings of royal government in England,[6] and the fact that Normandy also produced fine rolls,[7] the surprise might rather be that Ireland did not produce such rolls once the lordship had its own Chancery.[8] But that Ireland did not create such rolls is the inescapable conclusion, even given the paucity of the record evidence surviving from Ireland before the late thirteenth century.[9] Searches among the Irish Chancery material for references to Irish fine rolls are in vain. The material surviving from the closing years of Edward I's reign and the early years of his successor, Edward II, yields nothing.[10] Nothing in terms of references to fine rolls, that is; it is an easy matter to find evidence of fines, since they were recorded on the patent and close rolls in this period at least.[11] Having drawn a blank in a search for references to distinct fine rolls among these records, the question then became to ask whether distinct rolls had been produced at any time before the 1290s. A fire in 1303 at St Mary's Abbey, Dublin, where certain records of the Irish Chancery were being stored, perversely helps to answer that question. This fire destroyed up to thirteen years' worth of rolls and memoranda, except for two rolls of writs. But it is the detailed list of what remained that convinces us that the answer was no: among the bills of *allocate*, writs of various descriptions, letters of bishops and so on, no mention

---

[5] See D. Carpenter, 'The Fine Rolls, the Originalia Rolls and the Workings of Royal Finance', paragraph 1.2, available at http://www.finerollshenry3.org.uk/content/com mentary/historical_intro.html (accessed 9 April 2015).

[6] According to David Carpenter, the fine rolls were the earliest of 'the great series of rolls on which the English royal Chancery recorded its business': 'Fines and the Fine Rolls', paragraph 1.1, available at http://www.finerollshenry3.org.uk/content/commentary/historical_intro. html (accessed 9 April 2015). The importance of the fine rolls as a historical source may be judged by reading the wide range of articles featured on the Henry III Fine Rolls project website, available at http://www.finerollshenry3.org.uk/content/month/fine_of_the_month. html.

[7] Only that for 2 John is extant; it is published in *Rotuli Normanniae in Turri Londinensi Asservati Johanne et Henrico Quinto Angliae Regibus*, vol. 1: *De Annis 1200–1205, necnon de anno 1417*, ed. T. D. Hardy (London, 1835).

[8] A marginal comment in the extant Norman fine roll makes it clear that Irish fines were thought to belong on the English fine rolls. Referring to an order to the justiciar of Ireland to cause Richard de Thwit to have land to the value of £25 sterling outside the king's demesnes in exchange for the land of Thwit, which the king had granted to Richard de Haracurt, a scribe has noted 'that it ought to be written in the English roll' (*Rotuli Normanniae*, p. 77).

[9] See P. Connolly, *Medieval Record Sources* (Dublin, 2002).

[10] This article began life as a paper presented at the Leeds International Medieval Congress in 2009, i.e. before the appearance of CIRCLE. Initial recourse for the patent and close rolls was therefore made to *Rotulorum Patentium et Clausorum Cancellariae Hiberniae Calendarium*, vol. 1: *Pars Hen. II–Hen. VII* ed. Edward Tresham (Dublin, 1828). The volume claims Chancery content from the reign of Henry II but these 'Antiquissime littere patentes' are not the fragment of a patent roll. Recourse has latterly been made to CIRCLE.

[11] See, for example the payments for writs in CIRCLE, *Close Roll 2 Edward II*, nos 132–40, available at http://chancery.tcd.ie/roll/2-Edward-II/close (accessed 9 April 2015).

was made of anything relating specifically to fines.[12] The enrolled output of the Irish Chancery could have had a different shape in the period before the lordship was granted to Edward as part of his appanage in 1254, but this seems unlikely for reasons that will be given below, as well as the fact that the Irish Chancery does not appear to have produced its own letters until 1244.[13]

Establishing, or as near to establishing as we can get, that the Irish Chancery never produced fine rolls does not necessarily mean that there was never any intention of its doing so. The position of chancellor of Ireland was created during a political crisis in England and, as events played out, the Chancery may not have begun enrolment until 1244, when Ireland received its own chancellor.[14] But had Peter des Roches not himself been so quickly toppled from power, and Ralph de Neville, chancellor of England, not side-lined, could the Irish Chancery have followed a different course? Peter des Roches, bishop of Winchester, was an innovative administrator,[15] and Ralph de Neville, bishop of Chichester, combined 'an efficient mind' with 'sheer professionalism'.[16] Later in the century, in 1244 and 1258, there were clear associations between bishops and administrative reform.[17] Despite this potential, it is nevertheless unlikely that the creation of the position of Irish chancellor in 1232 was anything other than a move to outflank Hubert de Burgh.[18] Moreover, there were very good reasons why the Dublin administration, and in particular the Irish Chancery once established, did not need to produce fine rolls.

One reason arises from the dominant position of the Exchequer vis-à-vis the Chancery in Ireland. An Exchequer had been established in Ireland by 1210 at the latest,[19] and the Irish treasurer and his clerks had been managing the administration of the financial business (and thus fines) of the lordship for at least

---

[12] CIRCLE, *Close Roll 2 Edward II*, no. 416, available at http://chancery.tcd.ie/roll/2-Edward-II/close (accessed 9 April 2015).

[13] CIRCLE, *Henry III*, no. 1, available at http://chancery.tcd.ie/roll/Henry-III (accessed 9 April 2015). The first entry in the calendar is dated 29 April 1244.

[14] Robert Luttrell, who had been acting as Ralph de Neville's deputy as chancellor of Ireland, continued in office after the bishop's death: Richardson and Sayles, *Administration of Ireland*, p. 92.

[15] N. Vincent, 'The Origins of the Winchester Pipe Rolls', *Archives: The Journal of the British Records Association* 21 (1994), 25–42, at p. 29.

[16] J. and L. Stones, 'Bishop Ralph Neville, Chancellor to King Henry III, and his Correspondence: A Reappraisal', *Archives: The Journal of the British Records Association* 16 (1984), 227–57, at p. 232. The authors declined to comment in detail on 'Neville's influence on Chancery practice' but allude to the conviction of C. A. F. Meekings that Neville's hand lay behind the administrative changes during his chancellorship.

[17] D. Carpenter, 'Chancellor Ralph de Neville and Plans of Political Reform, 1215–1258', in *TCE II*, pp. 69–80. John of Crakehall, who was appointed treasurer by the baronial council in November 1258, and had close links with Robert Grosseteste, bishop of Lincoln, provides an example for the later period; see A. Jobson, 'Crakehall, John of (d. 1260)', *ODNB* (accessed 9 April 2015).

[18] This echoes the judgment of Richardson and Sayles, *Administration of Ireland*, p. 24, that 'it does not follow that the reorganisation of Ireland was based upon a considered plan.'

[19] Richardson and Sayles, *Administration of Ireland*, p. 21.

ten years before the appointment of Ralph de Neville as Irish chancellor. The treasurer and the barons of the Exchequer had theoretically had over twenty years in charge of the financial administration of Ireland prior to the appointment of Ralph de Neville, but in 1217 the justiciar, Geoffrey de Marisco, had to be ordered not to allow anyone to receive money from the revenues of Ireland, including the fines, unless at the Exchequer of Dublin and before the barons of the Exchequer without specific mandate to the contrary. Four years later it was 'inserted' into the agreement that the king made with the same Geoffrey, then in the king's prison in England, that all the revenue of Ireland was to be delivered into the safe keeping of the treasurer.[20]

This gave the Irish treasurer greater weight than the chancellor, a position he was able to maintain until the 1280s. The relative positions of treasurer and chancellor shifted following Stephen of Fulbourne's tenure of the office of treasurer.[21] The important point, however, is that the fine rolls were necessary in England because they were part of the mechanism by which the Exchequer came to know which debts needed to be collected and from whom, in order that the 'summonses' could be made out for the sheriffs. As an itinerant department, travelling with the king, the Chancery had the responsibility to keep the Exchequer informed of debts; this it did via the originalia rolls, estreats drawn from the fine rolls (the Chancery fair copy) and sent to the Exchequer.[22] In Ireland before 1232 the work undertaken by Chancery clerks in England was performed by Exchequer clerks. In September 1219, for example, Thomas fitz John and the treasurer were made responsible for all escheats and ensuring that all fines and debts were enrolled at the Exchequer.[23] The 1232 appointment of Peter de Rivallis to the office of chamberlain of the Dublin Exchequer probably provides a tolerably accurate guide to how fines were supposed to be dealt with in the 1210s and 1220s. In 1232 the chamberlain was to have a clerk to sit in the Exchequer of Receipt and keep a counter-roll of the king's Irish treasure. This clerk was also to be present in the Upper Exchequer when fines of the type the justiciar of Ireland was allowed to take were received by him, so that no fine was to be taken by the justiciar except in the presence of that clerk, who was to keep a counter-roll for comparison against the justiciar's roll. As Richardson and Sayles have it, this was a fine roll, but it was a fine roll produced under the aegis of the Exchequer.[24] The appointment of Ralph de Neville as chancellor of

---

[20] *RLC*, i, pp. 306, 476b.

[21] For Fulbourne, see P. Connolly, 'Fulbourn, Stephen of (d. 1288)', *ODNB*. The position of steward and treasurer in seigniorial administration in thirteenth-century Ireland was also a mirror image of that in England: B. Hartland, '"To serve well and faithfully": The Agents of English Aristocratic Rule in Leinster, c. 1272–c. 1315', *Medieval Prosopography* 24 (2003), 195–239, at p. 203.

[22] For the Originalia Rolls, see P. Dryburgh, 'Originalia Rolls', available at http://www. finerollshenry3.org.uk/content/commentary/originalia.html (accessed 9 April 2015).

[23] Richardson and Sayles, *Administration of Ireland*, p. 30.

[24] *PR 1225–32*, pp. 493–4. One cannot be certain, and of course the patent could very well be describing the situation that was imagined to pertain in Ireland before the appointment of

Ireland also came with the injunction that a clerk should keep a check on the justiciar's court.[25] Richardson and Sayles concluded that the intention here must have been that the chancellor's clerk should replace the chamberlain's clerk.[26] Whether that happened, however, is less clear. Much as the English example inclines us to think of fine rolls as Chancery productions, it seems likely that the power remained with the Exchequer in the short term.[27]

The appearance of fines on the earliest surviving Irish close and patent rolls has already been noted. Without detailed analysis of the fines surviving on these rolls against the fines recorded on the other records of the Dublin administration, notably the memoranda rolls and the rolls of justices, any detailed pronouncement on how fines were administered within the lordship would be guesswork. What can be said here is that in incorporating fines into the close and patent rolls, the Irish Chancery was reflecting the process that had taken place in the English Chancery in the early thirteenth century. Initially a set of rolls with a distinct purpose and content in England, the 'fine rolls gradually evolved from a simple but effective statement of expected revenue for the king's favour into a record of financial administration' as more and more business 'of direct relevance to the Exchequer' was recorded on them.[28] In other words, business that had previously been recorded on the close rolls was now being recorded on the fine

Rivallis, but on balance I think it is likely that a similar system was supposed to already be in place. This is the implication of the orders to Geoffrey de Marisco (see n. 20, above). Did what Richardson and Sayles term a 'fine roll' become incorporated into the Exchequer memoranda rolls? From the late thirteenth century onwards, and probably much earlier, information about fines was recorded on the memoranda rolls: J. F. Lydon, 'Survey of the Memoranda Rolls of the Irish Exchequer, 1294–1509', *Analecta Hibernica* 23 (1966), 49–134, at pp. 66–7. Information relating to Irish fines was certainly recorded on the English memoranda rolls: see *The Memoranda Roll of the King's Remembrancer for Michaelmas 1230–Trinity 1231*, ed. C. Robinson, PRS n.s. 11 (Princeton, 1933), p. 43. The wide-ranging grant of powers to Peter de Rivallis can also be found in the *CChR*, i, pp. 166–7. As the actual charter roll (TNA, C 53/26, m. 3) was damaged, the editor has supplied some text which alters the meaning of what the clerk supervising the justiciar in the taking of fines was doing. In *CChR*, i, pp. 166–7, the clerk is said to be keeping a counter-roll of what is paid to the justiciar as fines: 'and shall be present with the justiciar ... at the receipt of fines receivable by the said justiciar, and shall keep a roll of fines [paid so that] no fine be received by the justiciar without the treasurer.' The meaning from the patent rolls is quite different: 'et intersit ad fines recipiendos cum justiciario nostro H. Qui per eundem justiciarium capi possunt sine precepto nostro, et inde habeat unum rotulum contra predictum justiciarum; ita quod nullus finis capiatur per eundem justiciarum sine ipso clerico.' For a translation, see *CDI*, i, no. 1696. Those not familiar with these calendars should note, however, that the editor omitted information which did not pertain to Ireland. Many thanks are due to Dr Jonathan Mackman for supplying me with a digital image of this entry on the charter roll at short notice.

25   *CR 1231–34*, pp. 112–13.
26   Richardson and Sayles, *Administration of Ireland*, p. 38.
27   Later in the century it appears that it was the chancellor who was to make the estreats: *CDI*, ii, no. 2336.
28   See P. Dryburgh and B. Hartland, 'The Development of the Fine Roll', Fine of the Month October 2007, available at http://www.frh3.org.uk/content/month/fm-10-2007.html (accessed 9 April 2015).

rolls, which 'had the advantage of reducing the size of the increasingly unwieldy close rolls'.[29] Presumably the reverse was true in Ireland, and there simply was not the volume of business to justify another set of rolls – whether of fines or charters. Of course the discretion to make fines and grant charters only lay with the justiciar in as far as the king had delegated that power.[30] Business regarding fines and charters often took men to the king. For men based in Ireland this meant crossing to England, and the business they transacted there was sometimes recorded on the English rolls.

For favours which lay beyond the justiciar's remit[31] those seeking the king's patronage needed to make the journey to England, whether in person or by attorney. Until 1207, when King John extended the jurisdiction of the Irish justiciar to accept fines from those who wished to secure writs for actions such as *novel disseisin* and *mort d'ancestor*, the English fine rolls contained offers for the use of such writs in Ireland.[32] Thereafter, no such fines appear on the English rolls. Taking the patchy survival of fine rolls from John's reign into consideration,[33] the only other notable discrepancies in the subject matter of the Irish fines between the reigns of John and his son are grants of pardons of debts, terms for payment of debts, and respites on payments of debts, which were made in greater numbers in the son's reign. It was not only that Henry was perhaps more approachable on this subject than his father, but also that some of the debts respited had been incurred under John's rule.[34] Both kings received fines in return for their grace and benevolence.[35] King John, in addition, received various fines for prisoners to be delivered from gaol and from men petitioning to be allowed

---

[29]   D. Carpenter, 'Introduction to the Rolls', available at http://www.frh3.org.uk/content/commentary/historical_intro.html (accessed 9 April 2015).

[30]   For an example of a fine being made by the justiciar, see Royal Irish Academy, MS 12 D 9, fol. 51. The language here states that the fine, a simple fine for trespass, is made before the chief justice at Cork ('de fine facto coram capitali justiciario'). The language of the records cannot always be taken at face value, however, and many fines said to be made with the king in Ireland are clearly not actually made before the king's person there. See, for example, *Calendar of the Close Rolls preserved in the Public Record Office: Edward III*, 14 vols (London, 1896–1913), vii, p. 606, where Elizabeth de Burgh is said to have 'made fine with the king in Ireland by attorneys in Ireland'. This does, of course, raise the question of how often fines 'made with the king' in England were actually made in the king's presence. For a discussion of this, see P. Dryburgh, 'The Language of Making Fine', Fine of the Month June 2007, available at http://www.frh3.org.uk/content/month/fm-06-2007.html (accessed 9 April 2015).

[31]   None of the surviving indentures of appointment record the specific powers of thirteenth-century justiciars.

[32]   For examples, see *Rot. de Ob. et Fin.*, pp. 26–7, 30, 40, 66, 79, 180. In 1207 the justiciar was also given power to hold pleas of the Crown as well as civil pleas: G. J. Hand, *English Law in Ireland, 1290–1324* (Cambridge, 1967), pp. 6, 13. As well as making access to the civil pleas easier for the king of England's subjects in Ireland, this must have eased the administrative burden on the English Chancery.

[33]   Thirteen rolls survive for John's reign, covering some eight years.

[34]   There are notably a lot of respites of payment on the prests incurred during John's expedition to Ireland. For example, see *CFR 1229–30, passim*.

[35]   For comment on such fines, see Dryburgh and Hartland, 'Development of the Fine Rolls'.

to substitute others in their place as hostages.[36] Letters of protection without term were also requested from John. The remaining fines were concerned with the possession of land and the feudal incidents associated with it.[37]

Such matters quite properly belonged with the king. It is not hard to understand why men crossed the Irish Sea to obtain them. Of course, the physical journey was always a major and relatively expensive undertaking. Long absences from lands and possessions also left them potentially vulnerable to covetous neighbours, but there was no psychological barrier to getting the bags packed and ready.[38] Robin Frame has demonstrated how the king's court in England was the hub of the political world even for men with no lands in England or Wales. It is worth reciting his example of the Irish landholder John fitz Thomas (d. 1261), who travelled to the Henrician court in 1250, 1251, 1255, 1256 and 1258, before successfully securing the grant that he had obviously been pursuing in 1259.[39] That Robin Frame was able to base this important piece of research on material derived primarily from English record sources is testament indeed to his argument. In other words, it is not difficult to believe that there was a ready flow of men to the king's court from Ireland and back again in this period.

Nevertheless, it was not necessarily the case that all men mentioned in the fine rolls in association with Ireland made the journey to England. There are probably several different processes represented by the fines concerning Ireland recorded on the English fine rolls of John and Henry III. The simplest process was one-to-one, whereby the subject seeking the favour actually met and made a fine personally with the king (*fecit cum Rege*).[40] One would expect to find these fines randomly interspersed with other fines on the rolls, and this is, indeed, the usual pattern: Irish fines are sparsely distributed among fines from other areas.[41] As David Carpenter points out, 'routine fines for which there was a fairly settled

---

[36] For example, see *Rot. de Ob. et Fin.*, pp. 479, 554–5.

[37] For Henry III's reign, fines concerning Ireland and recorded on the rolls can be found by typing 'Ireland' into the Text Search on the Henry III Fine Rolls project website (available at http://www.finerollshenry3.org.uk/content/search/search_text.html) and setting the date range as appropriate.

[38] For an example of someone who did not want to make this journey in Edward I's reign, see 'Catalogue of Pipe Rolls', in *Thirty-Eighth Report of the Deputy Keeper of the Public Records in Ireland* (Dublin, 1906), p. 51.

[39] R. Frame, 'King Henry III and Ireland: The Shaping of a Peripheral Lordship', in *TCE IV*, pp. 179–202, at pp. 184–5.

[40] The versions of these fines calendared in *CDI*, i, no. 1273, omit to mention that these fines were made with the king, but before Hubert de Burgh and the bishop of Salisbury. For a discussion of certain authorisation notes in the fine rolls, see B. Hartland, '"Coram" as Authorization in the Henry III Fine Rolls, 1216–1224', Fine of the Month August 2007, available at http://frh3.org.uk/content/month/fm-08-2007.html (accessed 9 April 2015).

[41] Take, for example, the distribution of the first and second entries relating to Ireland contained in the fine roll for 1 John. The first entry is located on membrane 17, sandwiched between fines for Northamptonshire and Norfolk above, and Shropshire and Lincolnshire below; the second entry occurs on membrane 15. For the distribution of Irish fines through the fine rolls of Henry III's reign, see Table 2 in the appendix at the end of this chapter.

charge … were probably made simply with the Chancery staff.'[42] But after 1207 those travelling from Ireland to seek favours from the king could have secured writs for actions in Ireland. That their fines touched on areas within the king's patronage has already been discussed. It is likely that their fines were made with the king or, during Henry's minority, important ministers such as Hubert de Burgh.[43]

The other common process would have been for a deputation of one or more men at the court to act as proxies for one or more men back in Ireland, a one-to-many relationship. There are various indications that such practices took place, including some direct statements: for example, in 1234 the king notified the Irish administration that the ransoms of those taken during the Marshal rebellion in Ireland 'have been settled in the K[ing]'s presence by the Common Council of the K[ing]'s Barons on the arrival in England of Maurice fitz Gerald, justiciary of Ireland'.[44] The list of fifteen fines in a letter close sent to Ireland in February 1215 to be executed by the justiciar probably represents a similar process, the information on Irish affairs presumably being relayed to the king in this instance by the messengers who were constantly passing between the islands.[45] Another indication that a similar process had occurred may be found in the grouping of fines concerning Ireland in the English fine rolls. Such groupings are observable in the fine rolls of both King John and King Henry, but especially the former. The fine roll for 17–18 John (1215–16) has sixty-three Irish entries, largely split into two lists on membranes 9 and 8 of the roll;[46] the fine roll for 9 Henry III (1224–5) has four consecutive Irish entries.[47] The entries on the roll for 17–18 John are fines for a similar range of issues as the fines contemporaneously communicated to the lordship of Ireland by the letter close mentioned above: fines for seisin of land, for marriage and custody, for delivery from gaol and the release or exchange of hostages. Given the similarity in subject matter, it is likely that this second grouping of fines from 1215 were also made in England before the king, rather than representing an estreat of fines made before the justiciar and sent to England. The four entries on the Henrician roll concern men who were making fine for 'grace and seisin' or 'grace and benevolence' because they went against the king in the war of Hugh de Lacy.[48] Though the grouping is small, it is by both subject and region, and thus may indicate the involvement of a

---

[42] Carpenter, 'Introduction to Rolls'.
[43] See, for example, *CFR 1224–5*, nos. 174–6.
[44] *CDI*, i, no. 1227. For the administration of these fines, see *CR 1234–7*, pp. 165–6, 225, 307, 311.
[45] *CDI*, i, no. 529 (list of fines). The letter close enclosed another list of earlier fines which the justiciar was to distrain for. For the messengers, see *CDI*, i, nos 443, 526.
[46] *Rot. de Ob. et Fin.*, pp. 551–66.
[47] *CFR 1224–25*, nos 174–7. These may also be associated with entries 169–71, as all these fines occur only on the duplicate roll, where they are noted as 'Cancelled because it is in the close roll'. A later fine on the same subject was also cancelled for this reason (*CFR 1224–25*, no. 291).
[48] *CFR 1224–25*, nos 174–7.

proxy. Proxies must certainly have been used on some occasions when they are not named. It is, for example, otherwise quite problematic to account for how men taken prisoner in Carrickfergus Castle managed to fine with King John to be delivered from their various gaols.[49]

In view of the choice that existed about how individuals and communities might come before the king to make a fine, it is surprising that there are not more fines dealing with Ireland in the fine rolls of Henry III.[50] There must have been more fines concerning Irish matters. Looking at the late thirteenth and fourteenth centuries, a consideration of the appointments of attorneys to act in England while the principal was in Ireland, and of letters of protection issued for the same reason, indicates that, despite being dependent on fair winds, the Irish Sea was a reasonably busy communication route.[51] It was clearly not the case that men ventured from Ireland to England only infrequently. For example, between 1293–4 and 1295 thirty-four letters of attorney in Ireland for persons remaining in England, or in England for persons remaining in Ireland, were enrolled on the patent rolls.[52] Similarly, between 1295–6 and 1297 Sweetman noted letters of protection for forty-eight persons in or going to Ireland.[53] There is no reason to think that recourse was made to the king's court less frequently in the earlier period.[54] We must therefore presume that more fines concerning Ireland were made in England than appear on the English fine rolls. But where were these fines recorded? And why would some fines be recorded on the English fine rolls and others not?

At the heart of the problem lies the fact that there was no particular reason for a fine concerning Ireland to be recorded on the English fine roll unless it was to

---

[49] For such fines in 1215, see, for example, *Rot. de Ob. et Fin.*, pp. 554–5; *CDI*, i, nos 534, 539, 543. King John commanded that Philip of Oldcoates 'discharge all prisoners taken in the castle of Carrickfergus who are not knights or gentlemen, taking from them fine according to their condition and ability': *CDI*, i, no. 548.

[50] Only 0.5% of the fines of the whole reign are concerned with Ireland in some manner.

[51] This impression was gained while reading all the calendared records that could pertain to English landholding in Ireland in this period, during a period as Senior Research Associate on the English Landholding in Ireland, c. 1200 to c. 1360 project, at Durham University in 2002–5. See http://ahnet2-dev.cch.kcl.ac.uk/projects/english_landholding_ireland_c1200_ c1360 (accessed 9 April 2015).

[52] *CDI*, iv, no. 111.

[53] *CDI*, iv, no. 192.

[54] Reading the calendared rolls may give a false impression that the traffic across the Irish Sea was less heavy in the reigns of John and Henry III, since considerably fewer letters of protection and attorney are included than in the calendars for the later reigns. D. W. Sutherland, *The Assize of Novel Disseisin* (Oxford, 1973), pp. 54–5, notes that men going abroad on the king's service had 'always' been given protections from lawsuits in their absence in the form of letters close. The standard form of such letters may not have developed until the reign of Henry III, and earlier letters may have been enrolled on supplementary rolls that do not survive, or simply not enrolled as a matter of course. The discrepancy between the periods could also be due to differing editorial practices on the part of those editing the rolls. Letters of attorney may have become much easier and cheaper to obtain in the second half of the thirteenth century. I owe these suggestions to Professor Paul Brand.

be paid at the Exchequer in England.[55] There was no need for fines which were to be paid exclusively at the Dublin Exchequer to be recorded on the English roll. The king's administration in Ireland needed to know about the fine, and letters close might be sent to the lordship to this end, sometimes specifying that the fine needed to be enrolled at the Exchequer, as in the case of the king's grant of the land of Connacht to Richard de Burgh in 1234. Given the large sums involved, 3,000 marks for the fine, and 500 marks per annum for the land, it is hardly surprising that the English Chancery took a belt and braces approach to the recording of this fine: the letter close specifies before whom security should be made, and that the fine should 'be inrolled on the Rolls of the K[ing]'s Exchequer, Dublin', and the security taken certified to the king.[56] Unfortunately time and accident has been no kinder to the Irish Exchequer records from this period and stored in Ireland than it has to those of the Irish Chancery.[57]

Luckily we can fall back onto the records of the English Chancery in at least some instances. Repeated memoranda, and letters close and patent, sent from England to Ireland about this or that fine may strike us as inefficient, but without them certain fines would be lost to us, such as those that the money-strapped King John instructed his justiciar to distrain for in 1215.[58] Two fines from the 1230s may be used to further illustrate this point. In the first the king, having remitted his ire and indignation towards Geoffrey de Marisco and received him into his grace, undertakes to allow Geoffrey to render at the Exchequer in England the fine of 3,000 marks which he made with the king for having his grace and his lands, and any goods withdrawn from his lands and property while in the king's hands are to be allowed to him in his fine. Five months later the instructions to the justiciar were updated: now Geoffrey was to have respite of 1,000 marks of the fine, the remaining 2,000 to be paid in England, and the justiciar was to make 'diligent inquisition' as to how much of that fine Geoffrey could render in Ireland.[59] The second case

---

[55] It does not seem to have always been the case that a man needed to hold lands in England or Wales in order to pay his fine at the Exchequer in England. In 1238 Geoffrey de Marisco was to be distrained by his Irish lands to pay a fine 'for which he ought to have answered at the Exchequer in England', but which he did not pay, and which he could not be distrained for there 'as he has no lands in that country': *CDI*, i, no. 2445; *CR 1237–42*, p. 41. The Norman fine roll of 2 John (see n. 7, above) was right to say that Irish fines should be enrolled on the English roll if they were to be distrained for in England. In 2 John there may not have been an Exchequer in Ireland to do likewise there.

[56] *CDI*, i, no. 2219; *CR 1231–34*, pp. 534–5. Further instructions specified that the fine was to be paid in Ireland: *CR 1234–37*, p. 165.

[57] For periods when the Irish treasurer's account was audited at Westminster, TNA at Kew has copies of certain series. For records which were kept in Ireland, such as the pipe rolls, the 1922 fire destroyed almost all the original rolls. Our understanding of the Irish Exchequer should be much improved by the publication of a new edition of the Irish pipe roll for 14 John, being prepared for publication by the Pipe Roll Society by Dr Hugh Doherty. If funded, another project will lead to the publication of the Irish receipt and issue rolls.

[58] *CDI*, i, no. 529.

[59] *CFR 1234–35*, no. 371; *CFR 1235–36*, no. 81. An illegible marginal comment has been made beside this second order in the relevant originalia roll, showing that the clerks had cause to revisit this fine.

is similar: Hamo de Valognes, who had made fine with the king because he sided against him in Richard Marshal's rebellion in Ireland, is given terms to render that fine at the Exchequer in England. The justiciar is again to search his rolls to determine how much of the fine Hamo has already paid at the Exchequer of Dublin.[60] In both instances, without these changes being made to the terms of repayment and recorded on the well-preserved rolls of the English Chancery, we would know nothing of these fines. We must be grateful for all enrolled instructions sent to barons of the Dublin Exchequer telling them to respite or cancel this or that fine, or to search their rolls to find out how much had been paid in Ireland,[61] for many other instructions must not have been enrolled. This is evident, for example, in the instruction sent to the treasurer of Ireland and barons of the Dublin Exchquer in 1260 to quit the demands they made of John fitz John, the son and heir of John fitz Geoffrey, for 3,000 marks by which the latter had long ago made fine with the king for the custody of the land and heirs of Theobald Butler.[62] The mandate makes reference to letters produced by the Exchequer confirming the sum paid there by John fitz Geoffrey, a letter for which the mandate was not enrolled.

Ultimately, and from the Crown's perspective, the important fact about the enrolment of fines relating to Ireland was that they were enrolled and could be acted upon. The details of how and where that enrolment was managed were the concern of the clerks. Conversely, it was equally important that, when remitted, the fines which were no longer to be acted upon were removed from the rolls. But when dealing with the king's profits, Exchequer clerks did not act without what they regarded as sufficient mandate. Thus it was that they recorded Edward I's mandate to exonerate and annul the fine of the prior of the Hospital of St John of Jerusalem in Ireland in the pipe rolls, an order clearly sent to back up the previous decision of the justiciar and council of Ireland that they ought not to have fined the prior concerning the defence of the marches.[63] The instructions repeatedly sent across the Irish Sea to 'inspect the rolls' or 'make a search of the rolls of the Exchequer' also mean that, in spite of the loss of those rolls, there is one feature of the medieval Irish pipe rolls we can be sure of: like their English counterparts, these much-referenced documents would have been heavily annotated and very well thumbed.[64]

---

[60] *CFR 1235–36*, no. 485.

[61] I have not yet made a systematic study of the Irish fines recorded on these rolls. Looking at the published English close rolls it appears that the distribution of such references to Irish fines across Henry's reign was not even, with the majority of references occurring in the period up to 1247. The references are not very numerous, and sometimes they have been recorded on the close rolls as a by-product of the issuing of instructions to the justiciar of Ireland and the barons of the Dublin Exchequer about the fines. Sometimes, however, they are purposefully recorded, as with seven Irish fines recorded on the duplicate fine roll for 1224–5 and then cancelled 'Because in the close roll'. See Carpenter, 'Introduction to Rolls': 'The clerks were not always clear whether to enrol writs on the fine roll or the close roll.'

[62] *CR 1259–61*, p. 295.

[63] *Thirty-Eighth Report of the Deputy Keeper of the Public Records in Ireland*, p. 88.

[64] For example, the rolls were to be inspected to establish the debts of the earl of Pembroke in 1244, and searched to establish the debts of Peter de Geneva in 1246: *CR 1242–47*, pp. 271, 421.

Appendix

Table 2 Distribution of entries relating to Ireland in the fine rolls, 1199–1254

Fine Roll	Total entries relating to Ireland	Membrane	Consecutive entries relating to Ireland
1 John	18	17	1
		15	3, 3
		14	1
		12	2, 1
		11	1
		8	1, 1
		2	3
		16d.	1
2 John	12	22	1, 1, 3, 1, 1
		17	1
		15	1
		9	1
		7	1
		7d.	1
3 John	5	7	1, 1
		4	1, 1
		2	1
6 John	8	17	1, 1
		14	1, 1
		12	1, 1
		10	1, 1
7 John	4	17	1
		16	1
		11	1
		9	1
17–18 John	65	9	35, 3, 1
		8	16, 2, 1
		7	1, 2, 1, 1, 2
2 Henry III	3	7	1
		5	1
		4	1
4 Henry III	3	9	1
		2	1, 1
5 Henry III	1	6	1
8 Henry III	1	8	1
9 Henry III (C60/23)	8	4	7
		2	1
13 Henry III	1	9	1
15 Henry III	4	9	2
		6	2
16 Henry III	1	4	1
18 Henry III	2	4	1
		1	1
19 Henry III	2	12	1
		5	1

Table 2 *Continued*

Fine Roll	Total entries relating to Ireland	Membrane	Consecutive entries relating to Ireland
20 Henry III	9	17	1
		15	1, 1
		12	1
		4	2, 1, 1, 1
21 Henry III (E371/4)	1	4	1
24 Henry III (E371/7)	1	2	1
25 Henry III	2	7	1
		2	1
26 Henry III (C60/38)	1	14	1
26 Henry III (C60/39B)	1	1	1
27 Henry III (C60/40A)	4	10	1
		9	1
		8	1
		3	1
30 Henry III	1	15	1
31 Henry III	4	12	1
		9	1
		7	2
32 Henry III	2	13	1
		3	1
33 Henry III	4	12	1
33 Henry III		9	2
		3	1
34 Henry III	5	14	1
		11	1
		9	1
		5	1
		3	1
35 Henry III	7	20	1
		19	1, 1
		17	1
		9	1
		6	1
		4	1
36 Henry III	6	12	1
		8	1
		6	1, 1
		4	1, 1
37 Henry III	8	21	1
		15	1
		14	1
		13	1, 1
		12	1
		5	1, 1
38 Henry III	3	10	1
		8	1
		5	1

6

Auditing and Enrolment in Thirteenth-Century Scotland

Alice Taylor

Financial auditing and central record-keeping are neglected topics in Scottish historiography. Past studies have either concentrated on the fourteenth to the sixteenth centuries or, if they have dealt with the thirteenth century, have taken up only few pages in more general works. That being said, three assumptions have generally prevailed. First, Scottish kings started to have their accounts audited centrally at their own Exchequer by the early decades of the thirteenth century.[1] Second, the thirteenth century saw the emergence of a 'record-keeping bureaucracy': government conducted by royal officials who kept records of their activity.[2] Third, the model for both these developments was England, although Scottish practices were run on a smaller scale because Scotland was a smaller kingdom. This article will develop the first assumption, challenge the second, and show just how different auditing and record-keeping were in Scotland from its supposed 'model' of twelfth- and early thirteenth-century England.[3]

Until recently, little attention has been paid to the development of the Scottish 'Exchequer'.[4] One reason for this must be the absence of any original records of its activity, completely the opposite problem to that confronted by historians of England. The only evidence for the workings of whatever auditing system existed

[1] A. A. M. Duncan, *Scotland: The Making of the Kingdom* (Edinburgh, 1975), pp. 596–9, 606–7; A. L. Murray and C. J. Burnett, 'The Seals of the Scottish Court of Exchequer', *Proceedings of the Society of Antiquaries of Scotland* 123 (1993), 439–52, at p. 440; also *RRS*, i, p. 30.

[2] Most recently, R. Oram, *Domination and Lordship: Scotland 1070–1230* (Edinburgh, 2011), p. 363; A. L. Murray, 'The Scottish Chancery in the Fourteenth and Fifteenth Centuries', *Écrit et pouvoir dans les chancelleries médiévales: Espace français, espace anglais*, ed. K. Fianu and J. D. Guth (Louvain-La-Neuve, 1997), pp. 133–51, at p. 135.

[3] An article by David Carpenter has done much to illuminate financial administration, and government more generally, in thirteenth-century Scotland. The first half of this article confirms much of Carpenter's picture, and owes it, and the author, a great debt: D. Carpenter, 'Scottish Royal Government in the Thirteenth Century from an English Perspective', in *New Perspectives on Medieval Scotland, 1093–1286*, ed. M. H. Hammond (Woodbridge, 2013), pp. 117–59, at pp. 118–26.

[4] Carpenter, 'Scottish Royal Government'; see further J. M. Thomson, *The Public Records of Scotland* (Glasgow, 1922), pp. 1–24; A. L. Murray, 'The Pre-Union Records of the Scottish Exchequer', *Journal of the Society of Archivists* 2 (1961), pp. 89–117; A. L. Murray, 'The Procedure of the Scottish Exchequer in the Early Sixteenth Century', *Scottish Historical Review* 40 (1961), pp. 89–117; and other works cited in note 2.

in thirteenth-century Scotland is from transcripts made in the seventeenth century by Thomas Hamilton (1563–1637), first earl of Haddington, of the accounts of various royal officials from the years 1263–6 and 1288–90.[5] Haddington, however, abridged his material, sometimes providing quite full transcripts but on other occasions only listing the name and title of the particular official. The assumed inadequacies of Haddington's work have prevented modern historians from using them as anything other than a source of quite limited financial data. Yet one major argument of this paper is that the transcripts can reveal much about the procedures of financial administration, and question whether routine enrolment – or record-keeping more broadly – was a part of routine governance.

Similar problems with the source-base confront anyone who is interested in enrolment and the extent of Scottish central archives in the thirteenth century. Not one original roll – of whatever kind – survives. What we have are four inventories of the documents that were once kept in the king's 'Treasury' at Edinburgh Castle. The first was drawn up on 29 September 1282, when Alexander III was still king, by the king's clerks: Thomas of Chartres, Ralph de Bosco and William of Dumfries. The remaining three were compiled on the command of Edward I, after he had taken the title 'superior lord of the kingdom of the Scots'.[6] These Edwardian inquests are dated 23 August 1291, 30 December 1292 and 16 December 1296. Earlier historians and antiquarians used these inventories as the evidential basis for a sense of the complexity and sophistication 'reached' by the kingdom of Scotland before its destruction by Edward I. When William Robertson published the inventories in Edinburgh in 1798, he remarked 'such monuments of those ancient records are still preserved ... as prove incontrovertibly that Scotland, prior to the dispute about its Crown, had reached a pitch of internal polity not inferior to that of any kingdom of Europe'.[7] Despite the level of confidence placed in them, the inventories have never really been fully studied, although they must be the source of the historical assumption that government in Scotland during the thirteenth century showed evidence of record-keeping and enrolment akin to that in England, even if on a smaller scale. Yet it is argued here that the rolls listed in the inventory do not have to be seen as fully part of the process of direct government itself, but reveal instead its overall archival practices and priorities.

Given that the source-base is almost completely absent, it is thus understandable that, until relatively recently, structures of financial administration and other governmental activity, most notably its archival work, have been bypassed by scholars. This paper, along with an extensive one by David Carpenter published elsewhere, is aimed at restarting discussion. It will examine the 'Exchequer' record of the thirteenth century to reveal the workings of its procedures, and then use

[5] NRS, E 38/1. For some reason, they are usually referred to as rolls from 1264 and 1266, even though they clearly cover 1263 and 1265 as well.

[6] NRS RH5/8/1; RH5 8/2 (1282); TNA E 39/3/53; E 39/3/54 (1291); NRS, SP 13/1 (1292); TNA, E 101/331/5 (1296), printed in *APS*, i, pp. 107–18 (red foliation).

[7] W. Robertson, *An Index, drawn up about the year 1629* (Edinburgh, 1798), p. ix; Maitland Thomson, *Public Records*, pp. 2, 4.

that material, together with the surviving inventories, to discuss the practices of record-keeping and enrolment that went on in 'the lord king's chapel'. The paper argues that, while the auditing of the accounts of royal officials had begun by the early thirteenth century, this process was very different from that in England: it was mobile, fluid, and regional rather than fixed and universal. Moreover, the written records kept of accounting, along with outgoing letters, were not direct products of government *per se* but were rather *post factum* accounts.[8] The process of central record-keeping was thus at one stage removed from the process of government and administration.

Exchequer

First, the authority of our fundamental source, Haddington's transcripts, must be established.[9] Haddington's reputation is not good: he is berated for making scribal errors; for adopting a note-like approach to the material; and for abridging many of the accounts he only partially transcribed. But consultation of Haddington's original manuscript shows that he did take care throughout his work, scoring out his mistakes (when he made them) and copying the correct readings over the top. The main mistakes he made were when he expanded the names of the initials of the various officials, often incorrectly.[10] Moreover, the content of a few of his transcriptions is confirmed by the survival of extracts from accounts from the sheriffdoms of Banff and Aberdeen in a royal charter of Robert II drawn up for the bishopric of Aberdeen in 1382.[11]

Haddington also preserved the original order of the accounts he copied. This will be a particularly surprising remark to anyone who has consulted this material, because Haddington presented it in what looks like an extremely haphazard way: the order of individual accounts within the transcript is non-chronological and entries jump from year to year. This has led to the assumption that Haddington must have cherry-picked information from a number of sources, presumably one roll for each financial year (like the yearly pipe rolls of England).[12] Yet it would appear that Haddington was drawing on only two sources (one for the 1263–6

---

[8]   I will not be dealing with judicial records here, for reasons of space, but will do so in my forthcoming book, entitled *The Shape of the State in Medieval Scotland*, 1124–1290, chapter 7.

[9]   *ER*, i, pp. 1–34.

[10]   See, for example, NAS E 38/1, fol. 6r, in which Haddington began to transcribe the renders in kind from the waiting of four nights from Kinross (beginning *redditus vaccarum*) before stating that these renders were part of the waiting owed. He crossed out his mistake and began again with the words 'de waitinga', as at *ER*, i, p. 16. For his mistakes in expanding initials of the first-names of the officials, see Taylor, *Shape of the State*, chapter 7.

[11]   *Registrum Episcopatus Aberdonensis: Ecclesie Cathedralis Aberdonensis Regesta que extant in unum collecta*, Spalding Club, 2 vols (Edinburgh, 1845), i, pp. 157–61; for a summary of the lengthy dispute, see *ER*, i, pp. clxxv–clxxix; for further discussion, see Taylor, *Shape of the State*, chapter 6.

[12]   Although two copies were made, one for the chancellor, and called the 'chancellor's roll', see *Dialogus*, pp. 26–7.

material, a second from 1288–90) and, in both cases, followed their orders closely. About two-thirds of the way through the 1263–6 material, for example, Haddington stated that the remainder of the accounts (from various financial years) were on the dorse of the roll that he was copying.[13] That his source was a single roll containing financial accounts in non-chronological order is confirmed by references in the Aberdeen charter material that also state that some of their accounts are to be found on the roll's dorse, in roughly the same position as Haddington's.[14] Haddington's 'chaotic' and 'injudicious' arrangement seems to have been present in his original source and, although he often abridged content, he did not alter the order of that source and, indeed, generally took care in the presentation of its material.

We can thus use Haddington's transcripts with some confidence, although their limitations still have to be acknowledged. It is still not possible, because of their abridged state, to use them to calculate the precise sources of the income passing through this particular audit process, as one can in England. But we can use them to think about auditing structure and process. The accounts from the 1260s and 1288–90 reveal that they were heard by members of Alexander III's court, both lay and ecclesiastical, and were presided over by the household officers of chamberlain and chancellor.[15] There appears to have been an expectation that, if the audit was to take place at all, the chancellor and chamberlain had either to be present in person or, if they were not, to send a representative in their stead.[16] Officials of various kinds – from bailies to sheriffs to justiciars to the chamberlain himself – returned their accounts at the audit. The place they deposited their monies was called the *camera* ('the king's chamber'), and the clerks who recorded the proceedings, at least in some form, were called the 'clerks of the king's chapel'.[17] The whole proceedings were described simply as the business of the court: there was no Exchequer (*scaccarium*), merely the king's court and his financial *camera*.[18]

The first contrast to note with England is that sheriffs – and other officials – did not have to turn up to account each financial year. David Carpenter has recently argued that justiciars, who returned the profits of justice at the same accounting sessions, did not conduct their ayres twice a year, as was previously thought, but instead did so irregularly, the time between ayres being, on occasion, more than two years.[19] The timing of the ayres governed the timing of their accounts. Similar

---

[13] NRS, E 38/1, fol. 8v; *ER*, i, pp. 23–4.
[14] *Aberdeen Reg.*, i, p. 158.
[15] *ER*, i, pp. 11, 22, 45.
[16] For the *camera*, see *ER*, i, pp. 4, 41; for the *capella regis*, see *ER*, i, p. 51 and, more generally, G. W. S. Barrow, 'The *Capella Regis* of the Kings of Scotland, 1107–1222', *Miscellany V*, ed. H. L. MacQueen, Stair Society 52 (Edinburgh, 2006), pp. 1–11.
[17] There were no references to a *cancellaria* ('Chancery') nor a *scaccarium* ('Exchequer'), for which see below, pp. 92–4.
[18] *ER*, i, p. 45.
[19] Carpenter, 'Scottish Royal Government', pp. 133–7. For a small correction to Carpenter's position, see Taylor, *Shape of the State*, chapter 4.

conclusions can be made for other officials, including sheriffs.[20] This is perhaps more surprising, given that much revenue expected from particular estates and sheriffdoms was fixed and depended on annual rent and render extraction, either in kind or cash. Although the account rolls are littered with phrases saying that particular officials returned their accounts 'from that year' (*de illo anno*) or 'from one year' (*de uno anno*), there are also occasions when sheriffs were audited for an indeterminate period (described by the formula *de illo termino*).[21] In some cases, it is explicit that a sheriff was accounting for more than a single financial year, but it does not seem that this was a problem in any way; indeed, the lengthy financial period is merely recorded, not acknowledged as an exception. Gilbert de Hay, sheriff of Perth, returned his account via attorneys at the very earliest after 29 September 1263, despite his last account being over eighteenth months earlier, on 27 March 1262.[22] We see a similar level of flexibility in the collection of income by royal officials: render dates were generally Martinmas and Whitsun and, less frequently, Michaelmas.[23] The *financial* year could be calculated at either of these dates. Some officials returned their accounts for a financial year finishing at Whitsun, others at Martinmas, others at Michaelmas; others returned for three financial terms, starting at Whitsun one year and finishing at Martinmas the next.[24] Thus, the financial year and the period between audits all appear to have been relatively unfixed, although it seems to have been rare for an official to go for more than two years between accounts.

A second contrast with England, whose Exchequer met at Westminster, is that Scottish accounts were not heard at a single, central location. The material from 1263–6 shows accounts heard in many different places: in Scone, Arbroath, Linlithgow, Newbattle, and Edinburgh.[25] It is clear that some centres were used more often, such as Scone, but no one place held a monopoly. Nor were all places used for audit even royal centres: Arbroath, for example, was the burgh of Arbroath Abbey itself (even though the abbey was a royal foundation). Although the king's court did move to hear accounts, it still did so in a comparatively limited area, mainly confining itself to southern Scotia and Lothian.[26] There is no

---

[20]   The chamberlain, for example, who returned his account in 1264, was being audited for all the income received by all officials for three financial terms, that is, from Whitsun 1263 to Martinmas 1264: *ER*, i, p. 10.

[21]   For *de illo anno*, see *ER*, i, pp. 6, 12, 13; for *de uno anno*, see *ER*, i, pp. 3, 4; for *de illo termino*, see *ER*, i, pp. 1, 5.

[22]   *ER*, i, pp. 1–3.

[23]   For render days in charters, Whitsun was the most commonly specified, with 473 occurrences; then Martinmas (443); then Michaelmas (72); then Easter (61). These figures are from the database of *The People of Medieval Scotland*, found through 'browse' function, and 'factoid filter', see http://db.poms.ac.uk/browse/facet/renderdates/?resulttype=factoid&totitems (accessed 9 April 2015).

[24]   *ER*, i, pp. 2, 4, 5–6.

[25]   This has been noticed before: Duncan, *Making of the Kingdom*, pp. 606–7; Carpenter, 'Scottish Royal Government', pp. 121–2.

[26]   *ER*, i, pp. 1, 10–11, 18, 49–51 (Scone), 9 (Arbroath), 30, 37–45 (Linlithgow), 24–5 (Newbattle), 22, 34, 45–8 (Edinburgh), 40 (Haddington).

evidence to suggest that accounts were heard in the kingdom's west and north; thus, a sheriff of Inverness, Wigtown or Ayr would still have had to travel quite far to return his account. The general picture is of a mobile accountancy, but mobile within a fairly limited geographical area of the kingdom's heartland.

Furthermore, and again unlike in England, not all sheriffs were expected to account at the same session. The evidence for the 1289 audit session reveals that it was attended by the sheriffs of Berwick, Roxburgh, Selkirk, Traquair, Lanark, Ayr, Stirling, Linlithgow and Edinburgh, as well as the mason and carpenter who were then doing work on Stirling Castle.[27] All the accounts seem to have been heard in early February at Edinburgh.[28] It is notable that this southern venue was attended by sheriffs whose bases were south of the Forth within the jurisdiction of the justiciarship of Lothian. By contrast, another session held at Scone in 1290 heard the accounts of the sheriffs of Kincardine, Banff, Aberdeen, Forfar, Fife, Kinross, Perth and, perhaps surprisingly, Dumbarton.[29] Again we see a geographical focus to the attendees at Scone: all the sheriffs – bar one – were part of the justiciarship of Scotia. The exception was Dumbarton, a sheriffdom on the mouth of the River Clyde, west of Glasgow and south of Loch Lomond, and part of the justiciarship of Lothian.[30] The appearance of Dumbarton serves as an important reminder that whatever regional focus there was in the peripatetic Scottish accounting, it cannot have acted as a hard-and-fast rule. Presumably individual sheriffs had options about which session to attend, depending on when and where it was to be held.

By the time of the 1288–90 records at the latest, the host sheriff was responsible for bearing the costs of this peripatetic accounting. The 1288 session, held in March at Linlithgow, is a clear example of this phenomenon. The last official to account was William Sinclair, the local sheriff, who proffered sixty chalders of malt, of which a tenth went to the local nunnery of Manuel, and fifteen of which 'were freed to the service of the present auditors, that is the chancellor, and other clerks of the court'.[31] Thirteen and a half bolls of provender were also exempt from the sheriff's expenses because they were assessed as part of 'the expenses of the clerks and others who received provender for their horses in the present account', a nice indication of how the auditors travelled around.[32] Eels were clearly the preferred energy boost after a long day's auditing, for William also accounted for '280 eels ... by expenses incurred during the present account'.[33] If the costs of the audit were born by the local sheriff, it makes sense that the king's court would have moved around the kingdom in order to

[27] *ER*, i, pp. 45–8.
[28] *ER*, i, p. 46.
[29] *ER*, i, pp. 49–51.
[30] The sheriff here was also not in post at the time of the account: Walter Stewart, earl of Menteith, was described as 'once' sheriff of Dumbarton, when he returned his account (*ER*, i, p. 49).
[31] *ER*, i, p. 45.
[32] *ER*, i, p. 45.
[33] *ER*, i, p. 45.

hear them: no one sheriff could be expected to bear that much every year.[34] But it is important to stress the relative intimacy of this situation. By having local sheriffs bear the costs of the 'central' audit, the boundaries between local and central government became blurred. The scant evidence also suggests that the local sheriff would have sat as an auditor when the court came into his locality.[35] All this suggests that it would be misleading to describe Scottish accounting as a way in which the local was called to account by the centre: the centre travelled around and, in a very real institutional way, depended on the local for its own revenue collection.

For how long had the kings of Scots audited their accounts? The terms *camerarius* ('chamberlain') and *camera* ('chamber') are attested in the charters of David's reign (1124–53). But we should not confuse the presence of these officials with the auditing of accounts at which money was paid in and out of the king's chamber. It is generally assumed that auditing as a regular administrative process began either in the 1180s or by the 1200s.[36] As no original accounts survive, both these views are based on items listed in the, by no means comprehensive, inventory of the contents of Edinburgh Castle, drawn up in 1296.

The 1296 inventory lists a number of rolls that contain records of royal financial administration. Of these, attention has focused on the 'roll of Abbot Archibald'. This was said to contain 'ancient renders in pennies and ancient waitings' (hospitality income from certain estates).[37] Archibald was abbot of Dunfermline from c. 1182 to 1198; it is on the basis of this roll that the 1180s have been cited as the earliest date for the commencement of auditing and the recording of the accountancy session on a roll.[38] However, Abbot Archibald's roll may not have been a record of an account at all, but a list of expected revenues from certain estates that may – or may not – have been royal.[39] The roll is not called a *compotus* (an 'account'), the word generally used to describe an accounting process, which may not be an important absence in itself but is more significant given that other rolls listed in the same inventory are called *compoti* ('accounts'). This suggests that, had Abbot Archibald's roll survived, we would probably have categorised it as a similar type of document to the 'Alexander III Rental', a list of the value of the estates

---

[34] Because William Sinclair also served as sheriff of Edinburgh, he had to do the same all over again when the audit was held in Edinburgh in 1289: *ER*, i, p. 48.

[35] Nicholas de Hay, sheriff of Perth, served as an auditor at the Scone 1290 audit (*ER*, i, p. 49). He is, alongside Robert Cameron, described as a *miles*. It is of note that the office of sheriff of Perth swapped between the Hay and Cameron families throughout the second half of the thirteenth century: G. W. S. Barrow and N. H. Reid, *The Sheriffs of Scotland: An Interim List to c. 1306* (St Andrews, 2002), pp. 35–6.

[36] Duncan, *Making of the Kingdom*, pp. 213–14; cf. *RRS*, i, p. 30; cf. Murray and Burnett, 'Seals of the Scottish Court', p. 440.

[37] *APS*, i, p. 118.

[38] Duncan, *Making of the Kingdom*, p. 213.

[39] The difference between 'prescriptive' and 'probative' accounting is discussed in T. N. Bisson, *The Crisis of the Twelfth Century: Power, Lordship and the Origins of European Government* (Princeton, 2009), pp. 316–48.

in the sheriffdoms of Aberdeen and Banff, rather than an early example of the audit process.[40]

There are, however, six other items listed in the 1296 inventory that are each explicitly called *compotus*.[41] These were one roll of two membranes listing 'ancient renders in grain', headed by the account (*compotus*) of William Comyn, earl of Buchan. William was earl of Buchan from 1212 to 1233 so his account must have been returned during this period. The inventory also lists a roll of two membranes containing the account of William Freskin, sheriff of Nairn, returned in 1204; and one of a later sheriff of Nairn, returned in 1227. There were also two rolls, each of eighty-nine membranes, containing accounts of various sheriffs and other royal officials dating from 1218 to 1275 and from 1218 to 1242 respectively. Finally, there is a rather strange reference to a roll starting in 'the third decennovial year' (probably 1199) and ending in 1215. The choice of decennovial year is unusual and may have been an early experiment in dating before *anno domini* became standard.[42] All this suggests that certainly the recording of audits – if not the process of auditing itself – began in the last few years of the twelfth century and the beginning of the thirteenth.

If auditing had been a part of royal financial administration since the early thirteenth century, it did not develop into a form of continuous government: kings travelled to have their accounts heard in short bursts every so often. That auditing remained occasional in part explains why the process never became a separate institution of financial administration, as the Exchequer had done in England.[43] Scottish accounts were paid into the king's chamber; there was no institution of the Exchequer.[44] Indeed, the earliest reference to an 'Exchequer' (French: *leschequer, escheqier*) in Scotland is in a treatise written in French, known as 'the Scottish King's Household', apparently drafted between 1292 and 1296 (although the dating is not secure) which, as far as I can see, does not exactly resemble what we know about the king's household.[45] Its testimony on

---

[40] *Aberdeen Reg.*, i, pp. 55–6.

[41] *APS*, i, pp. 117–18.

[42] While 1215 is given in calendar year, the first date is rendered as *anno cicli xix iii*, the third year in a nineteen-year cycle (the *cyclus decennovalis*) dating back to Late Antiquity. There was a year one of this cycle in 1197; the third year of the cycle would thus be 1199, although this assumes that the accounting roll spanned less than a single decennovial cycle. I take this from the *Medieval Latin Dictionary*, which gives an example from 1238, described as the fourth year of the cycle; cf. *RRS*, ii, pp. 57, 67 n. 180, which calculates the date of 1205 from an 1843 work by N. H. Nicolas entitled *Chronology of History*. I am grateful to Richard Sharpe for discussing this with me and providing me with the evidence of 1238.

[43] H. Hall, 'The System of the Exchequer', in *Introduction to the Study of the Pipe Rolls*, PRS 3 (London, 1884), pp. 35–69, at pp. 35–6, 52–7. I have also found useful R. Cassidy, '*Recorda Splendidissima*: The Use of Pipe Rolls in the Thirteenth Century', *Historical Research* 85, no. 227 (2012), 1–12.

[44] A point already made by Carpenter, 'Scottish Royal Government', p. 121.

[45] M. Bateson (ed.), 'The Scottish King's Household and Other Fragments, from a Fourteenth-Century Manuscript in the Library of Corpus Christi College, Cambridge', *Miscellany of the Scottish History Society 2*, Scottish History Society first series 45 (Edinburgh, 1904), pp. 31–43, at p. 32; for the supposed date, see G. W. S. Barrow, 'The Justiciar', in

the Scottish Exchequer, stating that it met once a year in one place, in no way matches up to the practice recorded in Haddington's transcripts. It therefore makes much more sense to see this rather more intimate form of revenue collection, in which boundaries between centre and locality were blurred, not as having separate institutional form, but rather as part of the administrations of a peripatetic kingship in thirteenth-century Scotland.

Enrolment

This is an interesting base from which to approach the subject of enrolment. Enrolment is an important subset of the general practice of keeping records of governmental activity: it is a type of archiving whose form – in a roll – has a shifting resemblance to the actual practice it intends to record. In the case of the enrolment of financial accounts, rolls are assumed to be the direct and primary record of auditing procedure.[46] Yet enrolment can also be at further stages removed from process. For any type of outgoing document, such as charters or records of judicial proceedings, the enrolled item is a mere copy of an 'original' document; it is a written memory of an existing written document and thus is one stage removed from the process of drafting the original written record. The most important point about rolls – and central records in general – is that they are often seen to be part of the process by which kings started governing continuously.[47] The creation of central archives demonstrates the use of the written word as part of routine government that, accordingly, gave government more institutional permanence than could oral methods alone, or even single and disparate records that would not have been kept in the king's archives. Indeed, the keeping of written records allowed for past governmental activity to be theoretically a part of government in the present: the written record became an intrinsic part of the memory of kingship and always had the potential to be called upon. So if kings of Scots were adopting the façade of continuous government (through central accountancy), but that government really had little separate existence from the local, then how did they see the function of central archives in this more limited structure of direct administration? In the absence of the original rolls themselves, we must rely on the inventories, chance references in

The Kingdom of the Scots: Government, Church and Society from the Eleventh to the Fourteenth Century, 2nd edn (Edinburgh, 2003), pp. 68–111, at p. 75 and n. 2; for a reassessment, see D. Carpenter, '"The Scottish King's Household" and English Ideas of Constitutional Reform', The Breaking of Britain, Feature of the Month October 2011, available at http://www.breakingofbritain.ac.uk/blogs/feature-of-the-month/october-2011-the-scottish-kings-household/ (accessed 9 April 2015); see further, Taylor, *Shape of the State*, chapter 4.

[46] M. Clanchy, *From Memory to Written Record: England 1066–1307*, 2nd edn (Oxford, 1993), pp. 135–44.

[47] For the transition from 'brief spurt' governance and 'continuous government', see T. Reuter, 'Assembly Politics in Western Europe from the Eighth Century to the Twelfth', in *The Medieval World*, ed. P. Linehan and J. L. Nelson (London, 2003), pp. 432–50.

charters, and, of course, the transcripts of the accountancy records themselves. I will focus here on records of financial administration and the enrolment of royal charters.

It is clear that kings of Scots kept some of their records in rolls during the thirteenth century. But the body responsible for producing them was not called the 'Chancery' (*cancellaria*), as in thirteenth-century England, but the *capella regis* – the king's chapel.[48] By 1290 at the latest, there was at least one clerk with particular responsibility for the 'rolls of the royal chapel' and, by Edward I's period as superior lord, the clerk had been promoted from mere *clericus* to *custos* – 'guardian' or 'custodian' of the rolls.[49] Outgoing records of all kinds, including financial accounts, were compiled in the *capella regis*; there was no separation, as there was in England, between those records produced by the Exchequer and those of Chancery.[50]

It is clear that Haddington's source was a roll drawn up by a clerk (or clerks) of the king's *capella regis*.[51] But what part did these rolls play, if any, in the audit process itself? Were rolls compiled as the audit was taking place, as they were in England? There is no need to assume that Haddington's source was a direct record of the process of financial administration. Indeed, given its non-chronological order, it looks very much as though it was not produced at the audit itself, suggesting a relationship between the process of audit and the creation of central records different from that in England.

As stated above, Haddington's transcript of the accounts from the 1260s seems to have been made from a single roll that was arranged in non-chronological order.[52] Individual accounts returned in different years are scattered throughout the transcript. Accounts returned in 1264 are followed by those made in 1263; the roll then continues to record accounts returned in 1264, then 1266, then back to 1263 and so on. When it was thought that Haddington was copying from separate 'Exchequer' rolls, this erratic dating could be brushed away by blaming his editorial proclivities. But, if the layout of the transcript did follow the layout of the original roll, this *varia* approach has to be explained. The only

[48] The earliest reference to *cancellaria* is in the Ayr MS, datable to 1318×29, online MS available at http://www.stairsociety.org/resources/view_manuscript/the_ayr_manuscript/229 (accessed 9 April 2015). However, even here, the chapters containing the brieve formulae are called 'capitula capelle regis scocie'. They are divided into two types: those 'to be pleaded in court' (so, pleadable brieves), and 'brieves sent by the king from the Chancery (*de cancellaria*)': NRS, PA5/2, fol. 18v; now printed in *Scottish Formularies*, ed. A. A. M. Duncan, Stair Society 58 (Edinburgh, 2011), p. 11. See further Murray, 'Scottish Chancery', pp. 137–8.

[49] *ER*, ii, p. 51 (*clericus*); *APS*, ii, p. 111 (*custos*).

[50] For those produced by the Chancery, see, among many, N. Vincent, 'Why 1199? Bureaucracy and Enrolment under John and his Contemporaries', and D. Carpenter, 'The English Royal Chancery in the Thirteenth Century', both in *English Government in the Thirteenth Century*, ed. A. Jobson (Woodbridge, 2004), pp. 17–48 and pp. 49–69, respectively; for the distinction between Scottish and English procedures here, see Carpenter, 'Scottish Royal Government', pp. 121–2.

[51] *ER*, i, pp. 11, 19, 51.

[52] See above, pp. 87–8.

reasonable solution is that the original roll was a secondary record, one drawn up at a time removed from the process of accounting itself.

It is probable that this central roll either summarised or copied in full written records made at the audit itself. Haddington's transcript reveals that 'clerks of the chapel' attended the 1264 session and probably made records of its proceedings.[53] The 1296 inventory records two rolls of two membranes each, containing the accounts of two sheriffs of Nairn, one from 1204 and the other from 1227.[54] These may well have been the type of written account that fed into the central record. Furthermore, there are references to two large rolls containing accounts of various officials in the 1296 inventory. These were each of eighty-nine membranes: one covered 1218–72, the other, 1218–42.[55] There is no reason to think that the individual accounts therein would have been in strict chronological order; the evidence from Haddington suggests the opposite. The long periods each roll covered suggests that they were not fit for easy consultation.

The possibility that the rolls produced by the mid-thirteenth century were neither arranged chronologically nor drawn up to be direct records of the audit process itself is, rather surprisingly, strengthened by the contrast between the arrangement of Haddington's transcripts of the proceedings from the 1260s and those from 1288–90. Haddington seems to have been true to the order of the accounts returned between 1288 and 1290, even if he got understandably bored in transcribing all of their contents.[56] At the beginning of his transcription of 1288, for example, he noted to himself that 'the first comptis [on the document] ar revin blekked ['blackened'] and can not [sic] be red'.[57] The extracts Haddington made from 1288–90 are from three separate and clearly identifiable accounting sessions: one held in Linlithgow in 1288, another in Edinburgh in 1289 and a third at Scone in 1290.[58] These proceed on from one another in chronological order, with one exception: the accounts from Edinburgh in 1289 and Scone in 1290 are separated by seemingly miscellaneous accounts, one returned in 1290 and two in 1289 respectively.[59] The strange placing of these accounts in Haddington's transcript suggests that he was, as in his transcripts of the 1260s, following the order in his source, but that his 1288–90 source was arranged in a much more explicitly chronological way than his earlier one.[60] But the still haphazard arrangement of accounts even in the 1288–90 roll suggests that this too was a *post factum* document, compiled at a time later than the audit session itself.

53   *ER*, i, p. 11.
54   *APS*, i, p. 118.
55   *APS*, i, pp. 117, 118.
56   The accounts of John Comyn, earl of Buchan and sheriff of Banff, William of Meldrum, sheriff of Aberdeen, and Walter Stewart, earl of Menteith and one-time sheriff of Dumbarton, returned at Scone in 1290, are all blank: *ER*, i, p. 49.
57   *ER*, i, p. 35; for comment, see Murray, 'Pre-Union Records', p. 94.
58   See above, p. 90.
59   Sheriff of Wigtown (29 May 1290), at *ER*, i, p. 48; and the farmer of Dull (1289) and Nicholas of Hay, sheriff of Perth (1289), at *ER*, i, pp. 48–9.
60   See further, Taylor, *Shape of the State*, chapters 6 and 7.

Even if the mere outlines presented here are accepted, then the creation and role of central records of account were very different in Scotland from in England. Richard fitz Nigel's description of two, sometimes three, copies of the English pipe rolls being made at the very time of the meeting of the Upper Exchequer is evidence not only of a geographically centred accounting procedure (absent in Scotland), but of one in which the preparation of an authoritative written record was an intrinsic part of the process of accounting itself.[61] The contrast between English and Scottish procedure remains true despite the emerging view that the pipe rolls were on occasion not the record of unassailable accuracy described in the *Dialogus*.[62] That the pipe rolls sometimes contain mistakes does not detract from the intimate connection they reveal between the creation of a central written record and the otherwise oral process of account. In Scotland, however, the process of compiling central records was removed from the that of accounting. This is not to say that written records were not drawn up at the time of the audit – the accounts from the sheriffdom of Nairn may be our only lingering testimony of this – but that centrally kept records of the entire session were not drawn up at the time of the account. That happened later, as is witnessed by the arrangement in Haddington's transcript. These records are less ones of the immediate activity of government but, rather, should be seen as a later consolidation of that process.

What can then be said of other enrolment practices, in particular of outgoing charters, letters and memoranda issued under the king's name? The enrolment of royal charters by the English Chancery has long been thought an introduction made under John, although this is not uncontroversial.[63] In Scotland it was once thought that Alexander II's reign (1214–49) saw the introduction of central enrolment of royal charters. The evidence for this comes from a sixteenth-century transcript of royal charters, generally known to historians as 'Index A'. Index A proclaims itself to be part copied from a roll 'maid be King Alexander', whom Maitland Thomson identified as Alexander II.[64] Although the original roll is lost, it was long thought to be clear evidence of the enrolment of charters in the early thirteenth century. But Keith Stringer has recently shown that the one surviving charter text on Index A is inauthentic, containing charter diplomatic belonging to the fourteenth or fifteenth century, not the first half of the

---

[61] *Dialogus*, pp. 26–7, and reference to Thomas Brown's rolls, pp. 52–5; for the assertion that Thomas Brown's roll was a third copy of the pipe roll, see Vincent, 'Bureaucracy and Enrolment', p. 23 n. 27.

[62] M. Hagger, 'Theory and Practice in the Making of Twelfth-Century Pipe Rolls', in *Records, Administration and Aristocratic Society in the Anglo-Norman Realm*, ed. N. Vincent (Woodbridge, 2009), pp. 45–74.

[63] David Carpenter has argued that Chancery enrolment may have begun in the 1180s, possibly even earlier, for which see D. Carpenter, '"In testimonium factorum brevium": The Beginnings of the English Chancery Rolls', *Records, Administration and Aristocratic Society in the Anglo-Norman Realm*, ed. N. Vincent (Woodbridge, 2009), pp. 1–28, at pp. 24–7.

[64] *Registri Magni Sigilli Regum Scotorum: The Register of the Great Seal of Scotland*, ed. J. M. Thomson *et al.* 11 vols (Edinburgh, 1882–1914), i, pp. viii–ix; index A is printed in appendix II, with the relevant charters listed at Index A, nos 1–5, at p. 509.

thirteenth.[65] Stringer has thus concluded that the source of this part of Index A 'cannot be regarded as an entirely genuine product of Alexander II's chancery [*sic*]', despite its also containing references to potentially authentic land gifts of Alexander II, perhaps once confirmed in charters which no longer survive.[66]

This means that we have to look at evidence other than Index A for the introduction of the enrolment of royal charters. Attention has more recently been drawn to 1195, when limited dating clauses (containing only the day and the month of issue but not the regnal year) became a standard part of royal charter diplomatic during the reign of William the Lion. Geoffrey Barrow suggested that the introduction of limited dating clauses by 17 April 1195 could only be explained by 'the assumption that [from 1195] … the clerks of the chapel began to copy acts on rolls which were made up, or freshly headed, for each regnal year'.[67] If this had been the case, it would have meant that the kings of Scots kept charter rolls before they were introduced in England in 1199. Yet the introduction of limited dating clauses would explain only the absence of regnal years from the putative rolls, not from the sealed charters themselves. If consultation were ever a motivation for the introduction of charter rolls – whether in Scotland or in England – it would be impossible for an enrolled copy even to be found if the regnal year was missing from the original document. This does not prove that charter rolls were not introduced at the same time as limited dating clauses, but it does make Barrow's assumption rather more unlikely.[68] If the presence of dating clauses can be linked in Scotland to the creation of charter rolls, then it makes more sense to see 1222, when royal charters began to be dated by regnal year, as a more significant date than 1195.[69] But it will actually be argued below that the introduction of full dating clauses in 1222 was not linked to the process of keeping routine central records: there is not clear evidence for the enrolment of royal charters until the reign of Alexander III, and even this was a less routine and a more retrospective activity than it was in England.[70]

What, then, can the inventories tell us about charter enrolment? It should first be acknowledged that the four inventories are not identical in scope, purpose or content. The 1282 inventory was made on Alexander III's command (*ex precepto Regis*) and was preceded by an oral inquest into the whereabouts of the king's

[65]   *RRS*, iii.

[66]   I am grateful to Professor Stringer for sharing his conclusions with me in advance of publication.

[67]   *RRS*, ii, p. 58.

[68]   For a much more extensive treatment, see D. Broun, 'The Absence of Regnal Years from the Dating Clause of Charters of Kings of Scots, 1195–1222', in *Anglo-Norman Studies XXV: Proceedings of the Battle Conference 2002*, ed. J. Gillingham (Woodbridge, 2003), pp. 47–63, at pp. 50–7.

[69]   For the introduction of regnal year dating into the diplomatic of royal charters, see at present Barrow, '*Capella Regis*', p. 9; and, most importantly, Broun, 'Absence of Regnal Years', pp. 57–8, developed in D. Broun, *Scottish Independence and the Idea of Britain from the Picts to Alexander III* (Edinburgh, 2007), pp. 191–206.

[70]   For Scotland, see below, pp. 98–100; for England, see the works by Carpenter and Vincent cited above, notes 50 and 63.

documentation. One Simon Fraser confessed that he had taken certain papal bulls, once at the Edinburgh Treasury, to Melrose Abbey to be archived; the fact that this was recorded may suggest that this was not expected behaviour.[71] The inventory itself is divided into four sections, each concerned with the king's rights in relation to other powers: the first section deals with relations with the papacy; the second with Anglo-Scottish relations (listing, among many other items, treaties made with the English king since 1189); the third with the kings of Norway; the fourth with the magnates of his kingdom. The 1282 inventory thus tells us very little about governmental administration *per se* but a great deal about how the king's clerks made a statement about the king's historical legal position vis-à-vis other rulers and lords. In contrast, the three Edwardian inquests (of 1291, 1292 and 1296) have more simple aims: to list what they could.[72] This was not very much in the case of 1296, more in 1291, and really quite a lot in the 1292 inventory. All of these list once-existing rolls, a host of bags and chests of single-sheet documents, as well as precious jewels and items, relics and cloths that were also kept in the Treasury, including the staff used to invest Alexander II with the county of Northumberland in 1215.[73] It is thus from the inventories of the 1290s that we learn most about the depth of the Edinburgh Treasury, but we must not allow our own assumptions to lead us to place more attention on the listing of rolls rather than single sheets, and documentary evidence more generally over precious and symbolic items. All were part of a single archive. This point will be developed below.

The four inventories of the contents of the royal Treasury in Edinburgh Castle in fact reveal little similar to the rolls of letters patent and letters close found in England. This is despite the adoption of letters patent as an explicit category of document under Alexander II; indeed, each of the inventories of 1282, 1291 and 1292 all list individual – not enrolled – letters patent among their contents.[74] The inventories do, however, itemise rolls of charters, but these rolls are very different from the more systematic charter rolls first surviving in England from the first regnal year of King John (27 May 1199–17 May 1200). Indeed, some of the Scottish charter rolls are clearly the result of individual endeavour, not the more routine process of record. The 1291 inventory tells us of the existence of 'one roll of titles of all charters made by William of Dumfries'.[75] This appears to have been a calendar of certain charters made by William, who was described as Alexander III's clerk in 1282 and 'custodian of the rolls of the kingdom of Scotland' in 1291; it is thus possible that he compiled this retrospective calendar as part of his office.[76] In 1292 we find record of 'two rolls of memoranda' made by the chancellor, Thomas of Chartres, 'after the death of [Alexander III], king of

---

[71] *APS*, i, pp. 107–10, at p. 107.
[72] *APS*, i, pp. 111–18.
[73] *APS*, i, p. 112.
[74] *APS*, i, pp. 115–17, 118; *ER*, i, p. 20; *RRS*, iii, no. 273.
[75] *APS*, i, p. 112.
[76] *APS*, i, pp. 107, 110–11.

Scots'.[77] This sort of record-keeping was clearly made after, sometimes long after, the issue of the documents themselves. The rolls of charters and memoranda made by William and Thomas were not products of routine central government, but lists compiled later to bring together disparate documents.[78]

Where we do have evidence of rolls containing copies of royal charters that do not, at first glance, appear to have been compiled *post factum*, they are mixed up with other types of document. In 1292 we find record of 'one great roll of sixty-two membranes, written on both sides, containing various charters and confirmation of various kings of Scotland'.[79] But this 'great roll' also contained 'charters and recognitions and other written documents concerning lands and tenements which render to the king'; 'pleas in which justice was … amicably terminated'; 'agreements and *conventiones* over disputes occurring between the magnates and other men of the kingdom'; and other types of document besides. Had this roll survived, one might have found that these documents were grouped together for a purpose – perhaps to demonstrate the ins and outs of particular gifts, disputes and resulting settlements; on the other hand, it might have been a miscellaneous collection with no purpose other than to record disparate material in the same place. What it was not, however, is a roll that records even a proportion of the routine output of royal charters from the king's chapel organised according to regnal year.

Only by the reign of Alexander III do we have anything even remotely resembling the charter rolls of King John. It seems that a degree of charter enrolment had begun by mid-way through the minority of Alexander III: in 1253 Alexander's charter confirming the land of Smeaton to Dunfermline Abbey was copied into 'the roll of the lord king in his chapel' after a case of mortancestry had been brought by Emma, daughter of Gilbert, against the abbey.[80] The 1292 inventory records the presence of 'one roll of nine pieces, written on both sides, containing charters and confirmations of Alexander [III], last king of Scotland, of different years of his kingship'.[81] This is small fry indeed even compared to John's charter rolls, organised as they are as separate rolls dated by regnal year, the first, in three parts, containing a total of sixty-eight membranes; the second, for 2 John, containing thirty-five membranes; the third, for 5 John, containing twenty-six.[82] This standard was not maintained throughout John's reign:

---

[77]   *APS*, i, p. 115.
[78]   See also the roll of twelve membranes of 'recognitions and ancient charters of the time of King William and King Alexander', which included a list of 'those to whom the said kings gave their peace and those who stood with MacWilliam'. Both William and Alexander faced MacWilliam threats from the late 1170s to 1230; this roll, too, must have been a *post factum* roll, drawn up from a number of different sources of extremely varying date: *APS*, i, p. 114.
[79]   *APS*, i, p. 114.
[80]   *Registrum de Dunfermelyn*, ed. C. N. Innes (Edinburgh, 1842), no. 83; see also *Liber S. Thome de Aberbrothoc*, 2 vols, ed. C. N. Innes and P. Chalmers (Edinburgh, 1848–56), i, 294.
[81]   *APS*, i, p. 114.
[82]   *Rot. Chart.*; 1 John is preserved in three parts: TNA, C 53/1, 53/2, 53/3; 2 John is TNA, C 53/4; 5 John is C 53/5. The charter rolls for 3 and 4 John do not survive.

beneficiaries would have rushed to have their charters confirmed at the beginning of the reign, creating a far larger output of written documentation in the first few years than in those following.[83] We should not exaggerate the systematised production of a vast quantity of enrolled royal charters under John: the relationship between the issue of a charter and its entry on the roll is yet to be studied.[84] Even a summary survey of the structure and hands of John's charter rolls shows that charters were not copied into the roll in the order in which they were issued; enrolment appears to have been a more *ad hoc* process than we might imagine.[85] But there is still a vast difference between the amount of systematic enrolment in the Angevin Chancery, in which a separate roll was begun each regnal year, and the one small mention we have of charter enrolment under Alexander III. Here there were not enough charters copied onto the roll to justify the creation of a second, and its internal organisation may have been quite haphazard, containing 'charters and confirmations of Alexander III of diverse years of his kingship'.[86] Charter enrolment under Alexander III thus appears to have been extremely selective: only a small proportion of the king's charters would have been copied onto this roll. Nor was it necessarily organised by regnal year as the charter rolls in England were from the reign of King John, either because of this selectivity or because the Scottish king's chapel did not generate the same level of material. On the evidence of the inventories, it seems that the introduction of regnal years in 1222 in royal charter diplomatic was not caused by the enrolment of royal charters. This should not be surprising: full dating clauses were introduced to the diplomatic of Richard I's charters in 1189, but clear evidence of charter enrolment does not appear until 1199.[87]

The inventories also list many single-sheet items that are not evidence of the archiving of diplomatic correspondence, but are concerned with business internal to Scotland. These include charters issued by the kings of Scots, letters from burgh communities, and aristocratic letters and charters. Most of these documents touched the king's own interests, as is most obviously evidenced by the layout and structure of the 1282 inventory. But we can also see this focus in the

---

[83] There are 4 membranes in the charter roll for 15 John: 11 for 16 John; 10 for 17 John, 1 for 18 John (John died on 18–19 October 1216 and his regnal year began in 1216 on 19 May).

[84] As noted in Vincent, 'Bureaucracy and Enrolment', p. 38.

[85] See, for example, the charter roll for 9 John (1207–8: TNA, C 53/8), which contains a total of eight membranes with nothing written on the dorse. In 1207 John's regnal year began on 31 May. Membrane 3 contains eight charters and three clear changes of hand (although this preliminary conclusion is, of course, open to the onslaught of a full palaeographical study). Membrane 6 contains nine charters and at least six different hands of varying dates: (from the bottom of the membrane) 28 August, 19 October, 8 August, 25 October, 5 October, 27 August, 28 September, 16 June, 17 September. This demonstrates that, for example, the charters which follow 19 October, including some issued in June, could not have been entered before October.

[86] *APS*, i, p. 114.

[87] For the introduction of dating clauses in Richard I's charters, see P. Chaplais, *English Royal Documents: King John–King Henry VI, 1199–1461* (Oxford, 1971), p. 14.

other inventories that aim for comprehensive coverage of the Treasury's content. In 1292 it was recorded that the Treasury contained nineteen letters patent of the provosts and burgesses of nineteen Scottish burghs, kept between two boards, which temporarily quitclaimed the king of the money he owed them.[88] Other single letters concern land and offices once belonging to other individuals, now returned to the king: a letter of Margaret de Ferrers, countess of Derby, resigned the office of constable into the hands of Alexander III.[89] There are also references to aristocratic deeds that seem at first to have nothing to do with the king himself, but reveal themselves to be part of documentary chains concerned with a piece of land that eventually ended up in the king's hands. Thus, we have record in 1292 of a deed of William de Vieuxpont by which he granted *Shollesclyve* to his kins-man, William of Horndean, and his heirs.[90] But William of Horndean then gave (*dedit*) the lands of *Shollesclyve* to Alexander III, and this deed, surviving in two copies, was also listed as kept 'in a small box' in the king's Treasury. This suggests that William de Vieuxpont's original gift to William of Horndean was only in the Treasury because the land was now the king's, and all documentation con-cerning *Shollesclyve* had been handed over to him when William of Horndean donated the land. The overwhelming impression given by the documents listed in the inventories is thus that they are to do with the king's own business. The Treasury – or at least the Treasury as viewed by the inventory-takers – looks as much a repository for the king's personal rights and privileges as it does a record of direct and institutional government. Indeed, we see a clear reference to this process in a charter of Alexander III drawn up in 1271, when Nicholas Corbet, a knight, returned and resigned Manor in Peebleshire 'by his letters patent, sealed with his seal and the seals of many others of our barons', 'which we cause to be enrolled (*inrotularia*) in our chapel (*capella*) … at Kinclevin'.[91] Here, it was Nicholas's quitclaim that was enrolled, not Alexander's charter granting Manor to William of Badby. Nicholas's letters patent were enrolled to protect the king and the new beneficiary against any future challenge to the royal gift.

Conclusion

The auditing of the accounts of royal officials in Scotland seems to have begun by the early thirteenth century at the latest. But it was not a process that slav-ishly followed its English exemplar. There was no separate institution called the Exchequer in Scotland, royal officials did not have to account every year, and, most importantly, though the officials could go to the king's court, the king's

---

[88] *APS*, i, pp. 115–16. See further a box containing personal debts of the king and queen to various unnamed merchants: *APS*, i, p. 116.
[89] *APS*, i, p. 115.
[90] *APS*, i, p. 115.
[91] *Regesta Regum Scottorum: Volume 4, Part 1: The Acts of Alexander III, King of Scots, 1249–86*, eds. C. J. Neville and G. G. Simpson (Edinburgh, 2013), no. 166.

court also went to them. Scottish financial administration was peripatetic; it was not, as it was in England, carried out in one place (Westminster) at set times each year.

The records produced at these audit sessions were also very different from their English counterparts. Whereas the English pipe rolls were drawn up as part of the accounting process itself, Scottish financial accounts were far more haphazardly constructed. The reconstruction of Haddington's original source for the 1263–6 material and the 1288–90 material reveal that his source was, most probably, a consolidation of existing written records (however compiled) of past accounting sessions. They appear to have been entered on the roll with no regard, really, for future consultation. They were recorded simply because they were records. We should thus not see the account rolls of the thirteenth century as records of the immediate activity of government but rather as a later consolidation of that government, to record, at least in part, its past financial rights.[92] The same can be said for the so-called enrolment of royal charters. Inasmuch as enrolment was a routine part of royal charter production in England, Scottish kings did not adopt the practice during the thirteenth century; their enrolment was, like the enrolment of financial records, *post factum* and probably non-comprehensive. Not every item (or near enough) was included, but only those considered noteworthy at some point in the future.

Finally, all this should shed light on the relation between record-keeping – of which enrolment was a type – and the routine of administrative government. The Scottish inventories list many single documents that were deemed part of the Treasury at Edinburgh and, for Alexander's clerks in 1282, these were the most important part. These single sheets were often records of diplomatic correspondence and relations, but also included charters that recorded the king's patronage and the land surrendered to him; in short, they were the records of his legal rights and privileges. We should see the royal archive not only as the footprint of bureaucratic government but also as a more personal repository for safeguarding the rights and privileges of kings, in many ways far more similar to the great cartularies of monastic houses and bishoprics than historians of royal government might care to admit.

This is a point that should hold for not only the smaller structures of central government identifiable in Scotland but also those more unwieldy bureaucratic beasts, such as thirteenth-century England. Even an inventory as late as Bishop Stapleton's in 1323, concerning a royal archive as dense as early fourteenth-century England, shows that archiving and government are in many respects separate subjects, although they are both of course about the preservation of power,

---

[92]   These also include rights of another sort: the link with the saintly past, through the presence of the Black Rood associated with St Margaret, queen of Scotland; the link with the northern counties, not only the written record of the oaths sworn to Alexander II, but also the very staff with which he had been invested with Northumberland in 1215, all of which are recorded in the 1291 inventory: see *APS*, i, p. 112.

albeit through different but cognate means.[93] Stapleton's calendar includes many documents, both enrolled and in single sheets, which were not related to the day-to-day administration of government. All, however, were conceptualised together: Stapleton said in his preface that he compiled the *Kalendar* because the entire contents of the archive had been moved so frequently that it was hard to have any idea of their precise nature and location. The different types of document and record present in any central archive should thus be seen as outcomes of a process of record-keeping that was separate from – but did not exclude – the day-to-day administration of government. Record-keeping and governmental administration existed in relation to one another, but it was a relation that could vary in intensity and closeness. In the case of thirteenth-century Scotland, the processes of central record-keeping and everyday royal governance were less firmly entwined than we might once have imagined.

---

[93] F. Palgrave, *The Antient Kalendars and Inventories of the Treasury of His Majesty's Exchequer*, 3 vols (London, 1836), i, pp. iii–vii, 113–55.

7

Imitation and Independence in Native Welsh Administrative Culture, c. 1180–1280

Charles Insley

Welsh history of the thirteenth century tends to be studied through the prism of the events of 1277 to 1284, the seven years that saw first the emasculation of Wales' most powerful native principality, Gwynedd, and then its final destruction in the war of 1282–3. The Statute of Wales, sometimes known as the Statute of Rhuddlan, of 1284 set the seal on this process, converting the administration of what was left of native Wales into a simulacrum of English local government.[1] The century – or more – of Welsh history that preceded these events is therefore understood in their light, essentially as a series of processes that led to greater and more rigid English domination of Wales, and finally its conquest. It is not for nothing that Rees Davies's magisterial history of Wales in the central Middle Ages was published under the title *Conquest, Coexistence and Change: Wales 1063–1415*, nor that the date-frame for Davies's book began in 1063, the year that saw the death of Gruffudd ap Llywelyn, king of much of Wales, during the war with the English.[2] 1063 was also only three years before the Norman Conquest of England and, again, pre-vailing historiography sees the new Norman rulers of England adopting a deci-sively different, and certainly more aggressive and interventionist approach, to England's relationship with its Welsh neighbours than had their Anglo-Saxon predecessors.[3] Again, Rees Davies's Ford lectures, published as *The First English Empire*, began in 1093, the year that Rhys ap Tewdwr, king of Deheubarth, in south-west Wales, was killed by the Normans in Brycheiniog.[4] This sense of the arrival of the Normans marking something new in Anglo-Welsh relations is emphasised by the wistful words of the monk of Strata Florida who, in the late thirteenth century, compiled the version of the *Brut y Tywysogion* (The

---

[1]   *Statutes of the Realm, Published by Command of His Majesty King George the Third*, ed. J. Raithby, 9 vols (London, 1810–22), i, p. 55.

[2]   R. R. Davies, *Conquest, Coexistence and Change: Wales 1063–1415* (Oxford, 1987), republished as *Age of Conquest: Wales 1063–1415* (Oxford, 1991); *Brut y Tywysogion; or, The Chronicle of the Princes, Peniarth MS. 20 Version*, trans. T. Jones (Cardiff, 1952), *s.a.* 1063; the *Brut* calls Gruffudd 'head and shield and defender to the Britons'.

[3]   See, for example, L. Nelson, *The Normans in South Wales, 1070–1171* (Austin, 1966); D. Walker, *The Normans in Britain* (Oxford, 1995), pp. 47–74.

[4]   R. R. Davies, *The First English Empire: Power and Identities in the British Isles, 1093–1343* (Oxford, 2000).

Chronicle of the Princes) in Peniarth MS 20: 'with whom fell the kingdom of the Britons'.[5]

This process of 'domination and conquest' can be seen not just in political terms, but also in a wider cultural and administrative frame. Robert Bartlett regarded the period from c. 900 to c. 1350 as one which saw the 'Europeanisation' of Europe, in the sense of the political, social and cultural structures of Europe's heartland – essentially France and Germany – expanding and being exported to its periphery, whether Eastern Europe, southern Italy, the Iberian peninsula, Scandinavia or Britain and Ireland.[6] So, hand in hand with increasing English political domination of Britain and Ireland in the twelfth and thirteenth centuries, we also see a sort of 'cultural imperialism' as the cultural and social norms of the Anglo-Norman, Angevin and Plantagenet polities were imitated and adopted by the societies under English hegemony.[7] This may also be seen in the administrative structures and habits of these peripheral societies: an increased use of the written word in government, the use of English diplomatic forms, the use of seals and the emergence of administrative bureaucracies.

There is much to commend these historiographical paradigms, but it also needs to be noted that they are not without problems. It is perfectly arguable that the events of 1277–84 were not at all inevitable in the light of the preceding century and a half of increasing English hegemony in the British Isles, but rather were entirely contingent on rapidly changing political dynamics in the 1270s, in particular following the accession of Edward I in 1272. Indeed, it is far from clear that the English Crown was determined on the subjection of Wales until 1282 and, for much of the reign of Henry III, it seems that what the English Crown wanted from Wales was stability and a measure of control through reliable vassals, rather than the trouble of actually running the country itself. As Gwyn Williams pointed out as long ago as 1964, the 1241 treaty of Gwern Eigron between Henry III and the sons of Llywelyn ap Iorwerth (ruler of Gwynedd 1199–1240) in principle allowed for large parts of Gwynedd to escheat to the Crown should Dafydd, Llywelyn's 'legitimate' son by the Angevin princess Joan (half-sister of Henry III), die without issue.[8] This is precisely what happened in 1246, as the bishop of Bangor reminded Henry, yet the Crown was content for Gwynedd to be partitioned between the sons of Gruffudd, Llywelyn's older but 'illegitimate' son.[9] It is clear that there were significant advantages to the Crown in this arrangement; a Gwynedd partitioned between four sons (Owain, Llywelyn, Rhodri and Dafydd) was hardly likely to be problematic, not least

---

[5] *Brut Pen. 20, s.a.* 1093.

[6] R. Bartlett, *The Making of Europe: Conquest, Colonization and Cultural Change, 950–1350* (London, 1993), pp. 60–84, 269–91.

[7] Davies, *Age of Conquest*, pp. 110–210.

[8] *AWR*, no. 300; *CPR 1232–47*, p. 264; G. A. Williams, 'The Succession to Gwynedd', *Bulletin of the Board of Celtic Studies* 20 (1964), 393–413, at pp. 401–3.

[9] *AWR*, no. 312; C. W. Lewis, 'The Treaty of Woodstock, 1247: Its Background and Significance', *Welsh History Review* 2 (1965), 37–65; Williams, 'The Succession to Gwynedd', pp. 409–11.

because it was clear that none of Gruffudd's sons was entirely content with the situation. Not until 1255, following the battle of Bryn Derwin, did Llywelyn ap Gruffudd emerge as the dominant brother.[10]

The 'Europeanisation' model is also attractive and, to a large extent, works for Britain and Ireland. However, it perhaps assumes that cultural domination was structural and inexorable, and that the societies on the periphery of Europe really had little choice or agency about how this cultural domination was established. A study of Wales in the later twelfth and thirteenth centuries, while confirming that it was certainly drawn into an Angevin/Plantagenet cultural world, also suggests that the Welsh had some agency about precisely how they were drawn into this English – or Anglo-French – cultural orbit.[11] The purpose of the following discussion is to highlight some areas of the administrative culture of later twelfth- and thirteenth-century Wales that bear this point out; that indicate that while Welsh rulers and their administrators imitated on a significant scale elements of the administrative structures of their English neighbours, they did so on their own terms and in ways which were quite distinctive.[12] In particular, the diplomatic of Welsh princely and lordly *acta* suggests that, while Welsh rulers and the individuals who wrote their documents and kept their records adopted many of the norms of English documentary administrative culture, they did so in ways which suggest a dialogue between different administrative and documentary traditions, rather than one-way traffic.

The sources available to the historian of medieval Welsh administration are relatively thin, and can be broken down into four discrete categories: record sources (charters, letters, agreements and other administrative memoranda); legal material, including the main thirteenth-century compilations of Welsh law; literary sources, most importantly the significant body of poetry associated with the court poets of the twelfth- and thirteenth-century Welsh princes;[13] and historiographical sources, notably the connected set of annals compiled in the late thirteenth century and conventionally known by historians as *Brut y Tywysogion* and its satellites, in both Welsh and Latin (*Brenhinedd y Saesson* or *The Kings of the Saxons/English*, the *Chronica de Wallia* and *Annales Cambriae*).[14] The *Chronica*

---

[10] *Brut Pen. 20*, s.a. 1255; Davies, *Age of Conquest*, pp. 309–10.

[11] For a nuanced critique of Bartlett's model in relation to Wales, see A. H. Pryce, 'Welsh Rulers and European Change c. 1100–1282', in *Power and Identity in the Middle Ages: Essays in Memory of Sir Rees Davies*, ed. A. H. Pryce and J. Watts (Oxford, 2007), pp. 37–51.

[12] Pryce, 'Welsh Rulers and European Change', pp. 45–9.

[13] The major collection of princely poetry is preserved in the Hendregadredd manuscript (Aberystwyth, National Library of Wales, MS 6680B); *Llawysgrif Hendregadredd*, ed. J. Morris-Jones and T. H. Parry-Williams (Cardiff, 1933). For more recent editions of the works of the most important princely poets, see *Cyfres Beirdd y Tywysogion I: Gwaith Meilyr Brydydd*, ed. J. Caerwyn Williams and P. Lynch (Cardiff, 1994); *Cyfres Beirdd y Tywysogion IV: Gwaith Cynddelw Brydydd Mawr*, ed. N. A. Jones and A. P. Owen (Cardiff, 1995); *Cyfres Beirdd y Tywysogion V: Gwaith Llywarch ap Llywelyn 'Prydydd y Moch'*, ed. E. M. Jones and N. A. Jones (Cardiff, 1991); see also *The Welsh King and his Court*, ed. T. M. Charles-Edwards, M. E. Owen and P. Russell (Cardiff, 2000).

[14] *Brut Pen. 20*, trans. Jones; *Brut y Tywysogion; or, the Chronicle of the Princes: Red Book*

Majora of the thirteenth-century St Albans historian Matthew Paris also contains a significant amount of Welsh material from the middle years of the thirteenth century.[15] None of these sources is abundant, and much of the following discussion will focus on the first category, what we might term record sources.

One of the results of the conquest of Wales in 1283 is that many of its pre-Conquest records survive in post-conquest English governmental sources, as the circumstances of the conquest brought a rash of administrative and judicial activity, ranging from inquisitions and assizes through to more straightforward acts of confirmation; English royal Chancery and Exchequer enrolments, therefore, account for a major portion of the surviving Welsh princely *acta*, some 346 out of 618 included in the recent edition of the *acta* of the native Welsh rulers.[16] As well as what we might think of as 'normative' classes of Chancery documents – charter rolls, close rolls, patent rolls, fine rolls and the like – the events of 1277–84 and their aftermath also generated specific sets of records, notably the Welsh rolls series begun in 1277, following the treaty of Aberconwy, and the compilation of Welsh and Gascon material in an Exchequer manuscript known as 'Liber A', compiled at some point in the 1280s or 1290s.[17] Welsh records also survive in the muniments of the English religious houses with which Welsh lords had links, and in the muniments of Welsh religious houses.[18] The records of two Welsh houses in particular dominate the surviving pre-Conquest charter material: Margam Abbey in Glamorgan and Strata Marcella Abbey in Powys, the cartulary rolls and single-sheet charters of which are now preserved in the National Library of Wales.[19]

The pattern of survival of Welsh material is not just determined by the vicissitudes of Wales's post-1283 history, but also, to a lesser extent, by the century or so that preceded the Conquest. For most of the thirteenth century Gwynedd,

---

of Hergest Version, ed. and trans. T. Jones (Cardiff, 1955); *Brenhinedd y Saesson; or, the Kings of the Saxons*, ed. and trans. T. Jones (Cardiff, 1974); T. Jones, '*Cronica de Wallia* and Other Documents from Exeter Cathedral Library MS. 3514', *Bulletin of the Board of Celtic Studies* 12 (1946), 27–44; *Annales Cambriae*, ed. J. W. ab Ithel, Rolls Series (London, 1860).

[15] *Chronica Majora*; for discussion of Paris as a source for Venedotian politics, see Williams, 'Succession to Gwynedd', pp. 401–8.

[16] *AWR*.

[17] TNA, C 77; TNA, E 36/274 (Liber A); *Littere Wallie preserved in Liber A in the Public Record Office*, ed. J. G. Edwards (Cardiff, 1940).

[18] E.g. Leominster Priory cartulary (BL, Cotton MS Domitian A.iii [*AWR*, no. 238]); the register of Glastonbury Abbey (Cambridge, Trinity College MS R 5. 33 [*AWR*, no. 476]).

[19] Aberystwyth, National Library of Wales, Penrice MS 208 (*AWR*, no. 513); Penrice MS 225 (*AWR*, nos 345, 368–9, 387, 397, 539, 601); Penrice and Margam charters (*AWR*, nos 119, 122–3, 126–31, 133–4, 136–7, 142, 145–8, 151–5, 157, 159–65, 171–2, 174–7, 182–4, 186, 188–9, 199, 204, 219, 272); Penrice and Margam rolls 288, 290, 292, 293, 543, 2089, 2090, 2093 (*AWR*, nos 122–3, 127–8, 130–9, 142–8, 152–5, 157, 160–2, 165–6, 169, 170–3, 178, 180–1, 188–90, 617–18); Wynnstay Estate Records, Ystrad Marchell charters (*AWR*, nos 8–12, 16–17, 282, 483, 487, 496, 541, 544–5, 548, 551, 553, 555, 556, 563, 569, 575, 577, 581); *Cartae et Alia Munimenta quae ad Dominium de Glamorgancia Pertinet*, ed. G. T. Clark, 6 vols (Cardiff, 1910); R. B. Patterson, *The Scriptorium of Margam Abbey and the Scribes of Early Angevin Glamorgan* (Woodbridge, 2002); *The Charters of the Abbey of Ystrad Marchell*, ed. G. C. G. Thomas (Aberystwyth, 1997).

the northern principality, was much the most powerful native lordship in Wales; at various points its rulers were able to exercise hegemony over most, if not all, of Wales still ruled by native, rather than Marcher, lords. Although Welsh historical tradition would see Gwynedd's pre-eminence as something dating back to the rule of Rhodri ap Merfyn Frych, better known as Rhodri Mawr, or 'the Great' (d. 877), the hegemony of the thirteenth-century rulers of Gwynedd was largely a new phenomenon, emerging through the activities of Llywelyn ap Iorwerth, or Llywelyn the Great (c. 1199–1240), and his grandson Llywelyn ap Gruffudd (1246–82).

The political landscape of Wales during the twelfth century had been highly fluid, as native rulers came to terms with incursions by Anglo-Norman adventurers and, later on, the English Crown.[20] These incursions had seen the creation by the second quarter of the twelfth century of English/Anglo-Norman lordships across the South Wales coastal plain, as well as along the Anglo-Welsh border.[21] This period of incursion was followed by a period of consolidation and reaction, and some of these new lordships – in particular those in Gwent – were reincorporated into native Welsh polities in the middle years of the twelfth century.[22] During the period from 1135 onwards there was no single hegemonic native Welsh ruler, although particular individuals may have fancied themselves as such; a letter of 1165 produced by Owain Gwynedd (d. 1170) describes him as *rex Wallie*, while another describes him as *princeps Walliarum* (prince of the Waleses).[23] Owain Gwynedd was indeed a powerful ruler, but he was not unchallenged, and the ruler of the south-western principality of Deheubarth, Rhys ap Gruffudd (1155–97), or the 'Lord Rhys', was also a powerful and ambitious ruler whose *acta*, too, laid claim to wide-ranging authority.[24] Certainly, after Owain's death in 1170 Rhys was the most powerful ruler in Wales, a position to some extent acknowledged by Henry II, who is recorded as having appointed Rhys 'justice' of South Wales.[25] Rhys's southern hegemony collapsed on his death in 1197; indeed, it seems that Rhys's relationship with Henry II's successor, Richard I, was far less cordial and that Rhys's dominance was already on the wane by the 1190s.[26] Rhys's death was followed by internecine conflict within his dynasty and the fragmentation of Deheubarth between his sons and grandsons.[27] The mid-Welsh principality of Powys suffered a similar permanent

[20] Nelson, *The Normans in South Wales*.

[21] M. Lieberman, *The Medieval March of Wales: The Creation and Perception of a Frontier, 1066–1283* (Cambridge, 2010), pp. 23–137; B. Holden, *Lords of the Central Marches: English Aristocracy and Frontier Society, 1087–1265* (Oxford, 2008), pp. 13–45; Davies, *Age of Conquest*, pp. 82–107.

[22] Davies, *Age of Conquest*, pp. 45–51.

[23] *AWR*, nos 193–4 (*Rex Wallie*), 196 (*Princeps Walliarum*).

[24] C. L. G. Insley, 'Kings, Lords, Charters and the Political Culture of Twelfth-Century Wales', *Anglo-Norman Studies* 30 (2007), pp. 133–53, at pp. 145–50; *AWR*, nos 26 (*princeps Wallie*), 27 (*Walliarum princeps*), 35 (*princeps Suthwallie*).

[25] *Brut Pen. 20*, s.a. 1172; s.a. 1175; Davies, *Age of Conquest*, pp. 217–27; *AWR*, pp. 8–9.

[26] Davies, *Age of Conquest*, p. 223.

[27] Davies, *Age of Conquest*, pp. 223–7.

fragmentation on the death of Madog ap Maredudd in 1160, splitting into a number of lordships.[28] In the thirteenth century the most important of these Powyssian polities was northern Powys, sometimes called Powys Fadog after Madog ap Gruffudd (d. 1236), and southern Powys, sometimes called Powys Wenwynwyn, after its second ruler, Gwenwynwyn ab Owain Cyfeiliog.

In contrast to this twelfth-century fluidity, the thirteenth century saw Gwynedd emerge as the hegemonic Welsh principality, its rulers able to dominate and intervene in the affairs of their neighbours to the south.[29] It is also clear that both Llywelyn the Great and Llywelyn ap Gruffudd went to considerable lengths to 'institutionalise' their hegemonies. The *Brut y Tywysogion* records an occasion in 1238 where all the native lords of Wales gathered at Strata Florida, in Deheubarth, to swear oaths to Llywelyn the Great, and to swear fealty to Dafydd, his son by Joan, half-sister of Henry III; the same gathering effectively disinherited Llywelyn's older illegitimate son, Gruffudd, leaving him only in possession of Llŷn.[30] The choice of Strata Florida for this gathering was also testament to Llywelyn's power; it lay well outside his Gwynedd heartland, and was a major centre of Welsh historical writing. Impressive though this occasion might have been, it was also, essentially, a failure, since although the assembled lords were allowed to swear oaths to Llywelyn and Dafydd, their homage was specifically reserved by Henry III.[31] Despite Llywelyn's efforts in 1238, his death in 1240 was followed by the collapse of his hegemony and conflict between Dafydd and Gruffudd, a conflict into which other Welsh lords and ultimately the English Crown were all sucked.[32] In August 1241, at Gwern Eigron near Rhuddlan, Dafydd was forced to come to terms with Henry III, acknowledging that he and his brother held their portions of Gwynedd in chief from the Crown, handing over Gruffudd, who had been in captivity in Criccieth since September 1240, and returning to Henry III all the homages of Welsh lords held by Dafydd's father.[33] What is striking about the events of 1240–1 is the extent of Dafydd's isolation.[34] Not only was Gruffudd a popular figure, but other Welsh lords undoubtedly saw the strife between the brothers, and Henry III's intervention on behalf of Gruffudd, as a means of dismantling the hegemony constructed by Llywelyn; furthermore, Henry III was more than capable of manipulating Welsh aristocratic sentiment against Dafydd.[35]

Where Llywelyn failed in 1238, his grandson succeeded in 1267, in the aftermath of the Barons' War. Llywelyn ap Gruffydd aligned himself with the

---

[28] *AWR*, no. 37; Davies, *Age of Conquest*, pp. 227–36.
[29] Davies, *Age of Conquest*, pp. 236–5, 308–30; see, for instance, Llywelyn ap Iorwerth's grant of Llandimôr, in Morgannwg, to Morgan Gam (d. 1241), lord of Morgannwg (*AWR*, no. 239).
[30] *Brut Pen. 20, s.a.* 1238.
[31] *CR 1237–42*, pp. 123–5; series of letters dated 7 March 1238.
[32] Williams, 'The Succession to Gwynedd'.
[33] *AWR*, no. 300; *CPR 1232–47*, p. 264; *Brut Pen. 20, s.a.* 1241.
[34] Williams, 'The Succession to Gwynedd', pp. 398–403.
[35] Williams, 'The Succession to Gwynedd, p. 403.

Montfortian rebels; indeed, he subsequently married Simon de Montfort's daughter Eleanor. Some measure of Llywelyn's intent can be judged from a document sometimes called the 'Treaty of Pipton', agreed between Llywelyn and Montfort, which acknowledged Llywelyn as 'prince of Wales' and in this respect presaged the agreement made between Llywelyn and Henry III two years later.[36] Despite the collapse of the baronial cause following the battle of Evesham, Llywelyn was able to negotiate with Henry III from a position of relative strength.[37] The end result was the 1267 Treaty of Montgomery, agreed between Llywelyn and Henry III and brokered by Ottobuono, the papal legate.[38] Among other things, the treaty accorded English royal recognition of a title first recorded in 1258, that of 'prince of Wales';[39] moreover, the treaty gave Llywelyn the homage and fealty of all the Welsh barons of Wales ('omnium baronum Wallie Wallensium'), except for that of Maredudd ap Rhys (d. 1271), a grandson of the Lord Rhys and lord of Ystrad Tywi.[40] The net result was to create the principality that Llywelyn ap Iorwerth had tried and failed to achieve nearly thirty years earlier.

The importance and increasing sophistication of the government of thirteenth-century Gwynedd is also reflected in the documentary record; the surviving *acta* of the Welsh princes in the century and a half before the conquest of 1283 is dominated by the acts of the thirteenth-century rulers of Gwynedd: nearly 250 of the surviving 618 native Welsh *acta* were issued by Llywelyn ap Iorwerth and his successors alone. Not only, though, is this volume of material a reflection of the importance of Gwynedd in the thirteenth century, it also reflects an ever closer engagement with the English Crown and its administrative offices; much of the surviving correspondence issued by the rulers of Gwynedd was addressed to the English Crown or its agents. Even allowing for the fact that correspondence with the English state stood a much greater chance of preservation than anything else, this still points to key tensions at the heart of Anglo-Welsh relations in the thirteenth century: the increasing institutional strength of the rulers of Gwynedd, and their increasing involvement in the politics and political structures of the Plantagenet world.[41]

---

[36] *AWR*, no. 361; J. B. Smith, *Llywelyn ap Gruffudd, Prince of Wales* (Cardiff, 1998), pp. 167–70.

[37] Davies, *Age of Conquest*, pp. 313–15.

[38] *AWR*, no. 363; *CChR*, ii, p. 81; *Littere Wallie*, pp. 1–4; Davies, *Age of Conquest*, pp. 315–17.

[39] *AWR*, no. 328; an agreement between Llywelyn, *princeps Wallie*, the earls of Menteith, Buchan, Mar and Ross, William de Maxwell, chamberlain of Scotland, and others, that none of the parties will make agreement with the king of England or his magnates, unless all do; *AWR*, pp. 500–1; Smith, *Llywelyn ap Gruffudd*, pp. 110–14; G. W. S. Barrow, 'Wales and Scotland in the Middle Ages', *Welsh History Review* 10 (1981), 302–19, at pp. 311–12.

[40] Llywelyn purchased Maredudd's homage for 5,000 marks in 1270 (*AWR*, no. 398).

[41] A. H. Pryce, 'Anglo-Welsh Agreements, 1201–77', in *Wales and the Welsh in the Middle Ages: Essays Presented to J. B. Smith*, ed. R. A. Griffiths and P. Schofield (Cardiff, 2011), pp. 1–19; A. D. Carr, 'Anglo-Welsh Relations, 1066–1282', in *England and her Neighbours, 1066–1453: Essays in Honour of Pierre Chaplais*, ed. M. Jones and M. Vale (London, 1989), pp. 121–38, at pp. 127–38; D. Stephenson, *The Governance of Gwynedd* (Cardiff, 1984), pp. 1–54.

As has already been noted, some 618 *acta* survive issued by the various Welsh princely dynasties in the twelfth and thirteenth centuries; of these, roughly two thirds date from the thirteenth century. This pattern suggests two things: first, the increasingly routine use of the written word in the administration of native Welsh polities;[42] second, and related to this, is that the increasing volume of surviving material also, in part, represents the increasing engagement between native Welsh rulers and their English neighbours, both in terms of their English baronial counterparts and the English state.[43]

At first glance, the external and internal features of the surviving *acta* seem to bear out the supposition that diplomatic practice in Wales was largely imitative of contemporary English practice.[44] The formulation of the documents, and, indeed, their physical appearance, where they survive, correspond closely to the documentary norms of the Anglo-Norman and Angevin worlds. Welsh lords adopted equestrian seals, while many of the surviving documents begin with the sort of address clauses common in English royal and baronial *acta*.[45] There is clearly a significant degree of truth in this supposition; part and parcel of Welsh engagement with the Angevin political world was imitation and partial adoption of its documentary and administrative culture. However, closer analysis of the *acta* suggests that this picture of imitation and adoption of Angevin documentary norms needs to be refined, in particular to restore to native lords and their clerks and administrators some measure of agency in how they engaged with the documentary and, indeed, political culture of the Angevin polity.[46] The adoption of new documentary forms and new administrative practices was, in fact, less about the imposition of external influence, or a dialogue between 'native and non-native', than about the complexities of power politics within Wales.[47] What some Welsh lords seem to have realised by the later twelfth century is that the writ charter, for instance, gave scope for the establishment and representation of novel political claims.[48] In particular, we can see the emergence in the charters of new conceptions of identity and political authority; it is in the charters that we see the emergence of the terms *Wallia* and *Walenses* to describe Wales and the Welsh, rather than forms of Old Welsh *Prydein* and its cognates.[49] We also see

---

42 See Stephenson, *Governance*, esp. pp. 21–40, for a discussion of the written word in the administration of Gwynedd during the thirteenth century; Pryce, 'Welsh Rulers and European Change', pp. 40–1, 44–6.

43 Pryce, 'Anglo-Welsh Agreements', pp. 9–13.

44 Much of the best discussion of Welsh diplomatic of the twelfth and thirteenth centuries is by Huw Pryce in *AWR*, pp. 47–142; see also C. L. G. Insley, 'From *rex Wallie* to *princeps Wallie*: Charters and State-Formation in Thirteenth-Century Wales', in *The Medieval State: Essays Presented to James Campbell*, ed. J. R. Maddicott and D. M. Palliser (London, 2000), pp. 179–96.

45 M. Siddons, 'Welsh Equestrian Seals', *National Library of Wales Journal* 23 (1983–4), 292–318; *AWR*, pp. 86–7.

46 Pryce, 'Welsh Rulers and European Change', pp. 45–51.

47 Pryce, 'Welsh Rulers and European Change', pp. 46–50.

48 See Insley, 'Kings, Lords, Charters', pp. 142–50.

49 Insley, 'Kings, Lords, Charters', pp. 148–9.

the regnal styles of rulers such as Owain Gwynedd and Rhys ap Gruffudd reflecting rule not over peoples or ethnicities, but over territories, and new territories at that – Wales (*Wallia*), North Wales (*Norwallie*) and South Wales (*Suthwallie*).[50]

It is the surviving charters issued by Welsh lords, in particular those issued by members of the leading dynasties, that form the focus for the remainder of this discussion. The texts that survive bear ample witness to the complexity of the relationship between native and non-native documentary practice. It seems clear that the Anglo-Norman form of writ charter had established itself as the main diplomatic form for the conveyance of land or rights by the second half of the twelfth century, almost certainly related to the establishment of Benedictine and Cistercian houses in *Pura Wallia*, or native Wales.[51] This form, in contrast to the earlier solemn diploma, generally begins with an address before progressing to the notification, with the dispositive verb expressed in the first person singular or plural, often in the past tense. By the mid-twelfth century there are references to warranties in such documents, and the writ-charters also include dating clauses (sometimes referring to place of issue) and witness lists, generally quite short. In those houses which shared patronage between English and Welsh lords, such as Margam Abbey in Morgannwg, Goldcliff Priory in Gwynllŵg/Gwent, or Basingwerk Abbey near Chester, the charters issued by Welsh lords conformed closely indeed to the diplomatic of charters issued by the English Crown and English magnates.[52] Further into native Wales, the use of these new diplomatic forms was somewhat more eclectic and less standardised, but still, broadly, conformed to the diplomatic norms outlined above.

However, it is also clear that Welsh lords and Welsh communities were able to use these new forms to their advantage. The writ charter provided lords with opportunities to demonstrate their power – at the gatherings where such charters were enacted, but also through the use of imagery on seals. The charter also provided rulers with a vehicle to establish new claims to power, or new ways of articulating their power. This can be seen most powerfully with the way in which the rulers of Gwynedd in the twelfth and thirteenth centuries evolved novel and ambitious regnal styles in their *acta*.[53] If the writ charter was one of the ways in which the Anglo-Norman world intruded into Wales, it was also one of the most important ways in which native Welsh rulers engaged with the world beyond Offa's Dyke. Ambitious rulers perforce needed to articulate their power and identity in ways that had valency in the wider Anglo-Norman world, but this also created opportunities for such rulers to expand their claims within native Wales.[54]

What the foregoing discussion suggests is that by the beginning of the thirteenth century native rulers and those who drew up their *acta* were impressively

---

[50] Insley, 'Kings, Lords, Charters', pp. 148–9.

[51] *AWR*, pp. 59–70.

[52] E.g. for Morgannwg, see *AWR*, pp. 106–112.

[53] *AWR*, pp. 74–9; Insley, 'From *rex Wallie* to *princeps Wallie*', pp. 192–4.

[54] See Insley, 'Kings, Lords, Charters'; and Pryce, 'Welsh Rulers and European Change', pp. 43–5.

skilled at adapting the writ charter to their own ends, especially in terms of advancing new claims to power. The adoption of new documentary forms also presumes the supersession of older ones. The Welsh certainly had a diplomatic tradition that pre-dated the Norman arrival in Wales, but the evidence seems to suggest that this older native tradition was abandoned during the twelfth century.[55]

This older 'Celtic' (or 'Latin') charter tradition was first outlined by Wendy Davies.[56] Davies argued that there were a range of diplomatic features specific to earlier medieval charters from Wales, Brittany, Ireland and Scotland that allowed historians to talk of a distinctive tradition of charter drafting.[57] In particular, the key features identified by Davies were, 'first, a structure determined by the consistent inclusion of three constituent parts, disposition, witness list and sanction', and second, the consistent use of the third person in the disposition. Generally, this tradition was confined to charters of the eleventh century or earlier, although examples from the twelfth century survive. In particular, the sole surviving charter in the name of Madog ap Maredudd, king of Powys between 1131 and 1161, conforms to a large extent, as Huw Pryce noted, to Davies's Latin charter model.[58] Pryce also argued that this charter, a grant of land at Trefeglwys in Powys issued at some point between 1131 and 1151, marked, as far as we can tell, the end of the 'Celtic' charter tradition in Wales.[59]

This is true, but only up to a point. Madog's charter is certainly the last surviving charter that largely conforms to Davies's 'Latin charter' model. However, it is possible to see a sort of diplomatic 'penumbra' around the 'Celtic' charter tradition, in particular features that occur in Celtic charters but were not exclusive to them, and could thus be found elsewhere in Western European diplomatic. The risk here is that any identification of 'Celtic' or 'native' diplomatic elements is drawn too tightly and might exclude elements in charter drafting that were probably native to Wales, even if they also occur elsewhere across Europe. So, Madog's charter might indeed have been the last Celtic charter in Wales, but only for a particular definition of 'Celtic charter'. If the net of diplomatic elements that might derive from native, pre-Norman traditions is cast more widely, then further charters that contain native elements can be identified that date from well

---

[55]   W. Davies, 'The Latin Charter-Tradition in Western Britain, Brittany and Ireland in the Early Medieval Period', in *Ireland in Early Mediaeval Europe: Studies in Memory of Kathleen Hughes*, ed. D. Whitelock, R. McKitterick and D. Dumville (Cambridge, 1982), pp. 258–80, at pp. 266–7; A. H. Pryce, 'The Church of Trefeglwys and the End of the "Celtic" Charter Tradition in Twelfth-Century Wales', *Cambridge Medieval Celtic Studies* 25 (1995), 15–54, esp. pp. 49–50.

[56]   Davies, 'Latin Charter-Tradition'; W. Davies, *An Early Welsh Microcosm: Studies in the Llandaff Charters* (London, 1978), pp. 7–14.

[57]   Davies, 'Latin Charter-Tradition', pp. 262–3; For a critique of the 'Celtic Latin charter' see D. Broun, *The Charters of Gaelic Scotland and Ireland in the Early and Central Middle Ages*, Quiggin Pamphlets on the Sources of Medieval Gaelic History 2 (Cambridge, 1995), esp. pp. 38–47.

[58]   *AWR*, no. 480, pp. 119–20; Pryce, 'The Church of Trefeglwys'.

[59]   Pryce, 'The Church of Trefeglwys', 49–50.

into the thirteenth century. These elements are: first, the presence of vernacular boundary clauses; second, the phrasing used to introduce the beneficiary of the charter; and third, the presence of *arengae* in a small number of charters.

Some thirty-four of the surviving corpus of princely *acta* from the period (around 540 complete documents) are charters which have some form of boundary clause.[60] While this appears a small number, this perspective is skewed by the large volume of diplomatic correspondence that survives between the rulers of Gwynedd (in particular) and the English Crown. If this is stripped out of the corpus and charters or related documents alone are considered, then the proportion with bounds is about 17% of the surviving total; still small, but much more significant. Within these thirty-four, there are a variety of modes of expression, ranging from detailed and long perambulations – such as Rhys ap Gruffudd's 1184 foundation charter for Strata Florida, or Llywelyn ap Iorwerth's charter for Aberconwy (c. 1199)[61] – to very brief descriptions of length and breadth, such as Gwenwynwyn ab Owain Cyfeiliog's 1205 charter for Strata Marcella.[62] The majority fall somewhere in between, often based on the formulation 'as far as … as far as …'; an example of this is provided by Maredudd ap Rhobert of Cedewain's grant to the Cistercian nuns of Llanllugan, issued at some point between 1216 and 1236, where the bounds are delineated by local rivers.[63] Generally speaking, the majority of the boundaries are in Latin, with the boundary points themselves in Welsh, but some, especially those connected with Strata Florida, contain a significant amount of Old Welsh beyond the topographical terms.

The pattern of survival already discussed above, to some extent, affects the picture, since over a third of the thirty-four sets of bounds come from charters preserved in the archive of Strata Marcella/Ystrad Marchell Abbey in southern Powys.[64] This, in turn, is a function of the careful preservation of the Strata Marcella records by the Wynn family of Gwydir Hall during and after the sixteenth century. The records of other Welsh houses were less fortunate in the aftermath of the Edwardian Conquest of 1282–4, and the double catastrophes of the 1536 Act of Union between England and Wales and the subsequent dissolution of religious communities. The survival of five charters with bounds from the Cistercian abbey of Strata Florida/Ystrad Fflur in Deheubarth is simply due to the fact they were all wrapped up in Edward I's great *inspeximus* of the abbey's muniments issued in 1285.[65] Elsewhere we are dependent on chance survivals, such as the charter for the nuns of Llanllugan already mentioned, or one of the handful of charters that survive from Cymer Abbey in Meirionydd, which in the thirteenth century was one of the most important religious communities in

---

[60] See below, Appendix 1.
[61] *AWR*, nos 28, 218.
[62] *AWR*, no. 569.
[63] *AWR*, no. 18.
[64] See above, n. 17.
[65] TNA, C 77/6 (Welsh roll, 13 Edward I), m. 2; This *inspeximus* was confirmed by Edward II in 1320 (TNA, C 66/153 (patent roll, 14 Edward II, pt. 1) m. 5; *CPR 1317–21*, p. 527).

Gwynedd, though that fact is not immediately apparent from the number of its charters that survived.[66]

It seems overwhelmingly likely that the incorporation of boundary clauses, in a number of forms, into Welsh charters during the twelfth and thirteenth centuries was a relic of earlier, native diplomatic practice and one which in some ways was remarkably durable, surviving as it did almost to the conquest of native Wales. It is possible to dismiss the boundary in Maredudd ab Owain ap Rhys's confirmation charter for Strata Florida, dateable to between 1235 and 1265, as simply copied from Rhys ap Gruffudd's original charter of 1184 – which it almost certainly is – but Llywelyn ap Gruffudd's 1247 charter for Basingwerk Abbey and Gruffudd ap Llywelyn's 1226 charter for Strata Marcella both seem to be genuinely late uses of a boundary clause.[67]

Two pieces of evidence for the antiquity of bounds in the charters of native Welsh rulers can be presented. The first is that the material contained in the early twelfth-century *Book of Llandaff* incorporates both detailed perambulations and a mixture of Welsh and Latin in the boundary clauses.[68] While there are debates over the antiquity of the charter texts embedded within *Liber Landavensis*, it is, at the very least, possible that this material dates back to the ninth or tenth century.[69] The use of detailed perambulations and vernacular sections of texts of course has parallels with Anglo-Saxon diplomatic practice, where, from the later ninth/early tenth century, detailed and often long circuits in the vernacular were a hallmark of Anglo-Saxon royal diplomas. It is tempting to see the use of similar boundary clauses in Welsh charters as imitative, but this temptation should, perhaps, be resisted. The Llandaff material suggests that such practice in Wales was at least coeval with that in England.

The second piece of evidence lies in the variety of different types of boundary clauses; this, too, suggests a measure of antiquity, rather than a recent practice imported in the eleventh or twelfth century. The Strata Florida boundaries most resemble those of *Liber Landavensis*, in terms of length, detail and the mixture of Latin and Welsh. The boundaries for Llywelyn ap Iorwerth's charters for Aberconwy and Cymer also contain long perambulations which mix Welsh topographical terms with Latin directions.[70] Elsewhere in Wales different types of boundary clause can be seen. In Morgannwg, those charters – generally surviving from Margam Abbey – that have bounds incorporate brief descriptions, usually referring to major features such as rivers and streams, and do not include detailed perambulations.[71] In the material preserved in the Strata Marcella collection,

---

[66] *AWR*, nos 18, 229; J. B. Smith, 'Cymer Abbey and the Welsh Princes', *Journal of the Merioneth Historical and Record Society* 13:2 (1999), 101–18.

[67] *AWR*, nos 68, 282, 321.

[68] *The Text of the Book of Llan Dav, reproduced from the Gwysaney Manuscript*, ed. J. Gwenogvryn Evans with J. Rhys (Oxford, 1893); W. Davies, *An Early Welsh Microcosm*, p. 8.

[69] Davies, *An Early Welsh Microcosm*, pp. 7–8, 13–14, 28–32, 160–3; J. R. Davies, *The Church of Llandaff and the Norman Church in Wales* (Woodbridge, 2003), pp. 63–108.

[70] *AWR*, nos 218, 229.

[71] *AWR*, nos 134, 136, 137, 142, 184.

a variety of different boundary clauses can be seen, ranging from very detailed perambulations to the brief and laconic 'length and breadth' description already alluded to in Gwenwynwyn ab Owain's charter of 1205.[72] One might expect more consistency if the boundary clause was a diplomatic practice imported from England in the eleventh or twelfth century.

It is also important here to consider the way in which these charters were produced. While there is limited evidence of the development of some sort of secretariat in Gwynedd in the thirteenth century, it is very likely indeed that most of the charters here were produced by the beneficiary.[73] Where, in the case of Margam and Strata Marcella, the surviving archive contains a large number of charters from different grantors, this impression is confirmed.[74] What is striking, therefore, and important to note, is that those religious houses that seem to have made the most use of boundary descriptions and perambulations into the later twelfth and thirteenth centuries were new, Cistercian foundations, all daughter houses of Whitland. A note of caution needs to be sounded here, though, since those houses were perhaps the most likely to be systematic in their record keeping and, perhaps, to transmit their archives intact at the dissolution. Nevertheless, it is an important point that the preservation of elements of native, pre-Norman diplomatic practice in Wales seems to have been at the hands of the new, reformed religious orders, orders one might otherwise have thought to be a force for cultural assimilation in the other direction.[75] That said, it should also be remembered that some of the Cistercian houses in Wales functioned as centres of cultural memory; this is particularly true of Strata Florida, the likely *locus* for the compilation of the *Brut y Tywysogion* and its satellites; in this, Strata Florida seems to have inherited its role from the much older native foundation of Llanbadarn Fawr.[76] Aberconwy Abbey, in Gwynedd, also functioned as an important centre of cultural and dynastic memory; it had been founded by Owain Gwynedd's descendents and was where many of his family were interred.[77] By the time of the Edwardian conquest the Cistercians had become an integral part of the political, social and institutional fabric of native polities.[78]

---

[72] For detailed perambulations, see *AWR*, nos 541, 542, 555, 563; for Gwenwynwyn's charter of 1205, see *AWR*, no. 569.

[73] On the emergence of some sort of structured secretariat in Gwynedd, see Stephenson, *Governance*, pp. 26–39; *AWR*, pp. 132–42; Insley, 'From *rex Wallie* to *princeps Wallie*', pp. 194–6.

[74] Patterson, *Margam*, pp. 68–80; *Charters of Ystrad Marchell*, ed. Thomas, pp. 109–11.

[75] Bartlett, *The Making of Europe*, pp. 255–60.

[76] J. E. Lloyd, 'The Welsh Chronicles', *Proceedings of the British Academy* 14 (1928), 369–91; *Brut Pen. 20*, pp. xxxix–xliv.

[77] R. Hays, *The History of the Abbey of Aberconwy, 1186–1537* (Cardiff, 1963), pp. 5–6; G. Richards, 'The Church of St Mary and All Saints, Conway', *Journal of the History Society of the Church of Wales* 16 (1966), 28–80. Much of Aberconwy's history and, by association, that of its benefactors is preserved in the fourteenth-century cartulary chronicle of the abbey: BL, Harley MS 3725; 'Register and Chronicle of the Abbey of Aberconway from the Harleian MS. 3725', ed. H. Ellis, *Camden Miscellany* 1 (1847).

[78] D. H. Williams, *The Welsh Cistercians* (Tenby, 1984), pp. 32–42; D. H. Williams, *Atlas of Cistercian Lands in Wales* (Cardiff, 1990), pp. 10–18.

It might be argued that the main imperative for the preservation of boundary clauses in native charters was practical, and there is certainly something in this. Boundaries clearly did play an important part in the mechanism of dispute settlement; as late as 1280 resolution of a dispute between Cynan ap Maredudd and Strata Florida, brokered by the abbot of Whitland and Gruffudd ap Maredudd, lord of Ceredigion, hinged on a reading of the bounds of Rhys ap Gruffudd's original foundation charter of 1184.[79] Similarly, following the purchase by Ednyfed Fychan, Llywelyn ap Iorwerth's seneschal, of Rhosfynaich in 1230, bounds were included in Llywelyn ap Iorwerth's letter patent to forestall any dispute between Ednyfed and the heirs (*heredes*) – perhaps free proprietors – of the hamlet of Dineirth.[80]

However, there are other elements of twelfth-century Welsh diplomatic practice which might have their origins in pre-Norman custom and that have a less obvious practical aspect. Most significant of these is the phrasing used to introduce the beneficiary in the dispositive section of the charter. Very often, where the beneficiary was an ecclesiastic or religious community, the grant was made in the form 'to God, the Saint N and the community …'. This is in contrast to contemporary practice in English gifts and grants. Significantly, similar phrasing can be observed in the Llandaff material, and also in earlier Cornish charters from the tenth and eleventh centuries.[81] Although, in the most part, Anglo-Saxon charters for beneficiaries in Cornwall conform to the norms, inasmuch as there were any, of Anglo-Saxon diplomatic, it is significant that in the few cases where a Cornish religious community was the beneficiary, the grant was made to 'God, Saint N and the community'. The same is true of the one surviving indisputably native Cornish charter, an early tenth-century grant by a man identified as a *comes*, Maenchi, son of Pretignor, to St Heldenus.[82]

There are also a few twelfth- and thirteenth-century Welsh charters whose form departs from the basic 'address – notification – disposition – corroboration' form common to the vast majority of Welsh charters (as opposed to letters patent). Three charters, all from Powys, open with a verbal invocation, common in Anglo-Saxon charters but largely absent after 1100.[83] One of these Powyssian charters, a grant of 1191 by Gwenwynwyn ab Owain to Strata Marcella, also contains an *arenga*, which like a number of Anglo-Saxon proems, meditates on the importance of committing holy gifts to writing so as to ensure their commemoration. [84] Rather more narrative *arengae* can also be found in three charters

---

[79] *AWR*, no. 76.
[80] *AWR*, no. 260.
[81] Davies, 'Latin Charter-Tradition', pp. 263–6; Davies, *Early Welsh Microcosm*, p. 7.
[82] P. H. Sawyer, *Anglo-Saxon Charters: An Annotated List and Bibliography* (London, 1968), no. 1207; O. J. Padel, 'Two New Pre-Conquest Charters for Cornwall', *Journal of Cornish Studies* 6 (1978), 20–7; C. Insley, 'Athelstan, Charters and the English in Cornwall', *Charters and Charter Scholarship in Britain and Ireland*, ed. M. T. Flanagan and J. Green (Basingstoke, 2003), pp. 15–31, at pp. 20–1.
[83] *AWR*, nos 539, 542, 544; see below, Appendix 2.
[84] *AWR*, no. 544; see below, Appendix 3.

of Llywelyn ap Iorwerth, to, respectively, Cymer Abbey (1209), Ynys Llannog Priory on Anglesey (1221) and the Hospitallers of Dolgynwal (1225).[85] In these three the *arenga* takes the form not of a general meditation, but a specific discussion of why Llywelyn had chosen to make the grant.

Although the strong possibility exists that these diplomatic quirks represent the relics of an older diplomatic tradition, the issue is not clear cut. Although both the use of the verbal invocation and the *arenga* is indebted to the diploma, Huw Pryce has suggested that, in the case of Gwenywynwyn's charter at least, the temptation to see this as an example of native charter-writing practice should be resisted, since *arengae* do not appear to have been a feature of the Latin/Celtic charter tradition represented by Madog ap Maredudd's charter.[86] Instead, Pryce suggests a Continental, Burgundian model, perhaps via Strata Marcella's mother house, Whitland Abbey, and ultimately Clairvaux. This is quite possibly the case for Gwenwynwyn's charter, but it is possible that in the three charters from Gwynedd, all for – and possibly produced by – different beneficiaries, the *arenga* represents a relic of older traditions of charter-writing. The problem here is the desperate lack of pre-eleventh-century charter material from Wales, beyond the texts in *Liber Landavensis*. Pryce may well be right that a Continental model should be considered for the phrasing of Gwenwynwyn's charter, but the absence of similar formulation from material in Llandaff is not, in itself, conclusive proof that there was no Welsh origin.

The charters surveyed in this essay provide a microcosm of the way in which native society in Wales, its rulers and the men who drew up their *acta* engaged with the Angevin and Plantagenet worlds. These individuals were alive to the advantages new documentary forms offered in helping them to establish new claims to authority and to underpin their rule in increasingly systematic ways. It seems likely that by the mid-thirteenth century the rulers of Gwynedd possessed something which – if not a chancery in the strict sense – certainly had some of a chancery's functions.[87] Equally, those who drew up these princes' *acta*, even in Gwynedd, which was much the most structured Welsh polity, were able to integrate older documentary traditions with new ones. In part this may have been a function of practical necessity, but it may also have been for wider cultural reasons; the houses that produced many of the surviving *acta*, although belonging to European reformed orders, were peopled by Welshmen, who were deeply engaged in the political and cultural lives of the native lordships. In this respect we should set the diplomatic of Welsh princely *acta* in the wider context of literary and historical activity at these houses. It is surely no accident that Cistercian houses which produced the most idiosyncratic documents were also those which were centres of native dynastic memory, both before and after the conquest of 1283. As Pryce reminds us, it is important to see the dynamic in shaping Welsh political culture – including documentary culture – in the later twelfth and

---

[85] *AWR*, nos 229, 250, 256; see below, Appendix 3.
[86] *AWR*, pp. 124–5.
[87] See above, n. 73.

thirteenth centuries not in terms of a simple polarity between native and out-sider, or conservative and progressive, but in terms of political advantage. Welsh rulers and their administrators, while undoubtedly much less powerful than the English Crown, were not simply passive onlookers in the face of Angevin cultural imperialism; they were able to pursue their own agendas. Ultimately, the ways in which native society in Wales engaged with the Angevin and Plantagenet worlds were complex, and the traffic was not completely one way.

Appendix 1: Twelfth- and Thirteenth-Century Welsh Charters with Boundary Clauses

AWR[88] 18 (Cedewain): Maredudd ap Rhobert for Llanllugan, 1216×36

AWR 25 (Dehebuarth): Rhys ap Gruffudd for Strata Florida, 1165×82[89]

AWR 28 (Deheubarth): Rhys ap Gruffudd for Strata Florida, 1184

AWR 35 (Deheubarth): Maelgwyn ap Rhys for Strata Florida, 1198; confirmation of *AWR* 28

AWR 49 (Deheubarth): Rhys *Gryg* ap Rhys for Talley Abbey, 1197×1233

AWR 55 (Deheubarth): Rhys *Ieuanc* ap Gruffudd for Strata Florida, 1202

AWR 68 (Ceredigion): Maredudd ab Owain for Talley Abbey, 1235×65

AWR 76 (Ceredigion): Arbitration between Strata Florida and Cynan ap Maredudd ab Owain, 1280

AWR 134, 136 (Morgannwg): Morgan ap Caradog for Margam Abbey, 1199

AWR 137 (Morgannwg): Morgan ap Caradog for Margam Abbey, 1200×08

AWR 142 (Morgannwg): Morgan ap Caradog for Margam Abbey, 1205

AWR 184 (Morgannwg): Morgan ab Owain for Margam Abbey, 1215×22

AWR 218 (Gwynedd): Llywelyn ap Iorwerth for Aberconwy Abbey, 1199

AWR 229 (Gwynedd): Llywelyn ap Iorwerth for Cymer Abbey, 1209

AWR 260 (Gwynedd): Llywelyn ap Iorwerth for Ednyfed Fychan, 1230

AWR 282 (Gwynedd): Gruffudd ap Llywelyn for Strata Marcella Abbey, 1226

AWR 321 (Gwynedd): Llywelyn ap Gruffudd for Basingwerk Abbey, 1247

AWR 367 (Gwynedd): Llywelyn ap Gruffudd for Beddgelert Priory, 1267

AWR 467 (Gwynllŵg): Hywel ap Iorwerth for Glastonbury Abbey, 1179×84

AWR 473 (Gwynllŵg): Hywel ap Iorwerth for Iorwerth son of Caradog *Dapifer*, 1211×17

AWR 474 (Gwynllŵg): Hywel ap Iorwerth for Goldcliff Priory, 1211×17

AWR 483 (Powys Fadog): Elise ap Madog for Strata Marcella, 1183

AWR 539 (Powys Wenwynwyn): Owain Cyfeiliog for Strata Marcella, 1170

AWR 541 (Powys Wenwynwyn): Gwenwynwyn ab Owain Cyfeiliog for Strata Marcella, 1185

AWR 541 (Powys Wenwynwyn): Gwenwynwyn ab Owain for Strata Marcella, 1187

---

[88] *The Acts of Welsh Rulers, 1120–1283*, ed. H. Pryce with C. Insley (Cardiff, 2005).

[89] Mention only, in a confirmation of Henry II, 1165×82.

AWR 549 (Powys Wenwynwyn): Gwenwynwyn ab Owain for Strata Marcella, 1197×1216

AWR 552 (Powys Wenwynwyn): Gwenwynwyn ab Owain for Strata Marcella, 1199

AWR 555 (Powys Wenwynwyn): Gwenwynwyn ab Owain for Strata Marcella, 1200

AWR 563 (Powys Wenwynwyn): Gwenwynwyn ab Owain for Strata Marcella, 1201

AWR 564 (Powys Wenwynwyn): Gwenwynwyn ab Owain for Strata Marcella, 1202

AWR 563 (Powys Wenwynwyn): Gwenwynwyn ab Owain for Strata Marcella, 1204

AWR 569 (Powys Wenwynwyn): Gwenwynwyn ab Owain for Strata Marcella, 1205

AWR 616 (Senghenydd): Gruffudd ab Ifor for Margam Abbey, 1158×74

Appendix 2: Twelfth- and Thirteenth-Century Welsh Charters with Verbal Invocations

AWR 539 (Powys Wenwynwyn): Owain Cyfeiliog for Strata Marcella, 1170

AWR 542 (Powys Wenwynwyn): Gwenwynwyn ab Owain for Strata Marcella, 1187

AWR 544 (Powys Wenwynwyn): Gwenwynwyn for ab Owain Strata Marcella, 1191

Appendix 3: Twelfth- and Thirteenth-Century Welsh Charters with *arengae*

AWR 229 (Gwynedd): Llywelyn ap Iorwerth for Cymer Abbey, 1209

AWR 250 (Gwynedd): Llywelyn ap Iorwerth for Ynys Llannog Priory, 1221

AWR 256 (Gwynedd): Llywelyn ap Iorwerth for the Hospitallers of Dolgynwal, 1225

AWR 544 (Powys Wenwynwyn): Gwenwynwyn for ab Owain Strata Marcella, 1191

8

An Inventory of Gifts to King Henry III, 1234–5

Nicholas Vincent

Now that the fine rolls of Henry III's reign are emerging into the public domain, and now that we have a far clearer understanding of royal finances as recorded in the various enrolments of the Exchequer and Wardrobe, a question of significance looms even larger than it did in the days of Reginald Lane Poole or Sir James Ramsay: to what extent can the Exchequer accounts of income and expenditure be relied upon for an accurate assessment of royal revenue? It has long been recognised that the Exchequer accounts have to be used with care. Covering only that portion of the king's revenue derived from the county farms, from sheriffs, and from other such 'routine' sources as fines and the profits of justice, they omit an indeterminate but substantial proportion of the money that flowed each year into the king's coffers. The profits of war, of backstairs intrigue, of money raised in loans or from the regular pawning of the king's valuables, all of these sources of income, and more, go unreported in the standard Exchequer accounts.[1] In what follows, I shall examine just one such potential bounty: the gifts and precious objects presented to the king by courtiers and diplomatic contacts. Here I shall bring into play a record of such gifts produced over a period of six months in 1234–5. As we shall see, this record is of far more than merely financial significance.

Edited below, our list of treasures occupies one side of a membrane of parchment, today preserved amongst the Chancery Miscellanea of The National Archives (C 47/3/4/1). The parchment itself is holed and rodent damaged, leading to the loss of a small number of letters and words. First noticed in 1857, and resignalled in a 1964 guide to royal household records in the Public Record Office, its significance was not properly appreciated until the 1990s.[2] Since then

---

[1]   The most sophisticated handling of Henry III's revenues is that presented by R. C. Stacey, *Politics, Policy, and Finance under Henry III, 1216–1245* (Oxford, 1987); see also N. Barratt, 'Finance on a Shoestring: The Exchequer in the Thirteenth Century', in *English Government in the Thirteenth Century*, ed. A. Jobson (Woodbridge, 2004), pp. 71–86; R. Cassidy, '"Recorda Splendidissima": The Use of Pipe Rolls in the Thirteenth Century', *HR* 85 (2011), 1–12. For the Wardrobe, and for the slow development of anything approaching modern profit and loss accountancy, see the introduction to *The Wardrobe Accounts of Henry III*, ed. B. L. Wild, PRS n.s. 58 (London, 2012), esp. pp. xliii, li, with important remarks on pawning at pp. lii, civ, cxiv. For assistance with what follows, I am indebted to David Carpenter, Hugh Doherty, David Jacoby, Frédérique Lachaud, Tom Licence, Nigel Morgan, Jenny Stratford, and, especially, to Ben Wild and Louise Wilkinson.
[2]   In a chapter on Isabella, the daughter of King John, M. A. E. Green discussed 'a memorandum roll of presents given and received by Henry the preceding Christmas … Among these

it has several times been noticed in print, most substantially by Ben Wild, who in 2010 published the text that occupies the reverse side of the membrane on which our list is preserved.[3] The text published by Wild, which when rolled up would have formed the outer face of the roll, lists, in three columns with extensive annotation, nearly one hundred individual entries both of gifts made to King Henry III and of purchases made for the king's Wardrobe between 17 December 1234 and 7 May 1235. Most of these gifts were either of cups of silver-gilt plate, or of belts of gold or silver thread, the listing of cups and belts being accompanied by their equivalent sterling weight values. The total arrived at here approaches £139 in sterling weight: by no means a king's ransom, yet nonetheless a substantial supplement to Henry III's daily cash receipts.[4] As Wild remarks, the list of plate and belts published in 2010 is important for a number of reasons. As 'the earliest and fullest record of royal gift-giving to survive from medieval England', it reveals the role played by largesse at court, listing gifts to the king which, as the record itself makes plain, were in most cases then distributed by the king himself as gifts to others.[5] It covers a period of considerable significance in English history, yet one for which the corresponding Chancery *liberate* rolls, otherwise our chief source for royal gift-giving, are lost.[6] Following the collapse of the regime headed by Peter des Roches, bishop of Winchester, this marked the start of Henry III's first period of truly personal rule, a period during which Henry may have been particularly keen to display his pomp and circumstance.[7] A number of the items inventoried were offered as gifts to those such as Hubert de Burgh or the bishop of Carlisle, Walter Mauclerk, who had suffered under des Roches's regime.[8]

All told, under sixty headings the record edited by Wild lists ninety-eight items given to the king by thirty-five individuals, in turn redistributed among

was a table and tablets of Sardinian ivory, which the Countess of Ponthieu had given to the king, and a chess-table and chess-men, enshrined in a casket of ivory, which he had received from the prior of Jerusalem; also twenty-four zones of silk and goldsmiths' work, gifts to the king from Adam of Shoreditch, and other goldsmiths', referring here to 'Miscellaneous rolls in the Tower no. 31': see M. A. E. Green, *The Lives of the Princesses of England from the Norman Conquest*, 6 vols (London, 1849–55), ii, p. 13. For subsequent listing, see *List of Documents Relating to the Household and Wardrobe, John–Edward I*, Public Record Office Handbooks 7 (London, 1964), p. 77 ('Jewels, Plate, Books etc … Account of receipts and issues'), and for the citation of this list as early as 1981 for its philological significance, see below no. 10n.

[3]   N. Vincent, *The Holy Blood: King Henry III and the Westminster Blood Relic* (Cambridge, 2001), p. 23; N. Vincent, 'The Pilgrimages of the Angevin Kings of England, 1154–1272', in *Pilgrimage: The English Experience from Becket to Bunyan*, ed. C. Morris and P. Roberts (Cambridge, 2002), pp. 12–45, at pp. 35–6; N. Vincent, 'King Henry III and the Blessed Virgin Mary', in *The Church and Mary*, ed. R. N. Swanson, Studies in Church History 39 (Woodbridge, 2004), pp. 126–46, at pp. 135–6; B. L. Wild, 'A Gift Inventory from the Reign of Henry III', *EHR* 125 (2010), 514–69.

[4]   Wild, 'Gift Inventory', p. 538.

[5]   Wild, 'Gift Inventory', pp. 529–30.

[6]   The *liberate* rolls are lost for the years 18–20 Henry III (October 1233–October 1236).

[7]   Wild, 'Gift Inventory', pp. 530–1.

[8]   Wild, 'Gift Inventory', pp. 543–5, and cf. below no. 20n.

at least fifty-two beneficiaries of royal largesse.[9] The chronology of gift-giving is itself of significance, the list placing particular emphasis upon New Year's gifts (far more important than those made at Christmas).[10] The inventory also sheds light both on the activities of the king's Wardrobe officials and on the nature of royal record-keeping. The majority of cups and belts recorded as gifts to Henry III were kept by the Wardrobe for between five and nine months before being redistributed as gifts from the king. The fact that both their receipt and their eventual destination were recorded on the roll, in an inventory corrected and updated over a period of at least eighteen months, suggests that the Wardrobe assigned a unique mark to each incoming gift.[11] Furthermore, the very fact that such details were recorded suggests a court in which luxuries, although abundant, were judged worth individual listing; in other words, a court whose record-keeping was itself a function of resources judged far from limitless. As I have remarked elsewhere, compared to the medieval German emperors or the sheikhs of modern Arabia, the Plantagenet kings possessed financial resources that had to be very carefully stewarded. In these circumstances, necessity became the mother of administrative invention, leading to the precocious emergence of accounts and enrolments for Plantagenet England, records which are today the envy of historians from parts of Europe whose own financial resources the thirteenth-century Plantagenet kings might themselves have struggled to match.[12] The luxuries listed can themselves help to advance our knowledge of the materiality of royal largesse. No items of royal plate are known to survive from as early as the reign of Henry III. There is, however, a sword belt, no doubt similar to various of those listed in our inventory, which was offered as a diplomatic gift slightly later in Henry III's reign and is today preserved at Burgos in Spain.[13]

In administrative terms, the roll that survives to us, part edited by Wild, the rest edited below, can be categorised as the first surviving 'rotulus de particulis' intended to be employed in the drawing up of the Wardrobe's accounts as audited at the king's Exchequer. Many other such 'rotuli de particulis' are known to have been made. Of these, the vast majority for Henry III's reign have been lost.[14] From 1236, though, the Wardrobe accounts include a specific section, subsequently described as the 'jewel account' (*compotus de jocalibus*), offering a bald list of items of plate, textiles, rings, brooches, garlands and so forth, that remained in the king's custody.[15] This shows that such items were of sufficient monetary

---

[9] Wild, 'Gift Inventory', pp. 533–4, 536–7.

[10] Wild, 'Gift Inventory', pp. 535, 541–3, 545.

[11] Wild, 'Gift Inventory', pp. 537–8, 539–40.

[12] N. Vincent, 'Why 1199? Bureaucracy and Enrolment under John and his Contemporaries', in *English Government in the Thirteenth Century*, ed. A. Jobson (Woodbridge, 2004), pp. 17–48, at p. 20.

[13] Wild, 'Gift Inventory', pp. 535–6, and see here B. L. Wild, 'Emblems and Enigmas: Revisiting the "Sword" Belt of Fernando de la Cerda', *JMH* 37 (2011), 378–96.

[14] Wild, 'Gift Inventory', p. 540, and at much greater length in the introduction to *Wardrobe Accounts*, esp. pp. xxv–xxxv.

[15] *Wardrobe Accounts*, pp. xlix, 10–14, 26–9, and *passim*.

value to merit an account in their own right. In this context, it should be noted, 'jewels' (*jocalia*) are to be interpreted not in the sense of precious stones but as gifts and presents that might bring a smile to the face, a point of no small significance when it comes to our interpretation of the word *jocalia* as employed in other royal accounts, not least those of Henry III's father, King John.[16] From the period immediately before the introduction of 'jewel accounts' to the Wardrobe accounts enrolled in the Exchequer pipe rolls, at least two 'rotuli de particulis' survive from the single year 19 Henry III (October 1234–October 1235): the roll considered here (TNA, C 47/3/4/1) and another (TNA, C 47/3/3) that records textiles and items of clothing both for the king's own use and dispatched to Germany as the trousseau of the king's sister Isabella, who married the Emperor Frederick II at Worms on 15 July 1235.[17] Another such roll (TNA, C 47/3/43/3), datable only approximately to the period between May 1234 and October 1236, records the clothing allowances of 169 persons serving in the royal household.[18] As we shall see, gifts associated with Isabella's marriage also occur on both sides of the present gift roll. It is thus a possibility that, for reasons now unrecoverable, records touching upon Isabella's trousseau were preserved in the Wardrobe when all other such 'rotuli de particulis' were lost or destroyed. Alternatively, and perhaps more likely, the survival of these particular rolls was the outcome of the decision to commence the enrolment of Wardrobe accounts, and with them the pipe roll's 'compotus de jocalibus', from May 1234. This would make the surviving rolls the earliest in the series of 'rotuli de particulis' perhaps thereafter preserved in a degree of archival limbo.[19] Whatever the reason, the survival of such rolls for part of the year 19 Henry III must be considered fortuitous, shedding much light on the material realities of the court.

The text that presently concerns us, originally written on the inside face of the roll, shares all of the points of interest attributed to its companion list edited

[16] For a brief survey of the jewel lists of King John, see N. Vincent, 'The Great Lost Library of England's Medieval Kings? Royal Use and Ownership of Books, 1066–1300', in *1000 Years of Royal Books and Manuscripts*, ed. K. Doyle and S. McKendrick (London, 2013), pp. 73–112, at pp. 79–80, 104 n. 43. For various such lists that specifically refer to 'jocalia', see *RLP*, pp. 119, 145, 148b–149, the last of these including items such as silk belts that would not today be classed as 'jewels'. For a similar use, in April 1235, see *CR 1234–37*, p. 72. For the later jewel accounts of Eleanor of Provence, Henry III's queen, now TNA, E 101/349/6, 7, 12–15, 21, 23, 25, and E 101/684/56/1, see M. Howell, *Eleanor of Provence: Queenship in Thirteenth-Century England* (Oxford, 1998), pp. 78–80, 169–70.

[17] First noticed by Green, *Lives of the Princesses of England*, pp. 13–16. Edited by B. L. Wild as 'The Empress's New Clothes: A "Rotulus Pannorum" of Isabella, Sister of King Henry III, Bride of Emperor Frederick II', in *Medieval Clothing and Textiles VII*, ed. R. Netherton and G. R. Owen-Crocker (Woodbridge, 2011), pp. 1–31, and see also L. J. Wilkinson, 'The Imperial Marriage of Isabella of England, Henry III's Sister', in *The Rituals and Rhetoric of Queenship: Medieval to Early Modern*, ed. E. Oakley-Brown and L. J. Wilkinson (Dublin, 2009), pp. 20–36, at p. 30.

[18] As noted by Wild, 'The Empress's New Clothes', pp. 12–13.

[19] The audited accounts of the Wardrobe for the period 17 May 1234–3 May 1236 are today preserved on the pipe roll for the year 19 Henry III, whence *Wardrobe Accounts*, pp. 1–14.

in 2010. To these it adds several further elements. In essence, it continues the listing of gifts made to and from the king, but inventories a far more diverse series of objects presented on twenty-four specified dates between 6 December 1234 and 25 June 1235. All told, under twenty-six headings, the list details sixty-six individual presents made to the king, sometimes of single objects, sometimes of several or an unspecified number.[20] These gifts were made by twenty individuals, twelve of them from Henry's realm. Some were religious figures (the archbishop and the archdeacon of Dublin, the bishop of Carlisle, the prior of the Hospitallers, the abbots of St Osyth's and Bury St Edmunds, the abbess of Wherwell and the prioress of Amesbury), others were secular, such as the earl and countess of Cornwall, the countess of Warenne and the burgesses of Colchester. Eight of the donors were foreign, including the Emperor Frederick II, the countess of Ponthieu, the Master of the Temple in Jerusalem, the Hospital of Jerusalem, an unspecified group of Franciscans (perhaps from the Latin Empire of Constantinople), and three lesser individuals (Anselin de Norhoud, John of Saxony and Master Peter the surgeon). Three donors (the bishop of Carlisle, the prior of the English Hospitallers, and the countess of Cornwall) are recorded as making gifts on more than one occasion.[21] In turn, the roll records the redistribution of various of these gifts on twenty-one separate occasions between 1 January 1235 and 16 July 1236. Many gifts are specified as being retained for the king's own use or as being sent to the king's galleys, falconers, tailors or Wardrobe keepers.[22] Others were used as royal offerings to the saints or, in one instance, to the Oxford Dominicans.[23] For the rest, our roll reports eleven individuals as receiving gifts from the king. These included members of the king's own family (his brother Richard of Cornwall; his future queen, Eleanor of Provence; his sister, Isabella; his uncle by marriage, William of Savoy, bishop-elect of Valence);[24] Olaf, king of Man; the earls of Derby, Lincoln and Pembroke; and the relatively humble knight Aimery de Sacy.[25]

Various of these persons, both donors and beneficiaries, are also recorded giving or receiving gifts on the other side of the roll, as edited by Ben Wild.

[20]   For example, the thirty crossbows gifted to the king on 18 February 1235 (below no. 14), or the cross with an unspecified number of relics (below no. 22) given to the king on Easter Sunday, 8 April 1235.

[21]   The bishop of Carlisle on 1 and 6 January 1235 (below nos 5–6), the countess of Cornwall on 12 and 14 January 1235 (below nos 8–9), and the prior of the Hospitallers on ?26 December 1234, 1 March and 17 May 1235 (below nos 4, 16, 24).

[22]   Below nos 1, 5.1–3, 6, 10.1, 13.3, 13.26, 14 (for the use of the king's galleys), 17, 18–20, 23, 25.1, and possibly 13.5.

[23]   Below nos 13.4, 13.10 (Dominicans of Oxford), 13.11–12, 13.14, 13.16–17, 24.1.

[24]   Below nos 13.23 (a Turkish bow to Richard of Cornwall); 10.2–3, 11 (cloths and balsam for Eleanor of Provence and her uncle); 8, 16, 21 (cushions, gaming sets and a cross with relics for Isabella).

[25]   Below nos 5.4 (Aimery de Sacy), 13.7 (earl of Lincoln), 13.19 (king of Man), 13.20 (Earl Ferrers), 13.26 (Gilbert Marshal, earl of Pembroke), and cf. no. 13.5 (a camlet for W[alter] of Kirkham, which may in fact be not so much a gift as the delivery of an item for royal use to the keeper of the king's Wardrobe).

The bishop of Carlisle, for example, who in the present list is recorded giving goshawks and fur-trimmed items of clothing to the king on 1 and 6 January 1235, appears in the other record giving cups and items of plate on 1 January and, also on 1 January, receiving from the king a cup that was originally gifted by the bishop of Chichester.[26] Gifts to the king from the earl of Cornwall, from the prior of the Hospitallers, from the men of Colchester, and from the abbot of Bury St Edmunds are recorded in both lists,[27] as are gifts to the king's sister Isabella and to William de Ferrers, earl of Derby.[28] Our list includes a gift made to the king on 12 May 1235 by the mother of John of Saxony, described as the king's 'valletus'.[29] A month later, on 5 June, the companion list records that John was given a cup at the time of his knighting by the king.[30] Anselin de Norhoud, presented with a cup by the king on 11 March 1235, himself gave the king a golden cross with relics on Easter Sunday, 8 April.[31]

In diplomatic terms, our list is of significance not only for what it reveals of England's dealings with the Holy Roman Empire, and in particular for its extraordinary list of gifts made to Henry III by the Emperor Frederick II, but also for what it tells us of Henry's dealings with other powers, both neighbouring and distant.[32] It records, for example, gifts from the countess of Ponthieu, with whose daughter Henry III briefly contemplated marriage.[33] It sheds considerable light upon relations between England and the Latin East.[34] It adds to our knowledge of the circumstances in which Olaf, king of Man, renewed his homage to the English king in July 1235.[35] It illuminates the process by which Henry III entered into negotiations both for the marriage of his sister, Isabella, to the Emperor Frederick, and for his own marriage to Eleanor, daughter of the count of Provence.[36]

The only feature the objects recorded have in common is their portability; those who made presents at an itinerant court had to offer things that, although of high value, could be easily transported. The most common of

---

[26] Below nos 5–6; Wild, 'Gift Inventory', pp. 554–5 nos 15–17, 22.

[27] Below nos 12 (Richard of Cornwall, 8 February 1235), 18 (Colchester, 6 March 1235), 19 (abbot of St Edmunds, 17 March 1235), 4, 16, 24 (prior of Hospital, ?26 December 1234, 1 March and 17 May 1235); Wild, 'Gift Inventory', p. 558 no. 35 (Richard of Cornwall, 12 January 1235), p. 559 no. 40 (prior of the Hospital, 22 February 1235), p. 559 no. 41 (Colchester, 4 March 1235), p. 561 no. 47 (abbot of St Edmunds, 20 March 1235).

[28] Below nos 8, 16, 21 (gifts for Isabella, 1 March and 22 April 1235), 13.20 (for William de Ferrers, 11 July 1235); Wild, 'Gift Inventory', p. 552 no. 6, pp. 562–3 nos 53–4, 56, 58, p. 565 no. 67, p. 569 no. 94 (gifts to Isabella, 8 May 1235), p. 559 no. 40 (William de Ferrers, at Glastonbury probably on 25 June 1235, cf. below no. 13.12).

[29] Below no. 23.

[30] Wild, 'Gift Inventory', p. 553 no. 13.

[31] Below no. 22; Wild, 'Gift Inventory', p. 558 no. 37.

[32] For the emperor, below no. 13.

[33] Below no. 21.

[34] Below nos 15.1–7.

[35] Below no. 13.19.

[36] For the king's marriage, below nos 21, 26, and cf. below, n. 176.

the gifts listed below were textiles, recorded in twenty-eight instances.[37] The majority of these (eighteen individual entries) were delivered as part of a larger gift of treasures from the Emperor Frederick II to Henry III on 17 February 1235.[38] The emperor's bounty needs to be set in the context of the long list of cloths and finished items of clothing with which Isabella is recorded as leaving England on 11 May 1235, prior to her marriage with Frederick at Worms on 15 July.[39] Both lists include items of the very highest quality, not least, in the present instance, the emperor's gift of two cloths of gold decorated with images of eagles or peacocks, and of eight silk palls, or altar cloths, with geometric patterns.[40] It is important to note here that, although these gifts were part of a reciprocal exchange, the Wardrobe took care not to use any of the emperor's gifts of February 1235 in making up the trousseau with which Isabella was sent into Germany three months later. To have returned a gift, even accidentally, would have been a breach of good manners. This provides a further explanation of the care taken by the Wardrobe to inventory and mark each incoming gift. Only by such means could diplomatic embarrassments be avoided. Administrative invention was in this instance as much the product of courtesy as of financial necessity.

Besides cloth of gold and silk palls, we also find other textiles in our list: sendals/cendals (brightly coloured but inexpensive silks) of green or red, in two instances gifted by the emperor and described as sendals 'of Andros' (from the island of Andros in the Aegean, a major centre of silk production that was, from 1207, under the rule of members of the Dandolo family, victors of the Fourth Crusade);[41] red and yellow samite (heavier and more precious silk);[42] black and red camlets (expensive woollen cloth of uncertain composition, perhaps of camel or goat hair, woven in Syria), in one instance described as originating in Tripoli;[43]

---

[37] Below nos 1, 2.2, 3, 10.1–3, 13.1–18, 18, 19, 24.1–2.

[38] Below nos 13.1–18.

[39] Wild, 'The Empress's New Clothes', pp. 20–31, and for a general and dazzling description of the treasures sent into Germany with Isabella, see *Chronica Majora*, iii, pp. 319–21.

[40] Below nos 13.3–4, 13.11–18, and for another cloth of gold, see no. 24.1.

[41] Below nos 1, 10.2, 13.8–9, 23, and for cendal, see Wild, 'The Empress's New Clothes', p. 11. For my knowledge of the silk production of Andros, I am indebted to David Jacoby. In general, for silks at this time, see the two collections by D. Jacoby, *Trade, Commodities and Shipping in the Medieval Mediterranean* (Aldershot, 1997), and, as a special issue of *Techniques et culture*, 34 (1999), 'Soieries médiévales', especially the essay in the latter by F. Lachaud, 'Les Soieries importées en Angleterre (fin XIIe et XIII siècles)', pp. 179–92. For Andros, see also D. Polemis, 'Andros on the Eve of the Fourth Crusade', in *The Fourth Crusade Revisited: Atti della conferenza internazionale nell'ottavo centenario della IV Crociata, 1204–2004*, ed. P. Piatti (Vatican, 2008), pp. 11–17, esp. pp. 12–13.

[42] Below nos 8, 13.1–2.

[43] Below nos 10.1, 13.5, 24.2–3, and in general here, see below no. 10n. For camlet, defined as a 'textile with a warp-faced tabby weave … woven in mohair wool from the angora goat, imported from the Levant', see the 'Glossary of Historic Silk-Weaving Terms' in L. Monais, *Merchants, Princes and Painters: Silk Fabrics in Italian and Northern Paintings, 1300–1500* (New Haven, 2008), p. 301.

buckram (of fine cotton or linen), and woollen russet.[44] The condition of such cloths is sometimes referred to, either as 'finest' (*tenuissimus*) or in one instance as 'finest but worn' (*sccuriatus*).[45] In most instances, the quantity is unspecified, although the russet cloths of thirty-two and twenty-eight ells presented by the burgesses of Colchester may suggest bolts of material larger than those subsequently defined as standard.[46] Ben Wild has argued that there was a hierarchy of colours in use as court liveries, with Henry III himself favouring green costume, his messengers blue, others dressed in *mi-parti* robes of two colours divided vertically, and so forth.[47] In the present instance, the only cloths specifically stated to have been used for the king's costume were a pair of camlets from Tripoli (colour unspecified), and a cloth of gold with peacocks that was used to make an outer garment to be worn at the feast of Pentecost, 18 May 1236.[48] One of the attractions of cloth as a diplomatic gift, in addition to its combination of portability and value, was its suitability for both men and women. Of the four large (and we must assume precious) camlets presented in January 1235 by the master of the Temple in Jerusalem, two were used for robes for the king, one for the bishop-elect of Valence, and another to make a tunic for the queen.[49]

Besides textiles, the king was offered three items of finished apparel: stockings, boots and gloves from the bishop of Carlisle, all trimmed with fur.[50] Two gifts of silk cushions are recorded, two of otter skins (in both cases from Ireland), two of saddles, and one of a garland, the cushions and the garland being apparently gender-specific items deemed appropriate to be offered by women.[51] Other gifts were associated with the traditional royal pastimes of hunting and warfare: gifts of goshawks and of what can probably be identified as two pairs of elaborately decorated jesses for falconry, these latter again an appropriately feminine gift, offered by the countess of Warenne.[52] Of more masculine order were the presents of Turkish bows and a quiver for arrows, of silk spurs with iron buckles, of crossbows and maces.[53] There were two gaming sets, with chess and other gaming pieces. Unlike other gifts, these were offered both by men (the prior of the Hospitallers) and women (the countess of Ponthieu). In due course, both sets

---

[44] Buckram, below no. 13.6; russet, no. 18, and for russet, see Wild, 'The Empress's New Clothes', p. 10. The cloth striped on a dark blue field (no. 13.10) is otherwise undefined.
[45] Below nos 13.10–13.
[46] Below no. 18, and for an assize of 1272 specifying the standard size of a cloth ('pannus') as twenty-four ells in length, two in width (27.4m by 2.3m), see Wild, 'The Empress's New Clothes', p. 9. See also below nos 13.7 (eight ells), 13.13 (two ells), 19 (fourteen ells), and no. 10 (four camlets specified as 'large').
[47] Wild, 'The Empress's New Clothes', pp. 13, 17–18.
[48] Below nos 10.1, 13.3.
[49] Below nos 10.1–3.
[50] Below nos 5.1–3.
[51] Cushions, below nos 8, 23; otter skins, nos 20, 25.1; saddles, nos 13.19–20; garland, below no. 9.
[52] Below nos 3, 5.4, 6.
[53] Bows, bow case and quiver, nos 13.23, 13.25; spurs, no. 13.21; crossbows, no. 14; maces, no. 13.26.

were presented to Isabella, to add to the vast trousseau that she carried with her into Germany in May 1235.[54] An item listed merely as a 'pom' cannot be identified with any certainty, but was perhaps some sort of trinket, perhaps an amber pomander with gold fittings.[55] In all of this, it is worth noting the kudos that attached to items considered exotic because they were associated with distant or dangerous places: silk from the Aegean, camlets from Tripoli, Saracen work, Turkish bows, and so forth.[56]

Turning from the king's secular to his sacred interests, the list includes a quite extraordinary range of objects associated with the saints: statues of the Virgin Mary, and relics of at least six saints and a further seven holy places.[57] Even some of the apparently secular gifts had distinctly sacred uses: a silk wallet and two of the otter skins were subsequently used in the keeping of the king's relics, and the 'pharetram' covered with brushed silk and decorated with twelve Saracen arrow-heads, given by Frederick II, could have been intended either as a coffer or as a reliquary.[58] The gift of a glass vessel containing balsam should remind us that King Henry III occupied an uneasy position between the spheres of Church and State: balsam was essential to the making of chrism, the most precious of holy oils, used in the anointing of kings.[59] In this same junction between the realms of the sacred and the secular we can locate the 'stone against thunder', supplied with a chain to hang around the king's neck, gifted to Henry III by Peter the surgeon, perhaps as an ambassador from Henry III's future wife, Eleanor of Provence.[60]

Considerable personal significance attaches to the various relics and memorials of the saints reported in our list. Henry III's devotion to the Virgin Mary is well known, and perhaps derived from private and psychological causes linked to Henry's abandonment by his real mother, Isabella of Angoulême, at the age of only ten or eleven.[61] Our list includes an ivory statue of the Virgin, granted by the prioress of Amesbury (herself ruling a foundation dedicated to Mary, part of the wider and intensely Marian congregation of Fontevraud) – a gift made on 9 December 1234, a Saturday (the Virgin's day) and the morrow of the feast of

---

[54] Below nos 16, 21. Also noted in Wilkinson, 'The Imperial Marriage of Isabella the Empress', p. 31. For chess as a popular royal and aristocratic pastime, see J. C. Parsons, *Eleanor of Castile: Queen and Society in Thirteenth-Century England* (Basingstoke, 1995), p. 55, discussing Queen Eleanor's enjoyment of chess, noting Edward I's gift to her of a chess set in 1286, and her borrowing of a book from Cerne Abbey that might well have been a chess manual. For the sort of magnificence involved here in terms of board and pieces, see the illustrated catalogue *Spielwelten der Kunst. Kunstkammerspiele*, ed. W. Seipel (Vienna 1998), esp. 152–4 no.76, for the Kunstkammer's magnificent early fourteenth-century Venetian chess and backgammon set (KK 168).

[55] Below no. 4, and information from Jenny Stratford.

[56] Below nos 10, 13.19–23, 13.25–6, 21.

[57] Below nos 7, 12, 15.1–7, 17, 20; statue of the Virgin, no. 2.1.

[58] Below nos 1, 13.23, 22.

[59] Below no. 11.

[60] Below no. 26.

[61] Vincent, 'Henry III and the Blessed Virgin Mary', pp. 126–46, esp. pp. 143–4.

the Virgin's Conception.[62] In February 1235 the king was offered a substantial collection of relics by the Hospitallers including a glass vase with oil of Saydnaya set within a small silver image of the Virgin Mary. Saydnaya, in Syria, was home to an icon of the Virgin venerated alike by Christians and Muslims, and said to weep holy oil.[63] As this should remind us, the relics specified in our list include several that reveal ongoing contacts between England and the Christian East. Besides the oil of Saydnaya, the Hospitallers' gifts in February 1235 included portions of the Golden Gate of Jerusalem, of the Holy Sepulchre, of the altar on which Christ had been presented in the Temple, of the burning bush in which Moses saw God, of St Jerome, and earth from the hill of Calvary.[64] All of these would have helped to focus the king's mind on the fate of Jerusalem, restored to Christian rule since 1229 yet still acutely vulnerable to attack. As ever, this was a period of crusading recruitment, a call to which the king's brother, Richard of Cornwall, was eventually to respond with his crusade of 1240. Hence, no doubt, the prominence of the military orders among those making gifts to the king.[65] Others of the relics gifted at court also had eastern resonance, most notably the coffer given by a Franciscan friar, brother William, containing relics of saints George, Theodore and Pantaleon together with a spine from the Crown of Thorns.[66] At this time, before its sale to Louis IX of France, the Crown of Thorns remained in Byzantium as one of the most precious possessions of the Latin emperors of Constantinople. George, Theodore and Pantaleon were all Greek or Byzantine saints. What we have here, therefore, is almost certainly evidence of the continued recruitment campaign seeking support for the Latin empire of Constantinople, concurrent with similar efforts on behalf of the Christian kingdom of Jerusalem.

Closer to home, our list includes three relics of British saints: St Augustine of Canterbury, St Osyth, and St Patrick, in two cases gifted at locations close to the principal focus of these cults, in the third instance sent from Dublin.[67] Equally significant, the list helps to reveal Henry III's own devotion to English saints. Thus we find the king, a day after taking receipt from the Emperor Frederick II of a cloth of gold decorated with eagles, presenting this cloth at the high altar of Westminster Abbey. The king's gift was made on 18 February 1235, the feast of the translation of St Edward the Confessor, Westminster's principal royal saint.[68] On the same day a white silk with golden stripes, again given by the emperor, was divided into two portions, one of which the king gave to be placed on the image of the Virgin in Westminster's new Lady Chapel.[69] Another of the cloths gifted by the emperor, of red silk with white stripes, was presented in June 1236

---

[62] Below no. 2.
[63] Below no. 15.1.
[64] Below nos 15.2–7.
[65] From the Hospitallers, below nos 4, 15, 16, 24; and the Templars, no. 11.
[66] Below no. 7.
[67] Below nos 12, 17, 25.
[68] Below no. 13.4.
[69] Below no. 13.14.

to the shrine of St Benignus at Glastonbury. Once again the timing of this gift was significant: it was made on 26 June, the vigil of an obscure festival celebrated at Glastonbury commemorating the translation of the relics of Benignus, a semi-mythical fifth-century abbot (translated 27 June 1091).[70] On 3 October 1235, and again on 21 April 1236, the king deposited others of the emperor's cloths at Caversham in Berkshire, the first evidence of Henry III's devotion to an English shrine, sacred to the Virgin Mary, that was to remain a focus of royal attention throughout the 1230s and 1240s.[71] St Edward's shrine at Westminster was the also the beneficiary of a cloth of gold given originally by the prior of the English Hospitallers.[72] On the morrow of the feast of St Swithun, 16 July 1236, one of the emperor's silk cloths, this one with blue and yellow stripes, was deposited by the king in the chapel housing the relics of another Anglo-Saxon saint, St Cyneburh, in Gloucester Abbey.[73]

The significance of chronology here should remind us that the royal year was governed by near constant movement to and from locations that in many cases housed significant relics of the saints. In such a context, we should never attempt to write a narrative of the king's movements without a liturgical calendar very close to hand.[74] As our list makes plain, Henry III did not itinerate his realm at random but in many instances in order that his visits to particular churches should coincide with the feast days of their principal saints. Hence the significance of the evidence presented in our roll for royal awareness, or celebration, of such major Christian festivals as 1 January (the feast of the Circumcision, whose religious solemnities were deliberately intended to overshadow the previously pagan celebrations of the New Year, still marked by regular and lavish gift-giving),[75] 6 January (the Epiphany, yet another appropriate occasion for royal gifts),[76] Easter Sunday (an appropriate day for the king's taking receipt of a golden cross),[77] and Ascension day (for which in both 1235 and 1236 the king ordered new robes, and on which day, in 1235, he received rich gifts of cloth from the Hospitallers).[78] It had originally been intended that the king should wed his future queen on the feast of Pentecost, 27 May 1235, another great festival of new beginnings.[79]

---

[70] Below no. 13.12.
[71] Below nos 13.11, 13.16.
[72] Below no. 24.
[73] Below no. 13.17.
[74] For more general remarks here, see Vincent, 'The Pilgrimages of the Angevin Kings', pp. 21–6; Vincent, 'Henry III and the Blessed Virgin Mary', pp. 129–40; N Vincent, 'The Thirteenth Century', in *Ely: Bishops and Diocese, 1109–2009*, ed. P. Meadows (Woodbridge, 2010), pp. 26–69, at pp. 46–7.
[75] Below no. 5, and in general for the Christianisation of the feast of the Circumcision, see I. M. Resnick, *Marks of Distinction: Christian Perceptions of Jews in the High Middle Ages* (Washington, 2012), pp. 65–6.
[76] Below no. 6.
[77] Below no. 22.
[78] Below nos 10.1, 13.3, 24.1–3.
[79] Below no. 21n.

As this suggests, gifts and ceremonies were often carefully coordinated. The betrothal of the king's sister to the Emperor Frederick, for example, took place on 22 February 1235, the morrow of Ash Wednesday, at the beginning of the season of Lent. The gifts and luxuries intended to mark this occasion, however, had been exchanged a few days earlier, on Saturday 17 February, perhaps deliberately to avoid clashing with the Lenten solemnities.[80] On the first Sunday of Lent itself (Quadragesima Sunday) the Hospitallers took care to present the king with memorials of Christ and his church in Jerusalem.[81] Lent was very much the period during which minds were focused upon Christ's sufferings, and hence upon the fate of the crusades. Here we might recall that it had been at the very start of Lent, on Ash Wednesday, 4 March 1215, that the king's father, King John, had taken the Cross, vowing himself to the reconquest of Jersualem.[82] Since the time of his accession in 1216, Henry III had been pledged to fulfill his father's crusader vows. In due course, it was to be on the fourth Sunday in Lent, 6 March 1250, the day on which the introit *Laetare Jerusalem* was recited, that Henry renewed his vows and once again took the Cross.[83] The marriage of Henry's sister Isabella brought England even closer into the orbit of Frederick II, himself crowned king of Jerusalem since 1229, albeit as an absentee monarch. Among the gifts conferred by Frederick in February 1235 many would have served as reminders of his eastern dominion: silks, Turkish bows, Saracen saddles and maces.[84] Was it coincidence that led to the bestowal of one of these maces, on 29 September 1235, upon Gilbert Marshal, earl of Pembroke? Gilbert was an aspiring Christian warrior, originally intended for a clerical career but now all too keen to make a military reputation for himself, here suitably rewarded with arms upon the great feast day of St Michael, the warrior archangel.[85]

Nor was it only the greater international festivals that were commemorated. Henry III was strongly attached to the English saints, so we find clear evidence for the commemoration of such dates as 18 January (the feast of the translation of St Edward the Confessor, marked by gifts to Westminster),[86] and even 27 June (the feast of the translation of Glastonbury Abbey's otherwise obscure

---

[80] Below no. 13n.

[81] Below no. 15.

[82] The Barnwell annalist, in *Memoriale Fratris Walteri de Coventria: The Historical Collections of Walter of Coventry*, ed. W. Stubbs, Rolls Series, 2 vols (London, 1872–3), ii, p. 219. Wendover (in *Chronica Majora*, ii, pp. 584–5) errs in dating John's vows to 2 February 1215, the feast of the Purification of the Blessed Virgin Mary.

[83] *Chronica Majora*, v, pp. 100–2, and in general for Henry's vows of 1216 and 1250, see S. Lloyd, *English Society and the Crusade, 1216–1307* (Oxford, 1988), pp. 208–10, at p. 210 noting an exhortation of November 1234 from Gregory that Henry take the Cross, whence *Calendar of the Entries in the Papal Registers Relating to Great Britain and Ireland*, vol. 1: *1198–1304*, ed. W. H. Bliss (London, 1893), p. 141.

[84] Below nos 13.1–26, esp. nos 13.19–26.

[85] Below no. 13.26. For Gilbert's anxiety to prove his martial credentials, leading to his death in a tournament in 1241, see D. Crouch, *The English Aristocracy, 1070–1272: A Social Transformation* (New Haven, 2011), p. 217.

[86] Below no. 13.4.

St Benignus).[87] Hence too the significance of those occasions when the court seems to have miscalculated the dates of particular liturgical feasts.[88] The feast day of St George, for example, is traditionally assigned to 23 April. The fact that in 1235, despite himself receiving a gift of relics of St George, the king and his officials could assume that the feast fell on 21 April (a mistake shared in common with other English calendars) itself suggests that George was as yet by no means the best known of England's warrior saints.[89] Rather surprisingly, given the court's veneration of so many Anglo-Saxon saints, a similar confusion seems to have arisen over the calculation of the feast day of St Swithun in 1236, and perhaps over that of St Dunstan in 1235.[90]

Our roll, taken in combination with that edited by Ben Wild covering the same period, suggests that between December 1234 and June 1235 gifts were received at court in every month between December and June, with only one extended period of abstinence, between 17 May (the feast of the Ascension) and 15 June, when no gifts are recorded over a four week period.[91] It was not just the days of the year that were significant, either, but the days of the week. From the time of Henry III's minority, for example, there had been a concerted campaign to ensure proper observance of the Sabbath.[92] Saturday, the Sabbath eve, was a day believed particularly sacred to the Virgin Mary.[93] Hence the significance of our list in recording gifts made to the king on each of the seven days of the week, but with a slight preference for Sundays, nine of which are recorded as days of gifts (followed in popularity by Thursdays and Saturdays, with seven appearances each). What is particularly worth noticing here is that Sunday was considered an appropriate day for the receipt of gifts and was not otherwise a day of rest. Perhaps its solemnity and liturgical significance made it seem a particularly appropriate day for presentations that we must assume were public acts of court spectacle.[94]

Thus far we have considered the significance of our roll in financial, administrative, diplomatic, liturgical and ceremonial terms. One final aspect remains to be considered. The very last item on our list, the 'stone against thunder' given by Master Peter the surgeon, is perhaps the most remarkable of all the items recorded, not least because it carries us far beyond ceremonial routine into the personal psychology of the king. Magic talismans appear on several occasions during the reign of Henry III's father, King John. At Fontevraud, in April 1199, John is reported to have boasted of a stone that he wore around his neck, that had

---

[87]   Below no. 13.12.

[88]   For parallel examples, see N. Vincent, 'The Politics of Church and State as Reflected in the Winchester Pipe Rolls, 1208–1280', in *The Winchester Pipe Rolls and Medieval English Society*, ed. R. Britnell (Woodbridge, 2003), pp. 179–80.

[89]   Below no. 8, and cf. nos 7, 13.16; Wild, 'Gift Inventory', p. 563 nos 56–7.

[90]   Below nos 13.17, 23.

[91]   Below nos 24–5. The roll edited by Wild, 'Gift Inventory', records no gifts later than 7 May.

[92]   N. Vincent, *Peter des Roches: An Alien in English Politics, 1205–1238* (Cambridge, 1996), pp. 99, 172–3.

[93]   Vincent, 'Henry III and the Blessed Virgin Mary', pp. 137–8.

[94]   For gifts made on Sundays, see below nos 9, 14–15, 20, 22; Wild, 'Gift Inventory', p. 551 no. 1, p. 559 no. 41, p. 560–1 nos 45–6, p. 562 nos 50–1.

been granted to one of his ancestors and that would preserve him, so he claimed, against the loss of any of his lands.[95] The story here, recorded in the *Vita* of St Hugh of Lincoln, might be dismissed as exaggeration intended posthumously to blacken John's reputation, were it not for an entry on the *liberate* roll for 1201 recording a command to the justiciar then ruling in England to reward a man named Bartholomew, bearer of the present letters, with 20 shillings of land at Berkhamsted, his birthplace. This was a reward to Bartholomew for finding 'the precious stones and jewels that we used to wear around our neck'.[96] Was it perhaps one of these same stones, said to have the power to render its owner invincible in battle, that Hubert de Burgh was later to be accused of abstracting from the king's treasury to send to Llewelyn of Wales? Hubert's dealings here were among the charges laid against him at the time of his fall from grace in 1232.[97] Certainly some of John's jewels continued to be worn at the court of his son, Henry III, including a sapphire that John had borrowed for his lifetime from the monks of Bury St Edmunds and that in April 1234 Henry asked to be assigned to William, earl Warenne.[98] Henry's continued attachment to the memory of his father is worth noticing here, as is his trust in the supernatural and talismanic. As I have remarked in another context, Henry's attendance at the ceremonial burial of King John in his new tomb at Worcester, in May 1232, marked not so much the end of an era but a revival of the king's interest in the memory of his father, and in due course in the pursuit of the policies that John and his ministers, not least Peter des Roches, had become notorious for pursuing twenty years before.[99] But here the psychological possibilities go deeper still.

Reporting a violent thunderstorm that overtook the king out sailing on the Thames in July 1258, Matthew Paris tells us that Henry III had a morbid fear of thunder, a natural phenomenon that in medieval cosmology was generally associated with the demonic spirits of the upper air and therefore with divinatory practices claiming to use it as a means of future prediction.[100] Hence the significance

---

[95] Adam of Eynsham, *Magna Vita Sancti Hugonis*, ed. D. L. Douie and D. H. Farmer, 2 vols, 2nd edn (Oxford 1985), ii, pp. 139–40.

[96] *Rot. de Lib.*, p. 23, and cf. *Pipe Roll 4 John*, PRS n.s. 15 (London, 1937), p. 276, where the name is correctly given as Bartholomew.

[97] *Chronica Majora*, iii, p. 222.

[98] Vincent, 'The Pilgrimages of the Angevin Kings', pp. 38–9, citing *CPR 1232–47*, p. 43. For the Edmundsbury sapphire and a ruby, granted by King John to the monks in December 1203 but immediately taken back by him to hold for life in exchange for an annual pension of 10 marks, see *Rot. Chart.*, p. 114b. For gold rings associated with Henry's courtier Philip d'Aubigné, once again with apparently semi-magical attributes, see *CRR*, viii, pp. 35–6.

[99] Vincent, *Peter des Roches*, pp. 291–2; Vincent, 'Pilgrimages of the Angevin Kings', p. 27.

[100] *Chronica Majora*, v, p. 706 ('Rex autem huiusmodi tempestatem plus omnibus formidans'). For the demonic aspect of thunder, see V. I. J. Flint, *The Rise of Magic in Early Medieval Europe* (Oxford, 1991), pp. 108–15, 191–2, and from a much later period, S. Clark, *Thinking with Demons: The Idea of Witchcraft in Early Modern Europe* (Oxford, 1997), pp. 186, 241, 649. Set against this, and here deliberately following the more naturalistic clauses of Pliny, *Historia Naturalis*, bk. II, cc. 49–56, Alexander Neckham describes thunder as merely the report caused by the collision between two clouds, a terrifying sound likely to induce men to review their wrongdoings and think of the coming day of judgement: Neckham, 'De Laudibus

of Henry's declaration on meeting Simon de Montfort in the midst of this storm, as recorded by Paris, that he feared Simon 'more than all the thunder and lightning in the world'.[101] Master Peter the surgeon, the man who gave Henry his talisman 'against thunder', may be the same man subsequently recorded as physician to the queen, Eleanor of Provence. He was possibly of Gascon birth (perhaps from Jonzac in the Saintonge, north of Bordeaux).[102] His appearance at court in June 1235, coinciding with the opening of the negotiations for Henry's marriage to Eleanor, may suggest a pre-existing connection to the Provencal/Savoyard circles around Eleanor and her family.[103] If so, and if Master Peter came as an ambassador for the negotiation of Eleanor's marriage, then what could be a more appropriate symbol of the harmony of the projected union than a stone intended to calm one of the bridegroom's greatest personal fears? Meanwhile, the marriage to Eleanor would have served as yet another reminder of Henry's father, since, as Henry III informed Count Amadeus of Savoy, an alliance with Savoy would help cement a friendship first begun under their predecessors: a clear reference to the projected marriage between the future King John and a daughter of the then count of Maurienne/Savoy, negotiated as long ago as 1173.[104]

And so we return from the king's innermost thoughts to the rather more banal world of royal finance with which we began this essay. How can we put a value upon Henry III's sendals and camlets, his samites and otter skins? What price a spine from the Crown of Thorns? How much per ounce for the burning bush in which Moses saw God? Even had the Church permitted the sale of such objects (and from 1215, the sale of relics was officially forbidden), we would have great difficulty arriving at any sort of equivalent to the sterling weight of £139 that has been calculated for the reverse side of our roll, reporting a more prosaic collection of cups and belts gifted to Henry III over the same basic period. Our quinquiremes of Nineveh with 'sandlewood, cedarwood and sweet white wine' may defy any crude monetary valuation. Yet the charisma that they conferred upon Henry III's court was undeniable. Were it not for stray survivals such as the present roll, their extent and variety would be unknown. As a supplement to the financial resources recorded in pipe rolls and fine rolls, they can be considered, both literally and figuratively, beyond price.

divinae sapientiae', lines 97–118, and 'De Naturis rerum' c. 18, in *Alexandri Neckam de naturis rerum*, ed. T. Wright, Rolls Series (London, 1863), pp. 63, 397.
[101] *Chronica Majora*, v, p. 706 ('Supra modum tonitrum et fulgur formido, sed per caput Dei, plus te quam totius mundi tonitrum et fulgur contremisco'); cf. J. R. Maddicott, *Simon de Montfort* (Cambridge, 1994), p. 150.
[102] See below, n. 185, here relying upon an identification between Peter de Alpibus and Peter de Jonzac, disputed by the standard authorities.
[103] For these negotiations, first referred to in letters of 22 June, three days before the gift from Peter the surgeon, see below, n. 185.
[104] *Foedera, Conventiones, Litterae et Cujuscunque Generis Acta Publica*, ed. J. Caley *et al.*, 4 vols, Record Commission (London, 1816–69), i, pt. 1, p. 217 ('foedus amicitiae inter nos et vos ineundum sicut inter predecesssores nostros et vestros mutuus semper extitit'); for the marriage contract of 1173, see pp. 28–9.

Appendix: An Inventory of Gifts made to and by King Henry III of England (6 December 1234 – 16 July 1236)

A = TNA, C 47/3/4/1. Approximately 350mm × 520mm. This is the inner face when rolled up.

[1] Almonera. D(ie) mercurii proxima post <Aduentum Domini>[105] [*6 December 1234*] <de don>o abb(at)isse de Wherewell'[106] apud Wherewell'[107] i. almoneram de rub(eo) cend(allo) consu(ere)t(o) aurifil(o) ____ que postea liber-at(a) fuit ad inpon(en)d(um) relliq(ui)as

[2] D(ie) sabbati proxima ante fest(um) sancte Lucye [*9 December 1234*][108] de dono priorisse de Ambrebyr'[109]

    [2.1] ____ i. ymaginem eburneam de sancta Mar(ia) ex utraque parte inosam

    [2.2] ____ ii. bendas ad muniend(as) de albo filo contextas

[3] Die mercurii in vigil(ia) beati Th<ome apostoli> [*20 December 1234*][110] <de dono comiti>sse Warenn'[111] ii. paria iactorum ad austurcos de ser(ico) aurifil(o) cum noeleat(is) aur(eis) plen(is) ambr(eis) et cum turett(is) semiaureis et semical-cheis cum lo(s)ingiis et int(er)lo(s)igniis de serico et aurifil(o)

---

[105] Underscoring indicates the existence of connecting lines drawn in the MS, and dots indicate illegible passages. Where missing matter can be supplied editorially, it is given within angled brackets.

[106] Abbess Euphemia (occ. 1219–d. 1257), cf. *The Heads of Religious Houses: England and Wales*, vol. 2: *1216–1377*, ed. D. M. Smith and V. C. M. London (Cambridge, 2001), p. 617. Like the nuns of Amesbury (below no. 2), those of Wherwell were regular recipients of royal largesse, including, apparently in the present year, a promise of oaks from the Hampshire forest of Chute: *CR 1234–37*, p. 273.

[107] The king was certainly at Wherwell on 11–12 December 1235: *CPR 1232–47*, p. 132; *CFR 1235–36*, no. 63. From 3–10 December 1234, he was at Reading (*CChR*, i, pp. 188–90; *CLR 1234–37*, pp. 22–6; *CPR 1232–47*, pp. 84–5; *CFR 1234–35*, nos 61–7), visiting Wherwell on 12 December (*CR 1234–37*, p. 28). Wherwell lies 40 miles from Reading, so it is hard to explain the anomaly in dates here.

[108] At which time the court was at Reading: above, n. 107. Wild, 'Gift Inventory', p. 532, misdates this entry, reading 'sancti Hugonis' rather than 'sancte Lucye' to arrive at a date of 11 November.

[109] Unidentified – perhaps either Prioress Felicia (occ. 1227–c. 1238) or Ida (occ. 1256–1273), cf. *Heads of Religious Houses*, pp. 537–8. The nuns of Amesbury were promised thirty oaks from Chute forest in December 1235, implying a major programme of rebuilding: *CR 1234–37*, p. 217.

[110] On which day the court was between Windsor and Reading: *CPR 1232–47*, p. 85; *CR 1234–37*, p. 32.

[111] Matilda (d. 1248), daughter of William Marshal the elder, earl of Pembroke; widow of Hugh Bigod, earl of Norfolk; wife of William, IV earl Warenne (d. 1240).

[4] D(ie) martis in festo sancti <?Stephani> [?*26 December 1234*][112] <de dono prioris> Ier(usa)l(e)m in Angl(ia)[113] i. pom' de ambr(a) cum apparatu auri

[5] D(ie) lun' in festo circumcision(is) [*1 January 1235*] apud Geldeford'[114] de dono episcopi Karleoln'[115]

> [5.1] _____ i. par hosar(um) de allicto f(ur)ratas catt(a) montan(a) ____ liberat(i) fuerunt ead(em) die Germano scissori et retenti fuerunt postea ad us(um) r(egis)[116]
>
> [5.2] _____ i. par' botar(um) furratar(um) grisso ____ [*released as above 5.1*]
>
> [5.3] _____ i. par cyrotecar(um) furr(atarum) grisso ____ [*released as above 5.1*]
>
> [5.4] _____ i. austurcum mutatum _____ ead(em) die statim lib(er-atum) fuit Rad(ulfo) fil(io) Bern(ardi) austurcario[117] custodiend(um) et statim postea dat(um) fuit Emerico de Sacy[118] per r(egem)

[6] Die sabb(at)i in festo Epiph(ani)e [*6 January 1235*] de dono episcopi Karleoln' i. austurcum mutat(um) apud Wynton'[119] _____ eadem die ibidem statim lib(eratum) fuit Rad(ulfo) fil(io) Bern(ardi) austurcar(io) custodiend(um)

[7] Relliquie ___ Die mercurii proxima post festum s<ancti Luciani> [*10 January 1235*][120] <de dono fratris Wille>lmi de ordine minorum i. almonera in qua con(tinet)ur una capsa argent(ea) cum relliquiis de sanctis Georg(io), Theodoro, Pantelen(o) et aliis contentis et insertis eid(em), et de spina corone Domini in una capsa lignea et .... <i>nuolutam panno.

[8] Ceruical ___ Die veneris sequenti [*12 January 1235*] apud[121] .... <de dono comiti>sse Cornub'[122] i. ceruical(em) de samicto rub(eo) brusatto

---

[112]   For the court's presence at Kempton, following Christmas at Westminster, see *CPR 1232–47*, p. 86; *CR 1234–37*, p. 33.

[113]   Thierry de Nussa, cf. *CPR 1232–47*, p. 111.

[114]   For the court's presence at Guildford, see *CPR 1232–47*, p. 86.

[115]   Walter Mauclerk, bishop of Carlisle (1223–48), one of those attacked by the regime of Peter des Roches, and hence only recently reinstated at court. On 4 December 1234 the king had confirmed a major settlement made by the bishop over the barony of Gilsland: *CChR*, i, p. 189.

[116]   This same note of release extended so as to cover the two following entries, nos 5.2–3.

[117]   Cf. Wild, 'Gift Inventory', p. 558 no. 38.

[118]   For further gifts to Aimery de Sacy in December 1234, see *CR 1234–37*, p. 28. In April 1235 he secured a major wardship: *CPR 1232–47*, p. 101.

[119]   For the court's presence at Winchester, 4–7 January 1235, see *CPR 1232–47*, pp. 87–8.

[120]   On 10 January 1235 the court was at Southampton: *CPR 1232–47*, p. 88.

[121]   On 11 January the king was at Beaulieu. He is next recorded, at Clarendon, on 14 January: *CPR 1232–47*, pp. 88–9; below no. 9.

[122]   Isabella (d. 1240), daughter of William Marshal the elder, earl of Pembroke; widow of Gilbert de Clare, earl of Gloucester (d. 1230); first wife of Richard of Cornwall, younger brother of King Henry III. On 10 February 1235, while at Canterbury, the king granted

_____ Dominica in crastino sancti Georg(ii) [*22 April 1235*][123] dedit dominus rex Ysab(elle) sorori sue per man(um) W(illelmi) de Hauerh' ceruical(em) illud.

[9] Garland' ___ Dominica sequenti [*14 January 1235*] apud C<larendon'[124] de dono comitisse> Cornub' i. garlandesch(iam) de virga coopertam serico et aurifil(o)

[10] Camelot(ti) ___ Die mercurii proxima post festum sancti Vincent(ii) [*24 January 1235*] de dono magistri Milit(ie) Templi transmar(ini)[125] iiii. camelot(os) m(a)gnos de Tripoli[126]

    [10.1] ___ Die Iouis in octab(is) Ascension(is) [*24 May 1235*] apud Geldeford'[127] liberat(i) fuerunt G. scissori ad robam faciend(am) ad opus domini r(egis) anno xix°. ii. camelot(ti) per r(egem) [*over line*: et postea un(um) camelot(um) ibi cont']

    [10.2] _____ Die martis in crastino sancti Augustin(i) [*27 May 1236*][128] dedit dominus rex electo Valenc'[129] d<uos cam>elot(tos) ad robam sibi faciend(am) cum ii. cendall(is) loco suo con(t)entis.

    [10.3] _____ Die veneris proxima an(te) festum sancti Barnab(atis) [*6 June 1236*] apud Merewell'[130] [inclloe' *cancelled*] liberat' domin .... ad iupam fac(iendam) ad opus domine regine

[11] Balsam(um) ___ Eadem die mercurii [*24 January 1235*] de dono eiusdem magistri Templi unum vasculum vitreum cum balsamo _____ Balsam(um)

Richard of Cornwall the manor of Kirton in Lincolnshire, entailed upon his heirs by Isabella: *CFR 1234–35*, no. 131, and cf. *CChR*, i, p. 193. On 23 April, Isabella's claims to dower within the estate of the late earl of Gloucester were regulated by the king: *CR 1234–37*, pp. 80–1.

[123] Here apparently calculating the feast of St George as 21 rather than 23 April. The morrow of 23 April did not fall on a Sunday in any year between 1233 and 1239. However, cf. below no. 13.16, which seems to assume 23 April. On the other side of the present record, the Wardrobe correctly calculated the feast of St George as falling on 23 April 1235: Wild, 'Gift Inventory', p. 563 nos 56–7.

[124] For the presence of the court at Clarendon on 14 January 1235, see *CPR 1232–47*, p. 89.

[125] For grants made to the Templars by the king in Yorkshire, on 9 January 1235, see *CChR*, i, pp. 192–3.

[126] For camlet, a luxury cloth originating in the eastern Mediterranean of uncertain composition, perhaps of woven goats' or camel wool, see D. Jacoby, 'Camlet Manufacture, Trade in Cyprus and the Economy of Famagusta from the Thirteenth to the Late Fifteenth Century', in *Medieval and Renaissance Famagusta: Studies in Architecture, Art and History*, ed. M. J. K. Walsh, P. W. Edbury and N. H. S. Coureas (Farnham, 2012), pp. 15–42, esp. pp. 19–20, where the present entry is cited from its notice in the *Dictionary of Medieval Latin from British Sources*, ed. R. E. Latham *et al.*, fascicule II (C) (Oxford, 1981), p. 248 col. 3, *s.v.* 'camelotus'.

[127] Cf. *CPR 1232–47*, p. 202.

[128] This must be the morrow of St Augustine of Canterbury (26 May) 1236. In 1235 the morrow of St Augustine of Canterbury fell on Friday 27 May, and the morrow of St Augustine of Hippo on Wednesday 29 August.

[129] One of the earliest indications of the favour showered upon William of Savoy, bishop-elect of Valence, at the English court, for which see also *CR 1234–37*, p. 278.

[130] For the king's presence at Marwell on 6–7 June 1236, see *CPR 1232–47*, pp. 148–9.

illud die veneris proxima post f(estum) sancti Vincent(ii) [*25 January 1236*]¹³¹ dat(um) fuit electo Valenc' per precept(um) domini r(egis).

[12] Relliquie ____ Die Iouis proxima post f(estum) Purificationis [*8 February 1235*] apud Douor'¹³² de dono com(itis) Ric(ardi)¹³³ i. iunctam de digito beati Augustin(i) Angl(orum) apostoli.

[13] Die sabbati proxima an(te) festum sancti P<etri in Cathedra> [*17 February 1235*] <apud> ...... ann' per Petr(um) de Vin'¹³⁴

    [13.1] ____ i. samict(um) rub(eum)

    [13.2] ____ i. samict(um) croceum

    [13.3] ____ i. pann(um) ad aur(um) cum pauon(ibus) ____ Die iouis in festo Ascension(is) [*8 May 1236*] liberat(um) fuit pann(um) ille ad faciend(um) supertun(icum) ad opus domini r(egis) contra Pent(ecosten) [*18 May 1236*] per G. scissorem anno xx°.

    [13.4] ____ i. pann(um) ad aur(um) cum aquil(is) __ Dominica sequenti [*18 February 1235*]¹³⁵ apud Westm' in obl(a)c(ion)e domini r(egis) in maiori ecclesia ad maius altare pannum illum

---

131   The date of the gift to the elect of Valence was presumably after the king's marriage to Eleanor of Provence (14 January 1236, Henry and Eleanor having been betrothed since June 1235). The gift was most likely made in January 1236, since in 1237 the feast of St Vincent (22 January) fell on a Thursday, meaning that 23 January 1237 would most likely have been described as the morrow, rather than 'the Friday after' the feast. Balsam was essential, mixed with oil, in the making of chrism, itself used for the anointing of kings. For the care taken to preserve the oil of chrism even after the burial of Henry the Young King (d. 1183), King John (d. 1216) and Edward II (d. 1327), see D. A. Carpenter, 'The Burial of King Henry III, the Regalia and Royal Ideology', in Carpenter, *The Reign of Henry III* (London, 1996), pp. 427–61, at pp. 434–6. For Henry III's purchases of balsam in 1228, see *CLR 1226–40*, p. 71.

132   Cf. *CChR*, i, p. 192; *CPR 1232–47*, p. 91.

133   On 10 February 1235, at Canterbury, the king confirmed a major settlement between Richard of Cornwall and Gilbert Marshal over custody of the Braose heir and his lands: *CChR*, i, p. 192.

134   On 17 February 1235 the king was probably at or in the vicinity of Westminster: *CPR 1232–47*, pp. 93–4. Peter de Vinea had been empowered as early as November 1234 to act as plenipotentiary of the Emperor Frederick II in his negotiation for a marriage to Henry III's sister Isabella: E. H. Kantorowicz, 'Petrus de Vinea in England', *Mitteilungen des Instituts für Österreichische Geschichtsforschung* 51 (1937), 43–81; cf. J. P. Huffman, *The Social Politics of Medieval Diplomacy: Anglo-German Relations (1066–1307)* (Ann Arbor, 2000), pp. 249–51; Wilkinson, 'The Imperial Marriage of Isabella of England', pp. 23–4. The present record supplies one of the earliest notices of Peter's activities in England. On 22 February he acted as the emperor's proxy in exchanging vows with Isabella *per verba de presenti*, in the negotiation of her German dower and in the arrangements for a marriage portion to be assigned to her by Henry III of 30,000 marks: *Treaty Rolls 1234–1325* (London, 1955), nos 1–4, 8, 9, 12–17; *CR 1234–37*, p. 167; *Chronica Majora*, iii, pp. 318–19, and cf. Wild, 'Gift Inventory', p. 554 no. 16, p. 557 no. 33, p. 569 no. 97; Wild, 'The Empress's New Clothes', pp. 3–4.

135   For the date, Quinquagesima Sunday 1235, coincidentally the feast of the translation of St Edward the Confessor, when the king was at Westminster, see *CR 1234–37*, pp. 49–50; *CFR 1234–35*, nos 134–6; and cf. below no. 13.14.

[13.5] ___ i. camelot(tum) nigr(um) ___ Die Iouis in octab(is) Ascension(is) [*15 May 1236*] apud Geudeford'[136] anno xx°. dedit dominus rex domino W(altero) de Kyrk'[137] i. camelot(tum) illum

[13.6] ___ ii. bug(er)erann(a)

[13.7] ___ i. camelot(tum) rub(eum) contin(entem) viii. uln(as) ___ Die mart(ii) in crastino sancti Dunstani [*20 May 1236*] apud Merewell'[138] dedit dominus rex comiti Lincoln'[139] camelot(tum) illum anno xx°

[13.8] ___ i. cindall(eum) rub(eum) de Andre.[140]

[13.9] ___ i. cendall(eum) vir(idum) de Andre.

[13.10] ___ i. pann(um) radiat(um) de longo cum campo ind(eo) tenuissimo ___ Die veneris in festo cathedre sancti Petri [*22 February 1236*][141] dedit dominus rex fratribus predicatoribus Oxon'[142] pann(um) illum anno xx°.

[13.11] ___ i. pann(um) [*over line*, de serico] varii coloris radiat(um) in long(o) sine auro tenuissimo ___ Die mercurii proxima post festum sancti Michael(is) [*3 October 1235*] in oblatione domini r(egis) apud Kauersham[143] pann(um) ill(um)

[13.12] ___ i. pann(um) de serico rub(eo) radiato ex transuerso albo tenuissimo ___ Die iouis in festo sanctorum Ioh(ann)is et Paul(i) [*26 June 1236*][144] dedit dominus rex ad ponend(um) super feretr(um) sancti Bennugn(i) apud Glaston'[145] pann(um) illum

---

[136]   For the king's presence at Guildford that day, see *CR 1234–37*, p. 265; *CFR 1235–36*, no. 276.

[137]   Walter of Kirkham, keeper of the king's Wardrobe from 17 May 1234 to 27 October 1236.

[138]   For the king's presence at Marwell on 19–22 May 1236, see *CR 1234–37*, pp. 266–7.

[139]   John de Lacy, earl of Lincoln (d. 1240).

[140]   This and the next item refer to sendal or lightweight silk, which was produced on the island of Andros, the northernmost of the Cyclades in the Aegean. Since the Fourth Crusade the island had been placed under the rule of members of the Dandolo family of Venice. See here D. Jacoby, 'Silk in Medieval Andros', in *Captain and Scholar: Papers in Memory of Demetrios I. Polemis*, ed. E. Chrysos and E. A. Zachariadou (Andros, 2009), pp. 137–50, as drawn to my attention by Professor Jacoby.

[141]   When the king was himself at Oxford: *CR 1234–37*, p. 244.

[142]   Licenced by the king to carry off oaks from the estate of William de Longuespée at Bicester, Oxfordshire, 5 April 1235: *CR 1234–37*, p. 254.

[143]   The king's presence at Caversham on this day goes otherwise unrecorded. Nonetheless, for Henry III's keen devotion to and attendance at Caversham, at this time a major centre of Marian devotion, see Vincent, 'King Henry III and the Blessed Virgin Mary', pp. 135, 143. The present record supplies the first evidence of Henry's devotion to Caversham, and seems to have been followed by a second visit in April 1236, below no. 13.16.

[144]   The king is recorded at Glastonbury on 27 June 1236, having visited the abbey a year earlier, on 2 August 1235: *CChR*, i, p. 151; *CR 1234–37*, p. 124; *CFR 1235–36*, no. 355.

[145]   St Benignus, or Beonna, of Glastonbury, supposed by William of Malmesbury to have been St Patrick's successor as abbot of Glastonbury, was the subject of a *Vita* by William of Malmesbury that itself reveals confusion between the Glastonbury saint and the Irish St Benen/Benignus: *William of Malmesbury's Saints' Lives*, ed. M. Winterbottom and R. M.

[13.13] ___ i. pann(um) de serico tenuissimo burellat(um) et sccuriatum tenue(ssimo) de ii. uln(is)

[13.14] ___ i. toall(um) de serico albo radiat(um) auro ___ Dominica sequenti post festum Valentin(i) [*18 February 1235*][146] dedit dominus rex med(ietatem) toall(i) ill(ius) ad ponend(um) super ymaginem beate Marie apud Westm' in noua capella abbatie.[147]

[13.15] ___ i. toall(um) pounac(ii) coloris radiat(um) auro de serico.

[13.16] ___ i. pann(um) de serico radiat(um) minutis radiis variis ___ Die lun(e) proxima ante fest(um) sancti Georg(ii) [*21 April 1236*][148] in oblacione domini r(egis) apud Kauersham[149] illum pann(um) anno xx°.

[13.17] ___ i. pann(um) de serico cum latis radiis indis et croceis cum minutis radiis … d … auro ___ Die mercurii in festo [*recte* crastino] sancti Swithun(i) [*16 July 1236*][150] in oblacione domini r(egis) in capella sancte Kyneberge apud Glouc'[151] per preceptum domini r(egis) pann(um) illum anno xx°.

[13.18] ___ i. pann(um) de serico cum latis radiis croceis et rub(eis), indis et viol(etis)

Thomson (Oxford, 2002), pp. 344–67; J. Blair, 'A Handlist of Anglo-Saxon Saints', in *Local Saints and Local Churches in the Early Medieval West*, ed. A. Thacker and R. Sharpe (Oxford, 2002), pp. 495–656, at p. 515. A Glastonbury kalendar of the fifteenth century suggests that his feast day was celebrated at Glastonbury, as for the Irish St Benignus, on 3 November, but that Glastonbury also observed a distinct and equally solemn feast ('in iiii. cappis') for the translation of St Benignus on 27 June (commemorating the translation of his relics from Meare to Glastonbury in 1091), the day after Henry III's gift was deposited at the shrine: F. Wormald, 'The Liturgical Calendar of Glastonbury Abbey', in *Festschrift Bernhard Bischoff zu seinem 65. Geburstag*, ed. J. Autenrieth and F. Brunhölzl (Stuttgart, 1971), pp. 325–45, at pp. 326, 333, 338 (a reference that I owe to Nigel Morgan). For the cult, see also *The Chronicle of Glastonbury Abbey: An Edition, Translation and Study of John of Glastonbury's 'Chronica sive Antiquitates Glastoniensis Ecclesie'*, ed. J. P. Carley and D. Townsend (Woodbridge, 1985), pp. xxxviii–xxxix, 16–17, 68–71, 152–3 (his shrine given by King Harthacnut), 160–3 (the translation of 1091), 166–7, 282–3, p. xlii noting that he was sufficiently significant for the abbey's thirteenth-century seal to show Saints Patrick and Benignus flanking St Dunstan.

[146] When the king was at Westminster and left other gifts at the abbey's high altar, coinciding with the feast of the translation of St Edward the Confessor: above no. 13.4.

[147] For the statue of the Blessed Virgin Mary in the new chapel at Westminster, see Vincent, *Holy Blood*, p. 170.

[148] When the king is otherwise recorded only at Windsor: *CPR 1232–47*, pp. 142–43; *CR 1234–37*, p. 259.

[149] Noticed by Vincent, 'King Henry III and the Blessed Virgin Mary', p. 135, but there misdated to April 1235, and cf. above no. 13.11.

[150] The feast of St Swithun, 15 July, fell on a Sunday in 1235 (when the king was at Westminster), and on a Tuesday in 1236, when the king was between Tewkesbury, Evesham and Feckenham: *CPR 1232–47*, p. 154; *CFR 1235–36*, no. 384. The correct date for his visit to Gloucester should therefore be 16 July 1236, the morrow rather than the feast of St Swithun. The present entry, nonetheless, adds yet another date to the list of Henry III's known oblations to the English saints.

[151] For St Cyneburh/Kyneburgh, supposedly a late seventh-century martyred abbess of Gloucester, feast day 25 June, see Blair, 'Handlist of Anglo-Saxon Saints', pp. 523–4.

[13.19] ___ i. sellam ad equ(um) cum phal(ar)is de opere Sarracen(o) ___
Die mercurii in translatione sancti <Benedicti [*11 July 1235*][152]
d>edit dominus rex regi Mannens'[153] sellam illam cum phal(ar)is

[13.20] ___ i. sellam ad palefr(idum) cum phal(ar)is de opere Sarracen(o).
Ead(em) die mercurii [*11 July 1235, cf. 13.19*] dedit d<ominus
r>ex com(iti) de Ferrar'[154] sellam illam cum phal(ar)is.

[13.21] ___ i. par cyng(u)lar(um) de serico de opere Sarracen(o) cum
bucl(is) ferreis

[13.22] ___ i. pharetram cooperta serico brusdato cum xii. sagitt(is)
Sarracen(is)

[13.23] ___ ii. arciis Turkes(iis) cum ii. cord(is), de corio. Die veneris in
crastino cathedr(e) s<ancti Petri> [*23 February 1235*][155] <dedit>
dominus rex com(iti) R(icardo) fratri suo unum de ill(is) arcubus
cum corda anno xix°

[13.24] ___ i. tarkos(ium) de corio brusdato paruum

[13.25] ___ i. furrell(um) ad arcus Turkes' de samicto brusdat(o)

[13.26] ___ ii. macie ferr(ie) de opere Sarracen(o) ___ Die sabbati in festo
sancti M<ichaelis> [*29 September 1235*][156] <dedit dominus rex>
com(iti) G(ilberto) Maresch(allo) unam de ill(is) maz(iis) anno xix°
___ Die sabbati vigil(is) Pasch(e) [*29 March 1236*][157] .... de
Halap'[158] ad deferend(um) cum domino r(ege) anno xx°

[14] Dominica proxima post f(estum) sancti Val(e)ntin(i) [*18 February*

---

[152] The feast of the translation of St Benedict fell on a Wednesday, 11 July 1235, on which day
the king was at Westminster and there is clear evidence of a settlement with the king of Man,
as noted below, n. 153 (*CPR 1232–47*, p. 112). Although the parchment is badly damaged at
this point, it is perhaps still possible to make out the opening descender of the capital letter 'B'.
[153] Olaf ('the Black') (d. 1237), king of Man and the Isles (from 1226), to whom Henry III
issued letters of safe conduct on 13 April 1235 to come to England to parley before 1 August:
Foedera, p. 217; *CPR 1232–47*, p. 100. Olaf had spent the 1220s at war with his elder
brother Reginald, *alias* Ragnvald/Rǫgnvaldr Godredsson (d. 1229), who as king, in 1219, had declared
himself a vassal of Henry III as part of a settlement negotiated by the legate Pandulf: *Foedera*, pp.
156–7; R. A. McDonald, *Manx Kingship in its Irish Sea Setting, 1187–1229: King Rognvaldr and
the Crovan dynasty* (Dublin, 2007). Reginald had allied himself to the family of Alan of Galloway,
and Alan's death in 1234, combined with the threats to the lordships of the Irish Sea from
Scotland and especially from Norway, may have been what prompted Olaf to renew his contacts
with the English court. At Westminster, on 10 July 1235, Henry III issued a charter granting Olaf
an annual pension of 40 marks, wheat and wine from Ireland in return for his homage, the service
of fifty galleys in time of need, and an undertaking to guard the coast of the English north-west
facing Ireland: *CChR*, i, p. 209; *CPR 1232–47*, p. 112; and cf. *CR 1234–37*, pp. 356–7.
[154] William de Ferrers, earl of Derby (d. 1247).
[155] When the king was at Westminster: *CR 1234–37*, pp. 51–2; *CFR 1234–35*, no. 147.
[156] 29 September fell on a Saturday in 1235, but on a Monday in 1236. On 29 September
1235 the king was at Woodstock: *CPR 1232–47*, p. 118; *CFR 1234–35*, no. 460.
[157] When the king was apparently at or near Westminster: *CR 1234–37*, p. 252; *CFR 1235–
36*, no. 190.
[158] What appears to be a personal name here remains unidentified and partly undecypherable.

1235][159] .... xxx. balist(as) ligneas cum xxx. baldreis ___ Eadem die [*18 February 1235*] ibid(em) tradite fuerunt baliste ille cum baldr(eis) Thom(e) fil(io) Godefr(idi) et Paulino de <Winc>helese[160] ad muniend(um) galyas domini r(egis) per reg(em) per os G(odefridi) de Craucumbe

[15] Relliquie. Dominica proxima post f(estum) sancti Mathie [*25 February 1235*] de dono Elye Honne fratris Ioh(ann)is de Merc'[161] de dono Hospital(is)[162]

    [15.1] ___ i. vasculum vitreum cum oleo de Sardenay[163] [s... *erased*] est in parua ymagine argent(i) beate Marie

    [15.2] ___ i. partic(u)lam de Porta Aurea Ierosol' ___ sunt in quadam bursa de ser<ico in coffro> relliquiarum[164]

    [15.3] ___ i. partic(u)l(am) de Sep(u)lcro Domini

    [15.4] ___ i. partic(u)l(am) de altari in qua Cristus fuit presentatus.

    [15.5] ___ i. partic(u)l(am) de rubo quem viderat Moyses.

    [15.6] ___ i. partic(u)l(am) de Sancto Ieronimo.

    [15.7] ___ i. partic(u)lam de Monte Caluar(e) ___

[16] Die Iouis proxima post fest(um) sancti Mathie [*1 March 1235*] de dono prioris Ier(usa)l(e)m in Angl(ia)[165] i. s(ca)cc(ariu)m de ebore cum scacc(ariis) et tabellul(is) de eodem apud Straff[166] ___ Ead(em) die [*1 March 1235*] ibid(em) statim misit dominus Ysab(elle) sorori sue ipsum s(ca)cc(ariu)m cum sccacc(ariis) et tabellul(is)

159   When the king was at Westminster: *CR 1234–37*, pp. 49–50.
160   For Thomas fitz Godfrey of Winchelsea and Paulin of Winchelsea as keepers of the king's galleys at Winchelsea and elsewhere, see *CLR 1226–40*, pp. 389–90, 489; *CR 1234–37*, pp. 49, 68–9, 163, 468. On 17 February 1235, the day before the present entry, the king had ordered the constable of the Tower of London to release 3,000 crossbow bolts to Paulin (*CR 1234–37*, p. 49), in all probability reflecting continuing anxiety over Anglo-French relations in the aftermath of Henry III's new alliance with the Emperor Frederick II. From January 1235 until c. 1 March, Henry III responded to the arrest of various Englishmen, including the king's tailor, William Scissor, with a general order for the arrest of all enemy shipping in English ports: below, n. 170.
161   Both these men apparently otherwise unrecorded.
162   On 20 March 1235 the order of the Hospitallers was granted general letters of protection by the king: *CPR 1232–47*, p. 97. Matthew Paris (*Chronica Majora*, iii, p. 318) notes the involvement of two German Hospitallers, together with Peter de Vinea, in the negotiation of Frederick II's marriage to Isabella.
163   For the miraculous oil produced by an icon of the Virgin Mary at Saydnaya in Syria, see B. Hamilton, 'Our Lady of Saidnaia: An Orthodox Shrine Revered by Muslims and Knights Templar at the Time of the Crusades', in *The Holy Land, Holy Lands, and Christian History*, ed. R. N. Swanson, Studies in Church History 36 (Woodbridge, 2000), pp. 207–15; B. Z. Kedar, 'Convergences of Oriental Christian, Muslim and Frankish Worshippers: The Case of Saydnaya', in *De Sion exibit lex et verborum domini de Hierusalem: Essays on Medieval Law, Liturgy and Literature in Honour of Amnon Linder*, ed. Y. Hen (Turnhout, 2001), pp. 59–69.
164   The heading 'sunt in quadam bursa ... relliquiarum' linked by lines to the entries 15.2 and 15.7, perhaps intended to cover all of the entries 15.2–7. For the heading itself, cf. no. 17.
165   Cf. nos 4, 24.
166   For the king's presence at Stratford, from 28 February to 1 March 1235, see *CPR 1232–47*, p. 96; *CLR 1234–37*, pp. 54–5; *CFR 1234–35*, nos 152–5.

[17] <Rell>iquie. Die martis proxima an(te) fest(um) sanctarum Perpetue et Felicitat(is) [*6 March 1235*] apud Sanctam Osytham[167] de dono abbatis loci[168] i. os de tibia sancte Osythe ___ In cofforo relliquiarum

[18] Russet(as). Die martis proxima an(te) fest(um) sanctarum Perpetue et Felicitat(is) [*6 March 1235*] apud Colecestr'[169] de dono burg(e)ns(ium) Colecestr' ii. russet(as) integr(as) contin(entas) i. xxxii. uln(as) et alium xxviii. uln(as) ___ liberat(as) W(illelmo) Scissori[170] et W(illelmo) de Hauerh'.

[19] Mapp(a). Die sabbati proxima post festum sancti Gregor(ii) [*17 March 1235*] apud Sanctum Eadm(undum)[171] de dono abbatis loci[172] i. mapp(am) contin(entam) xiiii. uln(as) et ii. toall(as) et sunt in custod(ia) German(i) per manum Benne ___ Mappa liberata est Rad(ulfo) Mappar(io)[173] ad us<um regis> die sabbati an(te) festum sancte Margar(ete) [*14 July 1235*][174] anno xix°.

___ Toall(as) similiter

---

[167] For the king's presence at St Osyth's on 5 March 1235, see *CChR*, i, p. 194; *CPR 1232–47*, p. 96. Arriving from Colchester on 5 March, the king granted the abbey timber for the needs of its refectory: *CR 1234–37*, p. 56. A few days later, on 8 March, the canons obtained a charter from the king confirming their most recent acquisitions: *CChR*, i, pp. 194–5.

[168] Abbot David was in post from before 1221 to sometime after 1247: see *Heads of Religious Houses*, p. 456.

[169] For the king's presence at Colchester on 5 and 7 March 1235, see *CPR 1232–47*, p. 96; *CFR 1234–35,* nos 166–7. The present list, supplemented by the gifts of plate noted by Ben Wild ('Gift Inventory', pp. 534, 541), gives us some idea of the sort of gift-giving that accompanied the king's reception in the greater towns of England.

[170] W[illiam] Scissor is presumably the same man taken prisoner by the French sometime before 22 January 1235, whose capture provoked a series of orders for the confinement of enemy shipping to English and French ports, only lifted c. 1 March 1235: *CR 1234–37*, pp. 41, 54; *CPR 1232–47*, p. 96, and cf. above, n. 160.

[171] For the king's presence at Bury St Edmunds on 17–19 March 1235, see *CPR 1232–47*, p. 97; *CFR 1234–35*, nos 182–4; *CR 1234–37*, pp. 59–60. He arrived there by way of Bromholm, Norwich, Walsingham, Castle Acre and Thetford (*CR 1234–37*, pp. 58–9; *CFR 1234–35*, nos 175–80). This tour of the pilgrimage churches of East Anglia repeated, to some extent, a tour made a year earlier in ceremonial reversal of yet another tour, conducted in 1232. It was on the 1232 East Anglian tour that the former minister Hubert de Burgh had first been attacked. Since then, Peter des Roches and Peter de Rivalls had ruled England. When they in turn fell out of favour, in 1234, Henry revisited the same East Anglian shrines to proclaim their dismissal and the return of de Burgh and his associates: cf. Vincent, 'Pilgrimages of the Angevin Kings', p. 27. At Bury, on 18 March, the king continued this policy of reinstatement for those disgraced between 1232 and 1234, promising to honour his charters to the formerly disgraced bishop of Carlisle, and to observe dispositions within the Norfolk honour of Wormegay vouched for by Hubert de Burgh: *CR 1234–37*, pp. 59–60.

[172] On 19 March the king granted Abbot Henry (of Rushbrooke, abbot 1233–48, cf. *Heads of Religious Houses*, p. 26) and his monks a charter guaranteeing their right to two annual fairs in the Bury suburbs: *CChR*, i, p. 196; *CR 1234–37*, p. 61.

[173] For Ralph, recorded on 3 April having committed the king's table cloths (*mappa*) to the keeping of the reeve of Guildford, see *CR 1234–37*, p. 71.

[174] The dating here depends upon which St Margaret is in question, Margaret of Scotland (feast day 8 July), or Margaret of Antioch (feast day 20 July). Since Margaret was only officially canonised in 1250, St Margaret of Antioch seems the more likely candidate.

[20] … er'. Dominica in festo sancti Eadward(i) [*18 March 1235*] ibid(em) de dono archiepiscopi Dublin'[175] iii. pelles lutr(iorum). [*over line*, Germanus] Benne habet in custod(ia). Postea exp(endas) ad rel(liqui)as r(egis) per manum Germani

[21] … Die Iouis proxima post diem Palmar(um) [*5 April 1235*] de misso comitisse de Pontiuo[176] i. tabellarium de ebore de opere Sarrac(eno) cum tabellul(is) et scacc(ariis) ___ Postea delata fuit cum Ysabella sorore r(egis) in partes Alem(annie).

[22] Dominica in festo Pasch(e) [*8 April 1235*][177] de dono et missione Anselini de Norhoud[178] unam crucem aur(eum) cum relliquiis. Postea in All(e)man(i)a(m) ___ in coffar(io) relliquiar(um).

[23] Die sabbati proxima an(te) fest(um) sancti Dunstan(i) [?*12 May 1235*][179] de missione matris Ioh(ann)is de Saxon(ia) valleti domini

---

[175] Luke, archbishop of Dublin, was a former chaplain of Hubert de Burgh and therefore had himself been one of the targets of the reprisals against Hubert between 1232 and 1234: N. Vincent, *Peter des Roches*, pp. 261, 435, 437.

[176] Mary, countess of Ponthieu (wife of the count, Simon de Dammartin), had been licenced to visit England on pilgrimage in the autumn of 1233: *CPR 1232–47*, p. 25. By October 1234 there were indications that the king was considering a marriage with a daughter of Mary and Simon (*CPR 1232–47*, p. 74), negotiations for this marriage resuming in early April 1235, via the count's nuncios Bernard of Amiens and Peter de Famuchon, with the king sending his clerk, William of Wissant, on Easter Sunday, 8 April, to inform the count that he should send his daughter to England in order that she might be married and crowned queen on the feast of Pentecost: *CR 1234–37*, p. 175; *Foedera*, p. 216; Wild, 'Gift Inventory', p. 562 no. 51. In the meantime, the merchants of Abbeville and Ponthieu had specifically been exempted from the general embargo on cross-Channel shipping: *CR 1234–37*, pp. 38, 41, 47, 91. In the event, and thanks in part to lobbying in Rome by the king of France, the Ponthieu marriage plans came to nothing, being abandoned by June 1235 when the far greater prize of a marriage with Eleanor of Provence came into view: Howell, *Eleanor of Provence*, pp. 11–12; *Chronica Majora*, iii, pp. 327–8. Thereafter, the official annulment of the marriage plans with Ponthieu was to involve a long process in canon law, culminating in a judgement of 1254 disallowing the betrothal on the grounds of Henry III's consanguinity to Joan (who was by then queen of Castile) by common descent from King Louis VI of France. The judgement was printed by D. L. D'Avray, 'Authentication of Marital Status: A Thirteenth-Century English Royal Annulment Process and Late Medieval Cases from the Papal Penitentiary', *EHR* 120 (2005), 987–1013, at pp. 991–5, 998–1009.

[177] For the king's presence at Reading, 4–9 April 1235, see *CPR 1232–47*, p. 98; *CR 1234–37*, pp. 71–2.

[178] For Anselin de Norhoud/Norhout, who by June 1237 was in receipt of an annual fee from the king of £20, see *CLR 1226–40*, pp. 272, 293, 380. He had been licenced to come to England by royal letters dated 9 March 1235, issued on the same day as similar letters to Baldwin, count of Guînes, suggesting that Anselin was a northern Frenchman: *CPR 1232–47*, p. 97, and cf. Wild, 'Gift Inventory', p. 558 no. 37.

[179] The feast day of St Dunstan (19 May) itself fell in 1235 on a Saturday. Having seen off his sister, who departed for Germany from Sandwich on 7–8 May, the king returned via Canterbury and Rochester to reach Sutton-at-Hone in Kent by 12 May: *CPR 1232–47*, p. 103; *CR 1234–37*, pp. 90–1.

r(egis)[180] i. ceruical(um) [*over line*, de cendall(o)]. <P>osittum cum schuchon(is) de aur(i)fil(o).

[24] Die iouis in festo Ascension(is) [*17 May 1235*][181] de dono prioris Hospital(is) Iher(usa)l(e)m [Lond' *cancelled*] in Angl(ia)

    [24.1] ___ i. pann(um) ad aur(eum). Eadem die statim dedit dominus ad pendend(um) an(te) feretr(um) sancti Aedward(i) pann(um) ill(um).

    [24.2] ___ i. camelot(tum) nigr(um)

    [24.3] ___ i. camelot(tum) nigr(um).

[25] Die veneris proxima post festum sancti Barnab(e) [*15 June 1235*][182] de misso G(alfridi) de Turuill' archidiacon(i) Dublin'[183]

    [25.1] ___ iii. pelles lutr(arum) ___ liberat(os) Germano.

    [25.2] ___ i. vasculum argenti cum osse sancti Patricii

[26] Die lun(e) in crastino natiuitatis sancti Ioh(ann)is Bapt(iste) [*25 June 1235*][184] de dono mag(ist)r(i) Petri cyrurgici[185] i. lapidem contra tonitura in capsilia argente cum chac<ea> ad dependend(um) circa collum[186]

---

[180] For John of Saxony, who was apparently associated with the imperial mission to England in 1235, and was knighted by the king c. 5 June 1235, see Wild, 'Gift Inventory', p. 553 no. 13; and Wild, 'The Empress's New Clothes', pp. 15–16, 28–30 nos 108–13.

[181] On which day the king was at Westminster: *CPR 1232–47*, p. 105; *CR 1234–37*, pp. 91–2.

[182] On which day the king was at Woodstock: *CPR 1232–47*, p. 108.

[183] For Geoffrey de Turville, archdeacon of Dublin, royal treasurer for Ireland from at least February 1235, later bishop of Ossory (elected 1244, d. 1250), see *CPR 1232–47*, pp. 114, 429; *CR 1234–37*, pp. 165–6.

[184] On which day the king was at Woodstock: *CPR 1232–47*, p. 110. Wild, 'Gift Inventory', p. 532, misdates this entry to 26 June 1235.

[185] Presumably to be identified as Master Peter 'the leech' ('Leche'), also known as Peter de Jonzac (Charente-Maritime), a physician in royal service, apparently of Gascon birth. He first appears in the Chancery rolls a few weeks after the present entry, on 13 July 1235, where he was promised an annual pension of £5 at the Michaelmas Exchequer: *CPR 1232–47*, p. 113. In 1242 he received revenues from the king's estate at Bordeaux: *CPR 1232–47*, pp. 320–1. His final appearance is in 1255: C. H. Talbot and E. A. Hammond, *The Medical Practitioners in Medieval England: A Biographical Register* (London, 1965), pp. 248–9. Talbot and Hammond (pp. 244–5) seek to distinguish him from Peter de Alpibus, supposedly a native of Provence, who is recorded in England from 1241 and by the following year was serving as physician to the queen: *CPR 1232–47*, p. 275. However, the distinction is dependent upon the unlikelihood of any servant of Eleanor of Provence being found in England as early as July 1235, whereas we now know that the marriage of Eleanor and Henry III was under negotiation as early as June that year: it is first signalled in letters from Henry III to Eleanor's uncles Amadeus, count of Savoy, and his brother William, bishop-elect of Valence, dated 22 June, to be delivered by the prior of Hurley: *Foedera*, p. 217; Howell, *Eleanor of Provence*, pp. 11–12.

[186] As noted above, n. 100, a remarkable case of the present roll confirming what the chronicler Matthew Paris tells us was Henry III's morbid fear of thunder.

II

Government in Action

9

Another Fine Mess:
Evidence for the Resumption of Exchequer Authority in the Minority of Henry III

Nick Barratt

The reign of Henry III witnessed three key constitutional developments that still have relevance today, namely the emergence of Parliament; the confirmation that everyone, including the monarch, was subject to the rule of law; and the emerging concept that extraordinary taxation should be only be granted with the consent of the political realm. These fundamental changes to society were the result of deep dissatisfaction with royal government, and linked intrinsically to reissues of modified versions of Magna Carta, the first as a means to end the civil war after King John died in October 1216, and subsequently at the end of Henry's minority so that he could secure the grant of a fifteenth to conduct a defensive military campaign in Gascony. This second reissue was a particularly bitter pill for the king to swallow as he made his first foray into the world of politics, and one that shaped the way he managed his finances for the rest of his reign.

We know from other sources, such as the surviving pipe, receipt and memoranda rolls from the period, how much – or rather how little – revenue Henry III was able to generate from traditional sources throughout his reign, and that Magna Carta's restrictions on arbitrary exertions of the royal will were a major factor in the depressed levels of royal finance. Equally important was the fact that the administrative machinery of the Exchequer, harnessed under John to extract revenue at unprecedented levels, was dismantled during the conflict of 1215–17. It took the best part of a decade for it to recover its functionality and bring its records of audit up to date, by which time Magna Carta had become entrenched as the benchmark of good government, making it harder to exploit the Exchequer's revival for financial gain.[1] It can therefore be argued that the course of Henry's reign after 1225 was set by decisions made earlier by the regency council, and the associated reconstruction of the Exchequer and state finance, after 1216.

---

[1]   Discussed in N. Barratt, 'The Impact of the Loss of Normandy on the English Exchequer: The Pipe Roll Evidence', in *Foundations of Medieval Scholarship: Records Edited in Honour of David Crook*, ed. P. Brand and S. Cunningham (York, 2008), pp. 133–40; and N. Barratt, 'Finance on a Shoestring: The Exchequer in the Thirteenth Century', in *English Government in the Thirteenth Century*, ed. A. Jobson (Woodbridge, 2004), pp. 71–86.

Here I explore this crucial process with reference to an often overlooked source of financial data, the fine rolls, as they not only shed light on financial transactions and offerings to the king during this difficult early period, but also provide a different perspective on the way the Exchequer sought to re-establish itself after the chaos of civil war. Now that the fine rolls have been made digitally available online,[2] with supporting transcriptions and translations, it is possible to identify specific examples that clearly show how the style of management within the Exchequer changed over this time. The records also can be used to identify precisely the moment when retrospective reconstruction work came to a halt, and current events held sway over daily business once more. The fine rolls database makes it possible to search for specific words or phrases, which enables some basic statistical analysis about the nature of business recorded on the rolls. For example, searching for 'Exchequer' provides 4,826 hits for the period from 1217 to 1242, and each one of these entries tells us something different about the mechanics of government. Given that the fine rolls were a Chancery production, albeit with an overtly financial purpose, they reveal lines of communication between the key institutions at the centre of government, and record administrative transactions that far exceed the traditional notification of offerings and agreements made with the king. The fine rolls therefore play an integral part in the routine business of government, and the changing nature of entries throughout the minority period allows us to make some judgments about the state of the Exchequer and its functionality that its own records often mask.

In the period from 1217 to 1225 the Exchequer is mentioned on 786 occasions once duplicate entries have been stripped out, but there is a clear pattern when these figures are analysed more closely on an annual basis. Unsurprisingly given the continuing civil war, in 1217 there was only one recorded entry referring to the Exchequer by name; the number of entries between 1218 and 1222 remained fairly low, varying between forty-seven and seventy-six direct references annually. Yet there is a clear shift in the frequency of contact after 1222, jumping to 128 entries in 1223 and reaching 202 the following year, before returning to 146 in 1225. This is a marked increase from the previous period, as the reconstructive work drew to a close and the regency government began to prepare the adult king for direct rule. So the basic quantitative statistics suggest that the period 1222 to 1223 was a turning point in the nature of Exchequer business, or at least the volume of Exchequer business that impinged upon other aspects of the administration, and strongly suggest that a return to normality was imminent. By way of context, the frequency of entries remained steady at between 125 and 212 per year until 1236, when there was an enormous leap to 484 items of Exchequer business mentioned specifically; after 1239, the level remained well above 300 items per annum, reaching 523 in 1241.

Leaving the quantitative analysis to one side, the individual entries can be analysed to determine the nature of each transaction, and then categorised to demonstrate the various ways in which the Exchequer recovered its authority during the

---

[2] See the Henry III Fine Rolls project website, available at www.finerollshenry3.org.uk.

minority period. One key indicator that control had been re-established over royal debtors, and order brought to the accounting process, was the agreement of set regular payment terms for each debtor wherever possible. This was usually accompanied by the grouping of one individual's debts together in a single location on a pipe roll – often tidying up long-standing debts scattered across a range of counties. During the minority the Exchequer was acutely aware of the need to streamline and rationalise the summoning and audit process for older material, as well as identifying new content that had been generated up to the outbreak of war in 1215. Fixing payment terms with debtors, albeit at a low rate, at least had the additional benefit of bringing in a set level of revenue during the difficult early years of the minority, a vital component in the establishment of a regular income stream for the depleted coffers, while permitting the debtor to extend the debt for a more comfortable repayment period, in some cases taking advantage of the Crown's weakness.

The fine rolls contain numerous entries relating to this process of attermination, revealing the mechanics behind the entries in the pipe rolls. Many were fairly small debts, particularly in the first few years, but it was the grouping and attermination of large debts, often associated with fines made in the reign of King John or for feudal dues, that revealed a growing confidence in the Exchequer's conduct. This was especially true after 1221, when the amounts grew larger as payment terms grew shorter. This entry clearly shows the process at work:

> 13 November 1221
> Isabella de Bolbec, countess of Oxford, has made fine with the king, by £2,228 2s. 9½d., for having custody of the land and her son, the heir of Robert de Vere, formerly earl of Oxford, her husband, so that, beyond that fine, she will answer the king at the Exchequer for £1,778 11s. of the debt that the earl owed to the king for several debts. She is also to render 250 marks of the aforesaid monies at Hilary in the sixth year, 250 marks at Easter in the same year, 250 marks at the Nativity of St John the Baptist in the same year, 250 marks at Michaelmas in the same year, and £400 in the following year at the terms aforesaid, and £400 from year to year by the same terms until the aforesaid fine and debt have been paid in full.[3]

Yet the reality of the political situation meant that not all these vast sums were expected to be realised in hard cash, especially when the effects of the civil war and political upheaval were taken into account. In 1223, William d'Aubigny's fine for 6,000 marks was attermined at the rate of 40 marks per year, to be paid half at Easter and half at Michaelmas, as the next example shows. The corresponding entry for the fine appeared in the Lincolnshire pipe roll account from 1219 onwards,[4] but was left blank – that is, the debt was not called before the barons of the Exchequer – until the 1223 roll, when the attermination rate was inserted against the debt. The fine roll entry states:

---

[3]   *CFR 1221–22*, no. 23.
[4]   *The Great Roll of the Pipe for the Third Year of the Reign of King Henry III*, ed. B. E. Harris, PRS n.s. 42 (London, 1976), p. 126.

3 October 1223

The fine of William d'Aubigny. To the barons of the Exchequer. William d'Aubigny has made fine with the king by 40 marks, to be rendered each year at the Exchequer for as long as it pleases the king, for the 6,000 marks that he owes of the fine that he made with King John, the king's father, for his ransom, of which he is to render 20 marks at Easter forthcoming in the eighth year, 20 marks at Michaelmas next following in the same year, and 40 marks from year to year at the same terms for as long as it pleases the king. Order to cause the aforesaid fine to be enrolled and observed for as long as it pleases the king. They are not to penalize his steward because he did not pay any money at the Exchequer at this Michaelmas term in the seventh year.[5]

The uncertainty lies as to which William d'Aubigny was required to pay 6,000 marks. The Pipe Roll Society editions of the 1222 and 1223 pipe rolls incorrectly identify him as the William who was the fourth earl of Arundel.[6] His father, also William d'Aubigny, had been a staunch supporter of King John during the political upheaval in 1215 up to the point when the monarch abandoned Winchester to the advancing rebels, when he switched sides. However, it is clear that the 6,000 mark fine was imposed upon William d'Aubigny of Belvoir, a leading rebel and named as one of the twenty-five baronial 'enforcers' in the 1215 version of Magna Carta. William was placed in charge of Rochester Castle by the rebels, but after a staunch defence he was forced to surrender to John, who immediately threw him into prison and nearly hanged him. William only regained his liberty and forfeited estates by offering the enormous fine, and then fully embraced the royalist cause and was a leading commander at the battle of Lincoln in 1217.

Clearly in favour with the minority regime, William was granted fairly lenient repayment terms, and within months the Crown further reduced the amount to 15 marks per year.

17 August 1224

To the barons of the Exchequer. The king has granted William d'Aubigny that, of the debts that were exacted from him at the Exchequer, for which he made fine with the king to render 40 marks per annum, he is to render 15 marks to the king each year, namely a moiety at the Exchequer of Michaelmas and the other moiety at the Exchequer of Easter, until all aforesaid debts are paid to the king. Order to cause it to be enrolled and done thus.[7]

By this stage William had managed to find evidence that he had already paid some of this into John's chamber during the dying days of his reign: a total of £593 6s. 8d. between 12 July and 11 October 1216, the last payment being

---

[5]   *CFR 1222–23*, no. 294.

[6]   *The Great Roll of the Pipe for the Sixth Year of the Reign of King Henry III*, ed. G. A. Knight, PRS n.s. 51 (London, 1999), pp. 204, 230; *The Great Roll of the Pipe for the Seventh Year of the Reign of King Henry III*, ed. A. Jobson and C. F. Slade, PRS n.s. 56 (London, 2008), pp. 118, 212.

[7]   *CFR 1223–24*, no. 310.

made at Lynn on the day before the loss of John's baggage train and associated materials in the disastrous crossing of the Wash.[8]

Pledges were taken for many of the larger fines offered to the Crown, just in case there was any doubt about an individual's ability or willingness to pay the amount that had been imposed:

> 23 June 1222
> To the sheriff of Wiltshire. Eva de Tracy has made fine with the king by 200 marks, which is to be rendered at the terms given to her, for the trespass she made towards the king in that she married Hawise, her daughter, whose marriage pertained to the king, without licence. Order to receive pledges from Eva for rendering the 100 marks to the king at the terms given to her, and he is, with haste, under his seal, to cause the barons of the Exchequer to know the names of the pledges and for how much each of them will be pledge.[9]

In some cases more unusual deterrents were introduced to prevent default against a set repayment rate, as this early example shows:

> c. November 1217
> *Yorkshire. Cumberland.* Nicholas de Stuteville has made fine by 1,000 marks for his ransom, to be rendered at four terms, namely 250 marks at mid-Lent in the second year, 250 marks at Pentecost following, 250 marks at St Peter in Chains and 250 marks at Martinmas in the third year, namely so that if he does not keep the first term, he has bound his manors of Kirkbymoorside and Liddel under this form, that if he does not keep the first term, 50 librates of land are to be forfeited from the said manors. Similarly, if he does not keep the second term, 50 librates of land are to be forfeited from the same manors. Similarly, if he does not keep the third term, 50 librates of land are to be forfeited in the same manors. Similarly, if he does not keep to the fourth term, 50 librates of land are to be forfeited in the same manors. If the said two manors do not suffice to make good 200 librates of land, he will supplement the default from his other manors. Robert de Stuteville and Walter of Sowerby have mainperned for this fine in that if he does not keep a term, all of their lands are to be forfeited.[10]

Overall, the number of attermined debts rose during this period from only eighteen in 1218 to 235 in 1225, with the greatest increase coming from 1222 onwards once Exchequer authority had been reasserted.

Restoring order out of chaos was a key priority for the Exchequer, especially given the abandonment of the summoning and auditing of payments once civil war had broken out in 1215. The effect of the suspension of normal business, centred on the *adventus vicecomitum* at Michaelmas and preliminary proffer and views of account at Easter, is visible in the partially completed pipe roll for the last year of John's reign and the complete absence of a recorded audit for 1 Henry III, one of only a handful of occasions in Exchequer history that a pipe roll was

---

[8]   *The Great Roll of the Pipe for the Eighth Year of the Reign of King Henry III*, ed. E. Amt, PRS n.s. 54 (London, 2005), pp. 62–3.
[9]   *CFR 1221–22*, no. 206.
[10]   *CFR 1217–18*, no. 8.

not created. Re-establishing the pattern of activity throughout the Exchequer year was therefore of paramount importance.

From evidence contained in the extant memoranda rolls, we know how Exchequer officials planned the audit of the county accounts, in particular from the dates on which sheriffs and other accountants were provisionally given to appear before the barons of the Exchequer for the rigorous examination of their accounts and supporting material.[11] This evidence strongly suggests that normal business had been re-established by 1221, only to face further disruption caused by opposition to the regime from the Count of Aumale, incursions from Wales by Llywelyn ap Iorwerth, and the revolt of Falkes de Bréauté. Some of these incidents are reflected in the fine rolls; in particular, references to the grant of respite from paying or accounting for a debt enable us to gauge the impact of these political disturbances on the planning and delivery of Exchequer business.

It is no surprise to see that the number of entries relating to respite remained relatively low up to and including 1222, as the Exchequer vigorously strove to tackle the issue of recalcitrant debtors and impose its authority on as many of them as it could. No more than twenty-six grants of respite per year appear on the fine rolls before 1222; however, this jumped to over eighty entries per year in 1223, peaking at 119 in 1224 and remaining high in 1225. Thereafter, with the exception of 1228, the numbers of respites mentioned dropped to around sixty per year. The entries in 1224 and 1225 make it clear that many of the grants of respite were due to the political crisis; yet there are various other reasons why accountants were given additional time to appear at the Exchequer which reveal more about the way business was planned and conducted.

Some entries clearly relate to Crown debtors who were given more time to finalise their accounts and make payment, often linked to the time when Henry would 'come of age' and make such decisions himself:

5 October 1220

To the barons of the Exchequer. The king has given respite to John Lestrange, until the king comes of age, from the demand which they make from him by summons of the Exchequer for £79 10s. of the farm of the manor of Wrockwardine for 7½ years during the time of King John, the king's father, and for £24 of the farm of the same manor for the second and third years of the king's reign, and for the farm of the same manor which remains to be paid until the king comes of age. Order to cause John to have this respite until the king comes of age, as aforesaid.[12]

However, as the reign progressed, there usually had to be a compelling reason for an accountant to be assigned an alternative account date. There was a spate of entries in 1225 relating to the grant of the fifteenth, where sheriffs and other officials were permitted alternative dates to appear before the Exchequer so that they could prioritise the collection of the tax. Nonetheless, they were still expected to render the sums that were owed:

---

[11] *Receipt Rolls for the Seventh and Eight Years of the Reign of King Henry III*, ed. N. Barratt, PRS n.s. 55 (London, 2007), pp. v–xvi.

[12] *CFR 1219–20*, no. 276.

12 September 1225
On account of his business which the king has enjoined upon the sheriff of Oxfordshire to expedite, both in collecting the fifteenth and others things, he cannot render his account before the barons of the Exchequer on the morrow of Michaelmas in the ninth year. The king, therefore, has given him respite until the morrow of All Souls in the tenth year. Order to the barons of the Exchequer to cause him to have the aforesaid respite, admitting in the meantime his clerks that he will send with the money from the farm of his county and other things.[13]

It is also possible to glimpse some of the work that a Crown official was expected to undertake in the localities:

31 March 1225
To the barons of the Exchequer. Because Ralph Musard attends to the king's business in assessing and collecting the fifteenth in Bristol and elsewhere, and in making a perambulation of the forest and other business that the king has enjoined upon him, for which reason he cannot appear before them on the morrow of the Close of Easter to render his account, order to place his account in respite up to the aforesaid day [Easter] in one month.[14]

Other grants of respite were of a more practical nature:

30 July 1221
Order to the sheriff of Devon to place in respite the demand that he makes by summons of the Exchequer from William of Torrington, who has set out on pilgrimage towards Jerusalem, for the debts he owes the king, until the king is certain of his death or until his return from pilgrimage.[15]

Yet as the volume of business increased, the barons of the Exchequer were not above making the odd mistake, to the detriment of their timetable for the rendering of accounts:

8 December 1222
To the barons of the Exchequer. The sheriff of Herefordshire came to the king at Westminster in the octaves of St Andrew ready to render his account when they had left the Exchequer. Therefore, the king has given the sheriff a day to render his account at Hilary in one month. Order to permit him to have this day.[16]

Another accountant claimed an unusual excuse for non-attendance:

20 May 1225
Order to the barons of the Exchequer to place in respite, until fifteen days from Michaelmas in the ninth year, the demand for debts they make by summons of the Exchequer from W. archbishop of York, because the archbishop has set out for Alnwick where he is to be present to celebrate the marriage between Roger, son and heir of Earl H. Bigod, and Isabella, sister of the King of Scots.[17]

13   *CFR 1225*, no. 315.
14   *CFR 1224–25*, no. 140.
15   *CFR 1220–21*, no. 250.
16   *CFR 1222–23*, no. 29.
17   *CFR 1224–25*, no. 204.

The fine rolls open a window onto other areas of Exchequer practice during these crucial years of reconstruction, in particular the way that the staff of the Exchequer referred to its older records when conducting business. There is clear evidence from several fine roll entries that reference material was used to make decisions and plan forthcoming work, thereby demonstrating why it was so important retrospectively to audit and enrol the accounts.

The first such entry is from January 1218, and shows that not only was consultation made with other documents that have not survived – in this case the 'rolls of the Jews' – but also that the regents were entrusted with looking after important records not of their own making during the difficult early years:

> 3 January 1218
> To the barons of the Exchequer. It is evident to the king by an inspection of the rolls of the Jews that King John, his father, had granted to Mirabel, who was the wife of Elias the Jew of Gloucester, that she be quit of all the debts which Elias, her former husband, owed to the king, so that all of Elias's charters and the debts contained within them would remain to the king's father. And because those charters are in the custody of Earl W. Marshal, regent of the king and kingdom, at Gloucester, the king, wishing to uphold what was done by his father in this matter, order to cause the tenor of that grant to be upheld.[18]

The importance of the Exchequer's written memory is shown clearly by another entry from 1218, when attempts to clear up the mess left by the abandonment of normal record-keeping were getting firmly under way:

> 18 July 1218
> Order to R. bishop of Durham that since Simon fitz Walter made fine with King John … by 300 marks … in order to have the custody of the land and heir of Walter of Carew, with the marriage of the heir, so that in the time of King John Simon paid 300 marks at the Exchequer, according to the testimony of the rolls of the Exchequer of King John …[19]

During this state of flux, when records were being written and amended as old material was assessed and assimilated, we see an order for the usually sacrosanct pipe rolls to be changed to reflect actual events:

> 11 July 1218
> Because Robert of Cockfield has not kept to the fine he made with the king by 100 marks for having custody of the land formerly of Ralph Pikoc, of which he ought to have paid 50 marks at the Exchequer at Pentecost last past in the second year, but instead has refused to keep the fine, the king has granted the custody of the aforesaid land to Baldwin Filliol, who has made fine with the king for the same land by 50 marks to be paid at the Exchequer on the morrow of St Peter in Chains next forthcoming in the same year. Order to the barons of the Exchequer to receive this fine from Baldwin and to cause it to be enrolled in their rolls, and to cause Robert, who did not keep the fine which he made with the king by 100 marks, to be extracted from the rolls of the Exchequer.[20]

---

[18] *CFR 1217–18*, no. 17.
[19] *CFR 1217–18*, no. 154.
[20] *CFR 1217–18*, no. 152.

It is precisely because the Exchequer's archives were seen as the ultimate place of record that the need arose to expunge the old grantee's name to ensure that no future summons was made. Similarly, an examination of earlier rolls helped clear up confusion when accounting for old debts, or to take account of events that had happened in the previous reign.

> 14 April 1225
> The king, by an inspection of the rolls of the Exchequer, has learnt that Hugh Russell made fine with the king's father for having the hundred of Fawsley at farm by rendering 100s. annually, for which he has begun to make payment to the king of the arrears of the farm of the same hundred. Order to the sheriff of Northamptonshire to cause Hugh to have full seisin of that hundred.[21]

This clearly demonstrates why so much time was devoted to retrospectively creating pipe rolls that linked pre- and post-war debts, even if the process did not generate a large amount of revenue. The Exchequer was re-establishing its working archive, which it could then use to pursue individuals with more confidence, shifting the burden of proof for the discharge of a debt back towards the accountant rather than the Exchequer once any remaining areas of uncertainty in the records were eradicated.

Evidence, in the form of tallies, played a key part in the process. In this entry from 1225 the accountant William del Teyll was deemed quit because he was able to produce the relevant tally; this was particularly important because he had been involved in Falkes de Bréauté's revolt.

> 16 May 1225
> William del Teyll rendered 10 marks to the king in London by the hand of William de Castellis, on Friday next after Ascension in the ninth year, as he is able to establish by the tallies which he has for the fine that he made with the king for having his grace and benevolence because he was with Falkes de Bréauté. Order to the barons of the Exchequer to cause him to be quit.[22]

Another aspect of Exchequer practice revealed by the rolls was the diverse range of the accountants who were required to come in person to face the audit process. Receipt roll evidence from this period demonstrates that a far larger number of people appeared in person before the barons of the Exchequer to render their account than has traditionally been thought.[23] The fine rolls support this, given the range of orders sent out to enforce individuals to attend the Exchequer so that they could answer for their accounts. Many of these related to attermined debts, with a personal appearance serving to re-enforce the privilege granted to the accountant to have 'special terms'.

As with the professionalisation of the legal system, where the use of trained attorneys to represent their clients was to become standard, the bear-pit of the

---

21   *CFR 1224–25*, no. 160.
22   *CFR 1224–25*, no. 203.
23   *Receipt Rolls for the Seventh and Eighth Years of the Reign of King Henry III*, ed. N. Barratt, PRS n.s. 55 (London, 2007) pp. xix–xxv.

Exchequer and its complex processes also encouraged the nominal accountants to embrace the use of substitutes:

> 8 October 1224
> To the barons of the Exchequer. It is clear to the king by an inquisition taken by order of the king that the abbot of Cirencester used to answer by his attorney at the Exchequer for the debts of the king's predecessors ... by the return of the summonses of the Exchequer received by the hand of the sheriff of Gloucestershire from the bailiwicks of the seven hundreds ... Order to permit the abbot to answer the king at the Exchequer for the king's debts ...[24]

The fine rolls also cover other areas of Exchequer activity away from the principal role of audit. For example, we find information concerning payments out of the treasury. This particular entry was cancelled on the fine rolls, because it had already been copied onto the close rolls:

> 9 December 1225
> To E. the king's treasurer and the chamberlains. Order to deliver £500 out of the king's treasury to Walter of Kirkham and Walter of Brackley to acquit them of the expenses incurred by them and by the king at Christmas forthcoming.[25]

Fine rolls can give information about the flow of money directly into offices of the king's household, which is usually omitted from official Exchequer records of audit:

> 27 July 1224
> To the barons of the Exchequer. On Tuesday next before St Peter in Chains in the eighth year Henry son of Sigar rendered 40s. to the king in his Wardrobe at Bedford by the hand of Walter of Kirkham and Walter of Brackley for the men of Guildford, by which the aforesaid men made fine with the king for having licence to go towards their own parts and to be quit from coming to the army of Bedford.[26]

Importantly, the use of the Wardrobe as a means of rapidly gathering and disbursing cash was linked to moments of political crisis and warfare, as above, an echo of John's reign and a foretaste of what was to come with Henry's campaign in Gascony in 1242.

Re-establishing Exchequer authority throughout England was certainly not an easy task. The fine rolls contain clear evidence that the work of the Exchequer was hindered in the aftermath of the civil war. This entry, from May 1218, shows that rival factions were still at work at a high political level, and the obstructions that royal officials faced as a result; it also emphasises the fact that the Exchequer was still seen as the ultimate means through which the Crown sought to enforce compliance:

> 3 May 1218
> The count of Aumale, the earl Warenne, J. constable of Chester, the constable of Tickhill, Robert de Ros and Hugh de Balliol were summoned to come before the

---

[24]   *CFR 1223–24*, no. 408.
[25]   *CFR 1225–26*, no. 19.
[26]   *CFR 1223–24*, no. 286.

barons of the Exchequer at Trinity in fifteen days to answer why they have hindered the sheriff of Yorkshire in taking the king's pleas and doing as others ought to do and are accustomed to do in the same county to the king's advantage, so that he has been and is unable to pay his farm and to answer for the debts of the king and other things for which he has summons.[27]

These were difficult times, and a clear sense of frustration was expressed in this fine from April 1219, addressed to the sheriff of Yorkshire, who could no longer hide behind the recalcitrance of others:

23 April 1219
Order to the sheriff of Yorkshire that, as he loves himself, he is not to deliver any money arising from the king's debts, whether from fines, amercements, farms or anything else in his county, to anyone in the world by any letter or command, save than to the king at the Exchequer by the hand of the barons of the Exchequer, but, having collected and reserved those monies to the king's use, putting aside all delay and excuse, he is to be at the Exchequer at the day of account given to him, ready to answer the king there so fully that his lord has honour and the sheriff advantage, and lest the king should betake himself to his body and all his property, if he does otherwise.[28]

Despite this clear warning, the sheriff continued to drag his heels, warranting another blast six months later:

16 October 1219
Order to the sheriff of Yorkshire to come with all possible haste to the Exchequer ready to render his account for all that he ought to answer for there. He is distinctly forbidden to surrender or deliver any of the money arising from his bailiwick, whether from amercements, fines, debts, farms or other things, save to the king at the Exchequer or to the archbishop of York, as he is ordered by other letters of the king.[29]

On the other hand, supporters of the new regime could expect to receive favourable treatment, such as having their expenses cleared along with grants of respite from the necessity of preparing detailed accounts each year, as this entry shows:

12 May 1218
To the barons of the Exchequer. The king has granted R. earl of Chester and Lincoln, for the costs and expenses he has incurred in keeping the king's castles, that he and all of his bailiffs are to remain quit of all accounts, issues and farms that arise from the counties of Shropshire and Staffordshire and the honour of Lancaster ... up to the term which will be established by the legate and the king's council, save for the scutage assessed by the king's council in the second year ... The earl and his men are to send someone to the Exchequer at the set terms by the customs of the Exchequer, but are not to pay anything of the farms and issues of

27   *CFR 1217–18*, no. 52.
28   *CFR 1218–19*, no. 238.
29   *CFR 1218–19*, no. 425.

the counties, nor will they remain in arrears of the farms and issues up to the term which will be set, as aforesaid.[30]

Despite the fact that the earl and his bailiffs were freed from the requirement to answer for old debts, and remained quit for the specified accounts, they were still ordered to send a representative to the Exchequer; a case of 'keeping up appearances' in both senses.

Alongside the restoration of Exchequer authority, the other daunting problem facing the minority regime was the low level of royal revenue. A key step was the resumption of the royal demesne, recorded in a series of instructions issued to the county sheriffs at Michaelmas 1221, as typified by this entry for Cambridgeshire, which was also transmitted to all other sheriffs:

> 30 September 1221
> Order to take into the king's hand without delay all the king's demesne lands in Cambridgeshire, namely those demesnes of which King John, the king's father, was seised at the beginning of the war between him and his barons. They are also to take into the king's hand all his escheats, whether from the lands of Normans or from the lands of Bretons, or from other foreigners, and, similarly, all other of the king's escheats however they escheated, whether they came into the hand of the king's father before the war, in the war, or afterwards into the king's hand. They are to keep all those demesnes and all those escheats safely in the king's hand, so that they remove nothing therefrom until the king orders otherwise.[31]

Checks were made to ensure that these instructions had actually been followed, in the form of inquisitions into specific manors across the country in 1222:

> 24 June 1222
> By the counsel of the archbishop of Canterbury, the bishops of England, H. de Burgh, justiciar, and the earls and barons, it was lately provided that, from St Barnabas the Apostle last past, all of the king's demesne lands were to be taken into his hand. Order that, having taken with himself two law-worthy and discreet men of his county, he is without delay to go in person to the manor of Somerton and, by the view of the same men, take into the king's hand the twelve librates of land that Godfrey of Crowcombe holds in that vill, together with the issues then arising from the aforesaid day and the stock and new corn which Godfrey received therein, saving to him the rest of his chattels.[32]

Eventually, key lands, towns or manors were reassigned at fixed farms that had to be accounted for at the Exchequer by representatives. Bristol was granted to its citizens on an annual basis, while the men of Winchester were left in no doubt as to their conduct while they held their city at farm:

---

[30] *CFR 1217–18*, no. 69.
[31] *CFR 1220–21*, no. 346.
[32] *CFR 1221–22*, no. 213. For the original Latin text of this entry and the previous one, see *The Great Roll of the Pipe for the Fifth Year of the Reign of King Henry III*, ed. D. Crook, PRS n.s. 48 (London, 1990), pp. lvii–lxi.

17 November 1221

To the sheriff of Hampshire … He is to say to them on the king's behalf that they are to receive it in such a way and so behave themselves that the king will have no loss, and whatever is to be allowed to them when they come to the Exchequer for their account, the king will cause them to be allowed this by the consideration of the barons of the Exchequer and other faithful men.[33]

A great deal of thought went into the administration of some of the demesne lands, such as indicated in the lengthy grant of Cheltenham to its townsfolk:

24 March 1223

The king has granted his manor of Cheltenham to the men of Cheltenham to hold at farm for five years from Michaelmas in the sixth year, rendering £64 to the king in each of the five years at the Exchequer by the hand of each of them, of which they are to render a moiety at the Exchequer of Easter and the other moiety at the Exchequer of Michaelmas, so that the sheriff or his bailiffs will have no entry into the manor, unless to make attachments pertaining to the crown and to make the view of frankpledge, and so that, then, the sheriff or his bailiffs are to have no amercement or aid by reason of that view and are not to take anything therefrom. The men of the aforesaid manor will, however, have the hundred of Cheltenham within the farm of the manor with the customs that ought to and used to pertain to that hundred. Moreover, on Thursday of each week they are to have a market at the aforesaid manor and an annual three-day fair, namely on the eve, feast and morrow of St James, unless that market and fair are to the harm of neighbouring markets and fairs. The sheriff is also to render to them all issues of the same manor, which he has received, arising from Michaelmas aforesaid, saving arrears and debts to the sheriff from the time before Michaelmas. He is also to render to the same men the land newly brought into cultivation which he has received in the manor, and to cause the king to know how much he has caused them to have. They will also have all corn that the sheriff sowed in the land of the same manor in this the seventh year, for which they are to render to the sheriff the costs that he incurred in sowing the aforesaid land. Order to cause the men to have the manor by the aforesaid farm with the aforesaid liberty, hundred, issues, the newly cultivated land, and all corn sown in the land of the manor, and the aforesaid market and fair, as aforesaid, so that they are to be able to answer the king sufficiently for the farm at the terms given to them at the Exchequer without any impediment.[34]

Yet there was also an element of flexibility in arrangements as time progressed:

9 February 1224

9 Feb. Westminster. *Essex.* To the sheriff of Essex and Hertfordshire. Order to cause Stephen of Seagrave to have the moiety of the farms of sergeanties, frank-pledges and aids of sheriffs, sursises and perquisites and other issues of the aforesaid counties for half a year, namely from Michaelmas in the seventh year to Easter in the eighth year, so that he might answer the king sufficiently for the moiety of that half-year, namely for a quarter of a year. Alternatively, the sheriff is to retain fully the aforesaid issues of the aforesaid half-year, so that Stephen renders to him that

---

[33]   *CFR 1221–22*, no. 26.
[34]   *CFR 1222–23*, no. 110.

which he receives of the issues of the same half-year, and then the sheriff is to be respondent to the king for all issues of the whole of the half-year aforesaid.[35]

In essence, this curious entry seems to eschew traditional Exchequer control and delegates an element of autonomy to local officials to arrange matters among themselves.

Before the reign of Richard, the Crown had traditionally been reliant on income from the royal demesne. However, the damage done to this mainstay of state finance in previous reigns was irreparable and left a deficiency that could not easily be compensated for by other sources of income, as John's desperate attempts to exploit every possible financial avenue proved. Matters were not helped by the fact that there was a minority government for nine years after his death. This period of grace allowed Magna Carta to become a benchmark for acceptable government, but King Henry's three leading advisers were not able, given the precarious political situation, to attempt radical or innovative experiments to supply alternative sources of revenue. Instead, they were left with the traditional feudal dues, vacancies and estreats, fines, profits from the administration of justice, the forest and taxation by aids, carucages and tallages, as well as extraordinary levies.

The fine rolls contain plenty of evidence that the minority government was still willing and able to exploit the sensitive area of feudal incidents, including relief, wardship and the right to marry; but there was also a clear acknowledgement that times had changed, thanks to John's rapacity and Magna Carta's rules about what could be required – rules that reflected perhaps the most fundamental cause of concern among the king's advisors. Consider the following entry:

22 March 1219
Bedfordshire. Order to the sheriff of Bedfordshire that if Thomas of Gravenel finds him safe pledges for rendering 5 marks to the king at the Exchequer of Easter, which he owes the king at that term of the fine which he made with him for his trespass because he took to wife Joan who was the wife of Alan of Mumby, whose marriage belonged to the king's grant, without his leave, he is to cause him to have peace, making no distraint against him in the meantime and not permitting any distraint to be made against him.[36]

Doubtless John would have imposed severe penalties to regain 'the goodwill of the king' for such impudence, but the regents dared not step outside the limits expressed in Magna Carta, no matter how desperate they were for income.

John's harsh policies had, however, proved to be effective in raising revenue, and were not wholly abandoned. This can be seen from the tenor of the next entry following the death of Philip of Oldcoates, an order to the sheriff of Nottinghamshire and Derbyshire. The regency government moved swiftly to gather all Oldcoates's lands into the Crown's possession, admitting freely that these financial sums tied Oldcoates closely to the king:

---

[35] *CFR 1223–24*, no. 73.
[36] *CFR 1218–19*, no. 206.

2 November 1220
Phillip of Oldcotes, who was bound to the king in great debts, is dead. Order to take into the king's hand without delay all land Phillip held in his bailiwick, of whatever fee, with all chattels found therein, which he is to cause to be distinctly and openly recorded, so that he has one roll and the king's beloved and faithful Robert of Lexington, king's clerk, who the king has sent to him on account of this, the other roll.[37]

Once again, the fastidious record-keeping involved in this exercise was the key to enforcing the decision, and was repeated in all the counties where Oldcoates held land.

Desperation to gather income in the early days of the regime meant that strenuous efforts were made to recover old debts from the reign of King John; indeed, the Exchequer was expected to flex its institutional muscles:

19 January 1219
Order to W. archbishop of York to have before the Exchequer at the octaves of the Purification of the Blessed Mary, without difficulty, the 500 marks which he owes to the king and which King John, father of King Henry, lent to him before he set out for the Council of Rome, and which he promised to render upon his return from the same council, of which he has not yet satisfied King Henry or his father. The king has, moreover, ordered the sheriff of Yorkshire to compel the archbishop, by his lands and tenements, to pay the aforesaid 500 marks.[38]

On the same day another instruction was issued to follow up an Exchequer summons with the threat of distraint:

19 January 1219
Order to R. bishop of Durham and his associates, itinerant justices, to distrain the citizens of York to pay their debts to the king, for which they received summons of the Exchequer, and to induce them in each and any way that they can to make that payment.[39]

We can also gain a greater understanding of the ways in which the officials at the Exchequer dealt with other areas of royal finance that generated substantial bureaucratic activity, namely the general eyre and the collection of taxation. This entry from 1219 emphasises how many different lines of communication were required to carry out an eyre successfully:

21 June 1219
Order to the bishop of Lincoln and his associates, itinerant justices in the counties of Lincolnshire, Nottinghamshire and Derbyshire, that those who fell into mercy before them and can and ought to be amerced by them are to be amerced as is most expeditious for the king, and, those amercements having been recorded in writing, are to be sent under their seals to the sheriffs of those counties in which they are making their eyre, commanding and ordering them on the king's behalf to cause

---

37 *CFR 1220–21*, no. 3.
38 *CFR 1218–19*, no. 110a.
39 *CFR 1218–19*, no. 111.

distraint to be made for those amercements, and then to collect the money thus arising by the hand of two law-worthy knights who will expedite this best for the king, and they will nominate them in each county, so that the king will have the moiety at the Exchequer shortly forthcoming at St Peter in Chains in the third year by the hand of the same sheriffs and the two aforesaid knights, and the other moiety at Michaelmas next following, putting off all delay and excuse.[40]

It is interesting to note the implicit recognition that money was an important motive for sending itinerant justices to the counties, as much as the desire to ensure that everyone had access to royal justice.

Keeping track of the collection of scutage, tallage, carucage and extraordinary taxation, all of which generated dozens of rolls containing thousands of new names to be processed, was another task carried out by the Exchequer. The fine rolls show how instructions were sent out to various accountants to simplify their supporting records, particularly if the assessment and collection arrangements were complex:

11 March 1221
To the sheriff of Cambridgeshire and Huntingdonshire. Order that, putting off all excuse and delay, he is to cause the archbishops, bishops, abbots, priors and all prelates in his bailiwick to have, within mid-Lent forthcoming in the fifth year, that which he received in the name of carucage from their lands and fees, for which he has not yet answered those who had been assigned to this at the New Temple in London, and he is then to cause the barons of the Exchequer to know, upon his account at the Exchequer of Easter forthcoming, how much he answered for to the aforesaid assigns at the aforesaid place and how much he has caused the prelates and ecclesiastics in his bailiwick to have by the king's order.[41]

Nonetheless, time was taken for diligent enquiry, to ensure that the correct totals were received:

19 November 1223
Order to the sheriff of Gloucestershire to place in respite the tallage that the king caused to be assessed upon the vill of Cirencester, until three weeks from Hilary in the eighth year, because the abbot of Cirencester has been ordered to be before the king then or his justiciar, or the barons of the Exchequer, and is to have the charters that he has from the king's ancestors, in order to show by the same charters whether he ought to be quit of tallage or not.[42]

As with other areas of state finance, the Exchequer was increasingly prepared to use threats to collect what was due, particularly in times of crisis:

22 November 1224
Order to the sheriff of Kent to distrain all those who hold of the king in chief in his bailiwick by knight service to render their scutage to the king, namely 2 marks per shield for the army of Montgomery and 2 marks for the army of Bedford, so

---

[40]   *CFR 1218–19*, no. 307a.
[41]   *CFR 1220–21*, no. 103.
[42]   *CFR 1223–24*, no. 31.

that, as he loves himself and his own, he is to have that scutage at the Exchequer in the octaves of Hilary in the ninth year, excepting those who have quittance by the king's letters, and those for whom he rendered account at the aforesaid Exchequer.[43]

This summary of Exchequer recovery and the collection of royal revenue during the minority of Henry III shows the benefit of looking at sources beyond the Exchequer records themselves. Although much of the material confirms what we already know from pipe, receipt and memoranda roll evidence, there is a level of detail in these records that brings the workings of the Exchequer to life from a different perspective. Furthermore, fine rolls entries demonstrate the way that the Chancery and Exchequer worked closely in tandem to facilitate the recovery of governmental administrative machinery, revealing the complexity of the royal administration in a way that cannot be achieved by dealing with these key departments and their records in isolation.

---

[43] *CFR 1224–25*, no. 22.

10

Roger of Wendover, Prior of Belvoir, and the Implementation of the Charter of the Forest, 1225–7

David Crook

The *Flores Historiarum* of Roger of Wendover is one of the most important contemporary, or near contemporary, chronicles of the reign of King John and the first two decades of the reign of Henry III. However, for the earlier part of the period in particular, it is demonstrably inaccurate and untrustworthy on many points, which has led scholars to adopt a questioning attitude to material which cannot be verified from other sources.[1] Roger's work was continued by his successor at the Benedictine abbey of St Albans, Matthew Paris, who took over probably in May 1234, and for the period before that date used Wendover's work as a basis for his own history, the *Chronica Majora*, along with some additions of his own.[2] In 1944, V. H. Galbraith concluded that Wendover's chronicle was original from about 1201, when his main sources for the earlier period – Roger of Howden and Ralph of Diss (de Diceto) – came to an end, and was contemporary from then until 1235. Galbraith opined that 'the *Flowers of History* cannot have been begun until after 1204, while the probabilities are that Wendover only turned to history after 1219 when he was removed from his position as prior of Belvoir.' His material, thought Galbraith, is more trustworthy for the reign of Henry III than for that of John, and he wrote his account of John's time when his son, though still a minor, had already been on the throne for some years.[3]

The fundamental error in this account is the belief that the chronicler left Belvoir Priory (a dependency of St Albans Abbey) in or about 1219. This idea seems to have originated with the introduction to H. A. Coxe's edition of the *Flores*, published in 1841, and, despite clear evidence to the contrary, has been repeated ever since, down to and including the *Oxford Dictionary of National Biography* in 2004.[4] The *Gesta Abbatum*, which was put together from St Albans sources by Thomas Walsingham at the end of the fourteenth century, places

[1]   See, in particular, W. L. Warren, *King John*, new edn (New Haven, 1997), pp. 11–14; A. Gransden, *Historical Writing in England, c. 550–c. 1307* (London, 1974), p. 368; J. C. Holt, *The Northerners*, 2nd edn (Oxford, 1992), pp. 102, 107, 117, 141 n. 2; J. C. Holt, *Magna Carta*, 2nd edn (Cambridge, 1992), pp. 224–6, 406–11.
[2]   R. Kay, 'Wendover's Last Annal', *EHR* 84 (1969), 779–85.
[3]   V. H. Galbraith, *Roger Wendover and Matthew Paris* (Glasgow, 1944), pp. 16–21.
[4]   H. A. Coxe, *Rogeri de Wendover Chronica sive Flores Historiarum*, 5 vols (London, 1841–5), i, p. vi; Gransden, *Historical Writing in England*, p. 359; D. Corner, 'Wendover, Roger of (d. 1236)', *ODNB*.

Wendover's removal, which took place because 'he had wasted the property of the church with careless prodigality', during the abbacy of William of Trumpington. His rule lasted from 1214 to 1235, but the accounts of the different abbots in the *Gesta*, Trumpington's among them, do not take the form of a chronological narrative of their time in office.[5] The *Gesta* does, however, mention the abbot's visitation of various St Albans cells, including Belvoir, as having taken place 'in time of war', when, 'as customary', he received royal licence to go to the North. In the context this clearly refers to events at some date subsequent to the war of 1215–17.[6] This might, according to the Rolls Series editor of the *Flores*, H. G. Hewlett, indicate the events either of 1224 (siege of Bedford), 1227 (revolt of several earls against the king) or 1231–4 (Welsh campaign, Marshal's war). Hewlett concluded, however, that the reference to 'time of war' was too vague to fix the date of the visitation, and settled for a date sometime between 1224 and 1231. Assuming that Wendover's 'prodigality' was uncovered by the abbot's visit, and that his removal as prior came shortly after, this would have allowed him at least five years at St Albans to write his chronicle before his death on 6 May 1236 (recorded by Matthew Paris among a list of obits of St Albans priests and others from 1216 to 1253), although we now know from Richard Kay's work that he ceased to write in 1234.[7] More recent writers have had varying opinions as to the time of the chronicle's composition, usually assuming with Hewlett that it was after Wendover ceased to carry out his managerial responsibilities as prior of Belvoir (whenever that was), but allowing enough time for him to write it before his death. Kay thought that he began about 1220, Sir James Holt after 1225 and probably before 1230, and Antonia Gransden possibly as late as 1231, while Lewis Warren thought that his account of John's reign was written about ten years after that king's death.[8]

It is not certain when Roger became prior of Belvoir, but it was probably before the end of the reign of King John, possibly a little while before.[9] His geographical position at Belvoir gave him a good vantage point from which to observe events in the East Midlands, as Sean McGlynn has pointed out.[10] The

[5] *Gesta Abbatum Monasterii Sancti Albani*, ed. H. T. Riley, Rolls Series, 3 vols (London, 1867–9), i, pp. 270–2, 274.

[6] *Gesta Abbatum*, i, pp. 270–1: 'et, ut moris est, sicut praedicitur, tempore guerrae, accepta a regis licencia, versus plagam tetendit borealum'. The reference to the north relates to the abbot's visit to Tynemouth after he had been to Belvoir; no licence is recorded on the patent rolls.

[7] *Rogeri de Wendover*, iii, pp. viii–x; *Chronica Majora*, vi, p. 274.

[8] Kay, 'Wendover's Last Annal', p. 779; Holt, *The Northerners*, p. 3; Gransden, *Historical Writing in England*, p. 359; Warren, *King John*, p. 11.

[9] His predecessor, Master Ralph Simplex, died on 13 October 1217, but was by then a monastic archdeacon and could have left Belvoir some time earlier: *Chronica Majora*, vi, p. 270; *The Heads of Religious Houses in England and Wales*, vol. 1: *940–1216*, ed. D. Knowles, C. N. L. Brooke and V. London (Cambridge, 1972), p. 85.

[10] S. McGlynn, 'Roger of Wendover and the Wars of Henry III', in *England and Europe in the Reign of Henry III (1216–1272)*, ed. B. K. U. Weiler and I. W. Rowlands (Aldershot, 2001), pp. 183–206, at p. 186.

detailed account in his chronicle of John demanding and receiving the surrender of Belvoir Castle, adjacent to the priory, from the rebel William d'Aubigny's men on 27 December 1215, and his commitment of its custody to two of his Poitevin followers, Geoffrey and Oliver de Buteville, has all the hallmarks of an eye-witness account. Earlier in the year, at Michaelmas, the chronicler noted the provisioning of the castle by William d'Aubigny before he joined the rebels in London, while around Easter he gave a long and detailed list of those attending an armed gathering of magnates at nearby Stamford, although the authenticity of this has been questioned.[11] There is nothing by way of local or regional information in the chronicle before then, and it is tempting to imagine that it begins in 1215 because Trumpington, whose election to the abbacy of St Albans on 30 November 1214 is mentioned, was responsible for the chronicler's appointment as prior of Belvoir.[12] Under 1217 Wendover gives detailed information about the events surrounding the siege of Mountsorrel Castle (further east in Leicestershire), the violent passage of French infantry through the Vale of Belvoir, the three-day sojourn by the royalist army at Newark and the subsequent battle at Lincoln, followed by the siege of Newark Castle early in 1218 – together sufficient to indicate that local information from the region was available to him.[13] He even mentions the burial of a knightly casualty of the battle of Lincoln, Sir Reginald Crook, at nearby Croxton Abbey, and the story that a year earlier the abbot of Croxton had shriven the dying John at Newark Castle, when the king told him that he commended his body and soul to St Wulfstan, leading to his burial in Worcester Cathedral.[14] Local information continued to be included in subsequent years. In his annal for 1222 Wendover gives detailed information about severe weather in England, especially high winds and thunderstorms, a phenomenon also remarked upon by other contemporary chroniclers. He begins with a story about a lightning strike and fire on 8 February 1223 at the parish church of Grantham in Lincolnshire, the nearest market town to Belvoir Priory. After describing how the smell of burning resulting from the lightening caused those within the church to run outside, and the means by which the fire was extinguished, he ends the passage by remarking that physical traces of the event still remained in the church; this indicates that the account was written at least a few years afterwards, but that Roger still had access to local information, even if by then he had moved back to St Albans.[15]

The end of Roger's tenure as prior can be dated more easily than the beginning. He was still in office on 6 October 1224, when, after bringing an assize of *darrein presentment* against Geoffrey de Gresley, 'Roger prior of Beauuer' successfully claimed the advowson of the church of Norton, Leicestershire, by means

---

[11] *Rogeri de Wendover*, ii, pp. 114–15, 145, 164; Holt, *The Northerners*, p. 107.
[12] *Rogeri de Wendover*, ii, pp. 112–13.
[13] *Rogeri de Wendover*, ii, pp. 211–19, 226.
[14] *Rogeri de Wendover*, ii, pp. 196, 217.
[15] *Rogeri de Wendover*, ii, pp. 268–9.

of a final concord agreed in the Bench at Westminster.[16] His period of office had ended by 27 May 1226, as indicated in a document of that date whereby the abbey of St Albans presented Martin, brother of Winemer, the former archdeacon of Northampton, to replace him as prior because he had 'returned to the peace and quiet of the cloister on account of illness'.[17] This may have been a diplomatic cover for the financial mismanagement alleged in the *Gesta Abbatum*, and perhaps the abbot's visitation had only recently taken place, although 1226 can hardly be described as a 'time of war'.

It is therefore firmly established that Roger of Wendover was still prior of Belvoir during the year 1225. He began his annal for the year with an account of the process whereby the king, acting though the justiciar Hubert de Burgh, requested from the leading men of the realm a subvention to enable him to recover his recent continental losses in Gascony. They agreed to a tax of a fifteenth on moveable goods throughout England, in return for the concession of liberties.[18] This took the form, in February, of the reissue of Magna Carta and the Charter of the Forest, and their publication by proclamation in the counties, both immediately and again in May, when the first payment of the tax was due.[19] This process, though not its dual stages, was described in detail by Wendover.

> Charters having immediately been written and secured with the king's seal, one was sent to each of the counties of England, and to those provinces which were situated in a forest two charters were directed, namely one of the common liberties and the other of the liberties of the forest ... so that the charters of each of the kings are in no way found to be dissimilar.[20]

Roger was, of course, wrong in assuming that the Charter of the Forest had been issued in the time of King John at the same time as the first version of Magna Carta, and had in his annal for 1215 concocted a version of the later forest

---

[16]   TNA, CP 25/1/121/10, no. 92 [AALT_IMG 1936]; *The Heads of Religious Houses, England and Wales*, vol. 2: *1216–1377*, ed. D. M. Smith and V. C. M. London (Cambridge, 2001), p. 90; HMC, *The Manuscripts of the Duke of Rutland preserved at Belvoir Castle*, 4 vols (London, 1888–1905), iv, p. 143.

[17]   *Rotuli Hugonis de Welles Episcopi Lincolniensis*, vol. 3, ed. F. N. Davis, Lincoln Record Society 9 (1914), p. 150: 'propter ipsius debilitatem ad quietem et pacem claustri revocato'. The document is dated at 'Tinghurst in aula, vigilia Ascensionis Domini, videlicet vj kalendas Junii', i.e. 27 May, in the bishop's seventeenth episcopal year, 1226; it records a large number of witnesses, headed by John precentor of Lincoln and four canons of Lincoln. Under May 1226 Wendover noted the death of Richard Marsh, bishop of Durham, at the beginning of the month, but as would be expected made no mention of his own replacement at Belvoir: *Rogeri de Wendover*, ii, p. 307.

[18]   *Rogeri de Wendover*, ii, pp. 282–3. For the best account of these events, see D. Carpenter, *The Minority of Henry III* (London, 1990), pp. 379–86, 391–3, 403–4.

[19]   *RLC*, ii, pp. 70, 73b.

[20]   *Rogeri de Wendover*, ii, pp. 282–3: 'chartisque protinus conscriptis et regis sigillo munitis, ad singulos Angliae comitatus chartae singulae diriguntur, et ad provincias illas quae in forestis sunt constitutae, duae chartae sunt directae, una scilicet de libertatibus communibus et altera de libertatibus forestae ... ita quod chartae utrorumque regum in nullo inveniuntur dissimiles.'

charter of 1217, with 'John by the grace of God King of England etc.' as its grantor.[21] The 1225 account goes on to describe the arrangements made to hold perambulations of the forests to ascertain which areas had been afforested since the first coronation of Henry II in 1154, and which were, under the terms of the forest charter, immediately to be disafforested.

> Then a day was determined upon a month after Easter for twelve knights and legal men to be chosen from each county of the kingdom, who should on their oath go on to distinguish the new from the old forests, so that all those which should be discovered to have been afforested since the coronation of the present king's grandfather Henry should be immediately disafforested. And so, the council having broken up, the charters were sent each to their proper county where, by the king's written command, they were ordered under oath to be observed by all.[22]

After dealing with some other matters, Roger turned to the work of the forest officials and jurors who held the perambulations in the counties.

> In the same year, about a month after Easter, Hugh de Neville and Brian de Lisle, with other persons assigned for this, were sent throughout England for the purpose of choosing, in each of the forest districts, twelve knights or free and legal men to perambulate the bounds of the forests, and to determine on their oath what forests ought to remain as they were before, and which ought to be deforested.[23]

These letters were, as recorded on the patent roll, issued to Neville, Lisle, and also Master Henry of Cerne, with two, three or four named sub-commissioners for each forest county, on 16 February 1225. This was exactly six weeks before Easter that year, but Wendover's chronology was correct in that the returns were ordered to be completed by a month after Easter.[24] Also on 16 February the sheriffs of Yorkshire and Northumberland were instructed that no woods were to be felled or venison taken until the perambulations had been held and presented to the king.[25]

---

[21] *Rogeri de Wendover*, ii, pp. 127–32. On the texts of the two charters in the works of Wendover and Matthew Paris, whose information about the charters was dependent on Wendover, see J. C. Holt, 'The St Albans Chroniclers and Magna Carta', *TRHS* 5th series 14 (1964), 67–88; reprinted in *Magna Carta and Medieval Government* (London, 1985), pp. 265–87.

[22] *Rogeri de Wendover*, ii, p. 283: 'Tunc constitutus est dies certus ad mensem post Pascha, ut de singulis comitatibus regni duodecim milites et legales homines eligerunt, qui addito juramento novas a veteribus discernerent forestas, ut omnes illae, quae inventae fuerint afforestate post primam coronationem Henrici avi istius regis, statim deafforestentur; et sic, solute concilio, delatae sunt chartae singulae ad singulos comitatus, ubi ex regis mandato literatorio interposito juramento ab omnibus observari jubentur.'

[23] *Rogeri de Wendover*, ii, p. 286: 'Eodem anno, ad mensem de Pascha, missi sunt a rege Angliae Hugo de Nevilla et Brienus de Insula cum aliis ad hoc assignatis per Angliam, ut in singulis forestarum provinciis duodecim milites, vel liberi homines et legales, eligerentur ad deambulandum metas forestarum, ut per sacramentum eorum quae forestae remanere ut fuerunt prius et quae deafforestari debeant discernatur.'

[24] *PR 1216–25*, pp. 567–70.

[25] *RLC*, ii, p. 70.

There then follows one of the most remarkable passages in the whole chronicle, which exposes the feelings of relief experienced by all those affected by the forest law who were now to be freed from its restrictions.

> The king's commands being very soon executed, although not without great opposition of many, each and all used these liberties, selling the produce of their own woods, making assarts, hunting beasts, and ploughing the land which was before uncultivated, so that all disposed at their will in the disafforested woods; and not only the men, but dogs also, which were earlier accustomed to be expeditated, enjoyed these liberties. In short, the nobles, knights and free tenants used these common liberties, so that not one iota contained in the king's charter was excluded.[26]

No further reference to the forests is made in the chronicle until the point when the king repudiated some of the perambulations, immediately after declaring himself to be of age early in 1227.

> In the month of February in the same year, the king of the English, a council having been assembled at Oxford, before all those present he declared himself to be of legitimate age to be released from wardship, and to undertake the main performance of the kingly duties himself. ... At the same council too, the said king annulled and cancelled the charters of the liberties of the forests in all the counties of England, after they had been in practice throughout the whole of England for two years; and as a reason for this he alleged that the charters had been granted, and the liberties written and assigned, whilst he was under the care of a guardian, and had no power over his own body or his seal, and therefore as it had been an unreasonable usurpation it could no longer stand good.[27]

On 9 February 1227 the patent roll records orders by the king that the knightly perambulators of the forests in Nottinghamshire are to come before him to recognise that in making their perambulation they had trespassed against him and ask for his indulgence, because he could not remit this trespass against them or their heirs; the same orders were repeated in respect of the perambulators

---

[26] *Rogeri de Wendover*, ii, p. 286: 'Facta itaque in brevi regii exsecutione mandate, licet non sine magna contradictione plurimorum, concessibus libertatibus singuli usi sunt, de boscis suis propriis vendentes, essarta facientes, bestias venantes, terram arabilem de inculta sulcantes, ita quod de nemoribus deafforestatis omnes pro libitu disponebant; et non solum homines, verum etiam canes, qui prius expeditari solebant, has libertates se habere gaudebant. Communibus vero libertatibus magnates, milites et libere tenentes adeo usi sunt, quod nec iota unum in regis charta contentum exstitit praetermissum.'

[27] *Rogeri de Wendover*, ii, pp. 318–19: 'Eodem tempore rex Anglorum, mense Februario apud Oxoniam concilio congregato, denuntiavit coram omnibus se legitime esse aetatis, ut de cetero solutus a custodia regia negotia ipse principaliter ordinaret ... In eodem itaque concilio idem rex fecit cancellare et cassare omnes chartas de provinciis omnibus regni Angliae de libertatibus forestae postquam jam per biennium in toto regno fuerunt usitate; hanc occasionem praetendens quod chartae illae concessae fuerant, et libertates scriptae et signatae, dum ipse erat sub custodia, nec sui corporis aut sigilli aliquam habuerit potestatem, unde viribus carere debuit, quod sine ratione fuerat usurpatum.'

of Leicestershire, Rutland and Huntingdonshire on 19 March.[28] It seems that the men of these four adjacent eastern counties, in addition to Yorkshire, were thought to be the core of the movement against the established forest boundaries. Nottinghamshire and Huntingdonshire had been the most radical counties since 1218, when they both made perambulations of the forest in their counties before they were officially sanctioned on 24 July that year at Leicester, after which fully authorised Leicestershire and Rutland perambulations were immediately held on the following day. Nottinghamshire twice bought off attempts to hold a forest eyre in the county in 1221 and 1222, presumably wishing to reduce the forest area in accordance with the forest charter and their own wishes before an eyre was held, and in 1223 an attempt to hold a forest eyre in Yorkshire was thwarted when Walter of Sowerby and others appealed to the pope against it.[29] On 6 March 1224 arrangements had been made for a regard to be carried out by the foresters and twelve regarders in each of the forest counties, and twelve knights to view all the trespasses in contravention of the chapters of the regard.[30] This may have been the preliminary to a series of forest eyres held in some southern counties – Berkshire, Wiltshire, Somerset and Dorset – by Hugh de Neville late in that year, but none was held elsewhere before the attempt to implement the forest charter in 1225,[31] although Leicestershire did receive a session with a more limited scope in that period.[32]

The Leicestershire and Nottinghamshire forest perambulations of 1225 were both entered on the close roll in early 1227, presumably for reference.[33] The Nottinghamshire boundaries were settled soon afterwards, after two small adjustments to those given in the county's 1225 perambulation;[34] the boundaries of other counties may have been settled at the meeting of the perambulators with the king, held a week earlier than originally planned on 20 October 1227.[35] The Leicestershire jurors are not recorded as having attended, and it looks as if the original boundaries of the forest in that county remained in place for another eight years. Further consideration was given to the forest boundaries in a number of other forest counties in April 1228, when reference was made to the enrolment of the Leicestershire perambulation in the close roll of the previous year, but there is no indication that the Leicestershire boundaries were under active consideration.[36] In February 1229 another regard was ordered in the forests,

---

[28] *PR 1225–32*, pp. 109–10.
[29] D. Crook, 'The Struggle over Forest Boundaries in Nottinghamshire, 1218 to 1227', *Transactions of the Thoroton Society* 83 (1979), 35–45, at pp. 35–7; *Pipe Roll 7 Henry III*, ed. A. Jobson and C. F. Slade, PRS n.s. 56 (London, 2008), p. 162.
[30] *PR 1216–25*, pp. 482–3.
[31] *RLC*, i, pp. 633a–b, 655b–656; *Pipe Roll 8 Henry III*, ed. E. Amt, PRS n.s. 54 (London, 2005), pp. 156–7, 227–8; TNA, E 372/69, rot. 11, m. 1 [AALT_IMG 1230]; rot. 14, m. 2 [AALT_IMG 1244].
[32] See below, pp. 000–0.
[33] *RLC*, ii, pp. 207b–208.
[34] Crook, 'Forest Boundaries', pp. 39–40.
[35] *RLC*, ii, pp. 212b–213.
[36] *CR 1227–31*, pp. 100–4.

and a full set of the chapters of the regard was entered in the patent roll; they included, of course, the instruction to survey the sowing of assarts that had been undertaken since 1217.[37] The final phase in the history of the royal forest of Leicestershire began on 4 November 1234 at Woodstock, when three justices were appointed to enquire into persons who had hunted or coursed with dogs, or felled wood in the king's forests in Northamptonshire around Rockingham, Leicestershire and Rutland, 'on account of the liberties which the king by charter lately granted to the good men of the realm'. The justices were to meet to hold the enquiry at the abbot of Peterborough's manor of Ashton in Northamptonshire on 17 November, and the sheriff of each of the counties was to bring twelve knights with him to assist.[38] Whether this enquiry actually took place is not clear, but it is possible that the event prompted what followed.

On 3 December 1234, when the king was at Reading, the men of Leicestershire gave him £100 for a perambulation to be made of the forest adjacent to the boundary with Rutland. This was to be carried out by twenty-four knights, eight each from Northamptonshire, Rutland and Leicestershire, who were to have no lands within the forest, nor any blood-ties with those living in the forest, or with those who were present at the making of the previous perambulation. The aim was to define which areas were to be disafforested, and which were not. If the result was that disafforestation was not to take place, the king would retain the £100. If the result was that the area should be disafforested, the people would give him 50 marks, so that he would receive in total 200 marks.[39] On 21 February the sheriff of Leicestershire was officially notified of the disafforestation and ordered to have the charter read in the full county court. At the same time the hereditary forester of Rutland and Leicestershire, Hasculf son of Peter of Allexton, was told of the removal of the Leicestershire forest from his jurisdiction, and the justices of the next forest eyre in Rutland were instructed to read and hold to the terms of the charter.[40] Also in February 1235 it was noted in the fine roll that the men were due to pay 100 marks of this at mid-Lent (18 March), and the other 100 marks on 30 March.[41] These terms were evidently not met, because about 27 April, when the king was at Windsor, the sheriff of the county was ordered to distrain the men of the county to pay what they owed. The order noted that the fine had been made on their behalf by the prior of Launde and the abbot of Owston.[42] The delay in payment did not, however, delay the disafforestation of the county. On 20 February 1235 a charter was issued at Westminster to the effect that, since the king had earlier granted (in the 1225 forest charter) that all places which were afforested after the first coronation of Henry II should be disafforested, and the inquisition recently carried out stated that they had been,

---

[37] *PR 1225–32*, pp. 286–7.
[38] *CPR 1232–47*, p. 123.
[39] *CFR 1234–35*, nos 47–8. The first of these entries, in which the king was to receive 250 marks in total, was cancelled and replaced by the second.
[40] *CR 1234–37*, p. 51.
[41] *CFR 1234–35*, no. 146.
[42] *CR 1234–37*, p. 82.

Leicestershire was ordered to be disafforested.[43] This was a radical step, given that it was locally known that the forest in the county had been created by Henry I.[44]

The forest areas of three of the recalcitrant counties, Nottinghamshire, Leicestershire and Rutland, were close to Belvoir Priory. As prior, Roger of Wendover was responsible for managing the estates belonging to it, and in his performance of this task he was ultimately found wanting. A cartulary and some original charters of the priory remain in the custody of the duke of Rutland at Belvoir Castle, and the most important of them were edited and published by J. H. Round over a century ago.[45] The priory was founded by Roger de Toeny, the first lord of Belvoir, between 1076 and 1088, and was originally intended to be an independent house, but on the advice of Archbishop Lanfranc it became a dependency of St Albans.[46] Roger de Toeny and several of his Aubigny successors as patron were buried in the chapter house of the priory or in the monastic church itself, and in Wendover's chronicle the current lord of Belvoir was, of course, treated with respect. The priors of all the St Albans cells were presented by the abbot and instituted by the bishop, with rights of visitation reserved to the abbot, as illustrated by the events surrounding the replacement of Roger of Wendover in 1226.[47] Most of the property of the priory was in Leicestershire, but there were some holdings in neighbouring Lincolnshire and Nottinghamshire. In Nottinghamshire, four miles to the west of the priory itself, lay the village of Granby, in which the monks had been granted two carucates of land, one in demesne and one tenanted, with five tofts, by Oliver de Aincurt when he took the Benedictine cowl at the priory, under the name Robert. These were subsequently augmented by a further carucate and toft donated by his father, Walter, after Oliver's death between 1160 and 1168.[48] It has been established by Trevor Foulds that Oliver entered Belvoir within the two years after September 1157, and that he died in 1160.[49]

Granby was not in the forest of Nottinghamshire, whose southern boundary is generally accepted as having been the River Trent, which flowed six miles to the north of Granby at its nearest point.[50] This being so, it is somewhat surprising to find that, in the pipe roll of Michaelmas 1212, among the issues of the forest

---

[43] *CChR*, i, p. 193. The debt does not appear in the pipe rolls, so its payment cannot be traced: TNA, E 372/79, rot. 12; 80, rot. 10.

[44] *Select Pleas*, p. 45.

[45] *Manuscripts of the Duke of Rutland*, pp. 98–175.

[46] For the history of the priory from its foundation until the early thirteenth century, see BL, MS Sloane 4936, fol. 44; *Gesta Abbatum*, i, p. 57; *Victoria County History of Lincolnshire*, ed. W. Page (London, 1906), ii, pp. 124–7; *Heads of Religious Houses*, i, p. 85.

[47] *Gesta Abbatum*, i, pp. 275–7.

[48] *Manuscripts of the Duke of Rutland*, p. 135.

[49] *The Thurgarton Cartulary*, ed. T. Foulds (Stamford, 1994), p. lxx and n. 5; appendix nos 5–8, pp. ccix–ccxi.

[50] D. Crook, 'The Archbishopric of York and the Boundaries of the Forest in Nottinghamshire in the Twelfth Century', in *Law and Government in Medieval England and Normandy: Essays in Honour of Sir James Holt*, ed. G. Garnett and J. Hudson (Cambridge, 1994), pp. 325–40, at pp. 327–8.

eyre of Philip of Oldcotes and his associates, the vill of Granby accounted for a penalty of 6 marks for an unspecified forest offence. Payment of 5 marks had already been made, leaving 1 mark owing. That must have been paid off in the roll for 1213, which is missing, because the debt does not reappear in the roll for 1214.[51] Granby is the only Nottinghamshire settlement south of the Trent ever recorded as having been penalised for a forest offence. The reason for the penalty is not known, but it is possible that it can be explained by reference to a custom that men living up to a certain distance outside the forest boundaries in a particular county were obliged to attend forest eyres, and could therefore become liable for forest offences, even if they were procedural rather than substantive. There is no explicit evidence that this was the custom in Nottinghamshire, but in the 1209 Rutland/Leicestershire forest eyre a jury of Rutland knights stated that all the men of Leicestershire living within two leagues of the forest boundary were obliged to attend forest eyres.[52] If the penalty was levied completely or partly on the Belvoir Priory tenants in Granby, and if Roger of Wendover became prior in late 1214 or early 1215, as suggested, its imposition must have been a recent memory. If he became prior even only a year or two earlier, he might have been personally responsible for ensuring that it was paid.

The vill of Horninghold in Leicestershire, 23 miles south of Belvoir, formed part of the original de Toeny endowment of the priory, and the church there was added before 1154×59, when Pope Adrian IV confirmed it both to Robert, abbot of St Albans, and the monks of Belvoir. Under the uncertain circumstances of the civil war of the reign of King Stephen, when Leicestershire was an area of conflict between the rival earls of Leicester and Chester, the latter made himself 'advocate and defender' of the monks of Belvoir, and a guarantor of their manor of Horninghold, ordering that 'no-one is to interfere with them therein except through himself', while under Henry II the church there was successfully defended in the archbishop's court against the claims of Geoffrey de Normanville.[53] Horninghold was in the area of royal forest in the east of the county which was afforested by Henry I, probably about 1122, and which was contiguous to and administered with the king's forest in Rutland.[54] The Belvoir estate at Horninghold incurred forest penalties imposed in the eyres of the justices of the forest, beginning with that held by Alan de Neville in 1166–7, when there is a specific reference to an amercement of half a mark.[55] Most individual sums levied in forest eyres were hidden in large compendium entries, and so further Horninghold penalties cannot be traced in the subsequent pipe rolls down to the death of King John in 1216, but there can be little doubt that others were incurred. This is confirmed by the unique survival of a detailed list of

[51]   *Pipe Roll 14 John*, ed. P. M. Barnes, PRS n.s. 30 (London, 1955), p. 166; *Pipe Roll 16 John*, ed. P. M. Barnes, PRS n.s. 35 (London, 1962), p. 159.
[52]   *Select Pleas*, p. 6.
[53]   BL, MS Sloane 4936, fols 44, 46; *Manuscripts of the Duke of Rutland*, pp. 110–12, 136–7.
[54]   D. Crook, 'The Royal Forest of Leicestershire, c. 1122–1235', *Leicestershire Archaeological and Historical Society Transactions* 87 (2013), 1–23.
[55]   *Pipe Roll 13 Henry II*, PRS 11 (London, 1889), p. 162.

Leicestershire amercements imposed in the Rutland eyre held at Oakham on 3 March 1209, which provides far more information about such penalties than is available from any earlier forest eyre from any county, with the exception of the single surviving twelfth-century estreat which relates to the Shropshire forest eyre of 1179.[56] The penalties are given under several subordinate headings. Under 'Old waste in Leicestershire' there are entries for: 'from the vill of Horninghold half a mark'; 'from the prior [of Belvoir] of the same one mark'. Under 'Growing crops (*Imbladiamenta*) of the first regard in Leicestershire' there is: 'from the men of Horninghold 9s. 7½d. for 3 acres of wheat and 13 acres 1 rod of oats'. Under 'Growing crops of the second regard': 'from the men of Horninghold 8s. 3½d. for 16 acres and 1 rod of oats'.[57] These entries show that the prior and his tenants had created waste in the manor and had been cultivating oats and wheat on the reclaimed land, for which they were being charged by the forest eyre justices. It is unlikely that Roger of Wendover was prior of Belvoir at the time when these penalties were imposed, but from the point at which he took office he became responsible for Horninghold and its relationship to the forest law and those who administered it on behalf of the king.

After 1209 the next forest eyres were those held in 1212, including that in Nottinghamshire, but none was held in the Rutland and Leicestershire forest. Then the opposition to King John, which began in the summer of 1212, brought forest eyres to an end for what proved to be more than a decade. The conflict between the king and rebel barons eventually led to the issue of Magna Carta in 1215, followed by the war of 1215–17, the king's death in 1216, a subsequent reissue of a revised version of Magna Carta, and the victory of the supporters of the young Henry III at Lincoln in 1217. There followed the grant of a separate Charter of the Forest when Magna Carta was reissued for the second time in November 1217. Progress in implementing the terms of the forest charter, principally the disafforestation of areas afforested since 1154, was, as we have seen, slow until the mid-1220s, with the Crown resisting the attempts of the inhabitants of some forest counties to remove the operation of the forest laws from significant areas. Meanwhile, although no full forest eyres were held, some forest sessions of a lesser kind did take place, one of them in the Leicestershire portion of the forest of Rutland and Leicestershire. In the Warwickshire and Leicestershire account in the pipe roll for 1225, among a list of 'small particulars of the forest' imposed by Brian de Lisle, and at a time when it is certain that Roger of Wendover was in office as prior of Belvoir, the prior was charged with 8s. 3½d. for the sowing in Horninghold of 16 acres and 1 rod of oats, and separately 6d. for an acre of oats sown in Horninghold.[58] The most likely explanation for the imposition of these amercements is that they related to the long period between the Rutland eyre of

---

[56]   D. Crook, 'The Earliest Exchequer Estreat and the Forest Eyres of Henry II and Thomas fitz Bernard, 1175–80', in *Records, Administration and Aristocratic Society in the Anglo-Norman Realm*, ed. N. Vincent (Woodbridge, 2009), pp. 29–44.
[57]   TNA, E 32/249, rot. 30.
[58]   TNA, E 372/69, rot. 12 m. 2 [AALT_IMG 1235].

1209 and Lisle's session of 1224 or 1225. They confirm that the Leicestershire forest remained in existence in the year in which the clause of the Charter of the Forest relating to the forest boundaries was being implemented at last.

It is not clear whether Lisle's session took place before the Leicestershire perambulation of 1225 or not, because the account in which the amercements were recorded was not heard until 28 January 1226. The previous account had been heard in mid-November 1224, and we can only conclude that the session was probably held sometime between those dates, possibly earlier.[59] The larger area mentioned was exactly the same size as that sown before the eyre of 1209, and was charged at the same rate; a much smaller area sown with oats had been added subsequently, while the area sown with both wheat and oats before 1209 had apparently ceased to be cultivated. So, at about the time when Magna Carta and the Charter of the Forest were confirmed by the Crown in return for the tax grant, and the disafforestation of some forest areas was carried out following perambulations made by local juries (to the delight of the chronicler), Wendover was himself as prior subject to the administration of forest justice as a cultivator of reclaimed land. The passage in his chronicle celebrating the disafforestations of 1225 therefore represents the only recorded authentic voice of the forest landholder subject to the restrictions on agriculture imposed by the forest laws. His words were echoed by the actions of the abbot of Owston and the prior of Launde in taking a leading role in bringing about the demise of the royal forest of Leicestershire, a little more than a year before the death of their former colleague at St Albans. Their monastic buildings, unlike those of Belvoir Priory, lay within the forest, and their more extensive property there had suffered far more substantial financial losses during the century or so of the forest's existence.[60]

Further information about the activities of Belvoir Priory and its tenants at Horninghold comes from an estreat of the penalties imposed in the next Rutland forest eyre,[61] held in late July or early August 1249, over thirteen years after Roger of Wendover's death, but still partly relating to his period as prior. Under the heading 'Amercements of the assarts made in the county of Leicester and fines taken for having growing crops of the same assarts and for retaining assarts quit in perpetuity', the prior of Belvoir was charged 5 marks, with two named pledges: Gilbert de Empton and Robert of Hallaton. Under the heading for Leicestershire pleas of the vert, a Robert of Horninghold, probably a tenant of the priory there, was amerced 2 shillings for an offence in Stockerston. The sheriff's account for Warwickshire and Leicestershire in the pipe roll, audited on 6 October 1249,[62] recorded these entries, preceded by *t* to indicate payment in

---

59   TNA, E 368/8, m. 19 [AALT_IMG 2787]; *Pipe Roll 8 Henry III*, p. vi. Lisle was replaced as chief forest justice by Neville in March 1224, so it may have taken place when Lisle was still in office.
60   Crook, 'The Royal Forest of Leicestershire, *passim*.
61   TNA, E 389/87 (formerly E 370/43A).
62   TNA, E 159/25, rot 15 [AALT_IMG 0051]. The Rutland accounts for the years 20 to 33 Henry III were all heard together in the summer of 1250, and this must have been when the Rutland proceeds of the eyre were dealt with: E 372/94, rot. 8d [AALT_IMG 6096].

full, and marginated *Leyc*, as amounting to the substantial sum of £152 10s.[63] This note was followed by separate entries of larger unpaid sums owed by more important people. These did not include any entries for Belvoir Priory, but the prior of Launde received two penalties and the abbot of Peterborough was charged the large sum of 40 marks for having a wood. The Horninghold amercements must have been among those included in the compendium sum in the account.

At first sight the levying of penalties on the old Leicestershire forest in this eyre seems to be in clear contravention of the charter of 1235 confirming the disafforestation of the Leicestershire forest. At the time the charter was issued a specific instruction had been made that the justices of the next forest eyre in Rutland were to read and hold to the charter.[64] It must, however, have been concerned with forest offences committed between Brian de Lisle's forest session in 1224/5 and the time of the disafforestation a decade later, an explanation confirmed by parallel events in Nottinghamshire. In the 1229 Nottinghamshire forest eyre of Hugh de Neville and Brian de Lisle, the first to be held in the county since its new forest boundaries were confirmed in 1227, 'the men dwelling in those parts of Nottinghamshire which were disafforested by the forest perambulation made by the order of the king rendered account of 140 marks that they should be quit of all pleas of the forest levied upon them before that disafforestation except pleas of the venison'.[65] Their offer of a fine was evidently not matched by the men of Rutland and the former Leicestershire forest at the time of the eyre of 1249, since they were made to answer for the pleas of the years from 1225 to 1235. A quarter of a century after Roger of Wendover's delight at the disafforestations of 1225 and their liberating effects on the lives of the inhabitants of the newly disafforested areas, a final reckoning was followed by the permanent freedom of the inhabitants of eastern Leicester from the forest laws – laws which continued to afflict the inhabitants of the remaining forest areas for centuries to come.

---

[63] TNA, E 372/94, rot. 8d [AALT_IMG 6096].

[64] *CR 1234–37*, p. 51.

[65] TNA, E 372/73, rot. 5, m. 1d [AALT_IMG 3467]: 'homines manentis in partibus illis de Notinghams' que deaforestate fuerunt per perambulatione foreste factam per preceptum Regis reddunt compotum per c et xl m. ut quieti sint de omnibus placitis super eos levatis de foresta ante deaforestationem predictum exceptis tammodo placitis de venacione.' They paid £80, and owed 20 marks. On the Nottinghamshire forest in the period after the Charter of the Forest, see Crook, 'Forest Boundaries'.

11

Royal Government and Administration in Post-Evesham England, 1265–70

Adrian Jobson

On 4 August 1265, the Lord Edward's forces defeated Simon de Montfort's rebel army at Evesham.[1] This decisive battle marked the culmination of more than seven years of constitutional turmoil as the king, Henry III, struggled with his baronage for control over England's government. The revolution of April 1258 had seen a small cabal seize power and institute an ambitious programme of legislative and administrative reform.[2] Henry eventually overthrew the baronial regime in 1261, but there followed more than two years of political manœuvre as the balance of power shifted between the two sides. Only force could break the deadlock, and it was Montfort who initially emerged the victor from the ensuing civil war. Having captured the king at Lewes in May 1264, he became the realm's *de facto* ruler and his regime instituted some of the most radical reforms ever attempted in medieval English history.[3] Montfort's own arrogance and self-interest alienated many sympathisers, however, paving the way for a revival in royalist fortunes that eventually reached a climax at Evesham. Throughout these turbulent years the central administrative departments struggled to adapt to fluctuating political fortunes, but the constant upheaval unleashed forces that gradually weakened their operational efficiency until finally, in the early summer of 1265, they collapsed completely. This chapter will therefore examine the efforts to restore the central administration, undertaken between August 1265 and February 1270, primarily through the experiences of three key branches of government: the Exchequer, the law courts, and the Chancery.

The challenge facing the Crown after Evesham was truly formidable. For more than three months there had been no functioning Exchequer, and the royal finances had been reduced to a parlous state. Considerable debt had been incurred in the process of overthrowing Montfort's regime, and the crown

---

[1]   A. Jobson, *The First English Revolution: Simon de Montfort, Henry III and the Barons' War* (London, 2012), pp. 141–7. I am grateful to Richard Cassidy for his helpful suggestions in preparing this article.

[2]   *Documents*, pp. 96–113, 136–57. Most notably the Provisions of Oxford (1258) and the Provisions of Westminster (1259).

[3]   J. R. Maddicott, *Simon de Montfort* (Cambridge, 1994), pp. 352–3.

jewels pawned as security for loans.[4] Local royal officials had disbursed substantial sums in the king's cause, many of which had simply gone unrecorded as civil war engulfed the country. Equally confusing was the situation of the Crown's debtors: many individuals owed the king money, but their names and the amounts due were unclear. That the business of auditing accounts, the key Exchequer responsibility, had broken down completely further added to the administrative confusion.[5] While the events of June to August 1265 had been disruptive enough in their own right, they also served to exacerbate the continuing effects of several previous periods of administrative disturbance. From July to November 1263 there had been no treasurer or resident baron at the Exchequer, while the administration that immediately followed was 'provisional' in nature.[6] In 1264, moreover, not a single session had been held during the Easter term.[7]

Suffering from similar levels of disruption were the law courts. A general eyre, when royal justices travelled from county to county hearing civil and criminal pleas, had been originally commissioned in November 1260.[8] Baronial protests at Hertford and Worcester in the summer of 1261 had precipitated its temporary suspension, but following the eyre's resumption in January 1262 proceedings were commenced in several new shires.[9] Yet events eventually forced the visitation's permanent abandonment in May 1263, when unrest in the Welsh Marches prompted the suspension of proceedings at both Lincoln and Southampton.[10] Meanwhile physical attacks directed against the justices of the Common Bench had necessitated this court's adjournment for more than six months in 1263. The next year saw further disruption, as the political turmoil ensured that there were no sessions of the Bench for either the Easter or Trinity terms. The court *coram rege* (King's Bench) suffered similar operational dislocation, although to what extent it is now difficult to quantify.[11] In the spring of 1265 events once again forced the closure of the central courts. On 23 April the justices of the King's Bench held their final pre-Evesham session at Northampton. Shortly afterwards news of the Lord Edward's dramatic escape from Montfortian captivity reached Westminster, where, on 8 June, all litigation before the Common Bench was

---

[4]   M. Howell, *Eleanor of Provence* (Oxford, 1998), p. 213; J. A. Collingwood, 'Royal Finance in the Period of Baronial Reform and Rebellion, 1258–72' (unpublished PhD thesis, University of London, 1995), pp. 179, 189, 231.

[5]   M. H. Mills, 'Adventus Vicecomitum, 1258–72', *EHR* 36 (1921), 481–96, at pp. 489–90.

[6]   T. F. Tout, *Chapters in the Administrative History of England*, 6 vols (Manchester, 1920–33), i, p. 297.

[7]   Mills, 'Adventus', p. 489; *The Wardrobe Accounts of Henry III*, ed. B. L. Wild, PRS n.s. 58 (London, 2012), p. cliv. Exchequer business was further disrupted at Michaelmas 1264 when the earl marshal initially failed to appoint a deputy.

[8]   *CR 1259–61*, p. 451.

[9]   *RGE*, pp. 126–8.

[10]   *RGE*, pp. 127–8; Jobson, *First Revolution*, p. 86.

[11]   P. Brand, *Kings, Barons and Justices: The Making and Enforcement of Legislation in Thirteenth-Century England* (Cambridge, 2003), pp. 166–7.

immediately suspended.[12] Only days later Montfort's regime issued its last assize commission, in which Nicholas de Turri was ordered to hear an Oxfordshire plea of *novel disseisin*.[13]

Within a month the Chancery, the king's secretariat, had likewise ceased operations. This proved in practice to be a gradual process, the first manifestation of which can be found in the fine rolls. The last datable enrolment, noting Stephen Heym's offer of 1 mark for a writ *ad terminum*, was made on 22 June.[14] Four days later the final pre-Evesham entry was added to the roll: a writ of *liberate* for £16 13*s*. 4*d*., addressed to the bishop of Hereford's men.[15] On 28 June, a Chancery clerk recorded the last letter patent issued by the Montfortian regime. Concerning the defence of Sussex and Surrey, it ordered Simon de Montfort the Younger to 'aggrieve the rebels' in these counties.[16] Three days later, on 1 July, the Chancery's last known Montfortian enrolment was made. Ordering the knights of Herefordshire to rendezvous with Montfort's army, the entry was followed on the close roll by the heading 'Post Conflictum de Evesham.'[17]

For the Crown, the immediate priority after Evesham was to establish the security of its newly restored regime and to deal with those who refused to accept the changed political situation. New royalist sheriffs, such as Roger of Leybourne in Kent, were quickly appointed, while others, including John de Grey at Nottingham, received the custody of strategic royal castles.[18] Considerable numbers of letters and writs would need drafting to implement this key policy without delay, so the Chancery was swiftly reconstituted. On 8 August 1265, only four days after the battle, the first enrolment can be found on its departmental rolls. Noting the offer by Roger son of Richard for a writ *ad terminum*, the clerk making the entry on the fine roll left a noticeable gap after the last Montfortian enrolment, perhaps to emphasise the change of regime.[19] Two days later a new chancellor was in office. Charged with restoring the Chancery's operations, the man entrusted with this vital role was Walter Giffard.[20] An ardent royalist, he had enjoyed a successful career in the king's service before his election as bishop of Bath and Wells on 22 May 1264.[21] Giffard's appointment as chancellor was recompense for his unwavering loyalty, in tacit recognition of which he was the beneficiary of the first post-Evesham entry noted on the *liberate* rolls.

---

[12] *CR 1264–68*, p. 64; F. M. Powicke, *King Henry III and the Lord Edward*, 2 vols (Oxford, 1947), ii, p. 496 n. 2; S. Stewart, 'A Year in the Life of a Royal Justice: Gilbert de Preston's Itinerary, July 1264–June 1265', in *TCE XII*, pp. 155–66, at p. 159.

[13] TNA, C 66/83, m. 15d.

[14] *CFR 1264–65*, no. 515.

[15] *CLR 1260–67*, p. 179.

[16] *CPR 1258–66*, p. 434.

[17] *CR 1264–68*, p. 127.

[18] *CPR 1258–66*, p. 435.

[19] *CFR 1264–65*, no. 516; *CPR 1258–66*, p. 436. The patent roll records the grant of the treasurership of York to Edmund Mortimer on 7 August, but this is noted in an attached schedule rather than on the roll itself.

[20] *CPR 1258–66*, p. 435; *CLR 1260–67*, p. 179.

[21] R. B. Dobson, 'Walter Giffard', *ODNB*.

This writ, dated 10 August 1265, granted him 250 marks to sustain both 'himself and the clerks of the Chancery'.[22] Soon entries began to be made in the other series of Chancery rolls: on 13 August a letter close concerning Belia widow of Jacob Coprun was enrolled, while the grant of an annual market at Alvington in Gloucestershire, dated 4 September, was the first recorded on the charter rolls.[23] Over the following months the Chancery's business steadily increased, although it was several months before the volume of enrolments returned to its former level.[24]

Meanwhile the Crown had embarked upon the reconstitution of the country's legal system. The dispensing of justice was viewed as an intrinsic duty of kingship, and Henry III had sought to provide 'peace and justice' during the period of his personal rule in imitation of his patron saint, Edward the Confessor.[25] The collapse of law and order over the past months therefore made it imperative that the structures of law enforcement were quickly restored, both to demonstrate that Henry was once again the legitimate and unchallenged ruler, and to bring stability back to the shires.[26] On 8 August, four days after Evesham, the patent roll notes that Roger de Clifford had been appointed forest justice north of the Trent.[27] The following day saw the issuing of the first post-war assize commission, an order to Master Walter of Powicke to hear a plea of *novel disseisin* concerning a tenement in the Worcestershire village of Eastham.[28] In late August the Chancery enrolled its first judicial enquiry into the circumstances of a homicide, the death of Adam of Norton, authorising William of Englefield to investigate whether his killing had been committed in self-defence.[29]

Throughout the autumn of 1265 the restoration of England's legal apparatus continued. Judicial commissions were being issued in ever increasing numbers, while the scope of these inquiries was steadily expanded. In mid-September, for instance, the first post-war gaol delivery commission was enrolled, appointing four men, a mixture of royal justices and shire knights, to deliver Ilchester gaol.[30]

---

[22] *CLR 1260–67*, p. 179. This amount, payable at the next Michaelmas Exchequer, was the initial instalment of a 500 mark annual fee.

[23] *CR 1264–68*, p. 68; *CChR*, ii, p. 56. The decision to differentiate on the close rolls the post-Evesham enrolments from their Montfortian predecessors was clearly taken after 13 August, as Belia's entry precedes the heading 'post bellum Eveshamie'.

[24] In September 1265, for instance, there were forty enrolled letters close, while the number for the same month in 1257 was sixty-five: see *CR 1256–59*, pp. 362–7, 403–7; *CR 1264–68*, pp. 70–3, 129–30.

[25] Jobson, *First Revolution*, p. 2.

[26] M. Morris, *A Great and Terrible King: Edward I and the Forging of Britain* (London, 2008), p. 72; *Wardrobe Accounts*, p. clxxv. Henry's efforts to restore the Crown's battered image and authority also included, for instance, his ceremonial crown-wearing during October's celebrations for the feast of the Confessor. Similarly, in the months after Evesham, there was a dramatic increase in royal gift-giving that emphasised both his benevolence and largesse.

[27] TNA, C 66/83, m. 13d.

[28] TNA, C 66/83, m. 13d.

[29] *CPR 1258–66*, p. 489.

[30] TNA, C 66/83, m. 10d.

But the Crown's primary focus was now on the reopening of the central courts. On 9 September proceedings resumed in the King's Bench, its justices beginning with a plea concerning an assault on William de Aette's men and the taking of timber from his manor at Ayot in Hertfordshire.[31] This was followed, on 6 October, by the return of the Common Bench to Westminster.[32] A day later, at Thirsk in Yorkshire, Richard of Middleton presided over the first petty assize since the summer.[33] Thus, within two months, significant progress had been made by the Crown in its efforts to restore both the civil and criminal justice systems, although it was several more years before the overall volume of judicial business returned to pre-war levels. Yet the restoration process remained incomplete, for the moment at least, as the vindictive treatment of the defeated Montfortians provoked a violent backlash that made the commissioning of a new general eyre impossible.[34]

More intractable, however, was the chaotic state of the royal finances. On 6 August, two days after Evesham, the first decisive step was taken to restore the Crown's fiscal administration: Ralph of Sandwich, the Montfortian keeper of the Wardrobe, was dismissed from office.[35] This move, completed on the following day with Nicholas of Lewknor's appointment in his stead, brought the department responsible for the collection and disbursement of revenue for the king's daily requirements once more under direct royal control. Shortly afterwards the decision was taken to install Master Thomas of Wymondham as treasurer. Exactly when this occurred is uncertain but, since he received on 8 August what was only the second post-war letter patent of protection, the appointment was probably made at about this time.[36] Wymondham himself was in many ways a natural choice as treasurer. A Norfolk-born and university-educated career administrator, he first appears in official records in 1236 as a clerk to the treasurer Hugh of Pattishall.[37] Having transferred into royal service, he was subsequently rewarded with the post of precentor of Lichfield Cathedral.[38] Matthew Paris recorded that, in October 1258, Wymondham was appointed chancellor of the Exchequer.[39] Serving under two baronial treasurers, he remained in post at least until Michaelmas 1261.[40] That Wymondham had extensive experience of Exchequer practice was justification enough for his nomination, but there may

---

[31] TNA, KB 26/174, m. 1.
[32] Stewart, 'Preston', p. 159.
[33] TNA, JUST 1/1194, m. 5d.
[34] Jobson, *First Revolution*, pp. 152–5.
[35] *Wardrobe Accounts*, pp. clxvii, clxxiv.
[36] *CPR 1258–66*, p. 436.
[37] *CR 1234–37*, p. 243.
[38] *CPR 1232–47*, p. 191; John le Neve, *Fasti Ecclesiae Anglicanae, 1066–1300: Coventry and Lichfield*, ed. C. Brooke, J. Denton and D. E. Greenaway (London, 2011), p. 17.
[39] *Chronica Majora*, v, pp. 719–20. Wymondham's appointment may possibly date from February 1258, making him a royal rather than a baronial nominee, see R. Cassidy, 'The 1259 Pipe Roll', 2 vols (unpublished PhD thesis, University of London, 2012), i, pp. 127–8.
[40] TNA, E 159/36, mm. 3, 7. John of Chishall, Wymondham's successor, was sworn into office on 27 February 1262.

have been a political dimension too. The selection of an official who had formerly worked on implementing the reform programme could be viewed as a populist move to satisfy the Crown's more moderate opponents, while also affirming that the baronial fiscal reforms would not be abandoned entirely.

Yet even before Wymondham's appointment the Crown had already made some tentative progress in recovering control over its shrieval revenues. Several Montfortian sheriffs had been dismissed from office on 6 August in favour of trusted royalist supporters. John le Moyne, for instance, was installed in Cambridgeshire and Huntingdonshire, and his predecessor, John de Scalariis, was ordered to surrender these counties into his custody.[41] While such replacements were clearly vital in security terms, they also served a fiscal purpose, since it was the sheriff who accounted for the county farm at the Exchequer and collected debts owed to the king.[42] Throughout the early autumn this process of substitution continued until, by October 1265, fourteen replacements had been effected. Confusion surrounded the terms of office of the new sheriffs. Eleven were appointed on a custodial basis and answered for all the variable profits above the county farm, but the remainder were obliged to pay a fixed increment instead. This was soon remedied, however, as increments were imposed on all sheriffs appointed after 18 October.[43] That there was no single policy concerning the terms of office for this initial tranche of post-Evesham sheriffs was unsurprising; it was reflective of the chaos that still attended the Exchequer's operations.

October proved to be a crucial month for the Exchequer, as it now finally reopened. Yet this significant milestone on the road to administrative normalisation still suffered from the continuing political turmoil between the Crown and its enemies. Westminster Hall was the Exchequer's customary venue but, when the mayor of London and his fellow citizens arrived there on 30 September for the city sheriffs' Michaelmas appearance, they found it deserted.[44] In the recent conflict London had been staunchly Montfortian and the king, determined to reassert his control over the city, was busy mustering a besieging army at Windsor. Joining him there were the Exchequer barons, who held the *adventus vicecomitum* on the same day that London's mayor had made his unsuccessful journey to Westminster.[45] This important twice-yearly event in the Exchequer calendar, at which the sheriffs made their proffers for the coming half-year, marked the department's formal resumption of business. Financially the occasion was not a great success, because sixteen sheriffs failed to attend and only a single proffer of £50 was made. This figure was substantially lower than almost any other *adventus* proffer during the previous decade: at Michaelmas 1257, for example, £1,992 10s. was received, while £746 13s. 4d. was recorded at Michaelmas

[41]   *CFR 1264–65*, nos 652–63; *CPR 1258–66*, p. 445.
[42]   W. A. Morris, *The Medieval English Sheriff to 1300* (Manchester, 1927), p. 241.
[43]   Collingwood, 'Royal Finance', pp. 248, 250.
[44]   *Chronicles of the Mayors and Sheriffs of London, A.D. 1188 to A.D. 1274*, ed. H. T. Riley (London, 1863), p. 81.
[45]   TNA, E 159/40, m. 17; Jobson, *First Revolution*, pp. 151–2.

1263.[46] Yet the very act of holding an *adventus vicecomitum* within two months of Evesham, just as a royal army was being assembled for an assault on the capital, clearly demonstrates how far the Exchequer's recovery had already come.

On 13 October 1265 the Upper Exchequer began the process of auditing the annual shrieval accounts, a task that it had not undertaken since the previous February.[47] In selecting which counties to review, it is evident that the Exchequer barons were following a plan. Every shire audited over the coming year had been either solid Montfortian territory or one of the main theatres of war. This careful targeting by the Exchequer was intended to serve four interrelated purposes. First, it marked an important step towards the restoration of royal authority in these counties, as the former Montfortian office-holders were publicly called to account for their time in office. Second, these audits collectively constituted a highly potent political weapon that could be used to exact financial revenge upon the king's enemies and thus ensure their future good behaviour. Third, the weakness of the royal finances was such that it was vital that the Exchequer should recover the revenues lost from these shires. Last, the financial records of these counties were arguably the most chaotic and therefore would require the greatest investigation.

Essex and Hertfordshire, a joint shrievalty still held by the Montfortian sheriff Nicholas Spigurnel, was the first account to be audited. Originally this review had been scheduled for 9 October, but it was delayed for four days probably to coincide with the reconvened parliament.[48] This account, which took six days to complete, is the exemplar for the majority of those taken during the coming year. Almost every entry contains a marginal annotation noting a distraint. Others, however, such as the Gloucestershire account audited on 27 January 1266, contain no marginalia whatsoever.[49] In all, eight shrieval accounts were audited between Michaelmas 1265 and Michaelmas 1266. Of these, five were concluded before Christmas.[50] One shire was audited in late January, while the other two were heard in April and June respectively.[51] Every sheriff answered for a single year's revenues, with one exception: in Warwickshire and Leicestershire, Richard of Harrington accounted for the whole year ending Michaelmas 1265 as well as the final quarter of the previous one, while William Bagod had responsibility for the remainder.[52] That the shrievalty of Warwickshire and Leicestershire

---

[46] Collingwood, 'Royal Finance', pp. 167, 264; Cassidy, 'Adventus Vicecomitum and the Financial Crisis of Henry III's Reign, 1250–72', *EHR* 126 (2011), 614–27, at pp. 617, 624.

[47] TNA, E 368/38, mm. 12d–13d. Bedfordshire and Buckinghamshire was the last dated account.

[48] TNA, E 159/40, mm. 17, 19; 'Annales Monasterii de Waverleia', *Annales Monastici*, ii, p. 366; Jobson, *First Revolution*, p. 152.

[49] TNA, E 368/40, m. 19.

[50] TNA, E 159/40, mm. 19–21d. Essex and Hertfordshire (13 October), Hampshire (19 October), Lincolnshire (3 November), Warwickshire and Leicestershire (18 November), London and Middlesex (7 December).

[51] TNA, E 159/40, mm. 22–23d. Gloucestershire (27 January), Wiltshire (5 April), Kent (30 June).

[52] TNA, E 372/109, rot. 4; TNA, E 159/40, m. 19d.

was singled out for special scrutiny is not surprising: Montfort's comital estates were centred primarily in these two shires.[53] The Exchequer was deliberately reasserting its authority in the former Montfortian heartland. Overall, the total number of shires investigated was substantially lower than those for earlier years: in 1259, for example, twenty-one accounts were heard, while in 1262 nineteen were audited.[54] Such a marked fall in successful audits, a drop of approximately 60%, confirms that the Exchequer's operating efficiency was, for the first full fiscal year after Evesham, at a level far below that described in Richard fitz Nigel's *Dialogus de Scaccario* nearly a hundred years earlier.[55]

That the Exchequer's recovery was proving to be a complex undertaking can be seen even more clearly in the level of the king's annual income. Cash receipts were far below those of the late 1250s, although the lack of a surviving receipt roll means that a total figure cannot be calculated with any certainty. Nevertheless, if used cautiously, the payments made at the *adventus vicecomitum* can be indicative of any significant trend exhibited in the Exchequer's annual receipts. Thus in the year ending Michaelmas 1266, the sheriffs' proffers at the Lower Exchequer totalled only £380 19s. 8d.[56] Compared to the £3,184 16s. 8d. paid in 1257, for instance, this represented a fall in cash payments of more than 88%.[57] Other evidence supports this contention: the totals for 'authorised expenditure out of the Exchequer' as recorded on the *liberate* rolls underwent a similar decline, suggesting 'that reduced Exchequer receipts resulted in a reduction in the number of *liberate* writs that could be issued allowing Exchequer expenditure'. This fall in receipts was manifest, moreover, in the estimates for the king's overall annual income. James Collingwood has calculated that, based on the figures drawn from the pipe rolls, the Crown's total notional income for the year ending at Michaelmas 1266 was £21,553. Once credits for expenditure have been excluded, however, he argues that Henry III's income was actually £11,958.[58] These sums were both markedly lower than those recorded in 1255–63: in 1258–9, for instance, the Crown realised about £13,000, while the total notional income was approximately £25,000.[59] Clearly the royalist victory at Evesham had not yet been 'translated into a marked increase in cash revenue for the Crown'.[60]

---

[53] Maddicott, *Simon de Montfort*, pp. 33, 47–9.
[54] Mills, 'Adventus', p. 488; C. A. F. Meekings, 'The Pipe Roll Order of 12 February 1270', in *Studies in Thirteenth-Century Justice and Administration* (London, 1981), pp. 222–53, at p. 253.
[55] N. Barratt, 'The Exchequer in the Thirteenth Century', *English Government in the Thirteenth Century*, ed. A. Jobson (Woodbridge, 2004), pp. 71–86, at p. 72.
[56] Collingwood, 'Royal Finance', pp. 265–7; Mills, 'Adventus', p. 494. Mills suggests a substantially higher figure of £687 11s. The difference results from Collingwood's exclusion of several proffers that were offered 'but not delivered on the day of attendance'.
[57] Collingwood, 'Royal Finance', p. 167; Mills, 'Adventus', p. 494.
[58] Collingwood, 'Royal Finance', pp. 269, 280–1.
[59] Collingwood, 'Royal Finance', p. 147; Cassidy, '1259 Pipe Roll', i, p. 36. Collingwood has calculated figures of £27,704 and £43,254 respectively for 1259, but both totals are probably much too high.
[60] Collingwood, 'Royal Finance', p. 297.

Even though the Crown's income for the year ending Michaelmas 1266 was below than the earlier average, Wymondham and his colleagues could still view their first fourteen months in office as a qualified success. Substantially more money had been deposited at the Exchequer than during the previous year, when only £8,616 had entered the royal coffers.[61] Eight counties had been successfully audited, with their former Montfortian sheriffs being held accountable for even the smallest revenues or expenditure.[62] There was, under Wymondham's auspices, a concerted effort to trace the military expenditure incurred by the Crown's local officials during the recent conflict. Roger de Clifford, for example, received an allowance for what he expended on victuals, stipends, munitions, repairs and arms for Gloucester Castle. Similarly Philip Basset was granted a writ of *liberate* for the £92 12s. that he had disbursed on the 'repair of walls, bridges, engines and other necessary matters' at Oxford Castle 'during the disturbance and war in the realm.'[63] The Exchequer had also attempted to audit the accounts of those officials who had been given custody of individual royal manors or ecclesiastical estates during a vacancy. Clifford was called to account for the issues of several Gloucestershire manors, including Winchcombe and Churchdown, while Stephen Fromund was granted an allowance for the expenses he had incurred during his custody of Piddington in Oxfordshire. Henry of Wingham had been the subject of an enquiry, moreover, which confirmed that in 1248 he had delivered to William de Bitton, the incoming prelate, the temporalities of the bishopric of Bath and Wells.[64]

Meanwhile the Exchequer had begun the difficult task of tracing old debts. Only minimal progress, however, was made in the first year after Evesham. James le Savage, the former sheriff of Hampshire, had been pursued for the combined total of £176 11s. 5d. that he still owed from his time in office.[65] Similarly, the king had ordered the treasurer and his fellow barons to search through their rolls in order to establish exactly what debts were owed to him by Robert Bruce.[66] In the months after Evesham, Henry had actively rewarded his leading followers for their support during the war and it was the Exchequer that often implemented this crucial policy. Walter Giffard, the new royalist chancellor, was given an allowance for the £55 in arrears that his mother had owed the king before her death.[67] John de Turbervill was likewise pardoned 22 marks in arrears as a reward for his 'long and praiseworthy' service.[68] Several other individuals received financial relief as compensation for the damages they had personally

---

[61] Collingwood, 'Royal Finance', pp. 269–70.
[62] TNA, E 159/40, m. 14d. Simon de Pateshull, for instance, was ordered to account for a mark that he had received from the men of Eton in Buckinghamshire as a fine for their non-attendance in court.
[63] TNA, E 159/40, m. 9; *CLR 1260–67*, p. 202.
[64] TNA, E 159/40, mm. 1, 9, 10d.
[65] TNA, E 159/40, m. 3d. Savage had left office in November 1258.
[66] TNA, E 368/40, m. 2.
[67] TNA, E 159/40, m. 1.
[68] TNA, E 368/40, m. 2.

sustained: Philip Basset, for instance, received an acquittance of the arrears owed from his annual farm of Wycombe as part recompense for his losses during the war. Financial provision was even made for the widow of Richard le Lung, who had died in the king's service.[69] The Exchequer, on the king's orders, similarly provided relief for numerous towns that had suffered heavily during the fighting. Worcester, for example, had been sacked by Montfortian forces on 28 February 1264, while Gloucester had been besieged several times.[70] Thus the memoranda rolls record that the former did not have to pay its annual farm for another two years, while the latter was pardoned two separate debts totalling £69 and 100 marks respectively.[71]

Although the Exchequer's efforts at restoring the health of the royal finances during the year ending at Michaelmas 1266 proved to be only moderately successful, they were nevertheless a significant achievement given the continuing turmoil in the shires. Evesham may have been a royalist victory, but peace remained elusive. Several Montfortian garrisons, including Winchelsea and Kenilworth, refused to surrender. Royalist sheriffs found themselves unable to assert their authority as rebel bands roamed the forests in several shires, including Sussex and Oxfordshire.[72] Stoking the fires of unrest was the Crown's treatment of the former Montfortians, whose persecution through a vengeful policy of land confiscation rendered them destitute and embittered. Left with little alternative, the Disinherited, as they were collectively known, renewed the fight. On 25 November 1265 a seaborne raiding party from the Cinque Ports razed Portsmouth to the ground.[73] Meanwhile in Lincolnshire, diehard rebels such as Baldwin Wake sought sanctuary on the Isle of Axholme. Early 1266 offered little respite from the violence as the royalist regime went on the offensive. Sandwich was stormed by the king's forces on 15 January, while Winchelsea's fall in March prompted the Cinque Ports' capitulation. Over the subsequent months the royalists slowly drove the rebels from several shires and, by June, only Kenilworth Castle remained defiant.[74]

This widespread unrest inevitably had a serious impact upon the Exchequer's activities. Several sheriffs had cited the continuing disorder as an excuse during the Michaelmas *adventus* in 1265. Lincolnshire's sheriff, for example, reported that although his county's revenue had been collected, he was prevented from transporting it to Windsor 'propter turbationem regni'. Several boroughs, including Grimsby and Droitwich, expressed similar concerns.[75] In Worcestershire the sheriff reported that he had brought nothing with him 'for fear of the rebels in Kenilworth Castle.'[76] From Essex, Richard of Southchurch reported that his

---

[69] TNA, E 159/40, mm. 2, 3.
[70] Jobson, *First Revolution*, pp. 87, 108, 130, 138.
[71] TNA, E 159/40, mm. 1, 11d.
[72] Jobson, *First Revolution*, p. 154.
[73] TNA, E 372/110, rot. 5d; TNA, E 369/41, m. 1; Jobson, *First Revolution*, p. 154.
[74] Jobson, *First Revolution*, p. 155.
[75] TNA, E 159/40, m. 17.
[76] Cassidy, 'Adventus', pp. 624–5.

bailiffs were unable to carry out their office or levy fines because of the 'roaming evildoers' in his shire. Similarly, the constable of Ongar Castle had refused the escheator permission to execute an order issued by the Exchequer.[77] Even Westminster was considered at risk from 'discursum quorundam inimicorum', a threat that forced the central royal administration's temporary relocation to the relative safety of the bishop of London's palace near St Paul's Cathedral.[78] While the Exchequer resumed its operations 'in the bishop's chamber, the justices of the bench sat in his hall'.[79] Only on 23 May 1266 was it deemed safe for the departments and courts to return to their customary home at Westminster.[80]

For the Exchequer, however, the year ending Michaelmas 1267 proved to be equally disruptive. Kenilworth remained defiant until 14 December 1266, when starvation and the other surviving rebels' failure to break the blockade finally forced the castle's surrender after what had become the longest siege in English history. Meanwhile another rebel band, under John de Deyville's leadership, had occupied the Isle of Ely.[81] Throughout the winter of 1266–7 the fighting continued and, in February 1267, unsuccessful peace negotiations were held with the Ely rebels. A month later there were new revolts in Nottinghamshire and Northumberland. These were soon suppressed, but within weeks the royalist regime was threatened once more when Gilbert de Clare rebelled in April. London was swiftly occupied, while at Westminster the palace windows were broken and the contents looted.[82] King Henry assembled a large army in preparation for a lengthy siege of his capital, although it was never actually deployed as mediation ultimately delivered a peaceful resolution. Clare's followers were offered an amnesty on 15 June, while the Disinherited, under the Dictum of Kenilworth's amended terms, were allowed to recover their estates before the payment of a redemption fine. The war was now finally over.[83]

Taken together, these events had a detrimental effect upon the Exchequer's ability to function. Clare's rebellion forced its closure throughout the whole Easter term, a state of affairs that continued until Wednesday 22 June 1267, when it reopened its doors for business. Even when the Exchequer was in operation, its activities were often curtailed as the disturbances compelled the presence elsewhere of royal officials. Warwickshire's sheriff, for example, had not attended the Michaelmas *adventus* of 1266, presumably because of the continuing siege at Kenilworth.[84] Similarly, the first entry recorded on the memoranda roll notes

[77]   TNA, E 159/40, mm. 11d, 14d.
[78]   TNA, E 159/40, m. 13.
[79]   Powicke, *Lord Edward*, ii, p. 520.
[80]   TNA, E 159/40, m. 11d.
[81]   Powicke, *Lord Edward*, ii, p. 532; E. F. Jacob, *Studies in the Period of Baronial Reform and Rebellion* (Oxford, 1925), pp. 236–8.
[82]   Jobson, *First Revolution*, pp. 158–9.
[83]   C. H. Knowles, 'The Disinherited, 1265–80: A Political and Social Survey of the Supporters of Simon de Montfort and the Resettlement after the Barons' War', 3 vols (unpublished PhD thesis, University of Wales, 1959), i, pp. 58–64.
[84]   TNA, E 159/41, mm. 6d, 15.

that Robert of Lathom, the former sheriff of Lancashire, had failed to render his account on 30 September as his presence 'cum equis et armis' was still needed locally to enforce the observance of the peace.[85] There is at least one instance where a former Montfortian sheriff's non-appearance before the Exchequer barons was probably due to his incarceration in Gilbert de Clare's prison.[86]

Yet, despite the severe disruption to its operations, the Exchequer's recovery remained on course. Only four sheriffs had failed to attend the Michaelmas *adventus* in 1266: namely those for Nottinghamshire and Derbyshire, Warwickshire and Leicestershire, Shropshire and Staffordshire, and Lancashire. This represented a significant improvement on the attendance figures for the previous year, when a total of sixteen non-appearances were recorded.[87] Equally noteworthy was the progress achieved by the Upper Exchequer, which had successfully concluded nine shrieval audits before Easter 1267.[88] Essex and Hertfordshire was once again the first shrievalty selected for review, with its sheriff appearing before the barons on 30 September.[89] Four more audits were completed before Christmas, while another three concluded before the end of February.[90] In selecting the counties to be audited, the Exchequer barons adopted the previous year's policy and concentrated on those that had been either strongly Montfortian or had experienced heavy fighting. There was, however, some slight confusion surrounding the enrolment of the audit. All nine accounts are found on the pipe roll, the formal written record of the audit process, but that for London and Middlesex is not found in either set of memoranda rolls produced during the daily hearing of accounts to note matters of significant Exchequer interest.[91] Some membranes now lost could perhaps offer an explanation for this discrepancy, but it is more probably an indication that the Exchequer's internal processes were still in some disarray.

There was likewise a continued emphasis on unravelling the chaos of the wartime accounts. Credits were often issued to sheriffs and other officials for the military expenditure they had incurred in the king's service. Alan Basset, for example, received an allowance of £110 2s. in acknowledgement that he had spent an equivalent sum on the defence of Northampton. Confirmation that he had actually disbursed the money was nevertheless sought from both the Exchequer's own records and the testimony of the two overseers.[92] Compensation

---

[85] TNA, E 368/41, m. 1.

[86] TNA, E 32/137, m. 6d.

[87] TNA, E 368/41, m. 17; Cassidy, 'Adventus', p. 617.

[88] TNA, E 159/41, mm. 8–12d; TNA, E 372/110, rots 1–26d. Essex and Hertfordshire, Nottinghamshire and Derbyshire, Hampshire, Wiltshire, Kent, Northamptonshire, Gloucestershire, Worcestershire, London and Middlesex.

[89] TNA, E 159/41, mm. 11–12.

[90] TNA, E 368/41, mm. 9–14d. Nottinghamshire and Derbyshire (13 October), Kent (3 November), Hampshire (25 November), Wiltshire (1 December), Northamptonshire (20 January), Worcestershire (2 February), Gloucestershire (9 February).

[91] TNA, E 372/110, rots 11–11d.

[92] TNA, E 159/41, mm. 4–4d.

for damages sustained during the fighting was offered to both individuals and corporate bodies. Stephen Fromund was pardoned the issues from Piddington in Oxfordshire for two and a half years as recompense for the losses he had suffered during Simon de Montfort the Younger's sacking of Winchester in July 1265. Portsmouth had been burnt in November 1265, in recognition of which its inhabitants were now quit of their farm for five years. Old debts were sometimes pursued, although others were cancelled on the king's orders. William de Saint-Omer, for instance, was pardoned the £80 he owed, while Hawise of London received an allowance for the fine that she made with the king in 1258 following the death of her husband Patrick de Chaworth.[93]

The progress achieved by the Exchequer in its efforts to restore the health of the royal finances was more quantifiable. In terms of the money proffered by the sheriffs at the Michaelmas *adventus* in 1266, there had been an increase of only £4 compared to the year before. Even less impressive were the proffers of the boroughs, which had fallen over the same period from £192 to £55.[94] However, the Crown's overall annual income had actually experienced a significant increase. Collingwood has calculated that the king's total notional revenues for the year ending at Michaelmas 1267 amounted to some £36,002. Once credits for expenditure had been excluded, however, this left Henry with a cash income of £17,563.[95] In comparison to the previous year, this represented a 51% increase in his disposable income. However, this marked improvement soon proved to be transitory.

Even though the war was now officially over and the country at peace, in the year ending at Michaelmas 1268 the Crown's total notional income had fallen back to £22,031. Once credits for expenditure are excluded, this left the king with an even more modest sum of £12,475 in aggregated cash receipts. That there had been such a decline was the result of several factors, including the allocation of 'feudal' income to meet Henry's patronage needs, and a fall in demesne revenues.[96] Nevertheless the Exchequer had still made some progress in raising the level of payments made at the twice-yearly *adventus*. Some £353 was proffered by the sheriffs at Michaelmas 1267, while another £264 was paid in by the boroughs. At Easter 1268 they deposited a further £434 and £120 respectively. The Exchequer of receipt's earlier success at enforcing shrieval attendance had been maintained. Only three sheriffs failed to appear at the Michaelmas *adventus*, while only four missed the Easter proffer.[97] Meanwhile the Upper Exchequer had enjoyed equal success in its own efforts to hold the Crown's officials to account. Some fourteen shrievalties were audited, with the accounts being held at regular intervals throughout the year.[98] There were still some problems, however,

[93] TNA, E 368/41, mm. 1, 3d, 6d–7; *CFR, 1257–58*, no. 1067; *CFR 1258–59*, no. 61.
[94] Collingwood, 'Royal Finance', p. 263; Cassidy, 'Adventus', pp. 616–17.
[95] Collingwood, 'Royal Finance', pp. 280–1.
[96] Collingwood, 'Royal Finance', pp. 319–36.
[97] Cassidy, 'Adventus', p. 617.
[98] TNA, E 159/42, mm. 29–35d; TNA, E 372/111, rots 1–28d. Yorkshire, London and Middlesex, Northumberland, Oxfordshire and Berkshire, Norfolk and Suffolk, Bedfordshire

with the enrolment process, as three accounts found in the pipe rolls were not recorded on the memoranda rolls.[99]

Nevertheless the Exchequer was now confident enough of its position to initiate new enquiries into pre-war shrieval administration and behaviour. Orders were issued to the sheriff of Buckinghamshire and Bedfordshire, for example, authorising him to investigate whether his predecessor, Alexander of Hampden, had been impeded in the execution of his office.[100] Similarly the Exchequer renewed its efforts at 'clearing up outstanding shrieval account arrears'.[101] John Lovel, the former sheriff of Cambridgeshire and Huntingdonshire, was commanded to appear before the barons on 16 February 1268 to account for the three years that he had been in office. Others were given allowances for salaries they had been owed as custodial sheriffs: William de Engleby, for instance, was allowed reasonable expenses when answering for his tenure of Lincolnshire from 3 November 1258.[102] For treasurer Wymondham and his fellow barons, the year ending at Michaelmas 1268 had once again brought steady progress towards both financial and administrative recovery.

Meanwhile the year had also witnessed the final stage in the restoration of the legal system. This process had remained unfinished ever since the autumn of 1265, the disinherited Montfortians' armed resistance having precluded any possibility of the general eyre's return. But the onset of peace provided the long-awaited opportunity to commission a new general eyre. On 7 December 1267 the programme was announced in three letters patent. Consisting of three circuits, it was intended to be the 'most comprehensive of the reign'. Wiltshire and Yorkshire were the first counties to be visited, where, on 14 January 1268, Nicholas de Turri and Gilbert Preston respectively presided at their opening sessions. Six days later Richard Middleton began hearing pleas at Ilchester in Somerset.[103] Given the extended interval since the last general eyre and the enormous social upheaval experienced during the past decade, it was unsurprising that proceedings were more protracted than usual, although in fiscal terms it would prove extremely profitable for the Crown. Consequently the itinerant justices were still in session four years later when, on 16 November 1272, Henry III died at Westminster.[104]

Even before the general eyre had been commissioned, however, the royal administration had appointed special justices 'to hear and determine pleas concerning lands and tenements granted ... and trespasses committed in the time

and Buckinghamshire, Essex and Hertfordshire, Lincolnshire, Surrey and Sussex, Hampshire, Northamptonshire, Cumberland, Staffordshire and Shropshire, Cambridgeshire and Huntingdonshire.

[99]   TNA, E 372/111, rots 2–3d, 5. Cumberland, Staffordshire and Shropshire, Cambridgeshire and Huntingdonshire.
[100]   TNA, E 159/42, m. 19d.
[101]   Collingwood, 'Royal Finance', p. 316.
[102]   TNA, E 368/42, mm. 9d, 10d.
[103]   *CPR 1266–72*, p. 172; *RGE*, pp. 133–5.
[104]   *RGE*, pp. 134–5; Jobson, *First Revolution*, p. 166.

of the disturbance'. Ever since the 'wholesale and uncontrolled appropriation' of rebel estates that occurred immediately after Evesham, the control of these confiscated lands had been a bone of contention between the royalists and the Disinherited. Under the terms of the Dictum of Kenilworth, the latter could redeem their forfeited estates on payment of a redemption fine. In most instances the process was completed without difficulty, but in a 'hard core of cases' there was a need for 'judicial intervention'.[105] On 17 September 1267, therefore, letters patent for the commissioning of justices *de terris datis* were issued. Four circuits were constituted, each served by a mixture of professional and local justices.[106] Over the next five years they visited many counties until, in April 1272, this special eyre was finally suspended 'presumably because no new cases were coming forward'.[107]

Throughout the year ending at Michaelmas 1269 the restoration of fiscal administration remained broadly on course. The Crown had enjoyed a modest rise in its annual income. Collingwood has calculated that the king's total notional revenues amounted to some £25,059. Once credits for expenditure have been excluded, however, this left the king with a cash income of £14,561.[108] Similarly the proffers made at the biannual *adventus* were higher overall, with £138 and £892 respectively being paid in. Far less encouraging, though, were the figures for shrieval attendance at the Lower Exchequer. Seven had been absent from the Michaelmas 1268 *adventus*, although only two missed the Easter one.[109] In marked contrast, the Upper Exchequer had once again displayed significant progress in its efforts to audit the shrieval accounts. The accounts for some fifteen sheriffs were successfully reviewed by the resident barons and this total, although still markedly lower than that for the pre-war years, emphasised the considerable improvement that had already been achieved in the four years since Evesham.[110] There was still some confusion surrounding the enrolment of the accounts. Fourteen were recorded on the pipe rolls, three of which are not found in the memoranda rolls.[111] Conversely, the memoranda rolls contain an account for Worcestershire that was was not enrolled on the pipe roll, giving them twelve accounts in total.[112]

But it was the Upper Exchequer's systematic inspection of six specific sets of accounts that represented the real milestone on the path towards normal

---

[105]   S. Stewart, 'The Eyre *de terris datis*, 1267–72', in *TCE X*, pp. 69–80, at p. 71.

[106]   *CPR 1266–72*, p. 160.

[107]   Stewart, 'Eyre *de terris datis*', p. 72.

[108]   Collingwood, 'Royal Finance', pp. 318–19.

[109]   Cassidy, 'Adventus', p. 617.

[110]   TNA, E 159/43, mm. 25–31; TNA, E 372/112, rots 1–27d; Mills, 'Adventus', p. 488. Somerset and Dorset, Herefordshire, Surrey and Sussex, Cambridgeshire and Huntingdonshire, Worcestershire, Oxfordshire and Berkshire, Kent, Hampshire, Essex and Hertfordshire, Devon, Wiltshire, Norfolk and Suffolk, Warwickshire and Leicestershire, Northamptonshire, London and Middlesex.

[111]   TNA, E 372/112, rots 4, 6d, 26. Warwickshire and Leicestershire, Northamptonshire, London and Middlesex.

[112]   TNA, E 159/43, m. 27d.

operational efficiency within the department.[113] Usually the sheriff answered for a single year: on this occasion, however, the Exchequer scrutinised the accounts for multiple years. Devonshire, for instance, answered for the four consecutive years from 49 Henry III to 52 Henry III.[114] This new concerted effort to clear up old outstanding shrieval accounts was intended finally to draw a line under the administrative chaos of the recent past. While several more years passed before this process was eventually completed, the first step had already been made. Meanwhile innovations in record-keeping had been introduced into the Exchequer. In earlier years there were five distinct sections within the king's remembrancer memoranda rolls, namely the *communia, recogniciones, adventus vicecomitum, dies dati vicecomitibus* and the *compoti comitatuum*. In 1269, however, these were increased to eight with the introduction of separate membranes for the recording the *brevia*, affidavits and attorneys.[115] The purpose of these structural changes was to facilitate ease of use.

For the first four months of the year beginning at Michaelmas 1269 the Exchequer concentrated upon its primary functions of audit and receipt. Attendance was enforced at the Michaelmas *adventus*, when only two sheriffs were noted as being absent. Shrieval accounts continued to be audited: during this quarter year the Upper Exchequer fully reviewed a total of four shires.[116] Yet compared to previous years this represented a marked deterioration in operational efficiency over the same period. The problem was the department's legacy of old and desperate debts. Some were long-standing arrears, but it was those obligations contracted during the Barons' War that constituted the 'huge mass of debt'.[117] Each year these debts would be summoned, the 'abnormally large number' of which would be routinely 'copied into the summonses and on to the next account, at an expense of time and labour that inevitably reduced the number of accounts that could be audited'. The problem was becoming increasingly acute: the county accounts recorded in the pipe rolls for 51 and 52 Henry III, 'though more closely written, occupied between two and three times as much parchment as the accounts of a decade earlier'.[118]

Such was the scale of the problem that, in February 1270, there was a dramatic change in policy as radical measures were implemented to increase the speed of the recovery. Thomas of Wymondham was dismissed as treasurer on 6 February after almost five years in office. This was probably prompted, in part at least, by a wider generational transition as Henry III's veteran courtiers and

---

[113] TNA, E 159/43, mm. 25–25d, 27d, 30–31d. Somerset and Dorset, Herefordshire, Worcestershire, Devon, Wiltshire, Norfolk and Suffolk.

[114] TNA, E 372/112, rot. 9. William of Bickleigh, the incumbent sheriff, and his two predecessors rendered the accounts.

[115] TNA, E 159/43, mm. 16–19d.

[116] TNA, E 159/44, mm. 15–20. Staffordshire and Bedfordshire (7 October), Nottinghamshire and Derbyshire (21 October), Bedfordshire and Buckinghamshire (10 November), Norfolk and Suffolk (14 January).

[117] Mills, 'Adventus', p. 496.

[118] Meekings, 'Pipe Roll Order', pp. 236–7.

administrators made way for a younger generation that looked to the future Edward I for advancement.[119] Wymondham's successor was a man closely identified with the heir to the throne: John of Chishall. Having been recently elected as dean of St Paul's, in the 1260s he had already served as the chancellor of the Exchequer.[120] Six days after his appointment Chishall, with the royal council's agreement, initiated his plan to free the Exchequer of its burden of debt.[121] In the enrolled accounts on the pipe rolls, the long-standing use of superscript letters to denote desperate debts on the pipe rolls was maintained. But whereas in previous years these debts had been routinely copied over into the subsequent accounts, it was ordained that if the sheriff 'does not admit that he has received any money on a particular debt' then it was 'not to be copied onto the new account.' There it would be left unless a payment had been received, at which point the debt would be entered into the current account, while the earlier one was annotated with a note that it had been discharged. This scheme was first implemented in the Devonshire account, which was audited from 21 April 1270.[122] Chishall's initiative eventually proved successful and, within seven years, the crisis had been averted. For the first time in almost forty years every regularly accounting county had been audited, while the pipe rolls themselves had been reduced substantially in size.[123]

For central government and administration in England, the five years immediately following the royalist victory at Evesham were a period of recovery. Some departments, such as the Chancery, had been reconstituted within a matter of weeks. Others had found the restoration process more challenging: the law courts took over two years to become fully operational. Yet it was the Exchequer that had to overcome the greatest obstacles on the way to recovery. Left with a wartime legacy of administrative disarray and chronic indebtedness, the department's initial priority was the reassertion of its institutional authority. Once this had been largely achieved, attention then turned to unravelling the mess of the wartime shrieval accounts. Even though the continuing resistance of the disinherited rebels had significantly impeded its operations, the Exchequer still made steady progress as ever more accounts were audited and the Crown's income modestly increased. The growing problem of desperate debts eventually threatened that progress, so in February 1270 new measures were introduced that averted the crisis. In these, however, Chishall was building upon the solid foundations laid by his predecessor. That there was even a functioning Exchequer in 1270 for him to reform was entirely due to the efforts of Wymondham and his clerks. In the five years since Evesham, they had made remarkable progress in restoring order from chaos.

[119] Jobson, *First Revolution*, p. 165.
[120] T. F. Tout, rev. R. C. Stacey, 'John of Chishall', *ODNB*.
[121] *CPR 1266–72*, p. 407; Meekings, 'Pipe Roll Order', pp. 222–3.
[122] TNA, E 368/44, m. 18; Meekings, 'Pipe Roll Order', pp. 235, 238, 242–3. The scheme remained in operation until 1277, when the Exchequer reverted to 'traditional methods' and used *rotuli pullorum*, which were schedules containing desperate debts.
[123] Meekings, 'Pipe Roll Order', pp. 235, 242–3.

12

The Church and the King:
Canon Law and Kingship in England, 1257–61

Philippa Hoskin

The history of the late 1250s in England is dominated by legislation, particularly that of the baronial council. The long-term importance of the Provisions of Oxford and the Provisions of Westminster has been recognised and well considered. Yet another legislative process was also taking place in these years, in a series of Church councils: the process of developing a set of statutes for the English Church, which were finally presented to the pope for ratification in 1261. These statutes failed to obtain Pope Urban's consent, and were set aside, despite Archbishop Gray's claims that they were considered law by the English Church and recited before Archbishop Pecham's council of 1289.[1] Yet the legislation, and its two earlier recensions of 1257 and 1258, is of pivotal importance for the history of the development of the English Church. In a long-term, gradual process of compromise and change, they mark a crisis in attempts to demarcate the line between secular and ecclesiastical law. Although the specific issues were not new in 1257 and did not disappear in 1261, the concentration upon them in the first half of the thirteenth century, and the Church's willingness to oppose the secular court's claims, reflect the establishment of settled, permanent episcopal courts in the 1240s and 1250s and the need to decide their areas of jurisdiction; the bishops' views of secular authority and law are also illustrated, as is the parallel relationship between Prince and Church. The Church's process of legislation in 1257–61 demonstrates too the background from which the cooperation of bishops and barons was forged in 1264, while also revealing tensions which show that the alliance was always likely to be short lived.

In March 1257 Henry III called a council at Westminster for ecclesiastical and lay magnates. The constitution of the ecclesiastical section of this council was a broad one: Matthew Paris says that not only bishops and abbots but also archdeacons representing every diocese attended.[2] Here they heard Master Rostand, papal *nuncio*, lay out the details – and supposed advantages – of the Sicilian business: that is, Henry's attempt to take Sicily after accepting the papal

---

[1] J. W. Gray, 'Archbishop Peckham and the Decrees of Boniface', in *Studies in Church History 2*, ed. G. J. Cuming (London, 1965), pp. 215–19. The 1289 *council* description probably means the 1268 statutes (R. L. Storey, 'The First Convocation, 1257?', in *TCE III*, pp. 151–9, at p. 158; *C&S*, i, p. 664).

[2] *Annales Monastici*, i, p. 384; iii, p. 202.

offer of that kingdom for his second son, Edmund.[3] Unsurprisingly, given the costs of this venture and his financial promises to the pope, the king requested money from the clergy. According to the Burton annalist a taxation was proposed of a five-year tenth, half the income of benefices of non-resident clergy and all the income of benefices at a vacancy for the next five years, benefice income from those with exemptions and the portion of the goods of intestates which would have been set aside for their souls' good.[4] All this taxation added to the burden of papal taxes already granted to the king to fund his Sicilian plans.[5] The clergy were unwilling to agree. The same annalist tells us that they declared they were not obliged to make these payments, particularly as the king had entered agreements over Sicily unwisely, without common consent. Their money, they said, was 'the patrimony of the Crucified' which should, by divine law, be reserved for the poor, and unless they learnt to make filth into gold there was not, in fact, enough money in England to pay these demands, although this last suggests a misunderstanding, perhaps deliberate, about the amount being requested.[6] At a Church council probably held soon afterwards, in May, they attempted to compound their liability by making an offer of a single payment of 52,000 marks, in return for the restoration of the Church's liberties and the end of demands for those taxes known as 'graces': Paris claims that the list of fifty complaints (*gravamina*) concerning liberties infringed by secular authority that he recorded in his *Liber Additamentorum* was related to this meeting.[7] The king delayed making a decision over the offer.

In this situation, the archbishop of Canterbury's patience with the king apparently ran out. Boniface of Savoy, the queen's uncle, had already clashed with the king over the exercise of his ecclesiastical power and, despite his royal connections, was clearly committed to upholding the rights of the English Church. In July 1257, while Henry still hesitated, Boniface called a council of the province of Canterbury at London for August.[8] The king wrote immediately forbidding this. The kingdom, he said, was in danger, and all magnates, lay and ecclesiastical, should concentrate on support for his campaign in Wales.[9] The assembled clerics, however, agreed to continue their deliberations, noting the previous three-year financial oppression of the Church which they claimed had prevented proper pastoral care in the kingdom, resulting in sacrilege which should lead to excommunication

[3]   For the Sicilian business, see J. R. Maddicott, *Simon de Montfort* (Cambridge, 1994); R. F. Treharne, *The Baronial Plan of Reform, 1258–63* (Manchester, 1962), p. 50; M. T. Clanchy, *England and its Rulers, 1066–1272*, 2nd edn (Oxford, 1968), pp. 169–72; B. Weiler, 'Henry III and the Sicilian Business: A Reinterpretation', *HR* 74 (2001), 127–50.

[4]   *Annales Monastici*, i, pp. 386–91; W. E. Lunt, *Financial Relations of the Papacy with England to 1327* (Cambridge, 1939), pp. 276–7.

[5]   Lunt, *Financial Relations*, pp. 255–90.

[6]   *Annales Monastici*, i, pp. 390–1; *Chronica Majora*, v, pp. 580–5; Lunt, *Financial Relations*, pp. 251–2.

[7]   *Chronica Majora*, v, p. 621; vi, pp. 353–65.

[8]   *Annales Monastici*, i, p. 401; *C&S*, i, pp. 531–2.

[9]   *C&S*, i, p. 685.

and interdict of the guilty and their lands. They declared themselves ready to resist the 'oppressions of the Church' and, taking the *gravamina* of May, they identified among those complaints the outrages which they could not ignore except at the peril of their souls.[10] Although Cheney interprets the surviving documentation differently,[11] it seems probable from this declaration that Paris was correct in attributing the longer list of fifty *gravamina* to the earlier, May, meeting. The list is often very detailed and somewhat unstructured, with several points covering the same issue; it looks like a first attempt at gathering complaints and concerns. The August meeting was presumably intended to go through this list, and to hear other complaints,[12] in order to identify the most important issues for future consideration and negotiation. The final resulting document may well be that surviving in the Burton annals, made up of just fifteen points, which is described as articles conceded in the archbishop's council.[13] These covered the intrusion of clerks into benefices by the laity; summons of clerks before secular courts; secular abuses of sanctuary; infringements of the rights of criminous clerks; issues relating to probate; seizure of ecclesiastical property; the use of new and unapproved writs; concerns about the king's approach to ecclesiastical property, amercements of the clergy or their tenants; and demands for the clergy to perform suit of court. They reflected the main concerns arising in the longer document, excepting the detailed complaints about the process of ecclesiastical elections; possibly the existence of King John's charter of 1214 on this issue made this seem a less urgent problem to put to Henry, or upon which to make a formal agreement.[14]

The king would not give up his plans for Sicily, and in April the next year, still desperate for money to keep his promises to the pope, he summoned another royal council, at which the clergy present refused him a requested aid.[15] As in 1257, the royal council was soon followed by another Church council, possibly limited to the southern province if only because of the vacancy of the archbishopric of York. It was summoned for 6 June and may, as the Burton annalist claims, have met first at Merton, although its final documentation was issued at Westminster two days later.[16] In these two days the council made only small changes to the archbishop's draft document. This focused upon the issues laid down in the fifteen articles arising from the 1257 council, with the addition of some few detailed points taken from the earlier, longer set of *gravamina*, such as concerns about the position of the Jews in relation to the ecclesiastical courts.[17]

[10]   *Annales Monastici*, i, p. 404; *C&S*, i, pp. 535–6.
[11]   Cheney considers the fifty *gravamina* the council's final result: he does not comment upon the council's statement at the start of proceedings that they will discuss the 'articles and *gravamina*' which they clearly already have (*C&S*, i, p. 530).
[12]   *C&S*, i, pp. 537–9.
[13]   *Annales Monastici*, i, p. 403; *C&S*, i, pp. 534–5.
[14]   See *C&S*, i, pp. 40–1.
[15]   *Chronica Majora*, v, p. 676.
[16]   *Annales Monastici*, i, p. 412; *C&S*, i, p. 585.
[17]   Articles 32 and 33 of the 1257 *gravamina*, made into article 13 in 1258 (*C&S 2*, i, pp. 545, 580).

This was no longer a set of complaints, but of ordinances, concentrating not on wrongs done to the Church but on the punishments which would be meted out for those wrongs: the excommunication and interdicts mentioned as desirable penalties in general discussions in 1257 were now incorporated into the main document.[18] The whole was prefaced with a statement about the need to restore the liberties of the Church.[19] The document was not considered final, for provision was made in its last clause for later alterations.[20]

The parliament at Oxford, which led to the famous provisions seeking political reform and then to the baronial council of 1258–60, began just days after the sealing of these ecclesiastical ordinances,[21] and these political events may have been in part responsible for the dearth of Church councils in the next two years: Boniface was otherwise occupied, as a member of the Council of Twenty-Four.[22] In late 1260, however, the political situation, nationally and internationally, had changed. In Europe the Tartar invasion of Hungary had caused great alarm, increased by fears that the Tartars were forerunners of the Apocalypse, expected by many in the mid- and late thirteenth century. In November, Pope Alexander IV wrote to princes and prelates, seeking help and ordering the holding of Church councils to discuss how this threat could be met and how resistance was to be funded.[23] In England the baronial council was now a dead letter, although Henry still, in public at least, declared his commitment to his oath to keep the provisions. In this context Boniface called a council for 8 May 1261 at Lambeth.[24] On the table, in addition to the Tartar rebellion (about which there was only inconclusive discussion)[25] were the ordinances: the unfinished business of 1258. This alarmed the king, who arranged for Master John of Hemingford to be present as his representative at the opening of the council to make a formal statement of protest; he was followed by four more representatives, including the king's son Edward, who appeared on the last day of the council, to appeal on behalf of king and kingdom.[26] The king also made formal answers to accusations drawn largely from the 1261 documentation.[27] On 13 May the revised

---

[18] *C&S*, i, pp. 537–9.
[19] *C&S*, i, p. 573.
[20] *C&S*, i, p. 585.
[21] *Annales Monastici*, i, p. 163; for Oxford, see Maddicott, *Simon de Montfort*, pp. 156–62; D. Carpenter, 'What Happened in 1258?', in *War and Government in the Middle Ages: Essays in Honour of J. O. Prestwich*, ed. J. Gillingham and J. Holt (Woodbridge, 1984), reprinted in D. Carpenter, *The Reign of Henry III* (London, 1996), pp. 107–36.
[22] *Documents*, p. 101.
[23] *Annales Monastici*, i, pp. 495–9.
[24] *The Historical Works of Gervase of Canterbury*, ed. W. Stubbs, Rolls Series, 2 vols (London, 1879–80), ii, pp. 212–13.
[25] *Flores Historiarum*, ed. H. G. Hewlett, Rolls Series, 3 vols (London, 1886–9), ii, p. 465.
[26] *CPR 1258–66*, p. 151. For the king's representatives, see *Gervase of Canterbury*, ii, p. 213.
[27] *C&S*, i, pp. 687–92. Cheney notes that this document dates from 1261, and draws directly on the language of the statutes (*C&S*, i, p. 667). It is as likely, however, that it records responses during the council as after it as Cheney suggests. Article 6 of the statutes may be partly a response to the king's comments concerning benefices in article 1 of this document.

ordinances were issued by the council as statutes, intended as permanent law for the English Church.[28] The final document was based heavily upon that of 1258, with additional clarification added where necessary and a few articles added or removed. Concerns about amercements, for example, and more broadly about the treatment of bishops as secular lords, disappeared, and in their place was a more detailed consideration of testamentary law and practical arrangements to ensure that the Church's claims on criminous clerks were not undermined. The statutes included both much of the 1258 preface, as part of the first article, and a new preamble, again declaring the importance of ecclesiastical liberties and the Church's inability to persuade king or magnates to engage with them.[29] The document was taken to Pope Alexander by Boniface for ratification. In this he was unsuccessful. Henry was ahead of him, and had received papal permission to repudiate his oath to the provisions. Now, at Henry's urging, the new pope, Urban, refused to place his authority behind the statutes, although he noted to the king that there was nothing he could object to in the statements they made.[30] Historians have claimed that the statutes failed because Henry had obtained a papal concession that his officials should not be excommunicated while on the king's business, rendering many of the penalties of the statutes void,[31] but this seems not to have occurred to the pope himself as an objection.

The story of the Church councils of 1257–61 is, then, a story of failed legislation; a tale of long deliberation, drafting and discussion which came to nothing. This does not, however, mean that these documents are sterile ground for the historian, for their importance extends beyond the history of ecclesiastical law. Nor should they be read too closely against the English political events of the late 1250s. A comparison of the documents of 1257, 1258 and 1261 in their broader national and international context reveals how the English Church considered reform and its liberties at this date, and its attitude towards secular authority and kingship. In fact the statutes explain less about the bishops' involvement with the immediate events of 1258–61 than about the episcopate's later connections with Simon de Montfort's supporters in the mid-1260s.

Although the Church was part of the environment within which the political events of 1258 occurred, it is simplistic to view these documents as the ecclesiastical section of the baronial provisions. It is tempting to link Boniface's council of May 1258 directly to the political events of that month, articulating specific claims for ecclesiastical liberties so that the barons needed only to provide a more general statement of intent towards the Church. Although both the barons' and the bishops' documents of 1258 arose in the same political circumstances, and although there were clear links between the magnates and the prelates, Boniface's

---

[28] *C&S*, i, pp. 684–5.
[29] *C&S*, i, pp. 669–71.
[30] *C&S*, i, pp. 685–6; Henry moved against the bishops a fortnight after the statutes were issued: *CPR 1258–66*, pp. 152, 192, 197.
[31] Gray, 'Archbishop Peckham', pp. 215–19; Storey, 'The First Convocation, 1257', p. 158.

provincial council of 1258 was not consciously complementary to the baronial provisions, nor was it integrated into the documentation of the rebellion. Rather it was part of a long process of ecclesiastical complaint and protest in the thirteenth century, starting in the 1230s, continuing in 1253 and stretching after 1261 to the *gravamina* of 1267, 1280 and 1285, the clerical petitions of 1294, the statements in the *Articuli Cleri* of 1314, and the clerical complaints of 1328–9 and 1341,[32] all focusing on ecclesiastical liberties.

The aims of the barons and the bishops were not, in detail, the same. There were areas of agreement and common cause. The statutes of the Church and baronial complaints could overlap, as in the issue of lords forced to perform suit before the justices of the eyre on the first day of the summons.[33] Secular and ecclesiastical magnates did work together: in 1257 they produced a joint protest against the king's Sicilian proposal.[34] Members of the episcopate were secular lords by virtue of their episcopal estates, thus sharing the concerns of all large landholders in England, and in the late 1250s some were also heads of secular families in their own right: Fulk Basset's presence at the council of Oxford was by virtue of his headship of the Basset family, and Walter de Cantilupe was also head of his family during his nephew's minority.[35] Bishops were also members of the Council of Twenty-Four on both sides. Boniface also paid attention to the baronial legislation and adjusted his own statutes and provisions to take account of this. The episcopal concerns of 1258 over the amercement of bishops who had stood surety to bailed clerics arrested on a criminal charge, and those regarding the summoning of ecclesiastics to perform suit of court for lands held in frankalmoin unless they had specific charters of exemption, disappear by 1261: these issues had been addressed by the barons in 1259.[36]

However, there were as many areas of difference between secular barons and ecclesiastics as of similarity. There was a reason that the clause in the provisions about the liberties of the Church, like the first clause of Magna Carta, was vague.[37] Any attempt to create a more detailed list of ecclesiastical demands to be supported within a baronial reform movement was likely to tear the two parties apart. In 1258 baronial petitions for involvement in the election of heads of religious houses did not please the Church, nor did provisions concerning

---

[32] *Chronica Majora*, iii, p. 616; *C&S*, i, pp. 279–84; *Chronica Majora*, v, p. 359; *Annales Monastici*, i, p. 305; R. Vaughn, 'Excerpts from John of Wallingford's Chronicle', *EHR* 73 (1958), 70–7; *Annales Monastici*, i, p. 422; *C&S*, i, p. 469; *C&S*, ii, pp. 1132–3; J. W. Gray, 'Bishops, Politics and the Two Laws: The *gravamina* of the English Clergy, 1237–1399', *Speculum* 41 (1966), 209–45; J. H. Denton, 'The Making of the "Articuli Cleri" of 1316', *EHR* 101 (1986), 564–95.

[33] *Documents*, p. 82.

[34] J. R. Maddicott, *The Origins of the English Parliament, 924–1327* (Oxford, 2010), p. 159; *C&S*, i, pp. 388–95; *Annales Monastici*, i, pp. 386–8.

[35] *Annales Monastici*, i, p. 449; *Chronica Majora*, iv, p. 89.

[36] P. Brand, *Kings, Barons and Justices: The Making and Enforcement of Legislation in Thirteenth-Century England* (Cambridge, 2003), pp. 49–51, 82–3.

[37] *Documents*, p. 107.

alienations of land into mortmain.[38] There were parts of the episcopal protests of 1257–61 which were ignored or rejected by the barons, such as the use of oaths. Since 1253 the Church had declared that during parish visitations the bishop needed to take oaths from ordinary parishioners before examining them.[39] To the bishops this was a spiritual matter; individuals must tell the truth for their souls' health. To the king it was a cause of unease: the laity, as a group, should only make oaths to him. Bishops Grosseteste and Cantilupe were admonished for oath-taking.[40] The barons debated the issue in 1259, but left the situation as it was.[41] Always important to the medieval English Church was its right to try clerks accused of criminal actions. By the thirteenth century it was established that these should be handed over to their bishops by the secular courts, but uncertainty remained over precisely when the transfer should be made. Under Henry III, accused clerks were usually tried by secular process first and only given to the bishop for punishment.[42] This was unacceptable to the Church, but not to the barons. Bigod's special eyre dealt with accused clerks in exactly this way.[43] Other issues, such as laymen appearing in ecclesiastical courts when in dispute with the clergy, were not likely to appeal to the council, whose concerns were, naturally enough, secular ones. When considering the issue of benefices they first secured the rights of the patrons, not the Church.[44] The English Church was certainly focused on reform through legislation in the late 1250s; in this it pursued a process which ran parallel to that of secular reform in England, but could not be said to be a part of it.

These clashes between the secular and the ecclesiastical were an important motivation for episcopal legislation in a local and international context. Across Europe the development of the boundaries between secular and ecclesiastical authority – a legacy of the eleventh-century reform movement – were being defined and disputed, particularly in the twelfth and thirteenth centuries in legal terms as the study and development of Roman law, in parallel with canon law, provided a different vocabulary and context for scholastic discussion, not least in

---

[38] *Documents*, pp. 81–3; Brand, *Kings, Barons and Justices*, pp. 57–62.

[39] For 1253, see *C&S*, i, p. 470. For 1261, see *C&S*, i, pp. 678–9.

[40] *CR 1242–7*, pp. 543; *CR 1247–51*, pp. 221–2, 554.

[41] Brand, *Kings, Barons and Justices*, pp. 101–3.

[42] C. R. Cheney, 'The Punishment of Felonious Clerks', *EHR* 51 (1936), 215–36, at pp. 224–5; L. C. Gabel, *Benefit of Clergy in England in the Later Middle Ages*, Smith College Studies in History 14 (n.p. 1929), chapter 2; A. L. Poole, 'Outlawry as a Punishment of Criminous Clerks', in *Historical Essays in Honour of J. Tait*, ed. J. G. Edwards, V. H. Galbraith and E. F. Jacob (Manchester, 1933), pp. 239–46, at p. 240; R. H. Helmholz, *The Oxford History of the Laws of England*, vol. 1: *The Canon Law and Ecclesiastical Jurisdiction from 597 to the 1640s* (Oxford, 2004), pp. 511–14; *English Episcopal Acta 38: London 1229–1280*, ed. P. M. Hoskin (Oxford, 2011) nos 223, 286, 239, 241 and pp. xci–xcii.

[43] For the Oxfordshire eyre, see A. H. Hershey, 'An Introduction to, and Edition of, the Hugh Bigod Eyre Rolls' (unpublished PhD dissertation, University of London, 1991), ii, entries B415, 421, 444, 446, 450, 453.

[44] *Documents*, p. 129.

looking at the ruler's will in law.[45] Different interests increasingly highlighted the need to delineate the boundary between the laws of Church and State, the more so as individuals and institutions used conflicting claims and overlapping jurisdictions to their own advantages, sometimes bringing legal process to a standstill.[46] There was agreement between Church and Crown that such a boundary existed. The king in 1261 declared that he would not interfere with legislation concerning the purely spiritual,[47] and in the same year the Church formally stated that Crown and Church should pursue separate areas of authority.[48] The problem was as to where exactly the boundary lay. Attempts to separate secular and ecclesiastical law were hampered by their reliance upon each other. They guided the same people, and each was dependent upon the support of the other.[49] The importance of customary law, sometimes over-riding the written word, made finding this balance even more difficult. Custom was as important to the law of the Church as to common law, and although Gratian declared that custom was not in itself a reason to adhere to a practice – bad custom was just that – canon law expected to be revised or even replaced by good local custom.[50] In 1237 the papal legate Otto took advice on English custom before issuing his canons, and the Church agreed with little or no complaint to customary legal practice which was outside canon law. In advowson disputes it generally accepted the king's right to try the case, claimed on the grounds that the advowson was temporal property, and did not attempt to maintain canon law's position that advowsons, as spiritualities, came within ecclesiastical legal jurisdiction.[51] Attempts to define

[45]   For fuller discussion of this process, see, for example, J. Canning, *A History of Medieval Political Thought, 300–1450* (London and New York, 1996), pp. 84–124; A. Black, *Political Thought in Europe, 1250–1450* (Cambridge, 1992), pp. 152–5.

[46]   For example, the use St Augustine's, Canterbury, made of the ability to move between jurisdictions (see B. Bombi, 'The Role of Judges-Delegate in England: The Dispute between the Archbishops of Canterbury and St Augustine's Abbey in the Thirteenth Century', in *Legati e delegati papali: Profilif, ambiti d'azione e tipologie di intervento nei secoli XII–XIII*, ed. M. P. Alberzoni and C. Zey (Milan, 2012), pp. 221–60). For writs of Prohibition to halt cases, see G. B. Flahiff, 'The Use of Prohibitions by Clerics against Ecclesiastical Courts in England', *Medieval Studies* 3 (1941), 101–14; G. B. Flahiff, 'The Writ of Prohibition in the Court Christian in the Thirteenth-Century', *Medieval Studies* 6 (1944), 262–96; R. H. Helmholz, 'The Writ of Prohibition to Court Christian before 1500', *Medieval Studies* 297 (1981), 297–314; *Select Cases from the King's Court, 1272–1307*, ed. D. Millon, Selden Society 126 (London, 2009), pp. xxi–lix. For the prior of Eye's payment for such a writ in the regnal year of 126–61, see *CFR 1260–61*, no. 88.

[47]   *C&S*, i, p. 688.

[48]   *C&S*, i, pp. 670–1.

[49]   A. Harding, *Medieval Law and the Foundations of the State* (Oxford, 2002), p. 137; A. Harding, *The Law Courts of Medieval England* (London, 1972), pp. 43–9.

[50]   R. H. Helmholz, 'Conflicts between Religious and Secular Law: Common Themes in the English Experience, 1250–1640', *Cardozo Law Review* 707 (1990–1), 715–16; R. H. Helmholz, *Roman Canon Law in Reformation England* (Cambridge, 1990), pp. 12–20.

[51]   C. R. Cheney, *From Becket to Langton: English Church Government, 1170–1213* (Manchester, 1950), pp. 108–18; Helmholz, *The Oxford History of the Laws of England*, pp. 477–81; R. A. R. Hartridge, 'Edward I's Exercise of the Right of Presentation to Benefices as Shown by the Patent Rolls', *Cambridge Historical Journal* 2 (1927), 171–7; P. Heath, *Church*

secular and spiritual boundaries definitively were often apparently avoided, as the cause of tensions, but in the mid-thirteenth century such evasion became more difficult. As the English church courts developed from peripatetic, even *ad hoc*, assemblies into institutions with a fixed base within the diocese and identifiable dedicated staff and procedures, standardisation of court processes increased, handbooks of procedure were produced, and all areas of dispute and uncertainty concerning the jurisdictions of Church and State came under new scrutiny.[52] It was increasingly necessary for the practices and processes of the court to be set down. At the same time, the development of such courts and the need for precision in legal claims also encouraged a focus upon the exploration of law and the legal position of princes, popes and lower ecclesiastical and secular authorities which was taking place within the universities.

It is unsurprising, then, to find so many of the articles of 1261 pushing at these boundaries. Some of the debates which influenced the statutes, such as that concerning the hearing of civil cases related to the clergy, were of broad scope, with debate continuing across Europe.[53] Many others, although appearing sweeping in the statutes, concerned points where the dispute was in the detail not the principle. The first article of the statutes asserted the Church's right to try cases involving issues including parish boundaries, tithes and sacrilege. Were these claims in doubt? In fact only small areas were disputed. The king's response to this article reveals that parish boundaries were considered broadly the preserve of the Church, unless they were boundaries of royal chapels or liberties.[54] Disputes over tithes were also admitted to be ecclesiastical cases unless they related to such chapels.[55] The explanation added in the 1261 statutes to the 1258 wording, which states that the secular courts were claiming tithe disputes by calling them advowson disputes, makes it probable that these were those, apparently rare, cases involving more than a sixth of the tithes of a parish, which could potentially affect the right of advowson and were therefore claimed by the king.[56] The secular courts were not trying to establish a blanket jurisdiction in these areas, but arguing for specific exceptions to the general rule which placed such cases in the church courts. In discussing sanctuary, the Church claimed the right to ensure that those taking advantage of their protection were not so closely guarded that they received no food or drink.[57] With

---

and Realm, 1272–1461: Conflict and Collaboration in an Age of Crises (Oxford, 1988), pp. 124–5.

[52] J. A. Brundage, *The Medieval Origins of the Legal Profession* (Chicago, 2008), pp. 145–9. In the 1230s the legate Otto's canons reflected these new developments, establishing seals for offices within the courts and legislating for court officials (*C&S*, i, pp. 257–8). Episcopal statutes explore the use of apparitors, advocates and conveners of witnesses (*C&S*, i, pp. 179, 308, 356, 387, 493).

[53] R. H. Helmholz, *The Ius Commune in England: Four Studies* (Oxford, 2001), pp. 167–225; Harding, *Medieval Law and the Foundation of the State*, p. 127.

[54] *C&S*, i, pp. 687–8.

[55] *C&S*, i, p. 688.

[56] *Select Cases from the King's Court*, p. lxx.

[57] *C&S*, i, pp. 679–80.

this the king apparently concurred, stating the importance of maintaining sanctuary, a broad agreement in principle hiding a specific difference in meaning.[58] The particular issue was that of how long sanctuary should be allowed to continue. Canon law placed no limit upon this, while English secular custom said that after forty days the accused had to abjure the kingdom; from then attempts to starve the unfortunate individual out of hiding were legitimate, and it is probably these attempts to which the bishops referred.[59] Many more articles concern points where the broad-brush principles had already been agreed but the small details of law in specific circumstances remained to be negotiated.

The documents of 1257–61 are detailed negotiations of the boundaries of Church and State law, but they are also more than this. The creation of that boundary was, as Helmholz has pointed out, a long, slow process of compromise and discussion over several centuries, punctuated by only a few crises with overt hostilities.[60] Clearly those years 1257–61 marked such a crisis: what created it? The statutes are notable for their uncompromising confidence. The areas of difference may have been small but the Church was set on claiming them nonetheless. The statutes contain evidence of previous legal compromise, but no offers of such compromise in the present. The king's responses make it clear that he had no intention of giving way in these areas, either. An impasse had been reached, and this was due not to practical legal developments but to differing views of secular and ecclesiastical power.

By 1261 the bishops could look at Henry III and consider that he had failed in his secular and spiritual obligation to be a good king. Henry, they thought, neither ruled under the law nor demonstrated that he was a strong king. Debates about secular authority in the schools of the late-twelfth and early-thirteenth centuries examined the rights of the prince and emperor – or, in the English context, the king's rights – and explored good rule. In England the period 1215–58 has been described as dominated by the issue of whether the king was under custom;[61] that is, under customary law. Was the king, who made law and whose will was law, also bound by it? The answer was yes: once law had been made a just king should act according to that law. Moreover, the legal text traditionally known as *Bracton* noted that if the king infringed that law there were safeguards. The king had a duty to create and uphold good law: as John of Salisbury said, the tyrant oppressed the people, the good king ruled by law. Such good law had to be for the good of those he ruled: as Robert Grosseteste, former bishop of Lincoln, noted, a tyrant was a man who ruled in his own interests, a good king was one

58   *C&S*, i, p. 691.
59   Helmholz, *The Ius Commune in England*, pp. 56–69; J. C. Cox, *The Sanctuaries and Sanctuary Seekers of Medieval England* (London, 1911); A. Reville, 'L'abjuratio regni: Histoire d'une institution anglaise', *Revue Historique* 50 (1892), 1–42.
60   Helmholz, 'Conflicts between Religious and Secular Law', pp. 712–17.
61   K. Pennington, *The Prince and the Law, 1200–1600: Sovereignty and Rights in the Western Legal Tradition* (Berkeley, CA, 1993), p. 92.

who ruled in the interests of those subject to him.[62] If the king made bad law this could not be undone without his consent, and if he would not keep his own good laws he could not be forced to, but he could be challenged for the harm he had caused and instructed by his magnates, both secular and ecclesiastical, to make amends or face God's judgment.[63] That is, where the king infringed the law he could be 'bridled' by these his natural legal advisors, whom he should, indeed, already have consulted about large decisions where there was the potential for great wrongs to be committed; however, the extent to which that persuasive 'bridle' could be applied was not entirely clear.

The king also had financial obligations. A king needed sufficient income to rule: his income was required to give good gifts (not indiscriminately, but to his subjects)[64] and to protect his kingdom by defending it from attack, wielding the secular sword which Boniface and other English bishops considered him to hold at the will of the Church, which could also take it from him.[65] Some of the income for these duties came through taxation, but the long discussions in the schools about the prince's ownership of property had decided that private individuals held property absolutely and taxation was thus to be raised by consent.[66] In England the king's demands for regular taxes through the 1240s and 1250s, when he was obliged to call his council and to ask his magnates, clerical and lay, to grant him such taxes, established in fact the right of council to be consulted in this matter.[67]

Judged by these standards Henry had fallen far short, leaving the Church believing that it could, and should, guide him. The Church councils of 1257 and 1258 discussed, and were driven by, the king's need for heavy taxation; taxation which he required because he had, without taking advice from his natural counsellors, entered into military obligations which he could not sustain financially

---

[62] *Aristoteles Over de Vriendschap: Boeken VIII en IX van de Nicomachische Ethiek met de commentaren van Apasius en Michaël in de Latijnse vertaling van Grosseteste*, ed. W. Stinissen (Brussels, 1963), pp. 39–40.

[63] Harding, *Medieval Law and the Foundations of the State*, pp. 145–6; F. Schulz, 'Bracton on Kingship', *EHR* 60 (1945), 136–76; B. Tierney, 'Bracton on Government', *Speculum* 38 (1965), 295–317; E. Lewis, 'King above Law? "Quod Principi Placuit" in Bracton', *Speculum* 39 (1964), 240–69; C. Nederman, 'Bracton on Kingship Revisited', *History of Political Thought* 5 (1984), 61–77; C. J. Nederman, 'The Royal Will and the Baronial Bridle', *History of Political Thought* 9 (1988), 415–29; M. Blecker, 'The King's Partners in Bracton', *Studi Sensei* 96 (1984), 66–118, at p. 109; C. Radding, 'The Origin of Bracton's *Addicio de Cartis*', *Speculum* 44 (1969), 239–46.

[64] See Grosseteste on the Nicomachean Ethics, *Aristotles Over de Vriendschap*, p. 40.

[65] D. T. Williams, 'Aspects of the Career of Boniface of Savoy 1241–70' (unpublished PhD dissertation, University of Wales, 1970), pp. 118–24. Boniface may also have been influenced by Robert Grosseteste: Williams, 'Aspects of the Career', pp. 107–112. For Grosseteste's views, see *Letters of Robert Grosseteste, Bishop of Lincoln*, ed. F. Mantello and J. Goering (Toronto, 2010), pp. 366–9.

[66] Pennington, *The Prince and the Law*, pp. 124–5; B. Tierney, 'Origins of Natural Rights Language: Texts and Contexts, 1150–1250', *History of Political Thought* 10 (1989), 615–46 at p. 639.

[67] Maddicott, *Origins of the English Parliament*, pp. 227–32.

and which were not necessary for the defence of the kingdom whose peace he was to maintain. He was living beyond his means, and instead of giving to his people he was taking from them, beyond his natural right to do so.[68] The king's claimed insolvency had long been a source of concern in the kingdom and now, as far as the Church was concerned, matters had reached crisis point. Moreover, the king was not ruling justly. Boniface's prefaces of 1258 and 1261 draw extensively on the king's refusal to take counsel or to be ruled by either positive or natural law. In 1257, 1258 and 1261 the Church reiterated its grief that the king continued to ignore his promise to maintain Magna Carta.[69] The 1261 preface links this to divine law, noting the 'charter of freedom' granted to mankind by Christ in his death, which cancelled the 'chirograph of servitude' initiated at Adam's transgression and gave liberty from Heaven to the Church. This the preface compared to the 'charter of liberty' then renewed by 'faithful princes' on the earth.[70] The same preface expresses anger that Henry had ignored the repeated counsel of his bishops, as well as their petitions for the restoration of their liberties.[71] It also emphasises the role of divine law. Secular rule was intended to be in the pattern of divine rule, and was subject to the rule of heaven. Two laws were meant to work together: natural law – that is divine law, which would save man from sensual lust – and positive law, that is the law of man, which would guide people's weak wills.[72] Henry had infringed the liberties of the Church, he had forgotten his obligations to it and those who gave him his power; he had overthrown the Church's 'privilege of natural right'.[73] As the 1253 *gravamina* had it, he had turned natural authority upside down.[74]

All of these sins would bring down God's wrath upon Henry; it was the bishops' duty to lead him back to the right path. In challenging him they drew upon their past. Although this can be placed in a context of international thirteenth-century debate about secular authority and obligation, the broader English historical context was clear to Boniface and his bishops, who fitted their legislative attempts into the accepted pattern of persecution of the Church and of its eventual triumphs. Parallels with the past were claimed in the late 1250s: the bishops, defying Henry's demands in 1258, declared that Boniface would protect their rights just as Thomas Becket had in the twelfth century,[75] and in 1257 Matthew Paris described the *gravamina* of that year as 'similar to those for which the Blessed Thomas, archbishop of Canterbury, martyr, the glorious

---

[68] Grosseteste's commentary on the Nichomachean Ethics emphasised that a good king took only what was owed to him; a weak king or a bad king would take more: *Aristotles Over de Vriendschap*, p. 40.
[69] *C&S*, i, pp. 547–8, 585, 670, 680–1.
[70] *C&S*, i, p. 670.
[71] *C&S*, i, pp. 769–70.
[72] *C&S*, i, p. 770.
[73] *C&S*, i, p. 670.
[74] *C&S*, i, p. 469; *Annales Monastici*, i, p. 422.
[75] *Chronica Majora*, v, p. 632.

victor, fought'.[76] The preface to the 1261 statutes describes the archbishop as successor to those who had held the role before him. The recently canonised St Edmund of Abingdon is mentioned by name,[77] linking the Savoyard Boniface to a very English tradition and serving as a reminder of the good counsel Edmund provided the king in 1234, during the Marshall uprising.[78] But there are also reminders of earlier archbishops here: of Stephen Langton's struggle with John, and most importantly of Becket, defender of the liberties of the Church and one of the martyrs by whose blood, the same preface states, the liberty of the Church was defended against the princes of the world. The recently composed *vitae* of the new St Edmund, placing him in Becket's mould even though such a pattern barely fitted, were a further reminder of these links,[79] and Becket's martyrdom was depicted on the reverse of the very seal which Boniface attached to the statutes. These former archbishops were reminders to the episcopate of the 1250s of their duty to oppose secular power in the Church's interests when that Church was in danger. In fact, the Church was claiming the right to make and uphold law for itself when faced with a weak and all but tyrannical king, just as it felt Becket had.

Unsurprisingly, the king held another view of kingship, revealed in his answers to those 1261 statutes, and one with which rulers in other parts of Europe – and some contemporary theorists – would have agreed. He too saw himself as obliged to bring justice and peace to the kingdom, to protect the Church and to uphold divine law: in fact, his final statement in this document was that the Crown's special duty was to maintain the peace of the kingdom.[80] He agreed that the law of sanctuary should be upheld because to do otherwise was 'against God and Justice', and firmly stated his obligation to respect the Church's liberties.[81] This fits with Henry's use of his saintly predecessor, Edward the Confessor, as his role model from the 1230s on, when the saint's known concern for the peace and unity of the kingdom, and the Church, could be expected to be part of Henry's own perception of kingship,[82] or at least of the royal image which he wished to portray. These were royal duties with which the Church could agree; but Henry declared that he was not failing in these obligations, although fulfilling them in a way that the Church disliked. Like his French contemporary, Louis IX, he was prepared to uphold ecclesiastical law, but not to follow the demands of spiritual

[76] *Chronica Majora*, v, p. 637; Maddicott, *Origins of the English Parliament*, p. 146.
[77] *C&S*, i, p. 670.
[78] For further details, see C. H. Lawrence, *St Edmund of Abingdon* (Oxford, 1960), pp. 130–8.
[79] Lawrence, *Edmund of Abingdon*, pp. 168–81.
[80] *C&S*, i, p. 692.
[81] *C&S*, i, pp. 691, 688.
[82] D. Carpenter, 'King Henry III and St Edward the Confessor: the Origins of the Cult', *EHR* 122 (2007), 865–91, at pp. 877–80; P. Binski, 'Reflections on *La Estoire de Seint Aedward le Rei*: Hagiography and Kingship in Thirteenth-Century England,' *JMH* 16 (1990), 333–50, at pp. 346–7.

authority blindly.[83] He reaffirmed his obligations to defend justice but implied that they could only be performed by means objected to by the bishops, which included allowing him authority to summon clerks before the royal courts, even by amercement of their benefices, and the right to imprison even bishops who opposed him.[84] He would uphold justice himself, not assume that it had been done by the ecclesiastical authorities.

The king also had another obligation of which he now reminded the bishops: to ensure the retention of the Crown's liberties. His legislation reflected this: in 1256 he forbade alienation of lands held by tenants-in-chief unless they had royal permission: to do otherwise would be to damage the 'Crown and royal dignity'.[85] This was a duty impressed upon him by the papacy many years earlier, and which he returned to in his letter to the pope complaining of Boniface's 1261 statutes.[86] The king's duty was to be generous, but not so generous that he was left without the necessary income to retain his power; and Henry was accused often of over-generosity in the wrong places, no doubt making him sensitive upon the subject. Henry's refusal to allow the Church to impinge upon his chapels, and his determination to maintain his right to cases he declared related to goods and chattels, were informed by this duty. He presented himself, in fact, as a good king: a king under law, who emphasised past custom and royal rights in establishing his position. When he refused to concede that the bishops could claim writs *de excommunicato capiendo* by right, his reason was that there was no law to make him do so, by custom the writ was granted purely by grace and at the king's will. In France Louis IX had also objected to using the secular arm in all cases of excommunication, refusing to intervene in cases about property and stating that he would require proof that the excommunication was just.[87] Both Church and Crown thus claimed not only that they understood the duties of kingship, but also that they had the right in the circumstances of 1261 to define those duties. Henry did so on grounds that he was the king and fulfilling

---

[83] For Louis IX's disputes over temporal and spiritual authority and over the use of ecclesiastical sanctions in cases of temporal property, see G. J. Campbell, 'The Attitude of the Monarchy toward the Use of Ecclesiastical Censures in the Reign of Saint Louis', *Speculum* 35 (1960), 535–54; O. Pontal, 'Le Différend entre Louis IX et les évêques de Beauvais et ses incidences sur les Conciles (1232–1248)', *Bibliothèque de l'école des Chartes* 123 (1965), 5–34.

[84] *C&S*, i, p. 688.

[85] *English Historical Documents*, vol. 3: *1189–1327*, ed. H. Rothwell (Oxford, 1995), p. 360.

[86] *Royal and other Letters Illustrative of the Reign of Henry III*, ed. W. W. Shirley, Rolls Series, 2 vols (London, 1862–8), i, p. 551; T. Rymer, *Foedera, Conventiones, Litterae et cuiuscumque generis Acta Publica*, ed. A. Clark and F. Holbrooke, 4 vols (London, 1816–30), i, p. 234; *C&S*, i, p. 685; *CR 1259–61*, pp. 481–2.

[87] *C&S*, i, p. 689. The *gravamina* of 1253 also complain about the ways in which episcopal requests for these were ignored or not fulfilled (*C&S*, i, pp. 472, 541, 603, 689). Jurisdictional issues could hamper them: John Deyville, in April 1254, simply ran from county to county avoiding the sheriff's authority (*CFR 1253–54*, no. 366), while in Tynedale twenty years of significations went unimplemented through jurisdictional issues (P. Hoskin, 'Church, State and Law: Solutions to Lay Contumacy in the Anglo-Scottish Borders during the Later Thirteenth Century', *HR* 84 (2011), 559–71). For Louis IX, see Campbell, 'The Attitude of the Monarchy', pp. 545–54.

his obligations; the bishops because they were the king's natural advisers, who claimed he had strayed from his legal obligations to the Church. The issue then being fought over in these statutes was not just that of where the line should be drawn between Church and State authority, but of who should draw it and by what right.

The failure of the 1261 statutes – their rejection by the pope – was of vital importance to the structure of the rebellion of the later 1260s. The rejection left Boniface abroad at a crucial time of unrest, unwilling to return to England since his estates were attacked as those of a hostile foreigner. The English Church was thus left without its archbishop. Consequently it was in the hands of Walter de Cantilupe, the elder statesman of the Church and a close friend of Simon de Montfort. He had been bishop of Worcester since 1236 and as such was third in authority in the English Church. The bishop of London, who was dean of the province, was at this point a new and inexperienced bishop. Cantilupe's guidance of the southern province placed the Church largely behind the rebels in 1264.[88] The bishops may have been the more willing to follow this lead after the king had so clearly interfered in their liberties once more, crossing, in their view, that line between secular and ecclesiastical authority, and not acting as a good king ruling for the good of his subjects. Just as importantly, the Church's position concerning secular authority, and its relationship to the maintenance of ecclesiastical liberties, were clearly established by 1261. The Church's involvement with the baronial uprising was never likely to result in the regaining of its liberties; too much of what the Church requested in 1261 would not have been in the interests of secular magnates. Their belief, however, that the king could and should be brought under the law with not only counsel but also firm guidance, particularly legislative guidance, provided an ideological link with the baronial rebellions which enabled episcopal support for Simon de Montfort in the mid-1260s.

The English Church's attempts at legislation in the mid-1260s grew out of both general and specific concerns and must be seen in both a national and an international context. 1261 was a crisis point in the long, usually low-level, struggle between Church and State to claim areas of legislation at the borders of their authority, a dispute not unique to the English context. The particular opposition of 1261, though born out of a period of national concern which also led to secular opposition and legislation, and though influenced by many of the same issues, was, nevertheless, distinct from the process which led to the establishment of the baronial council. Part of the reason for the focus upon areas of difference at this date was the development of the consistory and other ecclesiastical courts as established institutions separate from episcopal and other households and with the need to set down processes and procedures. Yet the legislation also reflects the Church's attitude to secular authority, an attitude gained both from the international debates about the role of the prince in relation to the Church and his

---

[88]   P. Hoskin, 'Cantilupe's Crusade: Walter de Cantilupe, Bishop of Worcester, and the Baronial Rebellion', *Transactions of the Worcestershire Archaeological Society* 23 (2012), 91–102.

subjects. Both king and bishops expressed their positions on secular authority in 1261. The king exercised his authority through past custom and emphasised his duty to prevent infringement of his secular liberties. The bishops also pointed to the past and their recent history to depict Henry as a king failing in his duties and encroaching upon the liberties of the Church. Concern about the role and duties of the king – also an issue for the rebel barons – suggests common ground upon which the two bodies could meet, though in their specific aims they were divided as often as united. The 1261 legislation, although unsuccessful in gaining papal approval, had an enormous impact on the English Church of the next decade. It was the rejection of this legislation, with Henry's repudiation of his oath to the provisions, and Boniface's unfortunate isolation on the Continent, far from his sphere of authority, in the mid-1260s, that enabled the bishops, now led by the Montfortian Walter de Cantilupe, to unite with the barons at Lewes, with the ensuing consequences.

13

Women in English Local Government:
Sheriffs, Castellans and Foresters

Louise J. Wilkinson

When King John visited the cathedral city of Lincoln during the civil war of 1216, a remarkable meeting took place between the king and Lincoln's castellan. The castellan in question was a noblewoman by the name of Lady Nicholaa de la Haye, a twice-widowed heiress who was probably then in her sixties. That meeting made such a mark on the memories of Lincoln's citizens that, when records of a government enquiry which came to be known as the hundred rolls were compiled sixty years later from the testimonies of local jurors, the clerk faithfully preserved the details in writing for posterity. On King John's arrival at Lincoln, Nicholaa had offered him the castle keys and with them her resignation as castellan. As Nicholaa explained, 'she was a woman of great age and had endured many labours and anxieties in the ... castle and was not able to endure such [burdens] any longer.'[1] King John, for his part, had replied 'sweetly' (*dulciter*) to these protestations but instructed Nicholaa to keep the castle.[2]

This exchange between King John and Lady Nicholaa represented more than a simple exchange of social pleasantries. The king, it seems, recognised Nicholaa's talents in holding the most important royal castle in the area for his cause. Further proof of Nicholaa's high esteem in John's eyes came on 18 October 1216, presumably just hours before the king's death, when she was appointed joint sheriff of Lincolnshire, alongside Philip Mark, one of John's most notorious local officials.[3] Although Mark disappeared from the records as sheriff of Lincolnshire a little while after his appointment, Nicholaa retained that office until the end of May 1217, when she ably led the defence of Lincoln Castle against the supporters of the French prince Louis during the battle of Lincoln, one of the decisive battles that helped to draw the civil war to a successful close for those loyal to John's young son and heir, King Henry III.[4]

---

[1] *Rotuli Hundredorum*, 2 vols (London, 1812–18), i, p. 309. I am grateful to Professor David Carpenter, Dr Paul Dryburgh and Dr Adrian Jobson for their helpful comments on an earlier version of this chapter.

[2] *Rotuli Hundredorum*, i, p. 309. See also *Rotuli Hundredorum*, i, p. 315; C. Coulson, *Castles in Medieval Society: Fortresses in England, France, and Ireland in the Central Middle Ages* (Oxford, 2003), pp. 367–8.

[3] *RLP*, p. 199b.

[4] For an account of Nicholaa's career, including her role in the battle of Lincoln, see L. J. Wilkinson, *Women in Thirteenth-Century Lincolnshire* (Woodbridge, 2007), pp. 13–26.

The appointment of a woman to the office of sheriff was highly unusual. As I have argued elsewhere, King John's apparent lack of regard for convention in Nicholaa's case probably resulted from the scale of the rebellion in Lincolnshire and a dearth of suitable male candidates who had remained loyal to the Crown. In such circumstances, Nicholaa's position as a widowed local landholder who enjoyed an earlier association with the shrievalty through her second husband, Gerard de Camville, and a strong personal history of loyal service to John, made her a viable appointee.[5] It was not, however, entirely unknown in the thirteenth century for an heiress to transmit her father's claim to hold a royal castle or shrievalty to her husbands and sons. In neighbouring Norfolk, the constables of Norwich Castle often served as sheriffs of the county. On the death of William de Caisneto in 1174, his lands passed through his eldest daughter, Margaret, to her first husband, Hugh de Cressy, who was also awarded custody of Norwich Castle by the king.[6] When Hugh died,[7] Margaret married as her second husband Robert fitz Roger, who received seisin of her estates and subsequently served the Crown as sheriff of Norfolk and Suffolk, like his father-in-law before him, for a total of six years between 1190 and 1200.[8] Although Margaret outlived her second husband, and a royal charter issued on 22 December 1214 placed her in possession of her inheritance, the king retained Norwich Castle in his hand during his pleasure.[9] By the spring of the following year, Norwich Castle was held for the Crown by Margaret's adult son from her second marriage, John fitz Robert, who, also like his father before him, later held the office of sheriff.[10]

If Margaret de Caisneto did not personally serve as a castellan or sheriff in widowhood, there are some isolated examples of other women who were active as sheriffs in the reigns of Henry III and his son. Ela, the widowed countess of Salisbury, secured appointment as sheriff of Wiltshire in the late 1220s and 1230s, like her husband, father and grandfather before her, and attended the

---

[5]   Wilkinson, *Women in Thirteenth-Century Lincolnshire*, pp. 18–20.
[6]   *The Great Roll of the Pipe for the Twentieth Year of the Reign of King Henry the Second*, PRS 21 (London, 1896), pp. 37, 40. For further discussion, see J. H. Round, 'The Early Sheriffs of Norfolk', *EHR* 140 (1920), 481–96, at pp. 491–2.
[7]   Hugh still appeared in possession of lands in Blythburgh, Suffolk, in the first pipe roll of Richard's reign: *The Great Roll of the Pipe for the First Year of the Reign of King Richard the First*, ed. J. Hunter (London, 1844), p. 39.
[8]   Robert fitz Roger was in possession of lands formerly held by Hugh de Cressy in Blythburgh, presumably in the right of his new wife, in the pipe roll for Michaelmas 1190: *The Great Roll of the Pipe for the Second Year of the Reign of King Richard the First*, ed. D. M. Stenton, PRS n.s. 1 (London, 1925), p. 91. For Robert fitz Roger as sheriff, see *The Great Rolls of the Pipe for the Third and Fourth Years of the Reign of King Richard the First*, ed. D. M. Stenton, PRS n.s. 2 (London, 1926), pp. 33, 179; Round, 'The Early Sheriffs of Norfolk', pp. 492, 494.
[9]   *Rot. Chart.*, p. 203; *The Great Roll of the Pipe for the Sixteenth Year of the Reign of King John*, ed. P. M. Barnes, PRS n.s. 35 (London, 1962), pp. 168 (for Margaret in possession of Blythburgh), 175 (for Margaret's debt to the Crown of £1,000 for seisin of her inheritance).
[10]   Margaret's son from her first marriage had joined the rebel barons who fought against King John and his heir, and was among those captured fighting against Nicholaa de la Haye and the royalist forces at Lincoln in May 1217: Round, 'The Early Sheriffs of Norfolk', p. 495.

royal Exchequer at Michaelmas 1236 to deliver her accounts.[11] Later in the century Isabella de Clifford held the office of sheriff of Westmorland, alongside Idonea of Leyburn, her sister and fellow co-heiress to a local barony there. In the summer of 1286, according to the record of a case in the King's Bench, Isabella visited Appleby in person and delivered a writ to its borough court ordering it to cease investigating a murder.[12]

The appearance in the records of a small number of female sheriffs hardly indicates a large step forward for women's rights or a sexual revolution in medieval English government. Yet their presence does raise important questions about the opportunities that existed for women to exercise public authority over local communities in the Middle Ages, a subject that still commands relatively little attention in mainstream scholarship today.[13] This is not, of course, to deny that women were legally and socially disadvantaged in thirteenth-century England – they were. Medieval women, as the imperfect heiresses of Eve, were expected to be subordinate to men for most of their lives. Religious ideas about female imperfection were firmly upheld by the common law. When the author of the thirteenth-century legal text traditionally known as *Bracton* discussed the classification of the sexes, he noted how 'Women differ from men in many respects, for their position is inferior to that of men'.[14] Women from all social backgrounds often spent much of their lives as daughters and wives under the legal mastery of their parents, guardians and husbands. It was only in widowhood that a woman might enjoy a measure of freedom from male tutelage, and even that freedom might be lost if she remarried. Yet the occasional appearances of aristocratic widows like Nicholaa, Ela, Isabella and Idonea who served the Crown as its agents should not necessarily surprise us. These women all belonged to families who, as tenants-in-chief, came into direct contact with the king and his advisers, and who, as lords, dominated the English political landscape and cast their own webs of influence over local and national affairs. A survey of the rolls of the Chancery and Exchequer from the reign of Henry III reveals the names of other noblewomen who acted as royal officials in other capacities, most notably as castellans and foresters, in an age when women were usually denied access to public office on the grounds of gender. It is these ladies and the forms of authority they exercised that are the main topics of this chapter.

---

[11] TNA, E 372/81, m. 12d; L. J. Wilkinson, 'Women as Sheriffs in Early Thirteenth-Century England', in *English Government in the Thirteenth Century*, ed. A. Jobson (Woodbridge, 2004), pp. 111–24, at pp. 119–24.

[12] D. C. Jansen, 'Women and Public Authority in the Thirteenth Century', in *Queens, Regents and Potentates*, ed. T. M. Vann, Women of Power 1 (Woodbridge, 1993), pp. 91–105, at pp. 91, 96.

[13] Two notable exceptions are Emma Cavell and Linda E. Mitchell, who have illuminated some of the contributions made by aristocratic women to political life on the Anglo-Welsh Marches, most notably in Cavell's case as widows and lords who petitioned the English Crown in support of their rights and those of their tenants: E. Cavell, 'Aristocratic Widows and the Medieval Welsh Frontier: The Shropshire Evidence', *TRHS* 6th series 17 (2007), 57–82, at pp. 70–1.

[14] *Bracton*, ii, p. 31.

The women who held local office during the reign of King Henry III usually possessed a hereditary or 'quasi-hereditary' right to the position in question. (The term 'quasi-hereditary' is used here to cover offices that tended to pass from one generation to another within a family, but over which the Crown retained the overall right to confirm or veto appointments.) In fact, hereditary or 'quasi-hereditary' offices offered women the most accessible routes into local government in thirteenth-century England. This was often the case with constableships that had been held by the same family over successive generations. A claim to the constableship of Lincoln Castle, for example, was connected to the holders of the barony of Brattleby for most of the twelfth century. Lady Nicholaa de la Haye, the eldest daughter and co-heiress of Richard de la Haye (d. 1169), successfully transmitted this claim to her second husband, Gerard de Camville (d. 1215), and retained the castle for most of her widowhood.[15] On her death in 1230 Lady Nicholaa's office passed, via marriage, into the hands of the earls and subsequent countess-heiresses of Lincoln in the thirteenth and fourteenth centuries.[16] It was only in quite exceptional circumstances that a wealthy widow, usually one who controlled substantial estates in the same locality, was awarded the custody of a royal castle not closely associated with her natal or marital kin.[17] After the Barons' Wars of the 1260s Isabella d'Aubigny, countess of Arundel, served for a short period at the king's pleasure as constable of the royal castle of Portchester in Hampshire. She was expected to answer for the issues of the castle at the Exchequer and presided over a series of repairs to the buildings there, before surrendering this castle in the winter of 1270 to a new castellan, William Belet.[18] In a similar way Amice, countess of Devon, was appointed as constable of Hadleigh Castle in Essex between February/March 1269 and August 1270. As castellan Amice received orders to repair the mills, granges and other buildings pertaining to that fortress. In this case, however, it is not entirely clear whether Countess Amice effectively discharged the duties attached to her new office. In July 1270, just a month before the king decided to transfer the castle, together with all 'the weapons, victuals' and other things there, to a new custodian, the sheriff of Essex was ordered urgently to repair the mills and buildings at Hadleigh 'without fail'.[19] Perhaps Amice had neglected her obligations.

---

[15] See Wilkinson, *Women in Thirteenth-Century Lincolnshire*, pp. 14–24.

[16] *CChR*, iv, p. 213. For a brief summary of the history of the constableship of Lincoln Castle in this period, see F. W. Hill, *Medieval Lincoln*, new edn (Stamford, 1990), pp. 87–91, 262. See also Coulson, *Castles in Medieval Society*, pp. 367–71.

[17] For example, in 1280 the Crown awarded custody of Oswestry Castle to the widowed Isabella de Mortimer; the castle had formerly been held by her husband. See Cavell, 'Aristocratic Women', pp. 72–3.

[18] Isabel held the castle at the king's pleasure from 1267 to 1270, and received a grant of 16 marks per annum for the duration of her keepership from the issues: *CLR 1260–67*, p. 290; *CLR 1267–72*, no. 1922; *CPR 1266–72*, pp. 204, 496; *CFR 1270–71*, nos 57–8; L. L. Gee, *Women, Art and Patronage from Henry III to Edward III, 1216–1377* (Woodbridge, 2002), p. 15; Cavell, 'Aristocratic Widows', p. 74. Isabel held extensive estates in dower in the neighbouring county of Sussex and elsewhere: *CR 1242–47*, pp. 112, 116–17.

[19] *CFR 1268–69*, nos 163, 201–2; *CFR 1269–70*, nos 1155–6; *CLR 1267–72*, nos 691, 1580.

The responsibilities that some widows assumed as castellans grew directly out of their roles within marriage.[20] Noble wives often made a significant contribution to the governance of their families' lands, and sometimes assumed wide-ranging responsibilities in their husbands' absences.[21] Ladies of the greater and lesser aristocracy routinely assisted their husbands in the management of substantial households, and in widowhood they also often took direct personal control of their own domestic establishments and estates, answering directly to the Crown for military and other services owing from their lands.[22] The castle was still very much an aristocratic residence, a centre of lordship and a symbol of baronial authority in the reign of Henry III.[23] In spite of the increasingly palatial features and concessions to comfort that castle architecture was beginning to display, these structures still possessed important military and administrative functions in the twelfth and thirteenth centuries. Castles might offer a place of safekeeping for a noble family's treasure and plate. Their halls often provided meeting places for honorial or other local courts. They might also house armouries and prisons.[24] The fabric of each private castle held by an aristocratic family required constant upkeep and maintenance, as well as the presence of a garrison or basic staff, in ways not dissimilar to royal castles, who might be deployed locally to keep the peace or protect their lord, his *familia* and the local community during times of political unrest.[25]

As the wives of male castellans, some women were called upon to assist their husbands in their official duties in extension to their domestic responsibilities. For example, it might in an emergency be necessary for a lady to play an active

[20] See also C. Coulson's discussion of 'female castellans' and 'ladies of fortresses', which includes some interesting thirteenth-, fourteenth- and early fifteenth-century examples, in his *Castles in Medieval Society*, pp. 297–338 (esp. pp. 297–9, 305–7) and 366–82.
[21] For the role of noblewomen in estate administration, see, for example, R. E. Archer, '"How ladies ... who live on their manors ought to manage their households and estates": Women as Landholders and Administrators in the Later Middle Ages', in *Woman is a Worthy Wight: Women in English Society, c. 1200–1500*, ed. P. J. P. Goldberg (Stroud, 1992), pp. 149–81; J. C. Ward, *English Noblewomen in the Later Middle Ages* (London, 1992), ch. 6. For a model letter from an aristocratic wife to an absentee husband in a thirteenth-century formulary, whereby the wife promises to repeat her husband's wishes 'as orders', see *Lost Letters of Medieval Life: English Society, 1200–1250*, ed. M. Carlin and D. Crouch (Philadelphia, 2013), no. 76.
[22] See, for example, L. J. Wilkinson, 'The "Rules" of Robert Grosseteste Reconsidered: The Lady as Estate and Household Administrator in Thirteenth-Century England', in *The Medieval Household in Christian Europe, c. 850–c. 1550: Managing Power, Wealth and the Body*, ed. C. Beattie *et al.* (Turnhout, 2003), pp. 293–306.
[23] See, for example, M. W. Labarge, *Mistress, Maids and Men: Baronial Life in the Thirteenth Century* (London, 1965, rept. 2003), ch. 1; C. M. Woolgar, *The Great Household in Late Medieval England* (New Haven, 1999).
[24] R. A. Brown, *English Medieval Castles* (London, 1954), pp. 187–9. See also N. Denholm-Young, *Seignorial Administration in England* (Oxford, 1957), p. 92.
[25] See R. Liddiard, *Castles in Context: Power, Symbolism and Landscape, 1066 to 1500* (Macclesfield, 2005), ch. 4.

role in warfare.[26] There was a long history in both England and Normandy of aristocratic wives who supported their husbands' military activities.[27] After the forces of Ralph Guader, the rebel earl of East Anglia, were defeated at his manor of Fawdon in 1075, it was his wife, Emma, who held Norwich Castle for three months against three hundred royalist soldiers, assisted by slingers and engineers, before she finally joined her husband in Brittany.[28] The complicity of the countesses of Chester and Lincoln in a scheme involving their husbands, to capture Lincoln Castle during the civil war of Stephen's reign, is well known. The women secured admission to Lincoln by visiting the wife of the knight who had charge of that stronghold.[29] In Henry II's reign William of Newburgh praised Countess Petronilla of Leicester, who was captured with her husband at the battle of Fornham in 1173, for her manly qualities ('virilis animi femina').[30] Under Richard I it was Richeut, the sister of the royal chancellor William Longchamp and the wife of the castellan Matthew de Clere, who had charge of Dover Castle in 1191 and whose men attempted, on her orders, to apprehend Geoffrey, the newly ordained archbishop of York, when he landed in Kent.[31] This was also the year during which Lady Nicholaa de la Haye defended Lincoln Castle from Longchamp's forces during a forty-day siege, while Gerard de Camville was away in the service of John, count of Mortain.[32]

Aristocratic wives again came to prominence as acting castellans during the political troubles of Henry III's reign. In the summer of 1265, as the royalists made significant gains against her husband's forces in the Welsh Marches, Eleanor, the wife of Simon de Montfort, took up residence in Dover Castle. In the months immediately before and after her husband's death at the battle of

---

[26] The involvement of women in sieges was a long-running motif in historical writing. See, for example, P. Stafford, *Queens, Concubines and Dowagers: The King's Wife in the Early Middle Ages* (Athens, GA, 1983), pp. 117–20.

[27] M. Chibnall, 'Women in Orderic Vitalis', *Haskins Society Journal* 2 (1990), 105–21, at pp. 114–15. For further discussion, see J. A. Truax, 'Anglo-Norman Women at War: Valiant Soldiers, Prudent Strategists or Charismatic Leaders', in *The Circle of War in the Middle Ages*, ed. D. J. Kagay and L. J. A. Villalon (Woodbridge, 1999), pp. 111–26.

[28] *The Letters of Lanfranc, Archbishop of Canterbury*, ed. H. Clover and M. Gibson (Oxford, 1979), no. 35; L. Marten, 'The Rebellion of 1075 and its Impact on East Anglia', in *Medieval East Anglia*, ed. C. Harper-Bill (Woodbridge, 2005), pp. 168–82, at p. 168; A. Williams, *The English and the Norman Conquest* (Woodbridge, 1995), p. 63.

[29] *Historia Ecclesiastica: The Ecclesiastical History of Orderic Vitalis*, ed. M. Chibnall, 6 vols (Oxford, 1969–80), vi, pp. 538–41. For discussion, see S. M. Johns, *Noblewomen, Aristocracy and Power in the Twelfth-Century Anglo-Norman Realm* (Manchester, 2003), p. 18.

[30] *Chronicles of the Reigns of Stephen, Henry II and Richard I, vol. 1: Containing the First Four Books of the Historia Rerum Anglicanum of William of Newburgh*, ed. R. Howlett, Rolls Series (London, 1884), p. 179. See also J. Ward, *Women in Medieval England* (London, 2006), p. 112.

[31] *Giraldi Cambrensis Opera*, ed. J. S. Brewer, J. F. Dimock and G. F. Warner, Rolls Series, 7 vols (London, 1861–77), iv, pp. 388–90. See also *Radulfi de Diceto Decani Lundoniensis Opera Historica*, ed. W. Stubbs, Rolls Series, 2 vols (London, 1876), ii, pp. 96–7; *Wendover*, i, p. 193.

[32] Wilkinson, *Women in Thirteenth-Century Lincolnshire*, p. 18.

Evesham, Eleanor played a key role in coordinating the Montfortian war effort in the South East, paying for soldiers, facilitating communications between her sons, entertaining key supporters and overseeing Dover's defence.[33] According to the chronicler Thomas Wykes, it was the wife of Hugh Despenser, another important Montfortian, who held the Tower of London for the rebels in the summer of 1265, until news reached her of Hugh's death, whereupon she surrendered the Tower to the royalists.[34] The roles that these two women took upon themselves as their husbands' representatives in 1265 were of an extremely high profile, but they were mirrored by those adopted by other high-ranking wives once peace returned to England. In May 1267 William de Valence, the constable of Winchester Castle, dispatched a letter to his wife Joan, whom he addressed as 'his dear companion and friend', informing her that he was sending Sir Robert de Immer to defend Winchester and be under Joan's command. William's strong confidence in his wife's capabilities was clearly reflected at the end of this letter, when he explicitly gave her 'power' over Sir Robert and his associates and instructed her to 'ordain and arrange' all matters according to her best judgment.[35]

The fortunes of female foresters, like those of female castellans, illuminate some of the challenges faced by women who exercised – or who possessed a claim to exercise – local office directly. The archaic nature of forest administration in thirteenth-century England, an administration that continued to allow for the existence of hereditary keepers (or wardens) of areas of royal forest, and foresters in fee (hereditary foresters subordinate to keepers), provided some women with additional opportunities to wield political power as agents of the Crown.[36] It was here that a small number of ladies were able to find a niche by serving as conduits within baronial and knightly families for the transfer of forest offices from one generation to another, and by acting as custodians for their sons. They also, on occasion, served directly as keepers and foresters in fee in their own right, responding personally to royal writs, answering for revenues at the Exchequer and managing what were sometimes substantial tracts of territory in the king's name.

In the thirteenth century the keeping of forests and foresterships in fee passed down through the female line relatively frequently, in accordance with the passage of lands governed by inheritance customs that favoured patrilineal primogeniture. As in the case of certain shrievalties and constableships, there are examples of mothers who transmitted their claims to hold office within the royal

---

[33] For Eleanor's role in 1265, see L. J. Wilkinson, *Eleanor de Montfort* (London, 2012), ch. 8. See also L. Kjær, 'Food, Drink and Ritualised Communication in the Household of Eleanor de Montfort, February to August 1265', *JMH* 37:1 (2011), 75–89.

[34] 'Chronicon Vulgo Dictum Chronicon Thomæ Wykes', in *Annales Monastici*, iv, pp. 175–6; M. W. Labarge, *Simon de Montfort* (London, 1962), p. 260.

[35] *Royal and Other Historical Letters Illustrative of the Reign of Henry III*, ed. W. W. Shirley, Rolls Series, 2 vols (London, 1862–6), i, p. 311 no. dclvii; *Lost Letters of Medieval Life*, p. 238; L. E. Mitchell, 'Joan de Valence', in *Writing Medieval Women's Lives*, ed. C. N. Goldy and A. Livingstone (New York, 2012), p. 197.

[36] On keepers or wardens, and foresters in fee, see *Select Pleas*, pp. xvi–xix, xxiii–xxiv.

forest to their sons. On 13 June 1234, for example, the constable of Windsor Castle was ordered to ensure that Lawrence son of Matilda, who had recently paid the king a relief of 40 shillings, should be placed in seisin of Bagshot bailiwick in Windsor Forest. This bailiwick, so the entry on the fine roll recorded, had passed down to him 'by hereditary right' from his mother, Matilda.[37] In other records, Lawrence was styled Lawrence Kokerel.[38] Lawrence's decision, or the decision of the clerk who drew up the entry on the fine roll, to identify him as 'son of Matilda', presumably reflected the importance of his matrilineal connections as the basis for his title to this property. In a similar fashion, the lands, tenements and office of the Shropshire landholder Isabella of Bourton, who died before 28 April 1249, passed on her death into the hands of her son Ralph, who was then over the age of 40. An inquisition post mortem found that Isabella had held three and a half virgates of land in Pulley as a tenant-in-chief of the Crown in return for the service of keeping the forest of 'La Lye', presumably the hay of Lythwood within Long Forest.[39] Two entries on the fine roll, both dated 14 May 1249, record Ralph's smooth succession to his dead mother's properties in Shropshire and the king's order to Geoffrey fitz Warin, the steward of the forest, to place Ralph in 'full seisin of the bailiwick of forester of which the aforesaid Isabella was seised as of fee on the day she died'.[40]

There are also cases of foresterships that descended from fathers to daughters. In April 1257, for example, the husband of the eldest daughter and heiress of Hugh of Kilpeck promised to pay the king three marks of gold for the bailiwick of the Hay of Hereford and the wood of 'Coyttemor' in the right of his wife.[41] It was not unknown for multiple co-heiresses to inherit when there was more than one daughter in the same generation. On 6 July 1221 the sheriff of Northumberland was instructed to award Alice, Margaret, Juliana, Isabella and Constantina, the five sisters and co-heiresses of Philip of Oldcotes, seisin of their brother's lands in Northumberland, together with the king's coronership and forestership in the same county. Philip was a northern knight who had served as a trusted royal agent under John, and who had also held the office of sheriff of Northumberland between 1212 and 1220.[42] At the time of Philip's

---

[37]   *CFR 1233–34*, no. 224.
[38]   *CR 1234–37*, pp. 394, 507; C. A. F. Meekings, 'A Roll of Judicial Writs', *BIHR* 32 (1959), 209–21, at p. 215.
[39]   Isabella also held half a carucate of land as a tenant of the abbot of Shrewsbury in Bourton, Shropshire, and received income there from rents and a yearly tallage of villeins: *Calendar of Inquisitions Post Mortem*, vol. 1: *Henry III* (London: 1904), no. 136. For Lythwood, see M. L. Bazeley, 'The Extent of the English Forest in the Thirteenth Century', *TRHS* 4 (1921), 140–72, at p. 143.
[40]   *CFR 1248–49*, nos 215–16. In later records Ralph was referred to as 'Ralph the Marescal', the name that he shared with his father: *CFR 1262–63*, no. 760. For Ralph's father, see R. W. Eyton, *Antiquities of Shropshire*, 12 vols (London, 1854–60), vi, p. 178.
[41]   *CFR 1256–57*, no. 531. For the Hay of Hereford, see Bazeley, 'The Extent of the English Forest', p. 143.
[42]   *CFR 1220–21*, nos 226, 227. See also P. A. Brand, 'Oldcotes v. d'Arcy', in *Medieval Legal Records Edited in Memory of C. A. F. Meekings*, ed. R. F. Hunnisett and J. B. Post

death all his sisters, with the exception of Alice, were married. It therefore seems likely that their husbands, or perhaps one of their husbands, initially assumed the offices attached to the sisters' inheritance. In July 1221 the sisters and their husbands attorned Constantina and her spouse, Daniel fitz Nicholas, constable of Newcastle upon Tyne,[43] to represent all five co-heiresses in their dealings with the Crown. It was Daniel and Constantina who, upon agreeing to render the 80 mark fine demanded by the king, received a formal grant of Philip's properties and offices on the sisters' behalf.[44] It is, however, interesting to note that in a later case involving the four daughters and co-heiresses of Richard de Kingesl', who all stood to inherit a share of the forestership (*forestaria*) of Delamere Forest in 1245, the king approved a system of rotation, whereby each daughter, beginning with the eldest, took it in turns to receive the annual income from the office and to divide that income between her sisters.[45]

Not all co-heiresses were successful in asserting their claims to foresterships; the rights of younger sisters might sometimes be overlooked in favour of the elder, especially when it suited Crown interests and/or the rights of a powerful brother-in-law to manipulate inheritance customs to their own advantage. On 10 May 1204 King John granted Richard de Lucy, lord of Egremont, Ada his wife, and the heirs of Ada's body the forestership of Cumberland, on the same terms that it had been held by Ada's father, Hugh de Morville; it was, however, clearly stipulated that the forestership was not to be divided and shared with Joan, Ada's sister, and her heirs.[46] After Richard's death Ada remarried and took as her new husband Thomas of Moulton, another northern landholder,[47] who had agreed to pay 1,000 marks to the Crown in late July 1213 for the custody of Richard's daughters and their lands.[48] Upon her remarriage Ada successfully transmitted the forestership of Cumberland to her second husband.[49]

The benefits and advantages that might accrue to a husband who married the heiress of an office-holder are demonstrated by yet another case documented on the fine rolls. It was through marriage to Isabella, the sister and heiress of Thomas

---

(London, 1978), pp. 64–113, at p. 64; J. C. Holt, *The Northerners* (Oxford, 1961, rept. 1992), pp. 244–6.

[43] *RLC*, i, p. 459b; Brand, 'Oldcotes', p. 65.

[44] *CFR 1220–21*, no. 226; *CPR 1216–25*, p. 296.

[45] *CR 1242–47*, p. 336; C. R. Young, *The Royal Forests of Medieval England* (Leicester, 1979), p. 84.

[46] *Rot. Chart.*, p. 132.

[47] Ada married Thomas without royal licence. For a fine roll entry in which Ada appears as Thomas's wife, concerning her outstanding debt to the Crown for her fine to marry in John's reign, see *CFR 1217–18*, no. 221. For Thomas, see C. L. Kingsford, 'Moulton, Sir Thomas of (d. 1240)', rev. R. V. Turner, *ODNB*.

[48] *Rot. de. Ob. et Fin.*, pp. 482–3. On 11 July 1213, a little while after Richard's death, Ada agreed to pay the king £500 so that she might have her inheritance, dower and marriage portion and not be distrained to marry: *Rot. de. Ob. et Fin.*, pp. 474–5.

[49] In February 1227, upon his agreement to pay a fine, Thomas secured a royal confirmation of the earlier charter addressed to his wife and her first husband: *CFR 1226–27*, no. 111; *CChR*, i, p. 18.

of Birkin, that Robert of Everingham secured possession not only of all his dead brother-in-law's estates, but also of the keeping of 'the bailiwick of the king's forest of Sherwood as Thomas had on the day he died'.[50] Robert attended the royal court in November 1230, having agreed to pay a 200 mark fine, so that he might perform homage on his wife's behalf for her inheritance.[51] Although, as David Crook has shown, Isabella's right to the keepership of Sherwood was challenged as part of a wider campaign targeted at hereditary foresters in 1237, Robert and his wife successfully defended and maintained Isabella's rights.[52]

During Robert and Isabella's marriage, it was Robert who fulfilled the formal duties attached to the office of keeper of the forest and who executed the royal mandates that he received in this capacity.[53] It was only after Robert's death in 1246, when Isabella's status was transformed, in the eyes of the law, from that of a wife under her husband's *potestas* to that of a widow, a *femme sole*, that she successfully secured possession of her inheritance, centred upon the Nottinghamshire castle and barony of Laxton. It was also then that the king instructed Robert de Ros, chief justice of the king's forests north of the Trent, to surrender the keepership of Sherwood Forest to Isabella.[54] Thereafter, in widow-hood, Isabella executed the duties associated with this office. Indeed, a striking feature of the royal letters directed to her in this capacity, transcripts of which appear on the close rolls, is that they were addressed to her, rather than to a male deputy. The order to Robert de Ros was issued on 10 July 1246. When, just three days later, the king made two separate gifts of oaks from Sherwood to William de Grey and the prior of Torksey, it was Isabella who was instructed to see that William and the prior received their timber.[55] It was also Isabella who was instructed later that year to ensure that Walter Biset and Richard de Grey received royal gifts of deer from Sherwood.[56]

Intriguingly, the last letter close known to have been addressed to Isabella was an order issued on 17 October 1248, some four years before her death in 1252, which concerned a gift of four bucks and six does to Richard de Grey. By October 1251, if not before, Isabella's son and heir, Adam of Everingham, was in receipt of instructions from the king which were addressed to him as 'forester of Sherwood'.[57] Perhaps Isabella's tenure of office during the early years of her widowhood had, in part, been intended, from her point of view, to serve the dual purposes of safeguarding her inheritance for her son and preparing him for the responsibilities that went with the keeping of Sherwood Forest. It might,

---

[50] *CFR 1230–31*, no. 37.
[51] *CFR 1230–31*, nos 37, 38.
[52] D. Crook, 'Dynastic Conflict in Thirteenth-Century Laxton', in *TCE XI*, pp. 193–214, at p. 208.
[53] See, for example, *CR 1242–47*, pp. 16, 49, 90, 110, 131, 149, 152.
[54] *CR 1242–47*, p. 438.
[55] *CR 1242–47*, pp. 439, 440.
[56] *CR 1242–47*, pp. 452, 487–8.
[57] *CR 1247–51*, pp. 92, 521. For an earlier mandate on the close rolls, dated 8 June 1251, which was addressed to Adam and related to affairs in Sherwood, see: *CR 1247–51*, p. 455.

perhaps, be more appropriate to view her term in office as a temporary custodianship until Adam was able and willing to take over. On Isabella's death in 1252, an inquisition post mortem found that Sir Adam of Everingham, her son and heir, was of full age, and that 'the keeping of the forest of Sherwood pertained by hereditary right to the aforesaid Isabella'.[58]

Whatever the case, it is significant that Isabella was not, in fact, the first woman in her family to serve as a keeper of the forest. A precedent had been set earlier in the thirteenth century by her widowed kinswoman Matilda de Caux, who had secured the keepership of the Nottinghamshire and Derbyshire forests in hereditary right. In Matilda's case, however, there was an eighteen-year struggle to secure recognition as keeper of the forest, first with King John and, later, during the early years of Henry III's minority, with Philip Mark, the local sheriff. As a result, it was only from 1220 until her death in 1224 that Matilda truly held office, and her persistence in pressing home her claims at the royal court finally paid off.[59]

The high value that female keepers of the royal forest and foresters in fee placed upon their office is conveyed by the experiences of another woman, Agnes de Amundeville, and her son Ralph.[60] On 12 July 1238 John Biset, the chief justice of the forests south of the Trent, was ordered to restore to Agnes, who possessed a hereditary claim to a bailiwick in Feckenham Forest, seisin of that bailiwick, provided that she was able to find twelve persons to act as sureties and on the express condition that she would not transmit her bailiwick to any of her sons.[61] A later entry on the fine rolls reveals why the Crown was unusually reluctant to see the bailiwick pass on to the next generation. In March 1239 Agnes agreed to pay the king an annual fine of 1 mark so that she might have seisin of her bailiwick. As the record of the fine enrolled by the Chancery clerk noted, Agnes had asserted her right to the bailiwick after the king had removed Ralph, her son and heir, from office for a trespass involving the king's venison there. In the aftermath of her son's transgression, Agnes now sought to reassert her family's hereditary rights over Feckenham, and, apparently, to safeguard it for her lineage. The king advised John Biset that if Richard, Agnes's younger son, was able to find twelve free and law-worthy men who were willing to 'mainpern for him that he will keep the aforesaid bailiwick well and faithfully for Agnes',

[58] TNA, C 132/13/10(2).
[59] D. Crook, 'Maud de Caux and the Custody of the Forests of Nottinghamshire and Derbyshire', Fine of the Month January 2006, available at http://www.finerollshenry3.org.uk/content/month/fm-01-2006.html (accessed 14 April 2015). The area of forest which Isabella administered was smaller than that which Matilda had looked after. In 1225 and 1227 the forest in Nottinghamshire was restricted to what was known as Sherwood Forest: Crook, 'Dynastic Conflict', p. 208.
[60] For the bailiwicks and foresters in fee of Feckenham Forest in the thirteenth century, see *Records of Feckenham Forest, Worcestershire, c. 1236–1377*, ed. J. Birrell, Worcestershire Historical Society n.s. 21 (Worcester, 2006), map 1, pp. xv–xvi.
[61] *CR 1237–42*, p. 74.

then Richard was to be admitted to office in his mother's stead.[62] Thus, it was set down that Agnes would be a temporary custodian for her younger son. The king's willingness to entertain Richard as an alternative candidate is intriguing and betrays, perhaps, his preference for male, over female, office holders, as well as a mother's reluctance to exercise the duties connected with that office in person. It is, nevertheless, worth noting a later entry on the fine rolls, dated 24 April 1239, whereby Henry informed Biset that if Agnes could find no pledges for the rent that she owed him, the bailiwick would be liable to forfeiture if the rent remained unpaid at the Exchequer at Michaelmas.[63]

The difficulties that Matilda de Caux and Agnes de Amundeville encountered in making good their claims to office, whether they were acting on their own behalf or upon that of a son, were not altogether unusual. Another woman who was successful in securing royal recognition of her hereditary right to a forest keepership was Avice, widow of Michael de Columbars. In 1207 Michael had, for 200 marks, purchased from the Crown the right to Avice's marriage and her inheritance, including the forestership of Chute, formerly held by Avice's father, Elias Croc.[64] Elias came from a long line of men who had accounted to the Crown 'for several small forests in Wiltshire' since at least the reign of Henry I. The Crocs were, perhaps, the descendants of 'Croc the huntsman', a forester who received a charter from William Rufus.[65] Although Michael de Columbars served as keeper during his marriage to Avice, after his death his widow asserted her right to this office.[66] Avice's tenure of Chute was not, however, entirely without controversy. She became embroiled in a jurisdictional dispute with the Esturmy family, hereditary keepers of the neighbouring forest of Savernake, over their common boundary with Chute.[67] Avice resorted to the royal courts to establish her right. The case can be traced within the fine rolls. In November 1238 an entry noted that Avice had given the king three palfreys for a writ *coram rege* against Geoffrey Esturmy in order to ascertain by what warrant he held the bailiwick of Hippenscombe. In September 1239 another

---

[62]   *CFR 1238–39*, no. 127. For Ralph being deprived of his bailiwick, see *CR 1237–42*, p. 26. For Ralph's transgression, see also *CRR*, xvi, no. 149C. For other misdemeanours by him, see *Records of Feckenham Forest*, pp. 11, 14, 16.

[63]   In the meantime, the king restated his earlier order that Agnes should enjoy seisin of the property with the condition that it might be kept by her younger son: *CFR 1238–39*, no. 154 (24 April 1239). Richard was serving as forester in fee when an inquisition was made in 1242/6: *Records of Feckenham Forest*, p. 19.

[64]   *Rot. de Ob. et Fin.*, p. 409. See also 'Parishes: Tidworth, South', in *A History of the County of Hampshire*, vol. 4 (1911), pp. 391–4, available at http://www.british-history.ac.uk/report.aspx?compid=56838&strquery=Ellis Croc (accessed 15 April 2015). See also *The Great Roll of the Pipe for the Fourth Year of the Reign of King Henry III*, PRS n.s. 47 (London, 1987), p. 126, which refers to Michael de Columbars 'who has the daughter and heir' of Elias Croc.

[65]   Young, *The Royal Forests*, p. 15.

[66]   Letters patent of 11 April 1235 noted that Avice had performed homage for her bailiwick: *CPR 1232–47*, p. 100.

[67]   On the Esturmy keepers of Savernake Forest in Henry III's reign, see C. S. C. Brudenell-Bruce, *The Wardens of Savernake Forest* (Plymouth, 1949), chs 4 and 5.

entry recorded that Avice, having endured a dispute with Geoffrey, had been granted special permission to pay 'the 15 m[arks] by which she made fine with … [the Crown] for [having] the bailiwick of Hippenscombe' in four instalments, rather than one.[68] Geoffrey was not, however, the only member of the Esturmy family who caused problems for Avice over Hippenscombe. In 1259 another settlement was reached, this time between Henry Esturmy and Avice, over a moiety of the disputed area of jurisdiction.[69] When Avice finally died a little later that year, she left as her heir her adult son, Matthew, who stood to inherit from his mother a respectable portfolio of rights. According to the findings of her inquisition post mortem, Avice held properties in Hampshire that included a virgate of land pertaining to the forestership of Finkley, together with the bailiwicks of Finkley and Doiley. In the neighbouring county of Wiltshire, she held the manor of Chute as a tenant of the abbot of Hyde, in addition to the forest of Chute, which was held from the king in chief, and a moiety of the forestership of the bailiwick of Hippenscombe towards the south, pertaining to Chute.[70]

The evidence for Avice's time in office yields some valuable information about the daily responsibilities that those women who served as keepers of the royal forest were expected to assume. We have to remember that, as keepers, these women came into direct contact with the Crown. In the words of G. J. Turner, they were 'the executive officers of the king in his forests', to whom 'writs relating to the administration of forest business … were … addressed'.[71] As with Isabella of Everingham, from the moment that Avice assumed control of the forestership, it was Avice, rather than a male deputy or deputies, who became the recipient of frequent royal directives for the execution of specific duties associated with her office. For example, on 26 May 1238 Avice was ordered to receive John le Fol and Philip of Candover, whom the king had sent to course in Chute Forest and take seven harts there. As keeper, Avice was expected to see that the venison taken by the king's huntsmen was salted and carried to the royal castle at Windsor, so that it entered the castle stores there. On 5 December 1238 she was instructed to receive another royal huntsman, William fitz Walkelin, so that he might take another ten hinds from her bailiwick. Once again, she was to see that the venison was salted and dispatched, this time to Winchester, where the king planned to spend Christmas.[72] In addition to providing venison for the royal household's consumption, Avice was also instructed, on occasion, to administer gifts of deer on the king's behalf. On 9 December 1237, for example, she was directed to ensure that the hunters of Simon de Montfort, then a claimant to the

---

[68] *CFR 1238–39*, nos 12, 349. The three palfreys of the writ appear to have become the 15 mark payment. I owe this point to David Carpenter.

[69] *A Calendar of the Feet of Fines Relating to the County of Wiltshire, 1195–1272*, ed. E. A. Fry (Devizes, 1930), p. 53 no. 24. See also Brudenell-Bruce, *Wardens of Savernake Forest*, p. 50.

[70] TNA, C 132/22/12(2, 4).

[71] *Select Pleas*, p. xix.

[72] *CLR 1226–40*, pp. 334, 354.

earldom of Leicester and a trusted counsellor of the king, were permitted to take four hinds that Henry had given him in Chute Forest.[73]

Venison was not the only resource within Chute Forest. Avice's bailiwick was also used to furnish the Crown and recipients of royal favour with wood. When, in August 1238, the constable of the royal castle of Marlborough was overseeing repairs to the king's houses at Ludgershall, it was Avice who was commanded to ensure that the constable enjoyed reasonable estover from Chute by a view of foresters and verderers there.[74] The reference, in this case, to a view by foresters and verderers serves as a useful reminder that, in addition to delivering presents of venison and wood, Avice was expected to supervise the local forest administration, attend its various courts, and ensure that local officials detected and dealt with any persons who committed minor offences within her bailiwick. The work of female foresters, like that of their male counterparts, was carefully regulated by the Crown through a system of regular inspections. Every three years or so, twelve knights known as regarders sought answers to the chapters of the regard, a series of questions designed to ascertain and protect the king's rights, and identify any infringements of those rights within the forest.[75] A list of twelve chapters of the regard from Henry III's reign is preserved on the dorse of the patent roll for 1228–9, covering a range of issues, including:

	(i)	herbage in the king's demesne within the forest

- (i) herbage in the king's demesne within the forest
- (ii) hawks' and falcons' eyries
- (iii) mines and forges
- (iv) harbours for exporting timber
- (v) honey
- (vi) assarts
- (vii and viii) different types of purprestures
- (ix) wastes
- (x) holding views of the king's woods
- (xi) holding views of purprestures, assarts and wastes
- (xii) identifying individuals with bows, arrows, crossbows, braches and greyhounds that might injure the king's deer.[76]

The regard helped to keep the activities of the foresters in check, and its findings were reported to the next forest eyre. The plea roll of a forest eyre records

---

[73] *CR 1237–42*, p. 11. See also *CR 1237–42*, p. 22. As Jean Birrell's research into procuring, preparing and serving venison has shown, this was a highly valued meat that only graced the tables of the Crown and the aristocracy, and that might only be acquired by hunting: J. Birrell, 'Procuring, Preparing and Serving Venison in Late Medieval England', in *Food in Medieval England*, ed. C. M. Woolgar, D. Serjeantson and T. Waldron (Oxford, 2006), pp. 176–88, at p. 176.

[74] *CR 1237–42*, pp. 85–6.

[75] *Select Pleas*, pp. lxxv–lxxvii. On the early history of the forest regard, see E. M. Amt, 'The Forest Regard of 1155', *The Haskins Society Journal* 2 (1990), 189–95.

[76] *Select Pleas*, pp. lxxvi–lxxvii.

a forest regard in Chute Forest, relating to Avice's bailiwick in Doiley, Finkley and Freemantle. In this roll Avice was listed among those who coursed with dogs and greyhounds for hares and foxes.[77] As the Crown's chief agent in her bailiwick, Avice's name was also among those foresters in Wiltshire and Hampshire who, in the summer of 1255, were charged by letters patent with the task of aiding and advising the royal commissioners who had been appointed to sell off part of the forest to help relieve the king's debts.[78]

Women who were hereditary keepers of royal forests often enjoyed certain rights and privileges of their own, which differed from one area of jurisdiction to another. In return for the payment of fixed rents at the Exchequer, keepers were potentially able to exploit various sources of income within their bailiwicks.[79] An impression of the privileges that Isabella of Everingham enjoyed within Sherwood Forest can be ascertained from a later inquisition into those enjoyed by her descendant, Robert of Everingham, during the reign of King Edward I. In addition to 'the right to hunt the hare, the fox, the squirrel and the cat in the forest', Robert also possessed 'the right to the bark and crops of oaks which the lord king had given from his demesne woods by his writ', as well as 'the right to have after-pannage', 'the right to have the lawing of dogs not lawed' (3 shillings every three years 'from every dog not lawed'), and to demand payment for the transportation of millstones through the forest (a sum which the local jurors claimed brought Robert 20 shillings a year). Robert was also exempted from performing the services owed to the Crown for the ten knight's fees that he held from the king in chief 'on account of his custody of the forest and in return for finding his foresters at his own cost'.[80] The duties performed by male and female keepers of the forest were not without their rewards.

In conclusion, the appearance of female sheriffs, castellans and foresters clearly challenges traditional perceptions of the absence of women from the formal machinery of royal government in thirteenth-century England. In practice, hereditary or 'quasi-hereditary' shrievalties, constableships and forestrships offered women a 'way in' to local office in a world where women were not otherwise permitted to serve as royal justices, local jurors or government servants. This was usually as an extension of the responsibilities that they already enjoyed as local lords, managing their own private administrations and estate officials during widowhood and drawing upon earlier experiences and expertise gained in marriage. It was, undoubtedly, the experience of such aristocratic ladies, their knowledge of the localities in which they resided and, one suspects, their ability to command local loyalties that made the king, on occasion, prepared to overlook the supposed weaknesses of their sex and accept them as his agents.

---

[77] TNA, E 32/157, m. 7.
[78] *CPR 1247–58*, pp. 432–4 (Avice is mentioned on p. 434).
[79] Young, *The Royal Forests*, p. 78.
[80] *Select Pleas*, pp. 66–7.

14

The Origins of the Office of Escheator

Scott L. Waugh

English kings from the Conquest onward prized feudal incidents as sources of patronage and revenue, but it was not until Henry III's reign that an office devoted to administrating those rights – the escheatorship – was permanently established. Angevin kings relied on a variety of methods to find, seize, keep and account for the lands and rights to which lordship entitled them. They worked well enough to enable John's ruthless exploitation of those resources, driving the barons to formulate restrictions on the king's feudal authority, which became enshrined in Magna Carta. The Crown, however, did not relinquish its rights, and the turmoil in the wake of Magna Carta and John's death emphasised anew the importance of feudal incidents to the king. Between 1217 and 1250, therefore, the royal government experimented with different administrative configurations to manage its feudal assets. These efforts raised issues regarding the span of authority of different offices, relationships among officials, the role of the eyre, and how best to use the resources that came to the Crown. Through this process the office of escheator gradually came into being, until, by 1250, it had become a regular feature of the king's government in county communities.

The foundation of the escheatorships was one outcome of efforts by the council and Exchequer to address Henry III's chronic financial insecurity. Henry's fiscal problems and the Exchequer's response have been extensively investigated. Chief among the many historians of the period, Carpenter, Mills, Stacey and Vincent have exposed not only the harsh financial realities of these years, but also the political turbulence of Henry's court.[1] Favour and factionalism, along with Henry's political whims, strained the king's resources and made consistent fiscal policy difficult, and at times impossible. They also emphasised the court's insatiable appetite for patronage. Despite these adverse circumstances, the council and Exchequer launched a number of initiatives to bolster Henry's revenues, and these created a remarkable degree of stability in the 1240s. While the contribution that feudal incidents played in this financial recovery has been made clear, much less attention has been paid to the evolving administration of those

---

[1]   D. A. Carpenter, 'The Decline of the Curial Sheriff in England, 1194–1258', *EHR* 91 (1976), 1–32; R. C. Stacey, *Politics, Policy, and Finance under Henry III, 1216–1245* (Oxford, 1987); N. Vincent, *Peter des Roches: An Alien in English Politics, 1205–1238* (Cambridge, 1996); M. H. Mills, 'Experiments in Exchequer Procedure, 1200–1232', *TRHS* 4th series 8 (1925), 151–70; M. H. Mills, 'The Reforms at the Exchequer (1232–1242)', *TRHS* 4th series 10 (1927), 111–33.

rights. Accounts of the beginnings of the escheatorships have been sketchy and incomplete and have not related them to the broader effort at financial reform.[2] That is the goal of this paper.

The great advantage of feudal incidents was that they were a renewable resource. The king could rely on a flow of assets useful for either revenue or patronage, or both. Their availability, however, depended on the family cycle of births, marriages and deaths, and their usefulness depended on knowledge of their availability. Who had died? Did they hold of the king in chief? Did they hold of any other lords? Who was the heir or heirs; how old were they? The resources themselves, moreover, could vary greatly. Where were the lands of the deceased located? How much were they worth? What service did they owe? Had anything been alienated? Who were the tenants? Who was the widow? What was her dower? The uncertainty that the government faced can be illustrated by the fine of 100 marks that Wymund de Raleigh made with the king in January 1218 to have the custody of the lands of Michael Belet along with the custody and marriage of his daughter. As a result, the government ordered the sheriffs of Dorset, Surrey, and Berkshire to deliver to Wymund Michael's lands and custody of his daughter and heiress, 'if she is found within their bailiwicks'.[3] Ecclesiastical vacancies were less problematic since ecclesiastical institutions needed the king's authorisation to select a successor, but they were not routinely assigned to the custody of escheators at this time.[4] The successful exploitation of the king's seigneurial rights required, therefore, several different functions: acquiring information about deaths, births, marriages and vacancies; taking custody of lands and/or wards; supervising wards and widows; and managing and accounting for the property and stock.

Once lands were in hand a further question arose: how best to use the resources? There were four possibilities: they could be retained in royal custody and cultivated for profit, they could be leased, their custody could be sold to someone else, or given away. The last two applied as well to widows and wards. Their actual use depended on various circumstances, such as politics, finances or the length of the custody. While the government had a consistent need for revenue, Henry always needed patronage. These countervailing needs and pressures affected the way in which the Crown managed its feudal assets at any given time, resulting in a variety of schemes before it settled on a stable system of escheators.

---

[2]   H. C. Maxwell Lyte, introduction to *CIPM*, pp. vii–ix; E. R. Stevenson, 'The Escheator', in *The English Government at Work*, vol. 2: *Fiscal Administration*, ed. W. A. Morris and J. R. Strayer (Cambridge, MA, 1947), pp. 113–16.

[3]   *CFR 1217–18*, no. 21 (accessed 5 April 2015). The calendar is available both on the Henry III Fine Rolls Project's website (http://www.finerollshenry3.org.uk), and in the *Calendar of the Fine Rolls of the Reign of Henry III, 1216–1242*, ed. P. Dryburgh and B. Hartland, 3 vols to date (Woodbridge, 2007–9).

[4]   M. Howell, *Regalian Right in Medieval England* (London, 1962), pp. 60–109. Howell does not specifically detail administrative arrangements under Henry III, but her observations apply to his reign.

Escheats and Custodies, 1216–c. 1230

Henry III inherited a robust set of rights as a landlord, along with different mechanisms for managing them. The prime instrument for surveying the king's feudal rights was the eyre. The Assize of Northampton in 1176 laid out a series of articles into which the justices were to inquire, including heirs, escheats, lands and widows.[5] The extent of the information that could be uncovered through such an inquiry is visible in the *Rotuli de dominabus et pueris et puellis* dating from 1184–5. The justices inquired into widows and wards, whether they were married or in custody, their lands, whether *maritagium*, dower, or inheritance, and the stock on the property – an issue that would recur in subsequent investigations.[6] In 1194 Richard I launched another eyre, in the aftermath of John's rebellion, with an expanded number of articles.[7] They included an investigation of escheats, whether they were in the king's hands or alienated; if alienated, how, to whom; and how much they were worth. In addition, they asked about wardships that pertained to the king, the marriages of wards and widows, as well as lands, wards and escheats that had pertained to John. Like the inquest of 1185, the 1194 eyre focused on the economic state of the lands and how well they were stocked. The eyre gave the Crown a means of tracking lands and families under its lordship as well as an assessment of the economic value of its rights, though it recorded only the situation at one point in time.

The Crown also had to realise the potential value of the feudal incidents. During the year before the 1194 eyre, in an effort to capitalise on the sweeping number of forfeitures resulting from John's rebellion and an unusual number of deaths of tenants-in-chief, the government turned its escheats and custodies over to two custodians: William de Sainte-Mère-Église, south of the Trent; and Hugh Bardolf, north of the Trent.[8] As custodians they were expected to cultivate the lands and account for the issues and expenses, rather than simply paying a fixed lease. They did not have exclusive control of escheats and wardships, and sheriffs and special keepers were responsible for some of the lands in royal control. That kind of mixed responsibility was what Richard fitz Nigel had referred to in the *Dialogue of the Exchequer* when he described how the government handled escheats and wardships.[9]

John did not replicate Richard's national system of escheatorships, and instead relied on sheriffs, county escheators and special custodians to administer the lands in his custody. Between 1212 and 1215, for example, sheriffs were routinely ordered either to take custody of lands or to deliver lands to heirs, widows or grantees.[10] John, however, also appointed custodians of escheats or

---

[5] *Select Charters*, pp. 179–80, nos 4, 9. For background on the articles, see *RGE*, pp. 34–5.
[6] *Rotuli de Dominabus et Pueris et Puellis*, ed. J. H. Round, PRS 35 (London, 1913), pp. xvii–xlvii.
[7] *Select Charters*, pp. 179–80, nos 4, 9. For background on the articles, see *RGE*, pp. 34–5.
[8] *Rotuli de Dominabus*, pp. xvii–xlvii.
[9] *Dialogus*, pp. 140–5, 186–7.
[10] *RLC*, i, pp. 127, 127b, 128, 128b, 132b, 135–7, 139b, 145, 147b, 149, 151, 155, 161b, 166b, 173–4, 176b, 178, 181–2, 182b, 185b, 187–9, 190b, 192b, 194b, 196; *RLP*, p. 38.

escheators in individual counties across England, who dealt with all kinds of business relating to deceased tenants-in-chief, wards, widows, and outlaws.[11] At the same time, John gave responsibility for particular estates to individual keepers, who were supposed to account for the lands at the Exchequer.[12] In the early years of John's reign a wide range of individuals acted as custodians, including those responsible for vacant ecclesiastical holdings.[13] The system, if it can be called that, was effective enough to allow income from John's feudal sources to reach 19–20% of his annual revenue. Indeed, the increase was conspicuous and was attacked by the barons before the issue of Magna Carta. As a result, receipts from these sources did not reach comparable levels until the 1240s.[14] In surveying his feudal resources, John undertook one major inquest besides the eyre of 1208–9.[15] In 1212 he ordered sheriffs to inquire into all those who held in chief of the king, whether by military or serjeanty tenure, and into all tenements that had that been alienated, whether through marriage, gifts to the Church, or other grants.[16] Though narrower in scope than an eyre, the inquest produced a mass of information about tenants, holdings, families and alienations. In sum, John's government called on sheriffs, county escheators, special keepers and justices to enforce and manage his feudal authority. Some of the lands that came under its control were leased, some cultivated for profit, some sold, some given away; that pattern that was repeated with variations over the next thirty years.

In the immediate aftermath of the civil war ignited by John's predatory lordship, the government acted to make sure that it had access to escheats, wardships and marriages, as well as other incidents of royal lordship. Magna Carta may have placed significant limits on the Crown's prerogative, especially with respect to reliefs, but it said nothing about how the Crown could use lands that came into its custody, or what the king might charge for the custody of lands during a minority, or for the marriage of heirs or widows.[17] Indeed, the senior advisers of Henry III felt no compunction in collecting fines that John had levied, and immediately began granting and selling wardships and marriages. The fine rolls bristle with proffers, though it was several years before the king began extracting especially large fines. Similarly, in the short run, it had to rely on the methods that had been deployed by John and his predecessors to manage its assets.

The first step was to discover what was available, so the government launched

---

[11]   *Pipe Roll 14 John*, PRS 68 n.s. 30 (London, 1955), pp. 58, 68–9, 120; *RLC*, i, pp. 126, 126b, 127b, 128, 133, 137, 146b, 157b, 160, 161b, 183–4, 197, 219b, 597b.

[12]   *RLP*, pp. 45, 62: commissions to William de Cantilupe, 'dilecto nostro senescallo', to take custody of the land and honours of Hugh de Ferrers and account at the Exchequer in 1204, and to Hubert de Burgh in 1206 for the lands of Robert de Beauchamp in Dorset and Somerset.

[13]   *RLP*, pp. 37–8, 43–4, 50, 57, 63, 65, 67, 68–9, 73, 74–6, 78–80.

[14]   N. Barratt, 'The Revenue of King John', *EHR* 111 (1996), 835–55, at p. 847 (Table 5.1), and pp. 849–50; Stacey, *Politics*, p. 206, Table 6.1.

[15]   *RGE*, pp. 68–71.

[16]   *BF*, i, pp. 52–228.

[17]   Stacey, *Politics*, pp. 217–18.

a series of inquests to determine and, it was hoped, recover whatever had been granted, taken away or withheld from the Crown, as well as to prevent any further erosion of its assets. As David Carpenter has shown, from the outset of the minority and extending through Henry's personal rule, those around the king were punctilious in guarding and framing the king's rights with respect to his demesne and lordship.[18] Concerned about the loss of resources, the government set out to assert the Crown's rights over particular kinds of property, such as the lands of the Normans, and to recover royal lands and rights that had been alienated by John or usurped during the civil war, including wardships and marriages. Early inquests and management schemes therefore linked the royal demesne and escheats, a term that encompassed various feudal incidents. This concern over the alienation of lands and rights profoundly influenced the development of the escheatorships.

The investigations began in the autumn of 1217. On 29 September the government asked sheriffs to inquire into the royal demesne in their counties, to take whatever land they discovered into the king's hands, and inform William Marshal what lands they had taken and who held them. Some of the lands thus identified were resumed into the king's hands, though restored shortly afterwards, a pattern that would be followed in subsequent inquests.[19] In November, Nicholas de Lymsey, Amfred de Dene, and James de Skidmore were assigned to levy tallage on the king's demesnes in Kent, Sussex, Surrey and Hampshire, though they were also expected to conduct inquests into escheats and any lands that had been entered without licence, and take them into custody.[20] Sheriffs were instructed to assist the inquisitors in identifying escheated lands, how much they were worth, why they had escheated, and when. In the following year, the Crown launched the first eyre of the reign, an important step in reasserting royal authority.[21] The *veredicta* detailed information concerning the lands of the Normans, lands held by serjeanty tenure, alienated lands, purprestures, advowsons, wards, and widows.[22] Specialised inquests were also ordered in 1218–19, including one by John of Monmouth and Ralph Musard into purprestures made in the time of John and afterwards, as well as the stocking of demesne manors in Herefordshire.[23]

The pope's letter to the legate Pandulf in 1219 calling for the resumption of alienated lands and assets reasserted this strategy of restoring royal authority through the recovery of royal rights and property. At Henry III's second

---

[18] D. A. Carpenter, *The Minority of Henry III* (London, 1990), pp. 118, 142–5, 164–5, 186–91, 234–8, 281–9, 325–8.

[19] *RLC*, i, p. 336b; D. Crook, introduction to *Pipe Roll 5 Henry III*, PRS 86 n.s. 48 (1990), pp. xxxiii–xxxiv, lvii–lvix.

[20] *PR 1216–25*, p. 1.

[21] Carpenter, *Minority*, pp. 96–101.

[22] *RGE*, pp. 71–8; Crook, introduction to *Pipe Roll 5 Henry III*, p. xxxiv; Stacey, *Politics*, pp. 9–10; Carpenter, *Minority*, pp. 96–100; *BF*, i, pp. 244–88; *PR 1216–25*, pp. 206–8.

[23] *RLC*, i, p. 386b. For an inquest into knight's fees on the honour of Brittany in 1218, see *RLC*, i, pp. 360–1, 379, 385, 386b; *PR 1216–25*, p. 174; *CFR 1218–19*, no. 14.

coronation, on 17 May 1220, not only did the king swear to preserve the royal patrimony, but the barons present also swore to relinquish custody of royal castles and wards and to account faithfully at the Exchequer for their farms. A great council later that year, in August, set in motion another inquest into the royal demesne, escheats and the lands of Normans, but it does not appear to have resulted in any seizures.[24] These inquests served as a prelude to the measure taken in September 1221, in which the government ordered the sheriff and two knights in each county to take into the king's hands all demesnes that John held at the beginning of the civil war, all escheats, whether from Normans or other aliens, and any other escheats that had come into royal possession in the time of John or subsequently.[25] The order was the first attempt at a nationwide system for seizing and keeping demesnes and escheats, and as such formed a precedent for managing such lands as well as wardships. In this case, the sheriffs and custodians followed the instructions and, in the months after the initial mandate, the Crown issued numerous orders to sheriffs to restore lands that they had seized.[26] It is not clear whether any lands were retained in custody, or what role the knights played in the process. Overall, the policy of resumption in 1221 fell short and had to be abandoned, largely because the government failed to secure the support of the politically powerful, who were directly affected by its provisions.[27] The government tried again the following year, this time more successfully, having involved barons and gentry in formulating the policy.[28] Through its effort to resume into its hands alienated assets, the Crown linked demesne lands, escheats and custodies, but did not establish a distinct apparatus for identifying and managing those assets, so the measures did not lead to any changes in the management of demesnes or escheats.

Additional inquests were conducted throughout the 1220s, including an eyre in 1226–9.[29] Since the government was particularly interested in alienated lands or rights, it specifically raised the issue in the course of the eyre.[30] It took a

---

[24] *RLC*, i, p. 437, 9 August 1220; Crook, introduction to *Pipe Roll 5 Henry III*, pp. xxxiv–xxxv; Carpenter, *Minority*, pp. 142, 187–91, 203–7, 210–11.

[25] *CFR 1220–21*, nos 346–52; Carpenter, *Minority*, pp. 268–70; Crook, introduction to *Pipe Roll 5 Henry III*, p. xxxv.

[26] *CFR 1221–22*, nos 28, 41, 239, 281; *RLC*, i, pp. 478b–479b, 480b–481, 482b, 483b, 484b–487, 488, 490–1, 492b, 498b–499, 505–6, 513b, 514, 593, 595, 598, 613, 638b.

[27] Carpenter, *Minority*, pp. 268–70, 279–89.

[28] *CFR 1221–22*, nos 213, 219. The seizures included the manor of Benson in Oxfordshire, which had been granted to Engelard de Cigogné in 1218 and which Hubert had asked to be surveyed on 27 April 1221, perhaps testing the waters for the resumptions that would follow: *CFR 1218–19*, no. 52; *RLC*, i, p. 476.

[29] TNA, E 159/9, m. 14 (inquest into alienations in the honour of Lancaster); *RLC*, i, p. 569 (1223 sheriffs' inquest into royal customs and liberties); *RLC*, ii, pp. 69b (1224 sheriffs' inquest into lands of Normans and Bretons), 151–2 (1226 eyre), 153, 205–6, 213; *PR 1216–25*, pp. 83, 87, 142 (eyre); *BF*, i, pp. 353–92; *RGE*, pp. 78–86.

[30] During the eyre in Devon, Thomas of Moulton, Robert of Lexington and the other justices were instructed to inquire into lands, liberties and rights (*jura*) subtracted and alienated from the estate of the earl of Devon after it came into royal custody. They were to enquire who was responsible for the alienation, who now held the assets, and by what warrant they did so.

further step in 1228 when it set up an inquiry into lands that had been alienated to the Church without licence and ordered sheriffs to proclaim throughout their counties that no one holding in chief could alienate any portion of their estate to any religious house or person.[31] Impelled by necessity as well as by the papacy and legates, the minority government thus used a string of inquests, on the one hand to recover lands and rights that had been usurped or concealed during the confusion of civil war, and, on the other, to assert its prerogative with respect to those lands and rights, even if it could not always get its hands on the lands themselves.

While this information was important, the government also needed to administer the lands or rights that came under its control. At first Henry's government continued John's practice of having county keepers of escheats, though only a few were appointed and little is known about what they actually did. On 17 May 1217, for example, Simon Trussebut was named keeper of the king's escheats in Lincolnshire, and Richard Clerk and Walter de Verdon were added to the commission shortly afterwards.[32] The following year Ralph de Williton and Walter of Winchcombe, clerk, were similarly appointed in Gloucestershire.[33] It was made clear in both cases that the officials were custodians of the lands and were expected to account for the proceeds. In Lincolnshire the sheriff was directed to deliver lands to Trussebut, and in turn the government ordered Trussebut to provide lands to various grantees, sometimes out of the lands of the king's enemies.[34]

These are the only escheators to have been identified in these years, and references to their work disappear after 1218. For the next three decades sheriffs took the lead in administering the property that fell to the king through his rights as a feudal lord, whether escheats, wardships or royal demesne. Above all, the Crown continually called upon sheriffs to seize into the king's hands lands to which it had some claim: royal demesne lands, escheated lands of the Normans and Bretons, the temporalities of vacant abbeys and bishoprics, and lands held in chief on the death of tenants-in-chief.[35] Sheriffs sometimes acted on their own

---

They were then to restore the alienated assets in the state that they had been in when the estate first came into the king's hands: *CR 1227–31*, p. 64 (17 July 1228).

[31]   *CR 1227–31*, p. 88 (1 February, 1228). There is a writ to the sheriff of Yorkshire, but no inquest, in TNA, C 145/1 no. 36.

[32]   *PR 1216–25*, pp. 66, 70, 101, 119; *RLC*, i, p. 340; G. J. Turner, 'The Minority of Henry III, Part 1', *TRHS* n.s. 18 (1904), 245–95, at p. 287.

[33]   *CFR 1217–18*, no. 97 (17 May 1218); *PR 1216–25*, p. 154; *RLC*, ii, p. 362.

[34]   *CFR 1217–18*, nos 32, 64, 100; *RLC*, i, pp. 309–10, 314, 319, 320b, 367b, 363.

[35]   *CFR 1218–19*, nos 86a, 264, 365a; *CFR 1219–20*, nos 1, 46, 70, 91, 130, 152, 165–6, 279; *CFR 1220–21*, nos 2, 13–14, 69, 115, 120, 192, 265, 318, 343; *CFR 1221–22*, nos 1, 58, 78, 115, 125, 178, 181, 197, 213–19, 269, 274, 283; *CFR 1222–23*, nos 3, 146, 237, 280; *CFR 1223–24*, nos 78–9, 117, 128, 129, 154, 175, 186, 275; *CFR 1224–25*, nos 38, 43, 91; *CFR 1225–26*, nos 58, 105–6, 120–1, 128, 136, 156, 249, 256, 261, 299, 324, 343; *CFR 1226–27*, nos 58–62, 140, 146, 246; *CFR 1227–28*, nos 6, 8–9, 23, 61, 94, 158; *CFR 1228–29*, nos 94, 155, 171, 187, 203, 246, 297; *CFR 1229–30*, nos 14, 152, 164, 208, 378, 392, 389, 411, 430, 456, 463; *CFR 1231–32*, nos 25, 60, 160, 194, 227–9, 236, 242, 248,

initiative. Henry, for example, expressed his pleasure that the sheriff of Yorkshire took custody of the land of Walter de Chauncy, a tenant-in-chief who had died, and ordered him to retain the lands until otherwise instructed.[36] When Henry de Bohun, earl of Hereford, died *en route* to crusade, word got back to Gloucester, where the constable immediately took custody of the earl's lands in the county and notified the sheriff, Ralph Musard, who was at the Exchequer for the view of his accounts. Musard quickly wrote to Hubert de Burgh to let him know, and to explain that when he returned to Gloucestershire he would take custody of the earl's fortified house in Netherwent, Wales.[37] On 12 June the government ordered the sheriffs of Wiltshire, Herefordshire and Surrey to take custody of the earl's lands, before they were handed over to William Brewer in July.[38] Sheriffs also monitored the marital status of widows and wards to ensure that women did not marry without the king's licence.[39] The sheriff of Lancashire, however, overreached himself in 1223 when he seized the lands and goods of Cecilia, the widow of Thurstan Banaster, after she married Richard de Mohaut; he believed that they had married without the king's licence, but Henry then informed him that they married at his request and with his will and assent.[40] The incident is informative, on the one hand, of the scope of the sheriff's authority, and on the other of the problems of coordinating the actions of local and central officials.

From John's reign, at least, sheriffs also conducted inquests into the state and value of the lands they seized. In 1215, for example, John asked the custodians of escheats in Cornwall to appraise the lands formerly of William Botterel

---

308; *CFR 1232–33*, nos 3, 110, 120, 125, 126–7, 129–30, 207, 209–10, 341, 368; *CFR 1233–34*, nos 15, 253, 276, 293, 297, 302, 309, 354; *CFR 1234–35*, nos 75, 130, 199, 206, 213; *CFR 1235–36*, nos 20, 41, 136, 187, 205, 263, 475, 508, 539–40; *CFR 1236–37*, nos 107, 139, 141, 175, 189, 251; *CFR 1237–38*, nos 47, 84; *CFR 1238–39*, nos 54, 183, 251, 342; *CFR 1239–40*, nos 18, 40, 42, 108, 158, 218, 242, 270, 272, 276; *CFR 1240–41*, nos 33, 220, 230, 341, 343, 446–7, 477, 482, 509–10, 538, 568, 588, 611–12, 630, 676, 695, 711, 725–6, 743; *RLC*, i, pp. 293b, 297b, 301b, 304, 308–9, 329b, 338, 345, 347, 347b, 352, 355, 357–8, 394–5, 485, 531b, 552, 582, 592, 611–12, 616, 616b, 640b; *RLC*, ii, pp. 20, 34, 54; *CR 1227–31*, pp. 5–6, 18, 24, 31, 73, 155, 212.

[36] *CFR 1228–29*, no. 94 (December 1228). The land was in custody only a short time before the sheriff was ordered to deliver it to Walter's brother and heir, Roger, on payment of his relief in March 1229: *CFR 1228–29*, no. 155. See also *CFR 1227–28*, no. 197 (9 June 1228), in which the king showed his grace to the sheriff of Herefordshire because the sheriff had informed him of the death of Reginald de Braose.

[37] TNA, SC 1/1, no. 155; *Calendar of Ancient Correspondence Concerning Wales*, ed. J. G. Edwards (Cardiff, 1935), p. 5.

[38] *RLC*, i, pp. 419b, 423, 423b, 424, 424b. For similar examples, see *RLC*, i, pp. 293, 293b, 299b, 313, 329b, 330b, 337, 342b, 344, 345b, 347b, 352b, 354, 393, 399, 531b, 535b, 545b, 555, 560b, 563, 583.

[39] *RLC*, i, pp. 395, 561, 592; *RLC*, ii, p. 12.

[40] *RLC*, ii, p. 565 (12 October 1223): 'Scias quod Cecilia que fuit uxor Thurstani Banastre maritavit se Ricardo de Mohaut ad preces nostras et de voluntate nostra et assensu nostro. Et ideo tibi precipimus [quod] de tota terra et omnibus catallis ipsius Cecile que in manu nostra cepisti eo quod credidisti ipsam Ceciliam se maritasse Richardo sine assensu nostro; sine dilatione predictis Ricardo et Cecilie plenam seisinam habere facias et si inde cepisti postquam ea in manu nostra cepisti, id eis sine dilatione reddi facias.'

after the stock on the land had been sold. The lands were then to be given to Hugh Peverell de Stanford, who was to account for the lands at the new assessment. Boterell's lands had been farmed by the escheators prior to the grant, presumably fully stocked.[41] Concerned not only to maintain its control over land and rights but also to ensure an adequate flow of revenue, the minority government continued to use local inquests as a check on custodians and as a means to ascertain the level of relief that might be charged to heirs.[42] The writ to the sheriff of Cambridgeshire to take custody of the lands of Normans and Bretons in 1224 included a directive that his next account should include information about the lands: what was taken, their annual value, who held them, and by what warrant. An inquest might also be held on the death of a tenant-in-chief, when the sheriff was ordered to take the lands into custody. When William de Cahaignes died sometime before 22 February 1222, the government ordered the sheriffs of Somerset, Dorset, Northamptonshire, Oxfordshire, and Wiltshire to take possession of his lands and chattels and to inquire into the extent of the lands that William held in chief and their annual value. The valuation may have been intended as a benchmark for future accounts, for a few days later the king committed William's lands to the custody of the bishop of Salisbury, who was to account for the proceeds at the Exchequer.[43] Later that year, however, Henry changed direction and gave custody of the land and marriage of the heir to the bishop in return for a fine of £100.[44] By the 1230s and into the 1240s sheriffs were regularly, if not routinely, asked to extend the lands of deceased tenants-in-chief, as well as to conduct inquests into particular issues related to the king's lordship, including alienated lands.[45] Ordering and conducting inquests into demesnes, escheats and custodies became deeply engrained in administrative practice during these years.

As under John, however, while sheriffs did much of the routine work involving escheats and custodies, the Crown commissioned special keepers for certain

[41] *RLC*, i, p. 160, 183, 308b; *Pipe Roll 16 John*, PRS 73 n.s. 35 (London, 1962), pp. 60–2.

[42] *RLC*, ii, p. 6 (9 November 1224): orders to the sheriffs of Sussex and Surrey to take into the king's hands the lands, rents, stock, grain, and chattels on the lands belonging to Aumary de Crohun by view and testimony of 'proborum et legalium hominum' on each manor, and deliver them to R. Bishop of Chichester, whom the king had commissioned to keep the lands. The sheriffs were to make an appraisal of everything such that the sheriff had one roll and the bishop another ('ea omnia appreciari facias ita tunc quod tu habeas unum rotulum et dictus episcopus alium de omnibus redditibus, instauris, bladis et catallis in eisdem terris inventis').

[43] *CFR 1221–22*, nos 115–16, 119–20; *PR 1216–25*, p. 327 (28 February).

[44] *CFR 1221–22*, no. 312; *PR 1216–25*, p. 341; *Pipe Roll 6 Henry III*, PRS 89 n.s. 51 (London, 1999), p. 56; *Pipe Roll 8 Henry III*, PRS 92 n.s. 54 (2005), p. 164. Sheriffs also received orders to provide lands and dower to William's widow, Letitia: *RLC*, i, pp. 489b, 494b, 501, 506; *CFR 1221–22*, nos 181–2.

[45] *The Memoranda Roll of the King's Remembrancer for Michaelmas 1230–Trinity 1231*, ed. Chalfant Robinson, PRS n.s. 11 (Princeton, 1933), pp. xix–xx, xxv–xxvi, 24–5, 49–50, 56, 57–8, 75–6, 80–1; *Memoranda Rolls 16–17 Henry III*, ed. R. Allen Brown (London, 1991), nos 182, 1019, 1291, 2607, 2639 (alienation), 3011, 3091, 3098; *CIPM*, no. 30; *CIM*, i, pp. 1–15.

properties, usually large estates in hand because of a minority or vacancy. The arrangements for custody of the lands of the earl of Devon can serve as an example for the early years of Henry III. William de Redvers, earl of Devon, died around 10 September 1217. His heir was his grandson, Baldwin, who was then only a year old, so the Crown could count on a lengthy and potentially profitable custody.[46] Immediately on the earl's death, the government began making arrangements for the custody of the estate. On 15 September 1217 the king commissioned Henry de Pont-Audemer and Ralph of Norwich, clerk, to keep Plympton Castle, and then on 12 November he committed all the earl's lands and chattels in Devon to Henry during the king's pleasure.[47] Henry was a Norman who came to England in 1204 after administrative work in Normandy, to become one of John's leading judges. He was also an experienced custodian, having been responsible for the vacant see of Exeter in 1207 and the lands of Lucas fitz John in Hampshire, Surrey and Devon in 1218.[48] Henry's background was similar to that of many of those who acted as custodians of escheats or wardships in these years. Ralph de Williton, for example, received custody of the earl's lands in Hampshire, Dorset and Somerset on 12 November.[49] As already noted, he was one of the few county escheators appointed in 1218, and he would receive a similar commission in 1232. Ralph had been custodian of some of the lands of the bishop of Worcester during the interdict, acted as an attorney for the earl of Gloucester in 1219, was keeper of Berkeley Castle in 1220–3, was appointed constable of Bristol on 8 October 1224, and sat on numerous judicial commissions in Gloucestershire and neighbouring counties.[50] Because Ralph was engaged in other service, the king appointed Richard de Lokinton as keeper of the Devon lands in Ralph's place in December 1217. Richard may have worked with Ralph in Berkeley Castle and certainly sat with him as an assize justice on at least one occasion.[51] Richard was quickly succeeded as keeper by John Marshal,

---

46   G. E. Cokayne, *The Complete Peerage*, rev. V. Gibbs *et. al.*, 14 vols in 13 (London, 1910–40), iv, pp. 315–16, 318. The earl's son, Baldwin, died before the earl in 1216. His son Baldwin was not knighted and invested with the earldom until 25 December 1239.

47   *PR 1216–25*, pp. 91–2; *RLC*, i, pp. 343, 343b, 372. On 10 September the king ordered William Brewer jr., who was married to the earl's daughter Joan, to surrender the castle of Carisbrooke to the sheriff of Hampshire, to whom he had assigned custody of the castle: *PR 1216–25*, pp. 90–1; S. D. Church, 'Brewer, William (d. 1226)', *ODNB*, available at http://www.oxforddnb.com/view/article/3369 (accessed 4 April 2015). Ralph de Norwich was appointed keeper of the lands of Eustace de Vescy along with William de Duston on 14 November: *RLC*, i, p. 343b.

48   Vincent, *Peter des Roches*, pp. 101, 207; Ralph V. Turner, 'The Judges of King John: Their Background and Training', *Speculum* 51 (1976), 447–61, at pp. 449–50, 459; *RLC*, i, pp. 348, 352, 472.

49   *PR 1216–25*, p. 126; *RLC*, i, pp. 343, 372.

50   *CFR 1217–18*, no. 97; *RLC*, i, pp. 428, 490, 523, 555, 576, 588–90, 593, 604, 614, 624–5, 649–51; *RLC*, ii, p. 208 (tallage Bristol); *CR 1227–31*, p. 150; *CR 1231–34*, pp. 130, 143, 145–7; *PR 1216–25*, pp. 216, 395, 409, 474; *PR 1225–32*, pp. 89, 169, 509, 523; *CRR* viii, pp. 79, 176. See also *Complete Peerage*, xii:ii, pp. 643–5.

51   *PR 1216–25*, pp. 132, 409; *RLC*, i, p. 490.

to whom the king gave custody of all of the earl's lands in February 1218.[52] From the wording of the commission, it appears that Marshal was expected to account for the proceeds of the estate.[53] A month later, on 30 March, the king granted the castle of Plympton and all of the earl's lands in Devon to Falkes de Bréauté and his wife Margaret, in dower. Margaret was the widow of the earl's son Baldwin, and mother of the heir, whose custody the king had granted to Falkes and Margaret.[54] On 9 April 1219, Falkes was granted custody of the earl's lands in Surrey and Middlesex and received additional favours, including custody of lands belonging to deceased tenants of the earldom.[55]

When Falkes fell from grace in 1224 the government set out to retrieve what it had granted out from the Devon estate. In February and March, Falkes was ordered to surrender the castles of Carisbrooke and Christchurch and the castle and honour of Plympton, which as head of the honour of the earldom should not have been given to the widow as dower in the first place. Later that month the king committed custody of Baldwin, the earl's heir, to Walter de Fauconberg, stripping Falkes and Margaret of their last hold on the earldom, though it took repeated commands to get Falkes to relinquish the properties.[56] Margaret recovered her dower lands and inheritance, but only after offering the king a fine for the debts that Falkes owed the king. The king also retained all the chattels found on the dower lands, including the grain growing on them, which the king offered Margaret only if she answered for it at the assessed value.[57]

In the meantime, the government arranged for the custody of the earl's estate. In February and March 1224 it committed all the lands in Surrey, Hampshire, Dorset and the Isle of Wight to Waleran Teutonicus, on the understanding that he would cultivate the property and answer for the proceeds at the Exchequer.[58] Waleran was a household knight who performed a range of duties for the Crown, which included farming the stannaries of Devon for 200 marks a year.[59] On the death of William Marshal in 1231 Henry entrusted Waleran with safely

---

[52] *PR 1216–25*, pp. 136–7. Robert de Courtenay took custody of the lands on Marshal's behalf.

[53] The commission can be compared to an earlier commitment to Marshal of the lands of William de St John in Hampshire, where Marshal was sheriff, to sustain him in the king's service: *PR 1216–25*, pp. 38–9, 44 (appointment as sheriff).

[54] *PR 1216–25*, pp. 144–5; *RLC*, i, pp. 393, 408, 451, 457, 478b–479. Margaret was the daughter and co-heiress of Warin fitz Gerold, and Falkes owed £100 relief for her lands: *CFR 1217–18*, no. 98.

[55] *RLC*, i, pp. 358b, 408b, 455b, 457b.

[56] *PR 1216–25*, pp. 427, 429–30, 440, 456, 462–3.

[57] *CFR 1224–25*, nos 27–9, 96–9, 118. The Exchequer continued to hound Margaret for the debts until 1232: *CFR 1226–27*, nos 148–9, 164–5; *CFR 1231–32*, nos 274–6; *CFR 1232–33*, no. 51.

[58] *CFR 1223–44*, nos 91, 101–3; *RLC*, i, pp. 591 (31 March 1224), 597, 624b, 649b; *RLC*, ii, pp. 50b, 120b, 160b. He received a respite from accounting for the lands in 1226: *CFR 1225–26*, no. 285.

[59] *CFR 1220–21*, no. 86; *CFR 1221–22*, no. 302; *CFR 1222–23*, no. 288; *CFR 1225–26*, no. 101; *CFR 1235–36*, no. 80.

keeping the Marshal's castles and lands in Ireland and answering for the issues at the Exchequer.[60] Like Waleran, Thomas of Cirencester was a trusted agent of the Crown. On 13 September 1224 he was given custody of the honour of Plympton and ordered to stock the lands with funds received out of the lands of Falkes de Bréauté, which were now in the king's hands.[61] Thomas was also appointed custodian of the honour of Berkhamsted and constable of the castle sometime before November 1224, as well as keeper of various manors and rights pertaining to the earldom of Devon.[62] The government hoped to profit from the wardship. In his capacity as keeper, Thomas was expected to cultivate the lands, and he accounted for the costs of buying stock and keeping the properties in repair.[63] Throughout his career, Thomas performed similar duties for the king, and was named keeper of the lands of Hugh, count of la Marche, and his wife, Queen Isabel; keeper of the lands of Falkes de Bréauté, the earl of Salisbury, and Theobald Butler; and sheriff of Somerset and Dorset and Devon at different times.[64]

The last phase of the custody of the earldom of Devon came in 1226–7. On 29 October 1226, for a fine of 2,000 marks, Gilbert de Clare (the earl of Gloucester) was given permission to marry his eldest daughter to Baldwin, heir to Devon, and to have custody of £200 of the earl's lands until Baldwin came of age. On the same day the king instructed Thomas of Cirencester to carry out an inquest into the value of the lands and of the king's stock and corn on them, which he had agreed to give to Clare for his use as long as he accounted for the value of the stock at the Exchequer.[65] In June and July 1227 the king committed custody of the Isle of Wight and all the lands of the earl of Devon in the king's hands to Savaric de Mauléon.[66] Savaric, a Poitevin who had loyally served both John and the minority government, died before 12 August 1233, when custody of the lands of the earldom of Devon along with castles of Carisbrooke (Isle of Wight) and Christchurch were granted to the bishop of Winchester, Peter des Roches.[67]

---

[60]   *CFR 1230–31*, nos 138–9.

[61]   *RLC*, i, pp. 620b, 645b, 646.

[62]   *RLC*, i, p. 623; *RLC*, ii, pp. 7, 12, 16b, 35b, 46, 50, 54, 85, 90, 94, 118, 169b; *CFR 1223–24*, nos 361 (Plympton), 396 (Berkhamsted); *CFR 1224–25*, nos 43, 45, 83, 190, 287, 290, 303–4, 347; *CFR 1225–26*, nos 125, 197, 335; *CFR 1226–27*, nos 39, 291.

[63]   *RLC*, ii, pp. 85, 118, 141b; *CFR 1226–27*, no. 291.

[64]   *RLC*, i, pp. 621, 646; *RLC*, ii, pp. 3b, 32b, 46, 51b, 101, 120b; *PR 1225–32*, pp. 226, 431; *CFR 1223–24*, nos 203, 308; *CFR 1225–26*, no. 189; *CFR 1226–27*, no. 26; *CFR 1229–30*, no. 429; *CFR 1235–36*, no. 190; *CFR 1242–43*, no. 27.

[65]   *CFR 1226–27*, nos 1, 3, 36; *PR 1225–32*, pp. 87, 97–8; *RLC*, ii, pp. 157, 171; *Complete Peerage*, iv, p. 319, for the marriage.

[66]   *PR 1225–32*, pp. 129, 133–4, 179, 229, 425.

[67]   *CPR 1232–47*, p. 23. It is notable that custody was not given to Peter de Rivallis, who was the escheator at the time. For Savaric and the Mauléon family, see Sydney Painter, 'Castellans of the Plain of Poitou in the Eleventh and Twelfth Centuries', *Speculum* 31 (1956), 243–57, at pp. 249, 254; Robert Hajdu, 'Family and Feudal Ties in Poitou, 1100–1300', *Journal of Interdisciplinary History* 8 (1977), 117–39, at pp. 123, 132; Turner, 'Minority of Henry III, Part 1', pp. 256, 283. Richard of Cornwall was granted all the goods on the Devon lands in the Isle of Wight for which he was to answer at the Exchequer: *CFR 1232–33*, no. 316.

A couple of weeks later Henry turned custody of the Devon lands, along with all the plough teams, over to his brother, Richard of Cornwall, most likely as part of an effort to lure Richard away from supporting the Bassets in their rebellion against him in 1233.[68]

The long story of the custody of the earldom of Devon reveals several important points about the attitude of the Crown toward its feudal assets in these years. First, the Exchequer assumed that a wardship could be used for revenue by cultivating the property directly, rather than leasing the lands or accepting a fine for the wardship. Keepers were expected to stock the lands and keep a careful record of the stock, which in itself could bring profit when there was a change in keepership. The profit motive is clear as well in the enormous fine, one of the largest levied in these years, that the earl of Gloucester offered for the marriage and custody of a portion of the Devon estate. Within the Exchequer and king's council, therefore, there was a sense of how the king's rights and property could be used to the Crown's advantage. A second point, however, is that such intentions could be undermined all too easily by political influence. Falkes de Bréauté caused only a temporary interruption in the management of the Devon lands, but Henry's gift of the custody to des Roches and Richard of Cornwall diverted the benefits of the custody into private hands. Such grants were symptomatic of how favouritism could trump economic policy. Finally, the story reveals the existence of a corps of administrators with similar backgrounds and experiences capable of managing lands on behalf of the Crown. They were part of a growing body of local officials who enabled the Crown to extend its authority more widely in the counties and towns and to increase its demands on the population as a whole. They served as the precursors to the fully developed escheators.

Experiments in Managing Escheats and Custodies in the 1230s

Henry's financial plight worsened at the end of the 1220s because of his determination to lead an army to recover his patrimony in Poitou.[69] He needed all the revenue he could lay his hands on, which may explain why he instituted a new system for managing custodies and escheats as he prepared to embark. On 21 January 1230 Henry announced that he had committed to Ralph de Neville, the chancellor and bishop of Chichester, and Stephen of Seagrave custody of all of the king's escheats and wardships throughout England, for which they were to answer at the Exchequer, and ordered sheriffs to deliver all escheats then in custody and that fell in henceforward to the escheators.[70] In April Henry also made them keepers of the realm while he was in Poitou with the justiciar, Hubert

---

[68]   *CR 1231–34*, no. 252 (25 August); *CFR 1232–33*, no. 316 (28 August); N. Denholm-Young, *Richard of Cornwall* (Oxford, 1947), p. 27; Vincent, *Peter des Roches*, pp. 362, 390.
[69]   Stacey, *Politics*, pp. 165–73.
[70]   *CFR 1229–30*, no. 151.

de Burgh.[71] The two courtiers were logical choices to oversee the king's feudal resources. Seagrave came to the task with considerable background in and, presumably, understanding of the king's feudal rights. He had been one of the chief justices in eyre in the circuits of 1226–9, and had been among the royal councillors discussing financial affairs in the 1220s.[72] He was also sheriff in the counties of Northampton, Bedford and Buckingham, and Warwick and Leicester.[73] Like Seagrave, Neville had been involved in both royal finances and justice and, as chancellor, he had played a role in the supervision of demesnes, escheats and wardships.[74] In addition, as lord of a large estate, Neville was well informed about the issues of estate management, including the conduct of inquests into the properties of his deceased tenants.[75]

The changes in 1230, however, turned out to be modest. In the months after their appointment the king instructed Seagrave and Neville to deliver lands to heirs who had sworn homage and paid relief, to give escheats or wardships to grantees, to allow the executors of deceased tenants-in-chief access to their goods and chattels, and to assign dower to widows.[76] They may have also had custody of some demesne manors, but the arrangement is notable for focusing on escheats and wardships separately from the royal demesne.[77] In practice, Neville and Seagrave worked through sheriffs and a few local agents, and Henry apparently did not intend to retain custody of escheats or wardships for profit. Nevertheless, the government demanded to be well informed about the property that came under its control.[78] For example, on 5 September Seagrave wrote to the sheriff of Surrey ordering him to take custody of the lands, goods and chattels of Robert Testard; to provide a written inventory, which in other instances was to be witnessed by the coroners in the county; and then to answer for it all to Neville and Seagrave.[79] Another case involved Geoffrey de Say, who died when

---

[71]   28 April 1230, *PR 1225–32*, pp. 340–1.

[72]   *RGE*, pp. 78–86; C. A. F. Meekings, 'Six Letters Concerning the Eyres of 1226–8', *EHR* 65 (1950), 492–504; *BF*, i, p. 353; *CR 1227–31*, pp. 182 (1229), 227, 229, 241, 243–4, 320, 370, 379, 398, 402, 452, 508, 511, 525–6, 530, 534, 549, 552, 584; *PR 1225–32*, pp. 350, 449. See also W. Hunt, 'Seagrave, Sir Stephen of (d. 1241)', rev. P. Brand, *ODNB*, available at http://www.oxforddnb.com/view/article/25041 (accessed 4 April 2015).

[73]   *CR 1227–31*, p. 259; *Complete Peerage*, xi, pp. 597–601.

[74]   For his career, see F. A. Cazel, Jr, 'Neville, Ralph de (d. 1244)', *ODNB*, available at http://www.oxforddnb.com/view/article/19949 (accessed 4 April 2015).

[75]   W. H. Blaauw, 'Letters to Ralph de Nevill, Bishop of Chichester (1222–4), and Chancellor to King Henry III', *Sussex Archaeological Collections* 3 (1850), 35–76. Neville instructed his steward, Simon de Senliz, to hold an inquest concerning the lands of a deceased tenant, John de Neville, knight; Senliz, who was occupied at the time, turned the task over to a subordinate: pp. 53–5.

[76]   *CR 1227–31*, pp. 303, 327, 359, 377–8, 415, 418–19, 424, 435(4), 442–3; *PR 1225–32*, pp. 343, 388.

[77]   *PR 1225–32*, pp. 388, 404.

[78]   *CFR 1229–30*, no. 453 – order to sheriff to survey lands and send the valuation to Neville and Seagrave.

[79]   *CFR 1229–30*, nos 445, 459–60, 465; *CR 1227–31*, p. 435 (dower). Robert was son and heir of William Testard and received his inheritance in February 1230 (*CFR 1229–30*, no.

with the king in Poitou. Henry informed Neville and Seagrave that he had taken the homage of Geoffrey's son and heir, William, ordered them to give William seisin of his lands, and instructed them nevertheless to assess the value of the lands Geoffrey held of the king so that he could determine how much relief William should pay.[80]

Management, however, was complicated by the difficulties of communication while the king was in Poitou and by Henry's impulse to meddle in the process.[81] He did not delegate complete authority to his ministers at home. Several important estates came into the king's hands that spring and summer, in part because of deaths during the campaign. William de Say, Reymund de Burgh, Theobald Butler, Maurice de Gant, Nigel de Mowbray, Thomas Basset, Thomas of Birkin, and Robert de Bareville all died overseas, while others such as William de Braose, Ralph Musard, and Robert Testard passed away in England. Correspondence between Henry and his ministers shows that Henry primarily regarded the resulting custodies as opportunities to extend patronage.

The case of Robert de Bareville illustrates the problems. Just as he was about to embark for France, Henry informed Neville and Seagrave on 30 April that if the opportunity arose while he was overseas they should provide Peter the Poitevin, a servant of Hubert de Burgh, with £10 of land in escheats or wardships. After arriving in France, on 25 June he changed his mind and raised the sum to £15 or £20 of land.[82] Bareville accompanied Henry to France, where he died. On 5 July Seagrave ordered the sheriffs of Lincolnshire and Yorkshire to take into the king's hands all Bareville's lands, goods and chattels and to keep them safely until instructed otherwise.[83] It is not known how Neville and Seagrave learned of Bareville's death, but there followed a series of contradictory orders. A writ attested by Seagrave on 30 July stated that the king had granted Bareville's land in Ston Easton to Peter the Poitevin and ordered the sheriff of Somerset to give him seisin, presumably at Henry's insistence.[84] Nevertheless, Henry announced

208). Robert's son and heir, Thomas, paid 100s. relief and obtained his lands in October 1230 (*CFR 1230–31*, no. 10). For Testard, see also Vincent, *Peter des Roches*, p. 361.

[80]   *CR 1227–31*, pp. 431–2; *CFR 1229–30*, no. 456; *Complete Peerage*, xi, p. 470. Geoffrey had protection going with the king to Poitou: *PR 1225–32*, p. 357.

[81]   Writs attested by Seagrave begin on the close roll after 30 April: 'Hic incepit currere Sigillum de Scaccario', the first dated 8 May: *CR 1227–31*, pp. 351–2 (m. 6). The first writ attested by Segrave on the dorse is 9 May: *CR 1227–31*, p. 395 (m. 7d). On the patent roll (the 'Home Roll') Seagrave's writs begin around 6 June, 'Hic incepit sigillum de scaccario currere post transfretationem domini regis': *PR 1225–32*, pp. vii, 346. Writs attested by Seagrave run through to 27 October, when Henry attests a writ at Portsmouth: *CR 1227–31*, p. 379 (m. 1). Henry attests writs at Portsmouth on embarkation, 30 April: *CR 1227–31*, p. 395 (m. 7d). On the fine rolls, Seagrave began attesting writs around 24 April through October, when Henry returned: *CFR 1229–30*, no. 284; *CFR 1230–31*, no. 1. Henry issued a string of orders to Neville and Seagrave from France concerning a range of issues regarding the custody of lands. See, e.g., *CR 1227–31*, pp. 434–7.

[82]   *PR 1225–32*, pp. 32, 343; *CR 1231–34*, p. 415.

[83]   Protection going with the king to France: *PR 1225–32*, p. 360; *CFR 1229–30*, nos 392–3.

[84]   *CR 1227–31*, p. 366. Richard de Greinville held Stone Easton by bail (*ballio*) of King John, and Henry had granted the land to Bareville on 4 October 1229: *CR 1227–31*, p. 216.

from Bordeaux on 5 August that he had granted Bareville's land in Ston Easton to Henry son of King John and ordered Neville and Seagrave to give him seisin. Accordingly, on 25 September Seagrave ordered the sheriff to give him the land. Perhaps with some embarrassment or annoyance, Seagrave had to issue yet another writ on 2 October ordering the sheriff not to disseise Peter on account of the king's order to give Henry seisin of Stone Easton. If he had given Henry seisin as a result of the order, then he was to reseise Peter, notwithstanding the order giving Henry seisin.[85] It is not clear what happened to Henry's gift, but on 10 November King Henry formally granted the land that Bareville had held in Stone Easton to Peter for a sextary of gilly-flower wine rendered at Christmas.[86]

Theobald Butler likewise died in Poitou, with similar consequences.[87] On 19 July Henry wrote to Neville and Seagrave from France, instructing them to assign dower to Theobald's widow, Roesia.[88] A week later, on 26 July, he granted custody of Theobald's land in England and Ireland and the marriage of Theobald's heir to Henry's brother, Richard of Cornwall.[89] News of Theobald's death reached Seagrave before Henry's grant to Richard, for on 11 August the king ordered sheriffs across England to take Theobald's lands into custody and either keep them and account to Neville and Seagrave, or, in the case of Dorset and Somerset, turn them over along with goods and chattels to an intermediary, Thomas of Cirencester, who would in turn answer to Neville and Seagrave.[90] The instructions stipulated that coroners were to witness the seizure of lands and goods and their surrender to Thomas. They were also to hold half a tally and keep the other half recording the transfer, while the sheriffs were to provide an inventory of all that was found. Seagrave may have thought that the lands would be retained in custody for revenue, which would have been profitable, since Theobald's heir did not come of age for another fourteen years, in 1244. However, Henry's grant eventually became known and, four days after Seagrave's initial command to take the Butler lands into custody, he explained to the sheriffs that the king had granted the wardship of Butler's lands and heir to Richard, and ordered them to give Richard the lands as well as the heirs, if they were found in their bailiwicks.[91] Henry worked at cross-purposes with his ministers.

A similar case turned out differently. Maurice de Gant also died in Poitou and on 19 July Henry instructed Neville and Seagrave to take his lands into

---

Peter's connections at court proved fruitful in other respects: on 27 April Henry granted him the marriage of Isabella, eldest daughter of Gumbaud de Blankford, along with her portion of her father's estate: *PR 1225–32*, p. 385; *CR 1227–31*, p. 410.

[85] *CR 1227–31*, pp. 374, 424. The writs mistakenly identify Henry as King Henry's brother.

[86] *CChR*, i, 126. See also *CR 1227–31*, p. 517, for an indication that Peter was, indeed, in possession of land in Stone Easton in 1231.

[87] *CR 1227–31*, pp. 422–3. For Theobald's protection, see *PR 1225–32*, p. 360.

[88] *CR 1227–31*, p. 421.

[89] *PR 1225–32*, pp. 388, 421, 428, 430; Denholm-Young, *Richard of Cornwall*, p. 19.

[90] *CFR 1229–30*, nos 429–31 (11 August); *CR 1227–31*, p. 454.

[91] *CR 1227–31*, p. 370 (15 August 1230). Seagrave and Neville sent a similar writ to Richard de Burgh, justiciar in Ireland. In October, Richard was ordered to assign dower to the widow: *CR 1227–31*, p. 572. See also *Complete Peerage*, ii, p. 448.

custody.[92] It was not until 30 August that writs attested by Seagrave ordered the sheriffs of Lincolnshire and Somerset and Dorset to take custody of Gant's lands, corn and chattels, and turn them all over to Simon of Ropsley, who, like Thomas of Cirencester, would answer for them to Neville and Seagrave. The process was to be conducted by the view and testimony of the county coroners, involving the same system of tallies and written inventory stipulated in the Butler case.[93] Henry must have learned about the arrangements, since on 6 September, writing again from France, he ordered Simon to deliver all the goods and chattels found on the manor of Irnham, Lincolnshire, to Maurice's executors.[94] On 18 September Henry wrote to Neville and Seagrave, directing them to conduct an inquest into the claim of Andrew Lutterel, who was with the king in Poitou and had offered Henry 110 marks, regarding the descent of Gant's manors in Somerset. They duly conducted an inquiry, which supported Lutterel.[95] Finally, once Henry was back in England, he granted Hubert de Burgh temporary custody of Gant's manor of Irnham, on account of a debt Gant owed Hubert, and ordered Simon of Ropsley to deliver the manor to Hubert, thus ending Simon's period as custodian.[96]

These actions clearly show on the one hand the tight control over his assets that Henry, or perhaps Hubert de Burgh, insisted on maintaining from the court even while overseas, and on the other Henry's proclivity to dole those assets out to whoever stood closest to him.[97] The local arrangements, however, also underscore the importance of having experienced keepers such as Thomas of Cirencester, who could have supervised the properties to the king's profit. Simon of Ropsley was likewise a veteran local administrator and would be appointed county escheator in 1232. Despite the availability of competent managers, Henry let the experiment lapse upon his return. No further examples of escheats or

---

[92] *CR 1227–31*, p. 423; *PR 1225–32*, p. 360, protection going to Poitou.

[93] *CFR 1229–30*, nos 440–2.

[94] *CR 1227–31*, p. 372. Two days later a writ attested by Seagrave stated that Gant's widow, Margaret, was to have custody of two manors in Somerset to sustain her until dower was provided, and that Gant's executors were to have the goods and chattels found on the manors. The writ was a notification and was not directed to anyone in particular: *CR 1227–31*, p. 373. Gant's executors paid off at least some of his debts to king by 1231: *PR 1225–32*, pp. 435, 437.

[95] *CR 1227–31*, p. 437; *CR 1231–34*, p. 59; *CIM*, i, no. 30. For Lutterel's protection going to Poitou, see *PR 1225–32*, p. 360.

[96] *CR 1227–31*, p. 453. See *CR 1227–31*, p. 454, for reference to Robert de Gourney as Maurice's heir.

[97] For other examples, see *CFR 1229–30*, nos 378–9, 389, 391; *CR 1227–31*, pp. 357, 426, 435; *PR 1225–32*, pp. 346, 349 (Musard); *CFR 1229–30*, no. 411; *CR 1227–31*, pp. 193, 286, 348, 363, 366, 372–4, 376, 417–18, 420, 455; *PR 1225–32*, pp. 198, 324, 348, 359, 361; Vincent, *Peter des Roches*, pp. 260, 263 n. 10, 266 (Reymund de Burgh, nephew of Hubert); *CFR 1229–30*, nos. 445 (Testard), 453 (Palmer), 459, 460, 463–4; *PR 1225–32*, pp. 311, 359, 361; *CR 1227–31*, pp. 376, 435 (Birkin); *CR 1227–31*, pp. 377, 441; *CFR 1229–30*, no. 22; *CChR*, i, p. 126 (Mowbray); *CFR 1229–30*, nos 428, 465–7; *PR 1225–32*, pp. 357–9, 407; *CR 1227–31*, pp. 184, 205, 314, 377–8, 416–17, 436–7, 456, 459, 472, 542, 560; *CChR*, i, pp. 56, 200 (Thomas Basset and Gilbert, brother and heir).

wardships managed by Neville and Seagrave have been found after 1230. Neville continued to serve Henry as chancellor and Seagrave resumed his role as justice, conducting an eyre in Yorkshire in 1231, where he was expected to inquire into tenants-in-chief and those who held royal demesne lands.[98]

Sheriffs resumed their role as the primary custodians of the properties of deceased landholders.[99] On the death of tenants-in-chief, sheriffs were directed to take their lands into the king's hands, to assign dower to their widows, deliver their lands to heirs and conduct inquests into the value of their property.[100] In the case of William Marshal, who died on 6 April 1231, the king on 25 April instructed sheriffs across England to take Marshal's lands into custody, keep them safely, and cultivate the lands with the ploughs found there, which the king was retaining for his use.[101] While he ordered the sheriffs to provide lands to support Marshal's widow, Eleanor, on 28 May, he departed from usual practice on 23 June by assigning Thomas of Moulton and Henry of Bath, instead of the sheriffs, to determine the value of the Marshal estate and all its assets. Once they completed the appraisal, they were to assign Eleanor her dower and retain the remainder in the king's hands.[102] It appears that Henry anticipated keeping the Marshal inheritance under royal control, albeit by chicanery. In reaction, Richard Marshal, William's brother and heir, threatened rebellion, forcing Henry to relent and restore Richard's inheritance in August.[103] The intention may have been to work the property for profit, a motive that underlay the treatment of the Laigle inheritance at the end of 1231. Henry committed custody of all of the Laigle lands in Sussex, Surrey and Hampshire to John de Gatesdene, sheriff of Suffolk, on 26 December, admonishing him to keep the lands intact.[104] John

---

[98]   *RGE*, pp. 86–9; *Memoranda Roll 1230–1231*, p. 39: 'Memorandum quod debet mandari S. de Segraue quod … et similiter inquirat de tenentibus in capite in Ebor'sir' per quod seruicium teneant; et de terris alicuius de (eisdem) dominicis domini R. in eodem comitatu.'

[99]   On 17 April 1231, for example, Henry wrote directly to the sheriff of Lincolnshire explaining that Andrew Lutterel had offered a fine of 100 marks for Gant's manor of Irnham, and ordering him to deliver custody to Lutterel: *CFR 1230–31*, no. 145.

[100]   TNA, E 159/14, mm. 4, 13, 15; *CFR 1230–31*, no. 322 (the lands of Nicholas Verdun, who had been with Henry overseas: *PR 1225–32*, p. 359; *CR 1227–31*, pp. 410, 412); *CR 1227–31*, p. 572; *CR 1231–34*, pp. 4, 40; *CFR 1230–31*, nos 82, 96, 116, 167, 200.

[101]   *CFR 1230–31*, nos 156–7, 160–1, 174, 220, 237. Marshal's executors would be recompensed for the ploughs at a fair price. Henry committed custody of the Marshal lands in Ireland to his favourite Waleran Teutonicus on 12 April: *CFR 1230–31*, nos 138–9.

[102]   *CR 1227–31*, pp. 509, 520, 528, 591.

[103]   Henry promised William in 1230 that should William die in service overseas Henry would not impede Richard from succeeding to his inheritance; however, according to Wendover, at Hubert de Burgh's urging, when William did die in service, Henry refused to deliver the lands on the pretext that William's widow was pregnant. The Dunstable annalist also noted the unjust delay in giving Richard his inheritance: Vincent, *Peter des Roches*, pp. 271–3; *Wendover*, iii, pp. 13–14 (cited from another edition by Vincent); *Annales Monastici*, iii, p. 127; *PR 1225–32*, pp. 400, 429–30, 435–7; *CR 1227–31*, pp. 503–4. Henry had retained for his use a large number of ploughs and oxen from the Marshal lands: *CFR 1230–31*, nos 220, 237.

[104]   *CFR 1231–32*, nos 25, 32–4; *CR 1231–34*, p. 12; Vincent, *Peter des Roches*, p. 286.

retained custody of some of the Laigle inheritance, cultivated the lands and later accounted for the proceeds.[105] Clearly, some in the government were considering different ways of using feudal assets besides selling, granting or leasing them.

That thinking may have underlain another experiment announced in January and February 1232. The fine roll on 19 January notes that the king had committed the escheats in all the counties throughout England to teams of two knights, who were to answer at the Exchequer for the issues of the lands.[106] The scheme was fully laid out in a series of writs on the close rolls. On 8 February the teams were notified that they had been assigned custody of the escheats and wards in their counties, that the sheriffs had been ordered to give them full seisin of any escheats that fell in, and that the sheriff was to receive their oath in full county court that they would faithfully keep (*custodietis*) the escheats and wards and respond for them at the Exchequer. A parallel series of writs to the sheriffs notified them of these arrangements and ordered them to perform their part.[107] The system departed from recent practice by giving control to local knights, but since it was in place for only a short time there is little information as to how it was intended to function. In one case, the government wrote to both the sheriff and escheators in Somerset regarding the disposition of lands.[108] In another case, upon the election of a new abbot of Cerne, the king wrote to the escheators in Dorset to give him seisin of lands, rents and all other things.[109] The Laigle estate was excepted from the plan, John de Gatesdene retaining the lands to the king's use notwithstanding the new authority given to the local escheators.[110]

Like John de Gatesdene, the men appointed as escheators were knowledgeable about and experienced in local affairs. One clue to the origins of the plan is the fact that of the sixty-four knights appointed, forty-nine, or 75%, had served as a justice in one capacity or another at some point between 1228 and 1232. Some had lengthy judicial service. Robert de Rokele, a Kentish knight appointed as custodian of escheats in Kent, had been a steward for the archbishop of Canterbury, acted as an assize justice in Kent in 1224 and 1229, was summoned to sit on the Bench in 1234, and delivered the gaols in Kent in 1234.[111] As a justice, he

---

[105]   TNA, E 372/76 m. 5 (19 December to 24 June 1232), for four properties. The account records receipts from rents, pleas and perquisites of court, sales, etc., as well as payments to various servants: a master forester, four foresters, and 'messatores'. He also accounted for barley, wheat, peas and beans sown on lands, and other miscellaneous costs. Total £28 13s. 2d. John similarly accounted for issues and expenses of the manor of Kempton on the same roll, see TNA E372/76, rot. 5, AALT, IMG_3833.

[106]   *CFR 1231–32*, no. 57.

[107]   *CR 1231–34*, pp. 129–130 (8 February 1232), 'teste me ipso'.

[108]   *CR 1231–34*, p. 59 (10 May 1232), concerning manors that had belonged to Maurice de Gant.

[109]   *PR 1225–32*, p. 468; *CFR 1231–32*, no. 81 (1 April 1232).

[110]   *CR 1231–34*, pp. 32–3.

[111]   *CFR 1226–27*, no. 346; *CFR 1227–28*, no. 270; *CFR 1229–30*, nos 383–4; *CFR 1232–33*, no. 17; *CFR 1233–34*, no. 18; *CR 1227–31*, pp. 15, 53, 397–8, 402; *PR 1225–32*, pp. 71, 72, 156–59, 166, 206, 208–9, 212–13, 285, 289, 293, 301, 303, 305, 352, 366, 509, 511–12, 523.

served alongside Adam fitz William, among others. Simon of Ropsley, who was appointed to serve as custodian in Lincolnshire, had been placed on numerous judicial commissions in that county between 1226 and 1234.[112] In addition, he was a collector of the Fifteenth in 1226, the Fortieth in 1232 and the Thirtieth in 1238, and was involved in assessing and collecting tallage in Lincolnshire in 1227, 1233 and 1235. As already mentioned, he acted as a sub-escheator for Neville and Seagrave in 1230.[113] The experience of Simon of Ropsley and Robert de Rokele was not exceptional. Most of the men chosen in 1232 had worked on a variety of local commissions related to taxation or other issues as well as serving as justices.[114] A dozen had participated in the plan for escheats and demesnes briefly mooted in 1221.[115] These were the kinds of accomplished administrators who, on the one hand allowed the Crown to expand its demands on and operations in local communities, and on the other formed a corps of local leaders. Though their work was clearly grounded in their local interests, they also had close ties to the courts and Exchequer. The plan, in other words, appears to have been a serious attempt at building a new kind of organisation for the management of escheats based on the expertise of local officials, and it probably emerged from the council or Exchequer.[116]

Whatever the motive behind the enterprise may have been, it was soon pushed aside as Peter des Roches and his colleague Peter de Rivallis swept back into power in July 1232 and installed a new financial regime.[117] On July 16 the king granted Rivallis custody of all the escheats and wards throughout England to hold for his life, specifying that he was to account for them at the Exchequer. Henry ordered the sheriffs and the custodians of escheats appointed in January to be intendant to Rivallis for all escheats and wards that had and that would henceforth come into the king's hands.[118] A stream of orders on the fine rolls shows the change taking effect. On 20 July the king notified Rivallis that he had taken the homage of Henry de Pomeroy and ordered him, as keeper of the king's escheats, to deliver seisin of

---

[112] *RLC*, ii, pp. 146–7; *CR 1231–34*, pp. 155–61; *CR 1234–37*, pp. 545–54; *CFR 1226–27*, no. 282; *CFR 1233–34*, nos 126, 156; *CFR 1234–5*, no. 383.

[113] *CFR 1229–30*, nos 440, 442.

[114] *RLC*, ii, pp. 76–78, 146–7, 280–9; *CR 1227–31*, pp. 398–402; *CR 1231–34*, pp. 155–61; *CR 1234–37*, pp. 545–54; *PR 1225–32*, pp. 366–7.

[115] *CFR 1220–21*, no. 346; *CR 1231–34*, pp. 129–30: Ambelly (Suffolk), Balistarius (Lancashire), Baynard (Norfolk), Bello Campo (Worcestershire), Echingham (Sussex), Ferte (Cumberland), fitz Osbert (Norfolk), Furneux (Hertfordshire), Reigny (Somerset), Rossale (Shropshire), Romsey (Hampshire), Seculer (Hereford).

[116] Vincent, *Peter des Roches*, pp. 285, 350–1, implies that the commission was the work of des Roches, who reappeared at the Exchequer in January. This seems unlikely. Des Roches did not appear before late January, and his long absence from English administration meant that he was probably unfamiliar with earlier arrangements and the personnel involved (*Memoranda Rolls 16–17 Henry III*, nos 1452–3 (27 January 1232)). Vincent, however, is probably correct in linking the treatment of the Laigle inheritance in December to the new plan.

[117] D. A. Carpenter, 'The Fall of Hubert de Burgh', *Journal of British Studies* 19 (1980), 1–17; Vincent, *Peter des Roches*, pp. 262–5, 267–8, 270–9.

[118] *PR 1225–32*, p. 491. For Rivallis's career, see N. Vincent, 'Rivallis, Peter de (d. 1262)', *ODNB*, available at http://www.oxforddnb.com/view/article/23688 (accessed 4 April 2015).

his father's lands to Henry. The biggest prize came in September, when Rivallis was given control of all the lands and custodies that Hubert de Burgh had forfeited to the Crown, including the lands of the earls of Gloucester and Arundel and William d'Avranches.[119] Having regained control of wardships that he had lavished on de Burgh, Henry could reap the benefits of those lordships. On 28 September, for example, he ordered Rivallis to deliver custody of the lands and heirs of John of Walton, a tenant of the earl of Gloucester, to John son of Philip, who had offered £100 for the wardship and marriage.[120] After Robert le Moyne offered him two palfreys, the king was pleased to accept the fine of 132 marks that Robert had offered to de Burgh for custody of the lands and heirs of Peter of Watlington, and ordered Rivallis to take security from Robert for the horses and money and give him custody.[121] Similarly, on 28 September sheriffs across England were instructed to take custody of the lands of William of Eynsford, which had been in the keeping of John de Burgh, and turn them over to Rivallis.[122] William of Eynsford was a tenant of the archbishop of Canterbury, so his lands and heirs fell into royal custody during the vacancy of the archbishopric in 1231. Henry first granted custody of the lands and marriage of the heirs to John de Burgh for 700 marks.[123] Having recovered the wardship and marriage, Henry turned around and granted them to William Bardolf for £1,000, instructing Rivallis to deliver them to him.[124] Rivallis was also kept busy taking custody of the lands and heirs of recently deceased tenants-in-chief, such as Nigel de Mowbray (28 September 1231), Ranulf de Blundeville, earl of Chester (October 1232), Henry de Vere (7 February 1233), William Brewer (22 February 1233), and others.[125]

Rivallis was associated with every escheat and wardship that fell into the king's hands, as well as with all the transactions they entailed, such as delivering custody to others, assigning dower, securing relief, and giving heirs their inheritances.[126] Many of the actions involved delivering grants out of de Burgh's holdings to sustain various royal grantees, and later, similar grants out of lands forfeited by Richard Marshal and his adherents. Others were intended to undo actions

---

[119]   *CFR 1231–32*, nos 181, 217–20, 269–70.
[120]   *CFR 1231–32*, no. 250; *CFR 1232–33*, no. 182. For other examples of lands coming to the Crown as a result of the custody of the Clare inheritance, see *CFR 1231–32*, no. 272; *CFR 1232–33*, 110, 365–6 (William and Robert de Meysey).
[121]   *CFR 1232–33*, no. 16.
[122]   *CFR 1231–32*, nos 242–6; *CR 1231–34*, p. 114.
[123]   *CFR 1230–31*, nos 278–80, 282, 287, 289–91; *PR 1225–32*, p. 455; *Memoranda Rolls 16–17 Henry III*, nos 1437, 1691; *CR 1227–31*, p. 564.
[124]   *CFR 1231–32*, no. 292; *Memoranda Rolls 16–17 Henry III*, no. 3049.
[125]   *CFR 1231–32*, nos 248–9; *CFR 1232–33*, nos 3–5, 21–2, 108, 120, 125, 129–30, 215–16, 308–10; *CR 1231–34*, pp. 123, 164, 169–70, 173, 176, 189, 192, 197–8, 204, 210, 227–30, 245. For Rivallis taking custody of other lands, see *CFR 1232–33*, nos 8, 17, 24, 35, 47, 102, 111, 114, 123, 172, 175, 185.
[126]   As well as the actions cited above, see *CR 1231–34*, pp. 163–5, 168, 171, 173, 176–7, 179–80, 184–6, 192–3, 195, 197, 199–202, 204, 206, 208–11, 217, 227, 230, 238–9, 241–2, 248, 252, 255, 262, 265, 267, 275, 277, 281, 330, 332, 337, 345–6, 353–5, 373, 375, 390; *PR 1225–32*, p. 497; *CPR 1232–47*, pp. 12, 26.

that Hubert de Burgh had taken with respect to tenants. Rivallis also conducted inquests into the value of lands in his charge.[127]

Given the breadth of Rivallis's responsibilities and the number and ubiquity of the issues, it is difficult to see how the tasks were actually performed. Although the custodians appointed in January as well as the sheriffs were to be intendant to Rivallis, there is no evidence that as a group they continued to handle escheats or wardships. On 13 January 1233 the government explicitly prohibited sheriffs and their men from interfering with the custodians of the king's escheats and wards or meddling in the lands and wards, but did not identify those custodians.[128] In fact, however, sheriffs had often been and continued to be linked with Rivallis in administering the properties. For example, on 22 February the king ordered sheriffs to take custody of William Brewer's lands and deliver them with all goods and chattels to Rivallis.[129] He specifically instructed the sheriffs of Somerset and Hampshire to deliver certain lands to Brewer's widow, Joan.[130]

Aside from sheriffs, Rivallis relied on various agents to manage the lands under his authority. His principal associate was William Ruffus, who belonged to the group of county officials from which in 1232 the escheators were drawn. He had been asked to tallage the royal demesnes in three counties in 1230, had been a collector of the Fourtieth in Staffordshire in 1232, and had been commissioned as a justice in Staffordshire on several occasions between 1227 and 1232.[131] Ruffus took custody of some escheats and accounted for his custodianship at the Exchequer.[132] Bernard of Grimsby was often linked with Ruffus in various kinds of work associated with escheats, and rendered an account on behalf of Rivallis and Ruffus for properties in seventeen counties for just over a year, beginning in September 1232.[133] Ralph de Williton was another agent with extensive service as a royal custodian and official, as already mentioned.[134] Like Ruffus and many of his colleagues in 1232, he was a collector of tallage and sat as a justice in a variety of cases between 1227 and 1232.[135] Ralph, however, was closely tied to

---

[127] E.g. *CFR 1232–33*, no. 8.
[128] *CPR 1232–47*, p. 7. The directive was made a week after Rivallis's appointment as treasurer.
[129] *CFR 1232–33*, nos 129–30.
[130] *CR 1231–34*, pp. 198, 245, 451. With few exceptions, orders for the assignment of the widow's dower, the exercise of the rights of the executors and the partition of the estate among William's co-heirs were directed to Rivallis: *CFR 1232–33*, nos 214–16; *CR 1231–34*, pp. 227–30, 364.
[131] *CR 1231–34*, pp. 157, 421 ('custodi escaettarum suarum'); *CFR 1229–30*, nos 90–1; *PR 1225–32*, pp. 165, 206, 292, 352, 356, 523.
[132] *CR 1231–34*, pp. 262, 421; *CPR 1232–47*, p. 36; 'Account of escheats for the sixteenth, seventeenth and eighteenth years of the reign of Henry III', in *Roll of Divers Accounts for the Early Years of the Reign of Henry III*, ed. F. A. Cazel, PRS n.s. 44 (London, 1982), pp. 74–81.
[133] *CR 1231–34*, p. 194; *CLR 1226–40*, pp. 193, 195–6; *Roll of Divers Accounts*, pp. 74–81: account of Rivallis, 'Willelmus Ruffus pro eo per testimonium Bernardi de Grimesby'.
[134] *CFR 1217–18*, no. 97; *CR 1227–31*, pp. 65, 150; *CR 1231–34*, p. 130; *RLC*, i, pp. 428, 490, 523, 555, 576, 588–90, 593, 604, 614, 624–5, 649–51; *PR 1225–32*, pp. 89, 169.
[135] *RLC*, i, p. 208; *PR 1225–32*, pp. 509, 523; *CR 1231–34*, pp. 143, 145–7; *CFR 1223–24*, nos 4, 5.

Rivallis and so was also given custody of the castle and town of Devizes in July 1233. In that capacity, he was guardian of Hubert de Burgh and was ordered in August to assist the sheriff of Wiltshire in tearing down houses belonging to the rebels Gilbert Basset and Richard Siward.[136] Under Rivallis he had responsibility for fourteen properties, primarily in Essex and Hertfordshire, between 21 September 1232 and June 1233.[137] Finally, another justice and close associate of Rivallis, Robert Passelewe, not only worked as Rivallis's deputy treasurer but was also responsible for keeping some of Hubert de Burgh's lands, as well as the abbey of Bury St Edmunds.[138]

Some of the property that came under Rivallis's control was cultivated for profit, but the majority was held only temporarily and was bestowed on either heirs or friends. In some cases, as has been seen, the government added revenue by increasing the fines for wardships and marriages.[139] The different aspects of Rivallis's management are apparent in the six surviving accounts he rendered for a portion of his custodianship between 2 September 1232 and 14 October 1233, a little over a year.[140] Between those dates, lands remained in the king's hands for varying lengths of time. The escheat of Hubert de Burgh's estate and the custodies that he held at the time of his fall made up the bulk of the property, and the one-off sale of goods found on the estates – grain, sheep, oxen, horses, cattle – constituted a significant portion of the revenue. Keepers sometimes received orders to stock particular properties or incurred expenses for maintaining and cultivating the land. Rivallis was thus instructed on 11 November 1232 to purchase horses and oxen necessary for the cultivation of the lands of the count of Saint-Pol in England, and to make sure the lands were sown. He received a similar order the following January.[141] One of the count's properties – Shopland, Essex – was in Ralph de Williton's custody, and his expenses included £12 6s. 8d. for oxen, grain, and other necessities for the cultivation and sowing of the land, by a royal writ, which stipulated that the oxen, grain and other things would remain on the land.[142] Rivallis, Ruffus, Bernard of Grimsby and others received similar orders for stocking and cultivating lands and for carrying out repairs,

---

[136] *CPR 1232–47*, pp. 20, 27; *CR 1231–34*, pp. 274, 320–1, 325–6, 329; Vincent, *Peter des Roches*, p. 383; *Complete Peerage*, xii:i, p. 644.

[137] *Roll of Divers Accounts*, pp. 86–9.

[138] R. C. Stacey, 'Passelewe, Robert (d. 1252)', *ODNB*, available at http://www.oxforddnb.com/view/article/21507 (accessed 4 April 2015); *CFR 1232–33*, nos 148, 352, 384 (by Rivallis); *CFR 1233–34*, nos 86, 133; *CR 1231–34*, pp. 373, 379; *Roll of Divers Accounts*, pp. 81–2. Two other men, Hereburt of Burwash and Emery de Cancellis, also acted as custodians for Rivallis: *Roll of Divers Accounts*, pp. 82, 84–5. Cancellis had been sheriff of Sussex and a keeper of Tonbridge: *CR 1231–34*, pp. 427, 448.

[139] Vincent, *Peter des Roches*, p. 421, makes the same point.

[140] *Roll of Divers Accounts*, pp. 74–90.

[141] *CLR 1226–40*, pp. 187, 193.

[142] *Roll of Divers Accounts*, p. 89; *CLR 1226–40*, p. 220. The manor was in custody only a short time. On 22 October 1233 Henry granted Shopland to Henry de Tybetot and ordered Rivallis to deliver seisin along with grain and oxen, saving costs incurred in sowing the grain: *CR 1231–34*, p. 211; *CFR 1232–33*, no. 178.

indicating that the government took seriously the need to maintain some of the properties, especially those resulting from an ecclesiastical vacancy.[143]

Yet according to the accounts only a few lands – the honour of Arundel, the manors of Portslade and Shopland, and the lands of Bury St Edmunds – were managed directly. The remainder were either leased or granted out. Some lands, moreover, were only briefly in custody. The Crown held the estate of William Brewer, for example, only between February and June 1233, when it was partitioned among his co-heirs, though William Ruffus accounted for nearly £50 received from issues, perquisites of court, and rents for the Easter term from four different manors.[144] From the properties in nineteen counties in his custody between 8 September 1232 and 29 September 1233, Ruffus accounted for receipts of nearly £1,842, of which £786 came from the sale of goods, grain and livestock found on the lands, including roughly 260 head of assorted cattle, 2,600 sheep, 728 quarters of wheat, 285 of rye, 222 of barley and 965 of oats, and from de Burgh's cash. Rents, leases, tallage, mills and courts produced another £969. Rufus accounted for less than £90 from the issues of lands, and only claimed as expenses for the entire operation his annual fee of £30, and 20 marks for the fee of his clerical assistant. This was certainly not a formula for long-term revenue generation.

Rivallis's management of escheats and wardships was thus a mixed bag, and came to an end in less than two years. Peter des Roches fell from power on 15 April 1234 and Rivallis followed shortly thereafter, on 23 May.[145] On 15 April the king demanded that William Ruffus respond immediately and in the future to the king for the escheats and wardships in his custody, and cease reporting to Rivallis.[146] Ruffus was still called the keeper of the king's escheats in May, but by June he was removed from office and replaced.[147] He was forced to stand trial and had to purchase, for a fine of 80 marks, the king's pardon for the trespasses he may have committed while acting as Rivallis's bailiff.[148] The Crown was still seeking in 1244 to collect £307 in arrears on his account.[149] Ralph de Williton's fate was much the same. He was offered a pardon in return for a fine, but was not given immunity from those who had complaints against him for

---

[143]   *CLR 1226–40*, pp. 195–6, 197, 202 (Canterbury), 215, 223; *Roll of Divers Accounts*, pp. 81–2 (Bury St Edmunds); *CR 1231–34*, pp. 189, 365, 370, 373, 424 (Canterbury).

[144]   *Roll of Divers Accounts*, pp. 76, 77, 78. For the partition, see *BF*, i, pp. 395–401. Sheriffs were instructed to carry out the partition.

[145]   Vincent, *Peter des Roches*, pp. 234–55; D. Carpenter, *Struggle for Mastery: Britain 1066–1284* (Oxford, 2003), pp. 315–17; C. A. F. Meekings, 'Adam Fitz William (d. 1238)', *BIHR* 34 (1961), 8; *CRR*, xv, pp. xxiv–xxv.

[146]   *CFR 1233–34*, no. 196. The same order was sent to Robert Passelewe concerning the treasury of the Exchequer of London and other properties and wardships in his custody: *CFR 1233–34*, no. 198.

[147]   *CR 1231–34*, p. 421 (9 May).

[148]   *CPR 1232–47*, p. 95 (28 February 1235); *CFR 1234–35*, no. 161 (3 March); Vincent, *Peter des Roches*, p. 452 n. 105.

[149]   *CFR 1243–44*, nos 93, 283.

his service as Rivallis's bailiff.[150] In fact, several individuals did come forward claiming various abuses.[151] Ralph, however, was not harried for his accounts, as Ruffus was, perhaps because of his long service to the Crown. On 1 May 1236 Henry exempted him from being made a justice or put on juries, assizes, or recognitions.[152] He probably died within a year or so. First appointed county escheator in 1218, Ralph de Williton continued to perform similar functions for the Crown for nearly two decades, and so personifies the government's quest for a stable organisation of its feudal assets.

At one time, historians viewed the various arrangements that des Roches and Rivallis introduced as constituting fundamental financial reform, but recent accounts have been more skeptical. They portray the two as largely self-interested and determined to secure authority and resources for themselves and their followers and to destroy as far as possible de Burgh and his circle, in the manner of factional politics that had dominated the minority when des Roches was last in power.[153] Certainly, Rivallis's brief experiment in managing the Crown's feudal resources cannot be viewed as an administrative or financial reformation. Management was highly centralised in Rivallis's hands, similar to the scheme under Neville and Seagrave in 1230. Rivallis did produce considerable revenue for the Crown for a time, but most was a windfall from Hubert de Burgh's vast holdings and was realised by stripping the lands of goods and stock. Many of the properties were granted out to the regime's followers. The same happened to the lands that Richard Marshal and his adherents forfeited after Marshal's abortive rebellion. Other properties escaped management and accounting altogether, while many fell into the hands of des Roches and Rivallis themselves, perpetuating the cycle of factionalism and reward. The plan did separate the administration of and accounting for escheats, wardships and vacancies from the sheriffs, though sheriffs continued to be involved. Without a more extensive network of local escheators a truly independent system was simply unrealistic.

Rivallis also made the management of the Crown's feudal resources a topic of political discussion. Roger of Wendover reported a confrontation between Henry and his ministers sometime early in 1232, when Henry complained that he was too poor to pursue war against the Welsh.[154] In response, his ministers accused Henry of alienating feudal resources ('honores et custodias ac dignitates vacantes') that his predecessors had used to enrich the Crown. The assertion resonates with another confrontation that Wendover reported, concerning Henry's dispute with the archbishop of Canterbury in 1231 over the custody of the castle and town of Tonbridge, which had been held of the archbishop by Gilbert de Clare.[155] At that time, Henry declared that the custody of the lands of earls and

---

150   *CPR 1232–47*, p. 95.
151   *CRR*, xv, no. 1037.
152   *CPR 1232–47*, p. 144; *CR 1234–37*, p. 387.
153   Stacey, *Politics*, pp. 36–8, 38 n. 127; Vincent, *Peter des Roches*, pp. 351–62; Carpenter, *The Minority of Henry III*, pp. 13–15. For the older view, see the works of Mills and Powicke.
154   *Wendover*, iii, pp. 30–1, cited in another edition by Vincent, *Peter des Roches*, pp. 281–2.
155   *Wendover*, iii, p. 9; *Annales Monastici*, iii, pp. 125–6. The Clares held the honour of

barons belonged to the Crown until the heirs came of age, and that he could sell or grant those custodies to whomsoever he pleased. In asserting his right to pre-rogative wardship, Henry also summed up the prevailing attitude at court, where custodies were primarily viewed as patronage. The rebuke of his ministers a year later adumbrates a different view, albeit only sketchily. Whether it was a mani-festo for reform launched by des Roches and Rivallis, or merely a political salvo against Hubert de Burgh, the criticism became a standard element of political rhetoric in the following decade.[156] Indeed, politics may have put greater urgency on the need to find a viable mechanism for managing the king's feudal rights.

Escheators, Sheriffs and Keepers, 1234–46

With the fall of des Roches and Rivallis and the rehabilitation of Hubert de Burgh, the Crown instituted a different system of managing escheats and ward-ships. Between April and June 1234 the government replaced a wide range of officers with new men, some of them associates of de Burgh. On 4 June Richard de la Lade, king's clerk, was named custodian of the honours of Gloucester and Clare, recently recovered from Rivallis, and two days later Lade and Adam fitz William were given custody of the king's escheats in twenty-seven counties in southern England. They were to answer at the Exchequer for the proceeds of their custody, and sheriffs and bailiffs were told not to interfere with the escheats unless requested, and then only when necessary to provide aid and counsel to the escheators.[157] Although the appointment of fitz William and Lade was a product of the reaction against des Roches and Rivallis, it should not be read simply as repudiation of their regime, because both men had close ties to the former minis-ters. Lade seems to have begun his career as an attorney for the earl of Gloucester, Gilbert de Clare, and was presented to the church of Northill, Bedfordshire, by Clare in 1224.[158] Lade went on to serve as a clerk for Rivallis, who appointed him to manage the honour of Gloucester on his behalf and introduced him into

Tonbridge of the archbishop from the twelfth century, and the Crown gave custody to the archbishop in 1235: M. Altschul, *A Baronial Family in Medieval England: The Clares, 1217–1314* (Baltimore, 1965), pp. 19, 65 n. 35.

[156] Vincent (*Peter des Roches*, pp. 281–2) reads the statement as des Roches's manifesto. Wendover, however, greatly condenses the timeframe, moving from the statement about the king's use of escheats and custodies to the wholesale changeover in sheriffs and other officials, the removal of Ranulf de Breton in September 1231 (Carpenter, 'Fall', p. 7; Vincent, *Peter des Roches*, pp. 275–6), the rise of des Roches and Rivallis, and then Hubert's fall. Notably, in describing that fall from grace, Wendover emphasised de Burgh's need to account for the lands, liberties, marriages and other treasures that he had amassed: the kind of aliena-tion the courtiers complained about (*Wendover*, iii, pp. 31–2). For subsequent complaints about the king's use of escheats, wardships and marriages, see *Chronica Majora*, iii, pp. 240–1, 270, 294, 411–12, 477; *Chronica Majora*, iv, pp. 185–6.

[157] *CPR 1232–47*, pp. 54–5; Meekings, 'Fitz William', pp. 8–9; *CRR*, xv, pp. xxiii–xxviii.

[158] Altschul, *Clares*, pp. 65 n. 35, 238. Meekings says he was 'an official from the great Clare estates', 'Fitz William', p. 8.

the Exchequer, where, as marshal, he held the key to the treasury.[159] There was therefore a strong incentive to keep Lade in place to ensure continuity in the administration of escheats and wardships. Adam fitz William, a Hertfordshire knight, had a long career as a justice on assizes, eyres, and the Bench beginning in the 1220s, often in the company of William de Raleigh, who rose after the fall of des Roches and Rivallis to become the chief judge of the court *coram rege* and one of the king's leading councillors.[160] As justice, moreover, fitz William also came into contact with men, including some of the escheators, who were involved in local government and financial reform. In 1221 he had been named as one of the two keepers of demesnes and escheats in Hertfordshire.[161] Together, therefore, fitz William and Lade had the combination of judicial expertise, financial competence and official connections that played a significant role in the development of the Crown's policy towards its feudal assets.

What is most striking about the new program is the sharp increase, especially apparent in the fine rolls, in the number of orders addressed to the escheators, compared to any period before 1234.[162] The trend shows that despite political turnover at the top, the administration remained focused on finding ways to supervise profitably the king's feudal assets. Lade and fitz William largely acted as custodians of lands.[163] Although they occasionally seized the lands of deceased tenants-in-chief or the temporalities of vacant ecclesiastical institutions, most of that work was left to sheriffs, who then turned the properties over to the care of Lade and fitz William.[164] They thus worked in partnership with sheriffs, who

---

[159] F. M. Powicke, *King Henry III and the Lord Edward: The Community of the Realm in the Thirteenth Century*, 2 vols (Oxford, 1947), i, p. 107; Vincent, *Peter des Roches*, pp. 352–3, 356 n. 80; F. Pegues, 'The Clericus in the Administration of Thirteenth Century England', *EHR* 71 (1956), 529–59, at p. 537; Mills, 'Reforms at the Exchequer', p. 130; N. C. Vincent, 'The Origins of the Chancellorship of the Exchequer', *EHR* 108 (1993), 105–21, at pp. 107 n. 1, 118–19.

[160] Meekings, introduction to *CRR*, xv, pp. xxvi–xxxvii; Stacey, *Politics*, pp. 99–100, 104–6, 115–16.

[161] Meekings, 'Fitz William', pp. 1–15; *CFR 1220–21*, no. 351.

[162] *CFR 1233–34*, nos 251, 259–60, 280, 284, 287, 319–20; *CFR 1234–35*, nos 23, 74–5, 83, 89, 96, 98, 103, 106, 112, 129–30, 133, 135–6, 138, 149, 310, 369–70, 374–5, 396, 414, 431, 448, 461, 46–4, 495; *CFR 1235–36*, nos 1, 3, 30, 49, 65, 70, 95, 159, 160, 206, 224, 277–8, 298, 321, 333, 458, 460–1, 465, 532; *CFR 1236–37*, nos 8, 14, 63, 85; *CPR 1232–47*, pp. 62, 70, 104 (Lade), 130, 134–5, 185 (Lade), 383; *CR 1231–4*, pp. 463, 471, 481–3, 488, 492, 497–8, 503, 505–9, 510 (Lade), 514, 518, 519 (Lade), 521, 529, 535–9; *CR 1234–37*, pp. 6 (Lade), 10, 12, 17, 22 (Lade), 26, 41, 45, 47, 51, 56, 57, 78, 80, 91, 95 (Lade), 105–7, 114, 118 (Lade), 121 (Lade), 209, 223–4, 226, 230–1, 249, 266 (Lade), 324 (Lade), 385 (Lade), 406, 415 (Lade).

[163] Writs were directed to 'custodibus escaettarum' or, in one case, to 'custodibus gardarum et escaetarum': *CR 1231–34*, pp. 449, 539–40.

[164] *CFR 1233–34*, nos 253, 276, 293, 297, 302, 309, 354; *CFR 1234–35*, nos 75, 130, 169–70, 199, 206, 213, 369, 370, 372–5, 461–3; *CFR 1235–36*, nos 41, 205, 263, 475, 539; *CR 1237–42*, pp. 5, 9, 11, 15, 17, 20–1, 31, 54, 89, 92, 99, 112, 152, 157, 159, 164, 187, 228, 256–7, 267–8, 279, 288, 291–2, 295, 363, 385, 399, 403, 417–19, 442, 451, 460, 474. There was not a hard and fast rule, and the escheators were also ordered to seize lands: *CFR 1234–35*, nos 75, 129–30 (also sheriff), 133; *CR 1231–34*, p. 509.

were admonished not to withhold lands from the escheators or interfere with lands in their custody.[165] On 20 August 1234 the government had to order the sheriffs of Gloucestershire and Herefordshire not to interfere with the lands of the vacant bishopric of Hereford or of any escheats against the will of the escheator, and to relinquish all disposition of such escheats.[166] As Powicke stated:

> it is not always easy, as we read the numerous writs addressed to sheriffs and escheators, to see how the work was divided between them unless we remember that the main task of the escheators was to keep the escheats in good order and, so long as they had direct control over them, to account at the Exchequer for the proceeds.[167]

In their capacity as keepers, Lade and fitz William cultivated the lands, delivered property to heirs, widows, newly elected church officials, or grantees; and made gifts of goods or chattels at the behest of the Crown.[168] The majority of commands were addressed to fitz William and Lade jointly, but some were addressed to them individually, especially to Lade, and their work was somewhat differentiated. Fitz William alone, for example, accounted for the honour of Rayleigh and Hadleigh Castle in Essex, which had been in the possession of Hubert de Burgh, for the year beginning 11 June 1234. When Robert fitz Walter's estate, in whose household Adam had served and whose tenant he was, came into the king's hands on his death in December 1235, Adam was given custody. Adam's clerk was directly responsible for the property, but the government addressed writs to both escheators.[169] On the other hand, the government entrusted Lade with primary responsibility for the custody of the earldom of Gloucester, his former employer. On the death of Gilbert de Clare in 1230, Henry turned the estate over to Hubert de Burgh, and on Hubert's fall Rivallis acquired custody and gave Lade responsibility.[170] When Rivallis fell, Henry kept

---

[165]   *CR 1231–34*, p. 504 (20 August 1234): 'Mandatum est vicecomiti Glouc' quod de manerio de [Prestbury] vel de maneriis de episcopatus Hereford' vacantis vel de aliquibus aliis escaetis domini regis in ballia sua contra voluntatem escaetorum domini regis in aliquo se non intromittat, set omnino dispositioni eorum escaetas predictas relinquat ad respondendum inde ad Scaccarium domini regis.' Sheriffs and escheators often worked in tandem. See *CR 1231–34*, pp. 508, 588; *CR 1237–42*, p. 62; *CPR 1232–47*, p. 383.

[166]   *CR 1231–34*, p. 504. Several sheriffs in 1238 were instructed to take lands into custody unless the escheators had already done so: *CR 1237–42*, p. 52.

[167]   Powicke, *King Henry III*, i, p. 107.

[168]   Assigned custody and deliver lands: *CFR 1233–34*, nos 251 (also order to sheriff 250), 259–60, 280, 284, 287, 319–20; *CFR 1234–35*, nos 74, 96, 98, 103, 135–6, 149. Miscellaneous orders: *CPR 1232–47*, pp. 62, 70, 100, 104 (Lade), 131, 134–5, 185 (Lade), 383; *CR 1231–34*, pp. 463, 471, 481–3, 488, 492, 497–8, 503, 505, 507–9, 510 (Lade), 514, 518–19, 521, 529, 535–9; *CR 1234–37*, pp. 6 (Lade) 10, 12, 17, 22 (Lade), 26, 41, 45, 47, 51, 56, 57, 78, 80, 91, 95 (Lade), 105, 106–7, 114, 118 (Lade), 121 (Lade), 209, 223, 224, 226, 230–1, 249, 266 (Lade), 324 (Lade), 385 (Lade), 406 (fitz William), 415 (Lade).

[169]   Meekings, 'Fitz William', pp. 2–5, 9; *CFR 1235–36*, nos 65–6, 68, 70; *CR 1237–42*, p. 54; *CPR 1232–47*, pp. 100–1, 132; *CLR 1226–40*, pp. 258, 393; TNA, E 372/80 rot. 2, AALT, IMG_4343.

[170]   *Complete Peerage*, v, pp. 695–6, and 696 note 'd.'

Lade in place as keeper of the honour, and Lade accounted for the lands.[171] Lade, moreover, may have had primary responsibility for custody of the wards and escheats, since many writs were directed to him alone and because, unlike fitz William, who was still serving as a justice, Lade was able to devote most of his time to his duties as an escheator.[172]

Their accounts reveal that many of the lands that came into their custody turned over quickly, before any receipts came in, while in some cases they managed the properties directly for profit instead of leasing them.[173] Lade was given permission in July 1238 to buy as many oxen and horses as necessary for ploughing, as well as for grain to sow the lands and pay the servants on the Clare manors of Sudbury (Suffolk) and Eltham (Kent).[174] Lade rendered account for the honours of Gloucester and Clare from June 1234 to February 1237, which included rents, twelve manors, the soke of London, and three hundreds. He accounted for three manors only from June 1234 to 27 July 1234, when Henry granted them to Marshal, though Lade was again responsible for the manors from 17 December 1234, when the king took them back, until February 1237. Other lands were given to the archbishop of Canterbury. For those properties that Lade retained in custody, he oversaw the cultivation of demesnes, collected rents and leases, sold grain and livestock, and supervised the manorial officials.[175] For the honours of Gloucester and Clare, Lade reported gross receipts of £2,654 15s. 3d., with £732 18s. 4d. in expenses, and paid £1,752 9s. 7d. into the treasury.[176] Lade also had custody of the heir, Richard de Clare, and the Exchequer allowed him expenses for Richard's support as well as for medical costs when he was sick.[177] Clearly, the government understood that it could profit from the wardship of a great estate and, instead of granting it away, as Henry did when the Clare estate first came into his hands, it held on to most of the property and reaped the benefits.[178] The tension between the need for revenue, the need for patronage and the needs of families complicated the handling of escheats and wardships, but the government seems under fitz William and Lade to have found a reasonable balance.

---

[171]   *CR 1231–34*, pp. 442–3 (6 June 1234), 482, 483, 503, 519 (Lade); *CR 1237–42*, pp. 253 (2 December 1240), 450 (1242); *CPR 1232–47*, p. 54; TNA, E 372/80, rots. 1–1d, AALT, IMG_ 4339–42, 4411.

[172]   Meekings speculates that the business of escheats may have interfered too much with Adam's judicial responsibilities, so that his role as escheator diminished after May 1236. See Meekings, 'Fitz William', pp. 8–9, 10, 12.

[173]   TNA, E 372/80, rots. 1–2d, AALT, IMG_4411–12, IMG_4418, IMG_4339–46. They reported no receipts from twenty-eight properties.

[174]   *CLR 1226–40*, p. 342 (24 July 1238).

[175]   *CLR 1226–40*, p. 258 (20 March 1237), a writ of computate allowing Lade 5 marks annually for four bailiffs on four manors, 10 marks annually for the bailiff keeping the manor of Tewkesbury, and other expenses.

[176]   TNA, E 372/80 rot. 1, AALT, IMG_4340.

[177]   *CLR 1226–40*, pp. 247, 271, 275, 311, 369–70.

[178]   Richard de Clare performed homage and recovered his estate in 1243: *Complete Peerage*, v, p. 696. Henry granted custody of some of the estate to the archbishop of Canterbury: *CPR 1232–47*, p. 104 (8 May 1235).

The system, however, lasted only a short time. In 1236–7 there were signifi-cant shifts in policy with respect to the king's demesnes, escheats and custodies. First, on 1 February 1236, Roger of Essex, king's clerk, was appointed eschea-tor north of the Trent, explicitly designating two distinct spheres of authority. Second, in May, the government delegated authority over the king's demesne lands south of the Trent to Walter de Burgh and Warner Engayne, and to Robert of Crepping those north of the Trent, thereby taking those manors out of the hands of sheriffs.[179] Third, in April and May 1236, the government made sweeping changes in the shrievalties, dismissing curial sheriffs in favour of local men and revising the financial terms of their appointment.[180] It is worth noting that five of the new sheriffs had been appointed in the brief arrange-ment of county escheators in 1232 and so were familiar with managing feudal resources.[181] Fourth, orders to Lade and fitz William as escheators, which are plentiful through the autumn of 1236, almost disappear in 1237. After that and into the 1240s, there are only sparse references to escheators south of the Trent. Sheriffs resumed responsibility for handling escheats and wardships, ending the kind of centralised management of escheats and custodies that had been tried under Seagrave and Neville, Rivallis, and then Lade and fitz William. Finally, during the summer of 1240, the government removed the demesne lands from the hands of custodians, leased them out at new, higher rates mirroring the revenues obtained through direct management, and gave sheriffs responsibility for collecting the leases.[182]

Clearly, the government was struggling to find the right combination of local and central authority to manage its diverse portfolio of landed assets. As Carpenter and Stacey have demonstrated, the reforms played out in the context of changing political affiliations, in which William of Savoy sought to strengthen his position by pushing out an older, curial element and appealing to local com-munities for support. Taken together, these reforms greatly empowered local officials and could be undertaken because of the accumulated experience and expertise of such men in managing royal assets.

As suddenly as orders to Lade and fitz William appeared in 1234, they dried up after 1236. South of the Trent, sheriffs took over routine business of seizing, keeping and distributing escheats and custodies, and there are only a few refer-ences to unnamed escheators.[183] The Crown, however, assigned responsibility for some properties to special keepers. Indeed, Lade and fitz William remained active after 1236, but in their specific roles as custodians of the Gloucester and

---

[179] *CPR 1232–47*, pp. 145–6, 156, 160, 166, 173–4, 216; Stacey, *Politics*, pp. 73–91.
[180] Carpenter, 'Curial Sheriffs', pp. 17–19; Stacey, *Politics*, pp. 99–101.
[181] Hugh fitz Ralph (Nottingham and Derby), Robert Damory (Oxford), William fitz Gerebert (Wiltshire, January 1237), Peter de Tany (Essex and Hertfordshire) and Hugh le Poer (Worcestershire). See *CPR 1232–47*, pp. 141, 144, 172; Carpenter, 'Curial Sheriffs', p. 18 nn. 2, 3.
[182] Carpenter, 'Curial Sheriffs', pp. 19–20; Stacey, *Politics*, pp. 89–90.
[183] *CFR 1240–41*, no. 252; *CR 1237–42*, pp. 52, 62; *CPR 1232–47*, p. 181.

fitz Walter estates.[184] In March 1237 the king granted custody of the lands of Robert fitz Walter to William son of Richard, who had already been associated with fitz William, as well as custody of the honours of Peverel, London, Rayleigh and Hadleigh.[185] In Ireland and Chester the justiciars were given responsibility for escheats and custodies, as was John of Monmouth in parts of Wales.[186] Vacant ecclesiastical estates were invariably turned over to special keepers, who were expected to account for the receipts at the Exchequer. Similarly, custody of large lay estates was often assigned to special keepers.

Henry, always nervous about the availability of cash, wrote to the treasurer in February 1241 imploring him to put all receipts from the eyres then underway, as well as receipts from both ecclesiastical and lay custodies then in the king's hands (namely those of the archbishop Canterbury, the bishop of Winchester, the earl of Warenne, the earl of Lincoln, the earl of Gloucester, John fitz Alan, and John fitz Robert), into a chest with four locks, in the Tower of London.[187] Canterbury was in the custody of John Mansel and Bertram de Criol; Winchester in the custody of Paulinus Peyvre and Thomas of Newark; Warenne's estate in the custody of William de Monceaux, one of the earl's executors; Lincoln in the custody of the sheriff of Yorkshire, Nicholas de Molis, and after 1242 in the custody of the archbishop of Canterbury; Gloucester's in the custody of Richard de Lade; John fitz Alan's in the custody of the sheriff of Shropshire and John Lestrange, the justiciar of Chester; and John fitz Robert's estate was in the custody of sheriffs and Henry of Necton.[188] These were the primary keepers of the lands, but others played a role in managing the estates. Warner Engayne, Henry of Necton, and the sheriff of Norfolk, for example, all had a hand in running the Warenne estate along with Monceaux.[189] Criol, Peyvre, Newark, Monceaux, Molis, Necton and Engayne also served at different times as sheriffs or keepers of other lands, underscoring how the Crown had come to rely during the 1240s on a cadre of local officials to pursue its fiscal goals.

---

[184]   Lade: *CFR 1235–36*, nos 465, 532; *CFR 1237–38*, nos 6, 14; *CFR 1238–9*, nos 85, 101; *CR 1237–42*, pp. 64, 103, 257, 450. Fitz William: *CFR 1236–37*, nos 8, 16, 56, 63, 57, 75.
[185]   *CFR 1235–36*, no. 66; *CFR 1236–7*, nos 82, 188–190, 202, 258; *CFR 1237–38*, nos 13, 17, 57, 72, 88; *CFR 1238–9*, no. 217; *CFR 1240–41*, no. 512; *CFR 1241–42*, nos 399, 524–5; *CFR 1242–43*, nos 89, 323, 260; *CFR 1244–45*, nos 255, 266–7, 364–5; *CFR 1245–46*, nos 200, 241, 269; *CPR 1232–47*, p. 177; *CR 1242–47*, pp. 102–3, 106, 113. Adam fitz William died in 1238, when the king granted the wardship of his lands and marriage of his heirs, in royal control because of the minority of the heir of Robert fitz Walter, to Henry's favourite, John Mansel: *CR 1237–42*, p. 54 (20 May 1238). William son of Richard had died by 25 February 1246, and William son of Reiner was called keeper of Rayleigh: *CFR 1245–46*, no. 241.
[186]   *CFR 1240–41*, nos 402, 506–7, 735; *CFR 1241–42*, nos 116, 468; *CFR 1242–43*, no. 57; *CFR 1243–44*, no. 236.
[187]   *CR 1237–42*, p. 277 (20 February 1241).
[188]   *CFR 1237–38*, no. 33; *CFR 1239–40*, nos 102–3, 157; *CFR 1240–41*, nos 84, 157, 372, 381, 383, 422, 425; *CFR 1241–42*, nos 178, 256, 345–8; *CR 1237–42*, pp. 209, 211, 214, 271, 279; *CPR 1232–47*, p. 67; *CFR 1237–38*, no. 33; *CFR 1239–40*, nos 102–3, 157; *CFR 1240–41*, nos 84, 157, 372, 381, 383, 422, 425; *CFR 1241–42*, nos 178, 256, 345–8; *CR 1237–42*, pp. 209, 211, 214, 271, 279; *CPR 1232–47*, p. 67.
[189]   *CR 1237–42*, pp. 196, 212, 214, 219, 284, 349.

The query about revenues from these estates reflected the government's attentiveness to the problem of how to maximise its returns from lands that came into its custody. Clearly, some inside the administration were familiar with estate management and strove to ensure that properties were carefully maintained and well stocked. They pestered keepers, whether sheriffs, escheators or custodians, about the true value of the properties, the grain and stock on the lands, the cultivation of the land, the negotiation of leases, and anything related to the revenue that might be reaped. On occasion, they called on estate officials themselves to verify the appraised values of properties, to keep a check on the Crown's custodians, and even to continue to operate the manors on which they had worked.[190]

As has been mentioned, Roger of Essex was appointed escheator north of the Trent in 1236, and he continued in that role until July 1241.[191] It seems that whereas the government allowed the escheatorship south of the Trent to lapse, it continued with some form of custodianship for demesnes, escheats, and custodies north of the Trent through the 1240s. Essex's work mirrored that of the other escheators. He was given custody of the honour of Peverel, delivered lands to heirs, turned goods and chattels over to executors, and was asked to restore to an abbot lands mistakenly taken into custody when it had been falsely said that the abbot had died.[192] Robert of Crepping was also engaged in caring for royal lands after his keepership of the royal demesne ended, sometimes in capacities that resembled the role of an escheator.[193] He was made custodian of St Mary's Abbey, York, when it fell vacant in 1239, and was given custody of the lands of Stuteville, Bertram, and Aubigny on the deaths of the tenants-in-chief in 1241–2.[194] He was not called 'escheator', and sheriffs performed many of these tasks in parallel with him. Following Essex, Henry of Necton, who had been an attorney for Bury St Edmunds, assumed the duties of escheator in at least parts of the North.[195] In 1240 he was called the king's escheator in the province of York, but he was responsible for lands in Lancaster and Durham as well, perhaps under Roger of Essex.[196] Working with William Brown, Necton, as we have seen,

[190] *CFR 1226–27*, nos 29–30; *CR 1237–42*, pp. 284, 376.
[191] *CPR 1232–47*, p. 135.
[192] *CFR 1235–36*, nos 168, 277, 462; *CFR 1236–7*, nos 8, 68; *CFR 1237–8*, nos 11, 73; *CFR 1238–39*, nos 41, 138, 169–70, 362; *CFR 1239–40*, nos 23, 28; *CFR 1240–41*, no. 576; *CPR 1232–47*, p. 149; *CR 1234–37*, pp. 269, 283, 286, 313, 399–400, 427, 430, 499; *CR 1237–42*, p. 10; *CFR 1235–36*, no. 277, where he is treated as a kind of sub-escheator to fitz William and Lade.
[193] *CFR 1239–40*, no. 46 (deliver lands to heir, 1240); *CR 1237–42*, pp. 188 (deliver lands to heir, 1240), 455, 478–9 (dowers, 1242). For his appointment as custodian of the royal demesne, see *CFR 1235–36*, nos 537, 591; *CFR 1236–37*, no. 76.
[194] *CFR 1239–40*, no. 28; *CFR 1240–41*, nos 739a–c; *CFR 1241–42*, nos 14, 385, 408, 418, 534–5; *CR 1237–42*, pp. 478–9; *CR 1242–47*, pp. 79, 88.
[195] *CFR 1240–41*, nos 576 (Essex), 655 (Necton); *CR 1234–37*, pp. 200, 202, 227–8.
[196] *CR 1237–42*, p. 196, 'escaetori suo in provincia Eboraci'. On 19 July 1340 the Crown issued orders to the sheriffs of Yorkshire, Lancaster, Lincolnshire, Leicestershire, Northamptonshire and Dorset, as well as to the escheators in Yorkshire, to take custody of the lands of the earl of Lincoln: *CFR 1239–40*, nos 158–9.

was given custody of lands in the earldoms of Warenne and Lincoln and the bishopric of Durham.[197] The government asked Necton to perform all the tasks commonly associated with escheators and, consistent with its instructions to fitz William and Lade, expressed concern about the stocking of lands, indicating that it was expecting them to be cultivated for profit.[198] Yet, the government does not seem to have been committed to the system, and references to Necton disappear after 1241, except for instructions for him to account for his escheatorship.[199]

The Crown, moreover, continued to worry about the possibility of losing feudal assets through alienation or concealment, and so initiated inquests to uncover such losses. In 1237, for example, the government expanded the duties of de Burgh and Engayne by instructing them to seize any lands that had been given in marriage or in dower; or that had been sold or otherwise alienated out of the king's demesnes or out of lands held in villeinage by the king's villeins. When John of Monmouth was appointed the king's chief bailiff in the counties of Cardigan and Carmarthen, and South Wales, in 1242, he was required to summon knights, freemen and townsfolk to answer fourteen articles inquiring into the lands held in chief and the service due from them. These concerned lands that had been alienated from the royal demesne and those who held them; customs or liberties that had been withdrawn; children who ought to be in the king's wardship, those who had custody of them, their warrant, and how much land the wards had; women (*dominabus*) whose marriage pertained to the king, whether or not they were married, to whom, and the value of their land; and those who held escheats, serjeanties and purprestures, along with their value. The topics clearly derived from the articles of the eyre and anticipated the articles of the escheator's general inquest. While the results are not known, the king expected John of Monmouth to take into the king's hands any lands or liberties that the inquests revealed had been alienated.[200]

Two years later, the government ordered sheriffs in England to conduct two general inquests, one on 20 January and another on 22 March 1244. The second was narrower, inquiring into lands held by alien religious institutions

---

[197] *CR 1242–47*, p. 163; *CFR 1243–44*, no. 111, mandate to barons of Exchequer in 1244 to respite their account for the time that they were keepers of the lands and as escheators (*excaetatores*) in York. Durham: *CR 1237–42*, pp. 197, 200, 218–19, 224–5, 272 (after the election of a new bishop, 12 February 1241), 274; *CFR 1240–41*, nos 30, 242, 247. Lincoln: *CFR 1239–40*, no. 188 (for the county of Lancaster); *CR 1232–47*, p. 223. John de Lacy died before 19 July 1240, leaving Edmund, his son and heir, who was born around 1230. Edmund was still a minor in 1248, a ward of the king and his 'valettus', 1245–1251: *Complete Peerage*, vii, pp. 679–81. Warenne: *CFR 1239–40*, no. 297; *CR 1237–42*, pp. 197, 281–2, 376. William de Warenne died around 27 May 1240. John, his son and heir, was born around 1231, and was given seisin of his lands in 1248, though not yet of age: *Complete Peerage*, xii:i, p. 503. Custody of the Warenne lands in Surrey and Sussex was given to William de Monceaux in July: *CFR 1239–40*, nos 102–3.

[198] *CFR 1239–40*, nos 195, 197, 283; *CFR 1240–41*, nos 268, 232, 383; *CPR 1232–47*, pp. 258, 244, 262; *CR 1237–42*, pp. 196–7, 202–3, 223, 219, 376.

[199] *CR 1242–47*, pp. 25, 31, 163.

[200] *CPR 1232–47*, pp. 175, 276, 289, 292–3.

and lands of Normans, except those lands taken into custody as a result of the first inquest.[201] The writ of 20 January instructed sheriffs to seize any land held by those subject to the king of France, which would have included the lands of Normans, and to conduct inquests to discover whether such lands had been alienated, as well as to uncover any concealed escheats, marriages or serjeanties alienated without royal licence, which they were to take into custody. The order went to all counties except Cornwall. The mandate is notable not only for the extent of the inquiries but also for the emphasis the Crown placed on its proper execution, threatening the sheriffs that if they failed to carry out the instructions fully they would be punished so harshly that it would terrify anyone hearing about it. In fact, at least five sheriffs received fines of 100s. or 10 marks for failing to return the inquests as instructed or failing to seize lands as a result of the inquest, while in several cases they were merely instructed to take custody of lands uncovered in their inquests.[202] Though hardly terrifying, the fines did demonstrate that the government meant business, and throughout the spring of 1244 there are numerous references to the seizure of the lands of Normans and aliens and to alienated serjeanties. Some of the lands were returned to the holders, either because the inquests were in error or because the king pardoned the holder; some were granted to others; and some were retained in custody.[203] For those lands retained in custody, the sheriffs were required to value the grain sown on the lands, the produce of meadows, the issues of mills and the receipts from rents and other sources, as well as the costs of cultivation and operation.[204] The Crown, therefore, was interested as much in ensuring that it would profit from lands to which it had some claim as in keeping track of them.[205] Both problems argued that the government needed a more regular mechanism for supervising its rights and assets, alienations and concealments, than it had had hitherto.

[201] CR 1242–47, pp. 239–40. The inquest was accompanied by an order prohibiting the sale of wool to alien merchants, 27 March.
[202] CFR 1243–44, nos 66–7, 180–3, 189–90, 206–7, 209.
[203] CFR 1243–44, nos 164, 227, 262; CR 1242–47, pp. 162 (21 February 1244), 164–5, 167, 176, 180, 182, 185–6, 188–9, 191, 195, 199–201, 203–4, 210–11, 213, 237–40, 264, 269, 291, 313, 318, 407, 427, 437. For grants of such lands see, inter alia, CR 1242–47, pp. 212, 218, 220, 231. Holders of liberties may have also been involved. In 1245 an inquest reported that the abbot of Bury St Edmunds had seized a tenement in Cowlinge, Suffolk, held by James of Bullingham, on 25 March 1244 because James was an alien. Henry subsequently granted the tenement to Ernolin Venaunt, former yeoman of William, bishop elect of Valence. He also granted Bullingham's land in Surrey to William of Reading: CIM, i, vii, no. 25; CR 1242–47, pp. 327 (14 July 1245), 519.
[204] CR 1242–47, p. 258 (1 August 1244). The original orders to sheriffs showed a particular concern about the stock and moveables found on the lands, asking sheriffs on the one hand to make sure that they were in secure custody and on the other to appraise the lands both stocked and without stock ('extendi facias quantum valeant terre predicte instaurate omnimodis instauris et quantum deinstaurate'): CFR 1243–44, nos 66–7; CR 1242–47, pp. 239–40.
[205] In June 1246 the sheriff of Warwickshire and Leicestershire was ordered to conduct an inquest into whatever rights, liberties, rents and lands had been alienated since the civil war under John, and to take anything that had been alienated into the king's hands: CFR 1245–46, no. 477.

Emergence of the Escheatorships, 1246–50

That need impelled the government in 1245–6 to develop a new plan for monitoring and caring for escheats north and south of the Trent. This one proved lasting, and took hold first in the north. The king committed to Robert of Crepping, on 13 March 1245, care of all the escheats that were in hand and that would fall in henceforth, along with any lands that had been taken into custody as a result of inquests into the lands of aliens and alienated serjeanties in Yorkshire, Lincolnshire and Northumberland. The king repeated the March directive on 18 June and included the counties of Lancaster, Westmoreland, and Cumberland, thereby encompassing most of the north of England. Robert had to answer for the issues of the lands at the Exchequer, and the sheriffs were ordered to deliver them to Robert's custody. Sheriffs and others were also ordered to deliver specific properties to Robert for keeping.[206] The king, for example, ordered the sheriff of Nottinghamshire in November 1246 to hand the lands of Oliver de Aincurt over to Crepping and not to interfere with escheats in his bailiwick, but instead to allow the escheators to administer them freely and account for them at the Exchequer.[207]

Earlier, on 23 June 1246, the king's clerk Henry of Wingham was appointed escheator south of the Trent along with one knight in each county, called an escheator or co-escheator.[208] The appointment resembled Crepping's, though it was broader in scope. Wingham and the co-escheators were also directed to inquire into escheats and serjeanties in every county, to determine who held them, whether anything had been alienated from them without license, by whom, into whose hands they had come, and their yearly value. They were similarly to find out about serjeanties that had been alienated and taken into the king's hands, along with the tenants, issues and all particulars of alienated serjeanties. The mandate thus extended the policy of inquiring into concealed and alienated assets begun a few years earlier, and merged responsibility for keeping lands and conducting inquests. Bailiffs were ordered to aid Wingham and the co-escheators and to organise juries for the inquests. Each co-escheator was supposed to swear an oath of office to Henry and the sheriff of the county. Later in August, in a mandate that echoed the one Rivallis had issued in 1232, the government ordered sheriffs south of the Trent not to meddle in any wards or escheats that fell in, but to permit Wingham and his co-escheators to administer them.[209] Sheriffs were also told not to put local escheators on any assizes, juries or recognitions while in office.[210] Similarly, the government made it clear that Wingham's role

---

[206] *CFR 1244–45*, nos 210–13, 236–7, 342.
[207] *CR 1242–47*, p. 482.
[208] *CPR 1232–47*, pp. 482–3. For co-escheators, see, e.g., *CR 1242–47*, p. 467; *CR 1247–51*, p. 12.
[209] *CPR 1232–47*, p. 486 (23 August).
[210] *CR 1242–47*, pp. 455–6 (27 August 1246). See *CPR 1232–47*, p. 497 (20 February 1247), Peter of Goldington, escheator in Northampton, to be exempt from suits of counties and hundreds and from juries, assizes and recognitions, as long as he is escheator. Ironically,

was purely supervisory, noting that although he was appointed escheator south of the Trent, it was not intended that he actually manage the properties or answer for them. Instead, the county escheators were supposed to collect the issues and render account at the Exchequer, according to what Wingham commissioned them to do, though Wingham helped deliver funds to the king.[211]

As the general overseer, Wingham also replaced local escheators who left office, sometimes because they were old or feeble, and administered the oath of office along with the sheriff.[212] The bishop of Winchester, William de Raleigh, for example, asked the king in December 1249 to substitute someone else for Hugh of Arden, the escheator in Warwick. The king duly instructed Wingham, having removed Hugh from office, to appoint another in his place, administer the oath of office and inform the king of the individual's name. Henry Pipard replaced Hugh, and was in turn replaced by Thomas de Clinton in 1251 through the same process.[213] The county escheators were similar to the men who had been appointed local escheators in 1232, two of whom served again in 1246.[214] Several had been assessors and collectors of the Thirtieth in 1238.[215] Peter of Goldington, escheator in Northamptonshire, had sat as a justice alongside Adam fitz William, served with Henry in Poitou in 1230, and was a coroner in Hertfordshire.[216] The new system was directed from the centre but firmly embedded in county society.

The new escheators got down to work quickly. For example, on 20 August Henry announced that he had taken the homage of Henry, son and heir of Robert of Newburgh, for the lands that Robert held of the king in chief, and he ordered Henry of Wingham and his co-escheators in Somerset and Dorset to accept security from Henry for rendering his relief of £50 and to give him seisin of Robert's lands. Besides delivering lands to heirs, Wingham and the county escheators performed a familiar suite of tasks: assigning dower, delivering lands and heirs to grantees, giving executors access to the goods and chattels of the deceased, and caring for ecclesiastical properties during vacancies.[217] As the

---

on 15 December 1254, William le Moyne, yeoman of Henry of Wingham, received an exemption from being put on assizes, juries or recognitions, and from being made sheriff, coroner, escheator, or other bailiff of the king, against his will, as did Simon Murdac, knight, at Henry's instance: *CPR 1247–58*, p. 387.

[211] *CPR 1232–47*, p. 508; *CR 1247–51*, p. 83, order to Wingham and his co-escheator to send 400 marks to the king as quickly as possible, 28 August 1248. Similar orders: *CR 1247–51*, pp. 53, 302.

[212] *CFR 1246–47*, no. 320; *CR 1247–51*, pp. 64, 94, 101, 137, 155, 278.

[213] *CR 1247–51*, pp. 248, 277, 474.

[214] Alan Basset in Rutland and Simon de Furnell in Hertfordshire and Essex.

[215] *CR 1234–37*, pp. 545–54.

[216] *PR 1225–32*, pp. 217, 353, 362, 368; *CIM*, i, no. 290.

[217] *CFR 1245–46*, nos 582, 597, 601, 639, 650, 663, 666–7, 671–3; *CFR 1246–47*, nos 42, 57, 62, 103, 119, 134, 176–7, 182, 187, 203–5, 310, 351–2, 389, 402–6, 430–1, 502, 543–5; *CFR 1247–48*, nos 9–10, 24, 26, 40, 74, 84, 205, 209, 218, 237, 248, 265, 273–4, 290, 301, 358–9, 392–3, 400, 412, 445, 493, 545–6, 555, 565, 597, 604–5, 612; *CR 1242–47*, pp. 453–6, 460, 467–8, 475, 481, 484–6, 489–90, 506–7, 512, 514–15, 518, 521, 528, 530–2, 539–41.

original commission for the escheators indicated, they also seized alienated serjeanties. Occasionally the escheators south of the Trent worked in tandem with their colleague in the north when a tenant-in-chief's estate straddled the two jurisdictions.[218]

In 1247 the government changed the nature and scope of the escheatorship north of the Trent. Crepping's position had been extended until the end of 1246, but on 20 February 1247 the king committed all his demesne lands and all escheats in the counties of Nottinghamshire, Derbyshire, Yorkshire, Northumberland, Lancaster, Westmorland and Cumberland to the custody of Crepping and Thomas de Stamford.[219] Henceforth the government addressed orders concerning escheats, wardships or demesnes to the two officials jointly.[220] Henry amplified their commission on 12 January 1248 by adding co-escheators in each county, whom he exempted from assizes and juries, thereby replicating the system south of the Trent. Although the commission was directed jointly to Stamford and Crepping, it appears that Stamford was regarded as the senior partner. Just before the appointment, Stamford was addressed as the king's escheator in the North in a grant of 60 marks as his annual fee.[221] Although the Crown sent writs concerning escheats to both Crepping and Stamford throughout the spring, in March Stamford alone was responsible for appointing Peter de Vallibus as the co-escheator in Northumberland, and orders were regularly sent to Stamford and his co-escheators in various counties.[222] Crepping seems gradually to have withdrawn from the escheatorship, and in July 1248 he was ordered to deliver all of the king's stock in his custody to Stamford, the king's escheator in the northern parts.[223] The separation was formally acknowledged on 12 November, when Henry gave Stamford, along with the knights appointed as co-escheators, custody of all the king's escheats, wardships and demesnes in the counties of Nottingham, Derby, York, Northumberland, Lancaster, Westmorland and Cumberland.[224] The order also authorised Stamford to inquire into escheats, wardships and serjeanties to determine their value, who held them, whether anything had been alienated from them and by whom.[225] Conducting inquests of this kind was now assumed to be a routine part of the escheator's work, north and south of the Trent.

In establishing this new scheme the government intended to draw a clear distinction between the work of the escheators and that of the sheriffs. It mandated

---

[218] *CR 1242–47*, pp. 460–1, 467, 502, 510–11, 519.

[219] *CFR 1245–46*, no. 660; *CFR 1246–7*, no. 183; *CR 1242–47*, pp. 427, 429, 436, 441–2.

[220] *CFR 1246–47*, nos 310, 351–2, 357, 404–5, 447, 511–12; *CR 1242–47*, pp. 500, 505 (see *CFR 1245–46*, no. 565), 508; *CIM*, i, nos 43, 47, 53 (5 May 1247, writ to both escheators in Yorkshire).

[221] *CPR 1247–58*, pp. 6, 16 (14 May).

[222] *CR 1247–51*, pp. 36 (Vallibus), 39, 61, 66, 69, 73; *CFR 1247–48*, nos 176, 274, 302, 328, 352, 358, 360, 376, 402, 482, 494, 605.

[223] *CR 1247–51*, p. 69.

[224] *CPR 1247–58*, p. 32.

[225] After July 1250 the government routinely addressed writs to Stamford and his co-escheators for a wide range of actions typically assigned to escheators: *CFR 1248–49*, nos 2, 54, 189, 194, 250; *CFR 1249–50*, nos 460, 721; *CFR 1250–51*, 1–4, 5, 49, 390, 928.

sheriffs not to meddle in any wards or escheats falling to the king in their counties, and to allow Wingham and his co-escheators to administer them.[226] Nevertheless, it took a while to make the separation stick. Early in the process messages regarding the disposition of lands were sometimes sent simultaneously to both sheriffs and escheators. For example, after the king had taken the homage of James of Audley, on 19 November 1246 he ordered the sheriff of Staffordshire and Shropshire to give him seisin of all lands, castles and tenements which Henry of Audley, James's father, held on the day he died, having accepted security from James for his relief. Not only was the same order sent to John fitz Geoffrey, the justiciar of Ireland, but it was also directed to Henry of Wingham and the escheators in Shropshire and Staffordshire, without mentioning the relief. A similar sequence of orders was sent to sheriffs and escheators in various counties during the year, indicating that the government had not yet determined the precise boundaries for each official's sphere of authority.[227] In 1248 it drew the line more definitively. On 28 January the king ordered the sheriff of Kent to permit Henry of Wingham and his escheators in the county to extend the lands of William de Auberville, as he had formerly instructed the sheriff to do, and to have seisin of William's lands. The writ explained that by common counsel it had been provided that the extents and inquisitions that ought to be held into wards and escheats after they had come into the king's hands should be conducted by the escheators and not by sheriffs.[228] This mandate challenged a practice that reached back, as already noted, to the beginnings of Henry's reign. According to evidence in the *Calendar of Inquisitions Post Mortem*, until 1248 writs for extents and other matters relating to escheats and wardships were sent to sheriffs, with only a few exceptions.[229] The earliest writ addressed to Henry of Wingham that survives in the series is dated 1 October 1247, and several others were sent to him towards the end of the year, including one addressed to him and his co-escheator in Essex. During the same period, and even after the mandate in January 1248, the government addressed some writs for extents as well as other matters to sheriffs.[230] Nevertheless, over time the number of writs directed towards sheriffs declined, and the escheators gradually assumed full responsibility not only for the seizure and custody of escheats and wardships but also for gathering information about their value and disposition: the inquisition post mortem.

---

[226] *CPR 1232–47*, p. 486 (23 August 1246). A similar order was sent to the sheriff of Nottingham on 4 November 1246 to deliver lands of Oliver de Aincurt to the escheator and 'de cetero nihil se intromittat de escaetis regis in balliva sua, set permittat escaetores regis liberam earum habere administracionem, qui de exitibus earum regi ad Scaccarium suum respondere debent, sicut eis injunximus': *CR 1242–47*, p. 482.

[227] *CFR 1246–47*, nos 40–2, 56–8, 118–20, 134, 177–8, 181–2, 252–3.

[228] *CR 1247–51*, p. 105.

[229] Some were sent to the justiciar in Ireland for execution, and a few were addressed to Robert of Crepping, who was not identified as an escheator: *CIPM*, nos 19, 36, 49, 52, 64, 115, 117.

[230] *CIPM*, nos 87–9, 91–7, 100, 104, 106–14, 116–20, 122, 128–9, 131–3, 135, 138, 142, 144, 146–7, 149, 151, 154, 156–7, 161.

In this manner the escheator emerged as a fully formed office alongside the sheriffs, coroners, and other local officials. After a long series of administrative experiments, the government concentrated in the escheators' hands the primary functions related to monitoring and administering a significant range of the king's feudal rights. The escheators' basic work of securing, appraising and keeping track of properties, overseeing the conduct of wards and widows, and discovering concealments and alienations reflected the critical concerns of the minority government. The escheatorship was a product of the effort to stabilise and revive royal authority during Henry's minority.

The establishment of the escheatorships also signalled the movement of the management of the king's fiscal resources out of the court and closer to the communities in which they were located. Wardships, marriages, escheats or demesne lands could be most effectively supervised locally, while central or curial control was retained over the allocation of those rights and the revenues they generated. Instead of relying on curial keepers of escheats as under the Angevins, Henry's government gradually turned to local men to manage its feudal resources, though at times courtiers were nominally in charge of the overall process. In addition, the official functions of the escheator had to be delineated from those of other local officials, primarily sheriffs. On the one hand, therefore, the development of the office of escheator is a story of the decentralisation of functions away from the court, and on the other, one of the realignment of responsibilities among local officials. By 1250, the government had succeeded in bringing together the different functions associated with escheats and custodies – information, seizure and management – in one office, and this proved to be the most durable of Henry's experiments. In subsequent years the geographical boundaries of the escheatorships would change often and the king would augment the escheators' responsibilities, but the core content of their work remained much the same for the rest of the Middle Ages.

Index

Lucy, Richard de, lord of Egremont,
    forester, 220
  wife of *see* Morville
Ludgershall (Wiltshire), 225
Luka, Fortunatus de, royal jester, 26
Lung, Richard le, widow of, 188
Lusignan, family, 1, 9, 26; *see also* Valence
  Geoffrey de, 26
  Guy de, 26
  Hugh de, count of la Marche, 238; wife
    of *see* Isabella of Angoulême
Lutterel, Andrew, 243
Lymsey, Nicholas de, 231
Lythwood hay (in Long Forest,
    Shropshire), 219

Madog ap Gruffudd, 109
Madog ap Maredudd, king of Powys, 109,
    113, 118
Maelgwyn ap Rhys, 119
Maenchi son of Pretignor, 117
Magna Carta, 9, 15–16, 21, 29, 46, 55,
    149, 162, 227, 230
  Magna Carta (1215), 2, 13, 18,
    176
    cap. 2, 15–16
    cap. 7, 16
    cap. 8, 16–17
    cap. 17, 13
    cap. 18, 45
    cap. 39, 18
    cap. 40, 20
    cap. 52, 19
    cap. 61 (Twenty-Five Barons), 19,
      152
  Magna Carta (1216), 2, 176
    cap. 13, 45
  Magna Carta (1217), 2, 13–14, 176
    cap. 14, 51
    cap. 15, 45
  Magna Carta (1225), 2, 45, 51, 169,
    177
    cap. 1, 201, 207
  See also Forest Charter
Maitland, F. W., 55

Man, king of *see* Olaf
Manchester (Lancashire), church, 50
  manor, 50
Mandeville, Geoffrey de, 14–15
  wife of *see* Gloucester
Manor (Peebleshire, Scotland), 101
Mansel, John, 257
Manuel (Scotland), nunnery, 90
Marche, count of *see* Lusignan
Maredudd ab Owain, 119
Maredudd ab Owain ap Rhys, 115
Maredudd ap Rhobert, 114, 119
Maredudd ap Rhys, lord of Ystrad Tywi,
    110
Margam (in Morgannwg, Glamorgan),
    abbey, 107, 112, 116, 119–20
Margaret, queen of Scotland, wife of
    Alexander III, 20, 64
  brother of *see* Henry III
Marisco, Geoffrey de, justiciar of Ireland,
    75, 81
  See also Marsh
Mark, Philip, sheriff of Nottinghamshire
    and Derbyshire, 212, 222
markets, 1, 10, 35, 70, 161, 182
  See also under fines
Marlborough (Wiltshire), castle, 225
  Statute of (1267), 53
marriage, 1, 14, 16–19, 64, 79, 110,
    124–7, 129, 132, 135, 153,
    155–6, 162, 213–16, 220–1, 223,
    226, 228–31, 234–5, 238–9, 242,
    247, 249, 259–60, 265
  See also under fines
Marsh, Richard, bishop of Durham, 156,
    163
  See also Marisco
Marshal, Gilbert, earl of Pembroke, 125,
    132, 142, 255
  John, 236–7
  Richard, earl of Pembroke, 244, 247;
    rebellion of (1234), 79, 82, 167,
    251
  William (d. 1219), earl of Pembroke,
    62, 156, 231